STAR WARS

DOCTOR APHRA

WORST AMONG EQUALS

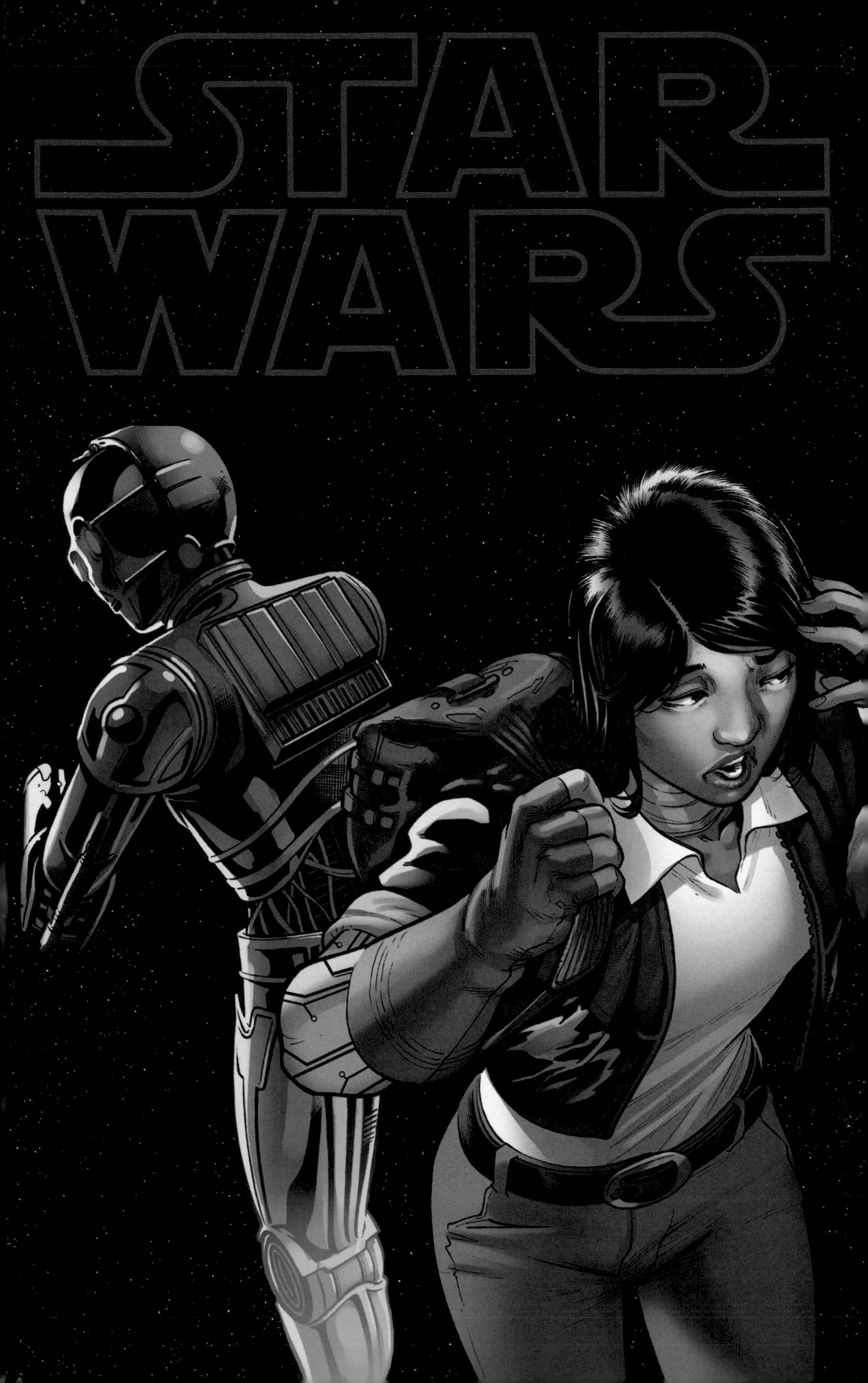
STAR
WARS

DOCTOR APHRA

WORST AMONG EQUALS

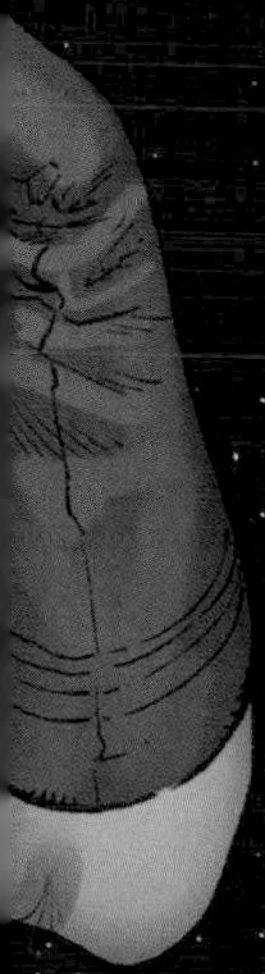

Writer SIMON SPURRIER

ANNUAL #2

Artist/Cover CASPAR WIJNGAARD

ISSUES #26-31

Penciler EMILIO LAISO
WITH ANDREA BROCCARDO (#31)

Color Artist RACHELLE ROSENBERG

Cover Art ASHLEY WITTER

Letterer VC's JOE CARAMAGNA

Assistant Editor TOM GRONEMAN

Editors MARK PANICCIA
WITH HEATHER ANTOS (ANNUAL #2)

Special thanks to KIERON GILLEN

Editor in Chief C.B CEBULSKI

Chief Creative Officer JOE QUESADA

President DAN BUCKLEY

For Lucasfilm:

Senior Editor ROBERT SIMPSON

Creative Director MICHAEL SIGLAIN

Lucasfilm Art Department PHIL SZOSTAK

Lucasfilm Story Group JAMES WAUGH, LELAND CHEE,
MATT MARTIN

Collection Editor JENNIFER GRÜNWALD
Assistant Editor CAITLIN O'CONNELL
Associate Managing Editor KATERI WOODY
Editor, Special Projects MARK D. BEAZLEY
VP Production & Special Projects JEFF YOUNGQUIST
Book Designers ADAM DEL RE
WITH STACIE ZUCKER
SVP Print, Sales & Marketing DAVID GABRIEL
Director, Licensed Publishing SVEN LARSEN

STAR WARS: DOCTOR APHRA VOL. 5 — WORST AMONG EQUALS. Contains material originally published in magazine form as STAR WARS: DOCTOR APHRA #26-31 and ANNUAL #2. First printing 2019. ISBN 978-1-302-91487-5. Published by MARVEL WORLDWIDE, INC., a subsidiary of MARVEL ENTERTAINMENT, LLC. OFFICE OF PUBLICATION: 135 West 50th Street, New York, NY 10020. STAR WARS and related text and illustrations are trademarks and/or copyrights, in the United States and other countries, of Lucasfilm Ltd. and/or its affiliates. © & TM Lucasfilm Ltd. No similarity between any of the names, characters, persons, and/or institutions in this magazine with those of any living or dead person or institution is intended, and any such similarity which may exist is purely coincidental. Marvel and its logos are TM Marvel Characters, Inc. Printed in the U.S.A. DAN BUCKLEY, President, Marvel Entertainment; JOHN NEE, Publisher; JOE QUESADA, Chief Creative Officer; TOM BREVOORT, SVP of Publishing; DAVID BOGART, Associate Publisher & SVP of Talent Affairs; DAVID GABRIEL, SVP of Sales & Marketing, Publishing; JEFF YOUNGQUIST, VP of Production & Special Projects; DAN CARR, Executive Director of Publishing Technology; ALEX MORALES, Director of Publishing Operations; DAN EDINGTON, Managing Editor; SUSAN CRESPI, Production Manager; STAN LEE, Chairman Emeritus. For information regarding advertising in Marvel Comics or on Marvel.com, please contact Vit DeBellis, Custom Solutions & Integrated Advertising Manager, at [illegible]. For Marvel subscription inquiries, please call 888-511-5480. Manufactured between 4/19/2019 and 5/21/2019 by LSC COMMUNICATIONS INC., KENDALLVILLE, IN, USA.

10 9 8 7 6 5 4 3 2 1

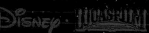

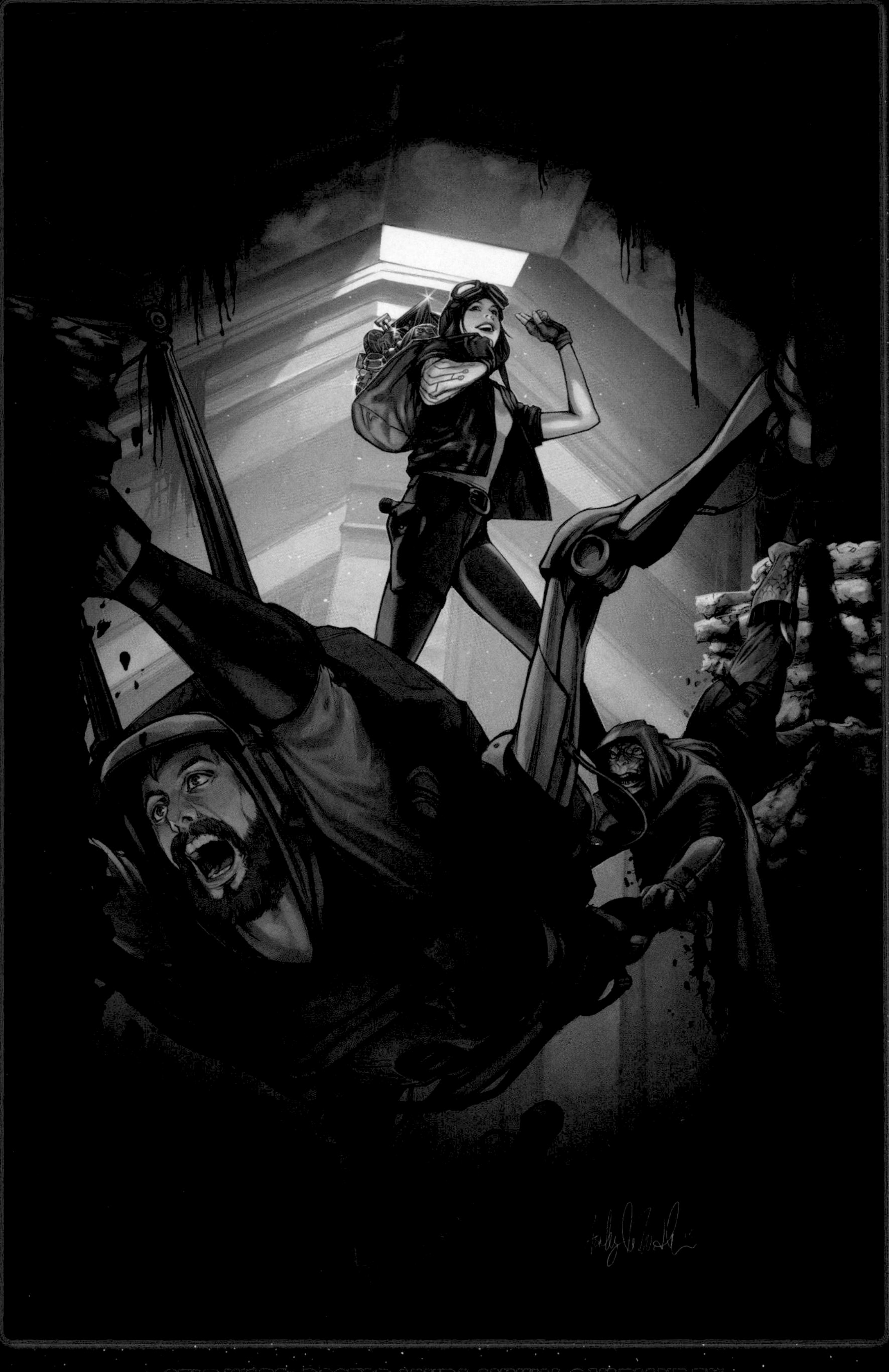

STAR WARS: DOCTOR APHRA ANNUAL 2 VARIANT BY
ASHLEY WITTER

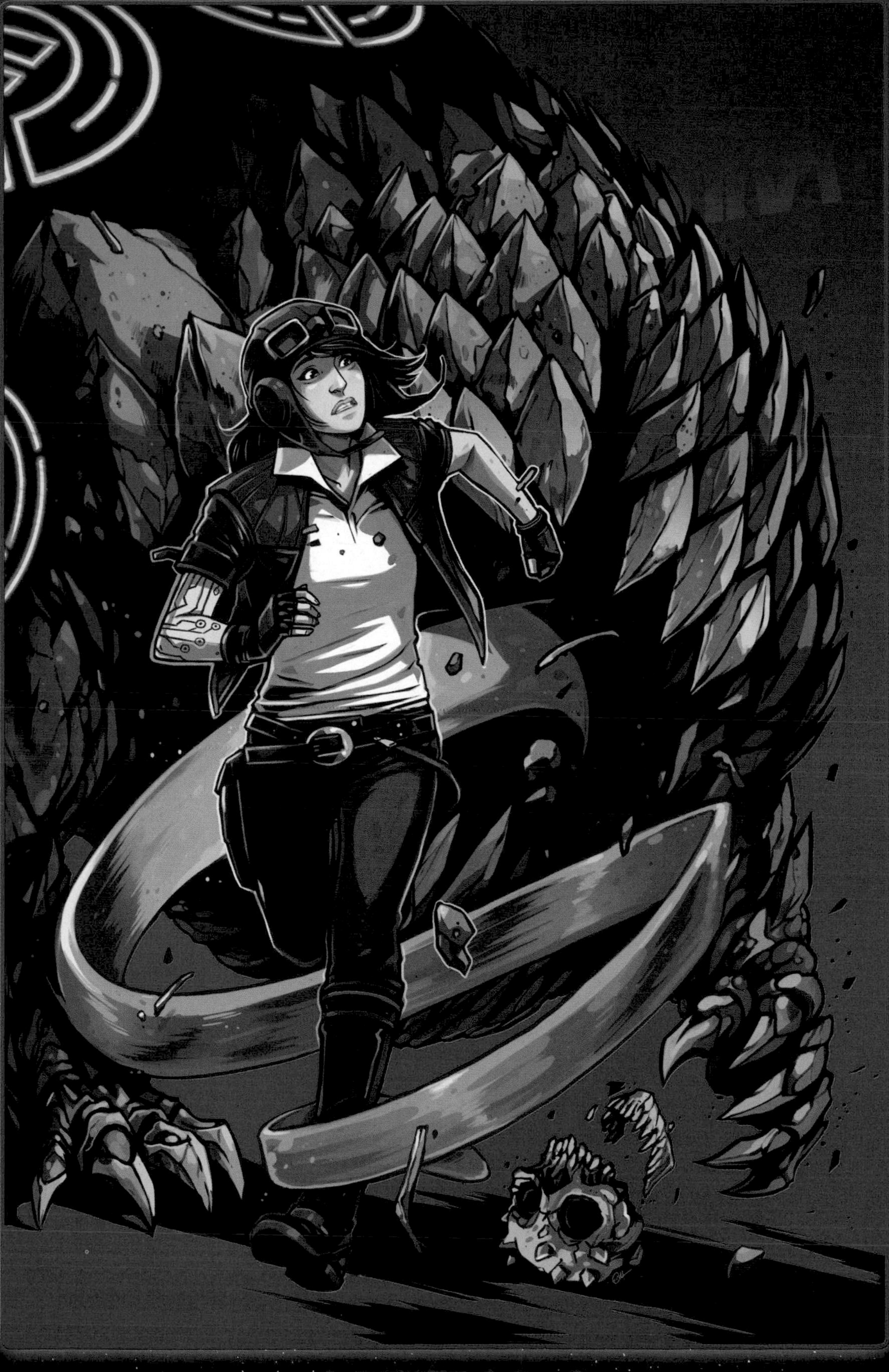

ANNUAL 2

DOCTOR APHRA ANNUAL II
WINLOSS AND NOKK

The evil Empire rules the galaxy with an iron fist.
But the more Imperial forces tighten their grip,
the more star systems slip through their fingers.
Criminals and fringe factions thrive!

Rogue archaeologist Doctor Aphra is no stranger
to risk in the pursuit of credits and thrills, ever
on the hunt for the rarest and most valuable
artifacts in the galaxy.

Others, like monster-hunting team Winloss
and Nokk, make their living even more
dangerously....

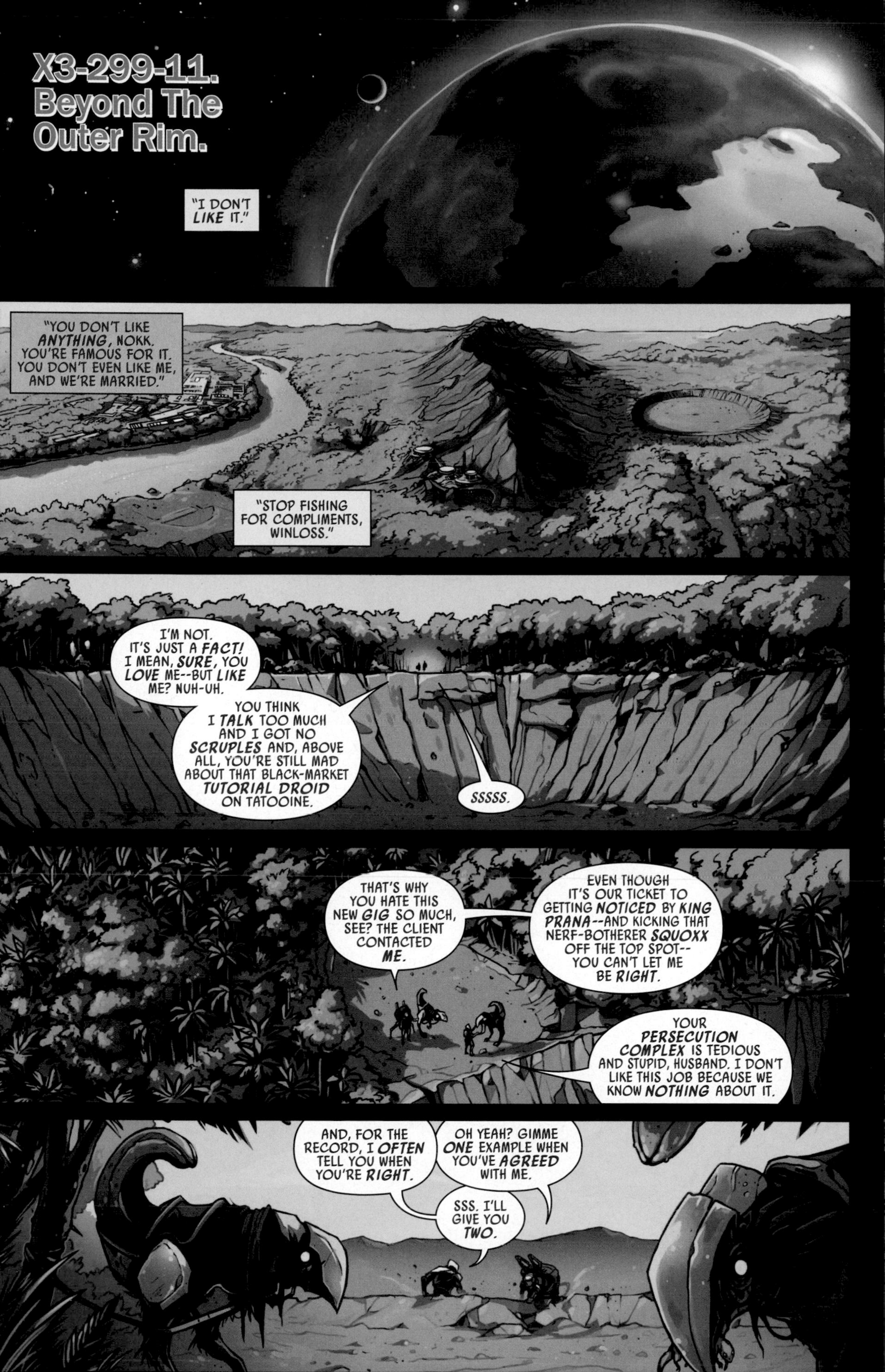
X3-299-11. Beyond The Outer Rim.
"I DON'T LIKE IT."
"YOU DON'T LIKE ANYTHING, NOKK. YOU'RE FAMOUS FOR IT. YOU DON'T EVEN LIKE ME, AND WE'RE MARRIED."
"STOP FISHING FOR COMPLIMENTS, WINLOSS."
I'M NOT. IT'S JUST A FACT! I MEAN, SURE, YOU LOVE ME--BUT LIKE ME? NUH-UH.
YOU THINK I TALK TOO MUCH AND I GOT NO SCRUPLES AND, ABOVE ALL, YOU'RE STILL MAD ABOUT THAT BLACK-MARKET TUTORIAL DROID ON TATOOINE.
SSSSS.
THAT'S WHY YOU HATE THIS NEW GIG SO MUCH, SEE? THE CLIENT CONTACTED ME.
EVEN THOUGH IT'S OUR TICKET TO GETTING NOTICED BY KING PRANA--AND KICKING THAT NERF-BOTHERER SQUOXX OFF THE TOP SPOT--YOU CAN'T LET ME BE RIGHT.
YOUR PERSECUTION COMPLEX IS TEDIOUS AND STUPID, HUSBAND. I DON'T LIKE THIS JOB BECAUSE WE KNOW NOTHING ABOUT IT.
AND, FOR THE RECORD, I OFTEN TELL YOU WHEN YOU'RE RIGHT.
OH YEAH? GIMME ONE EXAMPLE WHEN YOU'VE AGREED WITH ME.
SSS. I'LL GIVE YOU TWO.

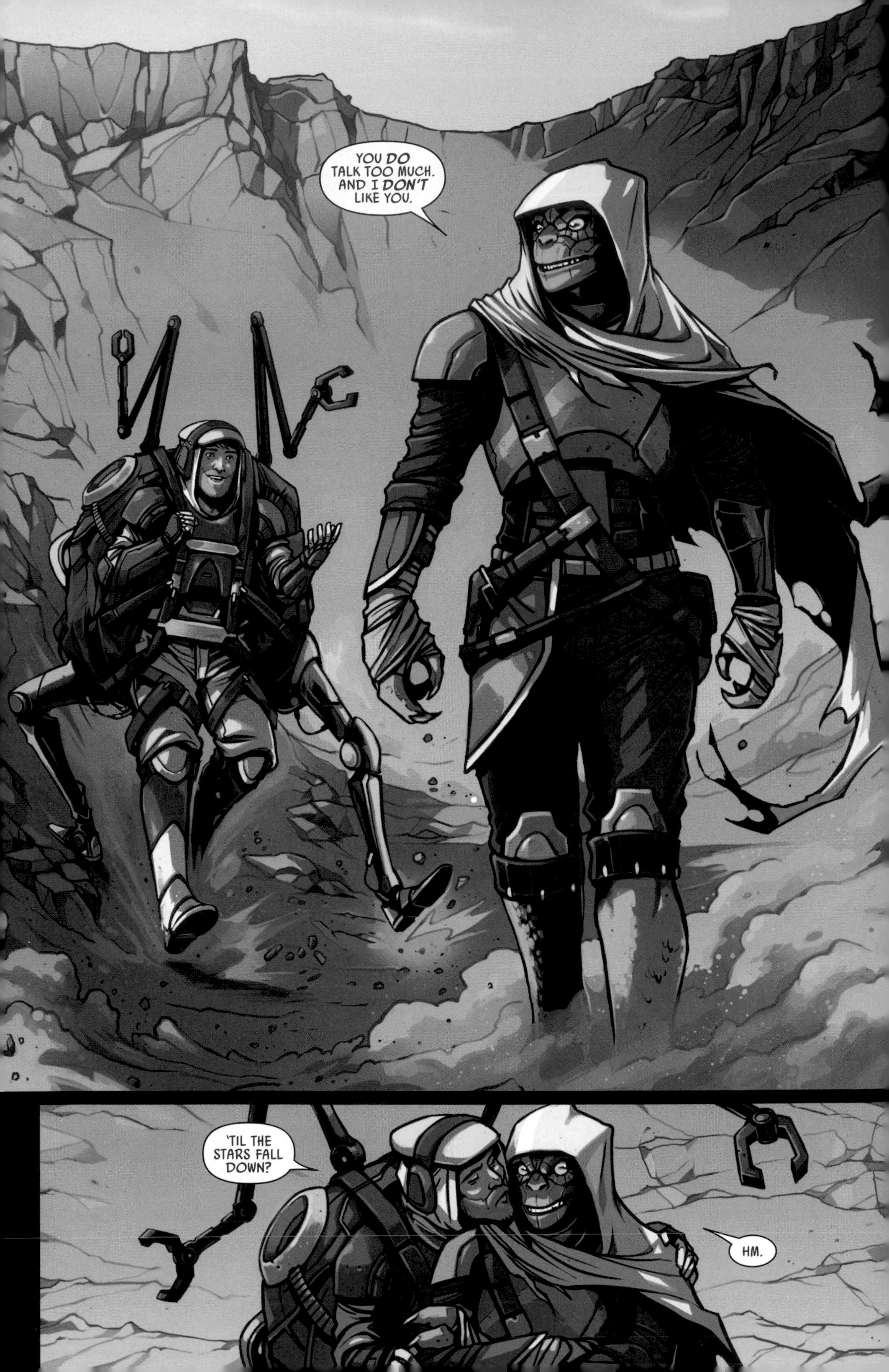
YOU DO TALK TOO MUCH. AND I DON'T LIKE YOU.
'TIL THE STARS FALL DOWN?
HM.

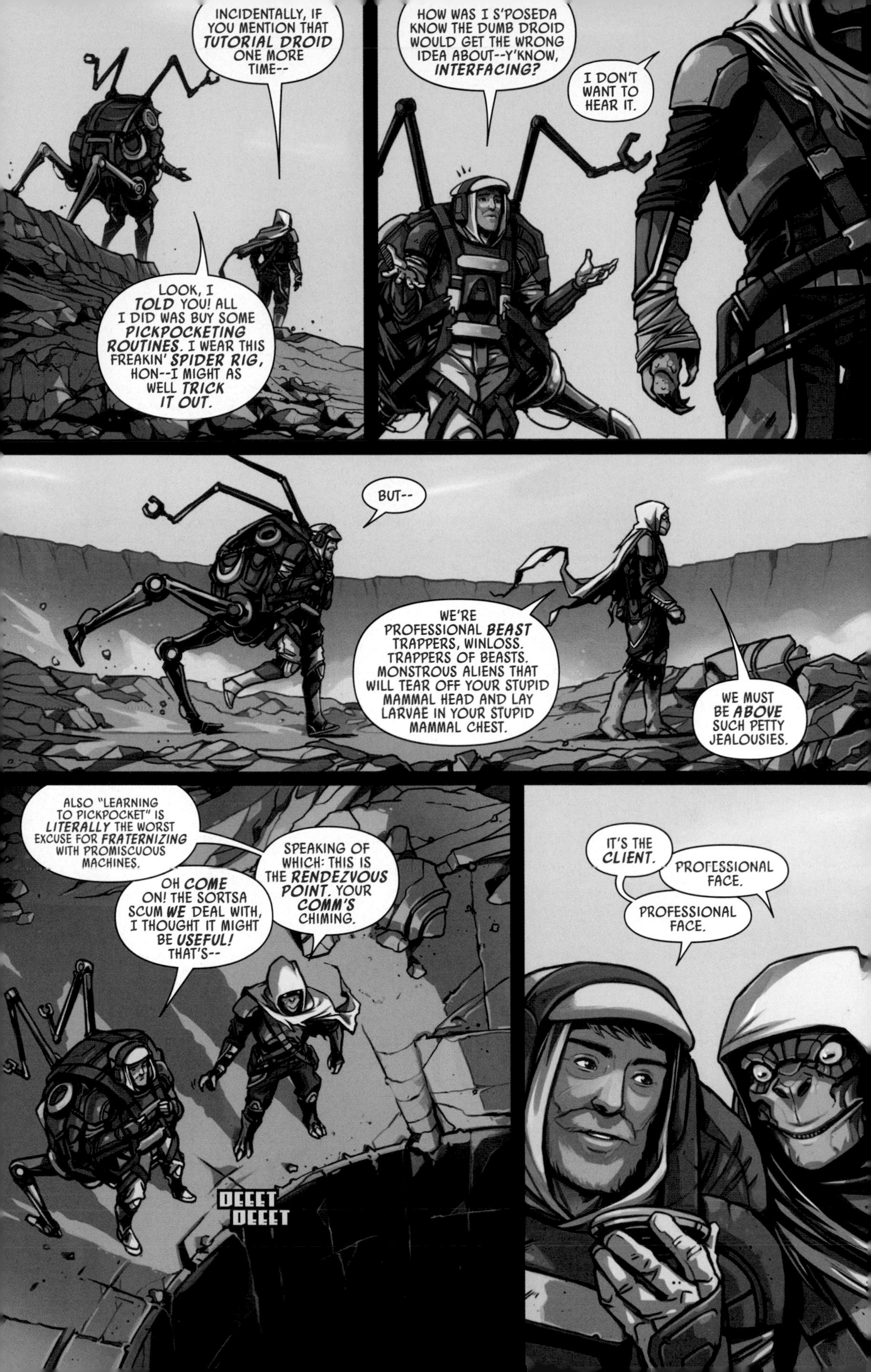
INCIDENTALLY, IF YOU MENTION THAT TUTORIAL DROID ONE MORE TIME--
LOOK, I TOLD YOU! ALL I DID WAS BUY SOME PICKPOCKETING ROUTINES. I WEAR THIS FREAKIN' SPIDER RIG, HON--I MIGHT AS WELL TRICK IT OUT.
HOW WAS I S'POSEDA KNOW THE DUMB DROID WOULD GET THE WRONG IDEA ABOUT--Y'KNOW, INTERFACING?
I DON'T WANT TO HEAR IT.
BUT--
WE'RE PROFESSIONAL BEAST TRAPPERS, WINLOSS. TRAPPERS OF BEASTS. MONSTROUS ALIENS THAT WILL TEAR OFF YOUR STUPID MAMMAL HEAD AND LAY LARVAE IN YOUR STUPID MAMMAL CHEST.
WE MUST BE ABOVE SUCH PETTY JEALOUSIES.
ALSO "LEARNING TO PICKPOCKET" IS LITERALLY THE WORST EXCUSE FOR FRATERNIZING WITH PROMISCUOUS MACHINES.
OH COME ON! THE SORTSA SCUM WE DEAL WITH, I THOUGHT IT MIGHT BE USEFUL! THAT'S--
SPEAKING OF WHICH: THIS IS THE RENDEZVOUS POINT. YOUR COMM'S CHIMING.
DEEET DEEET
IT'S THE CLIENT.
PROFESSIONAL FACE.
PROFESSIONAL FACE.

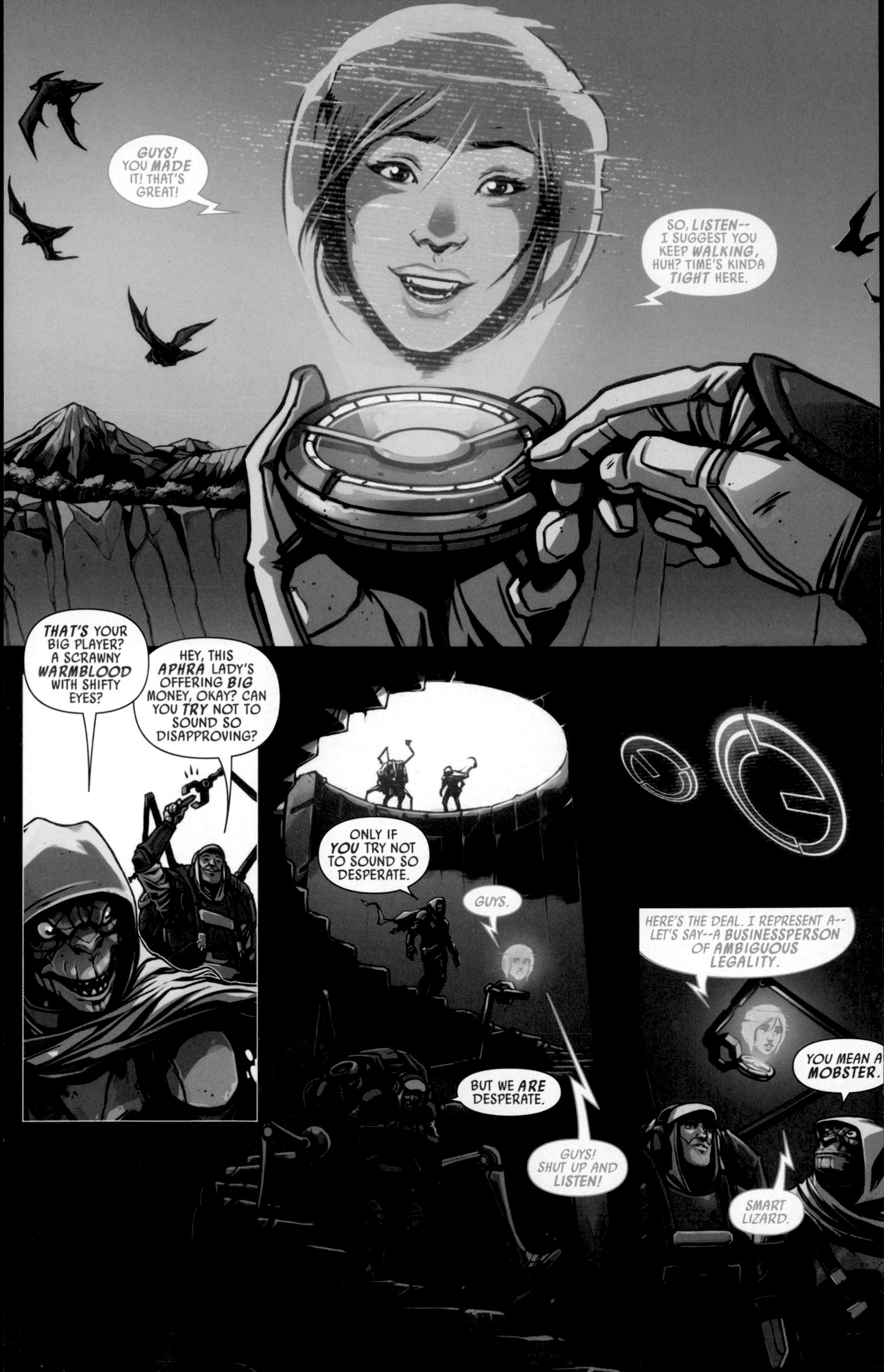
GUYS! YOU MADE IT! THAT'S GREAT!
SO, LISTEN-- I SUGGEST YOU KEEP WALKING, HUH? TIME'S KINDA TIGHT HERE.
THAT'S YOUR BIG PLAYER? A SCRAWNY WARMBLOOD WITH SHIFTY EYES?
HEY, THIS APHRA LADY'S OFFERING BIG MONEY, OKAY? CAN YOU TRY NOT TO SOUND SO DISAPPROVING?
ONLY IF YOU TRY NOT TO SOUND SO DESPERATE.
GUYS.
BUT WE ARE DESPERATE.
GUYS! SHUT UP AND LISTEN!
HERE'S THE DEAL. I REPRESENT A-- LET'S SAY--A BUSINESSPERSON OF AMBIGUOUS LEGALITY.
YOU MEAN A MOBSTER.
SMART LIZARD.

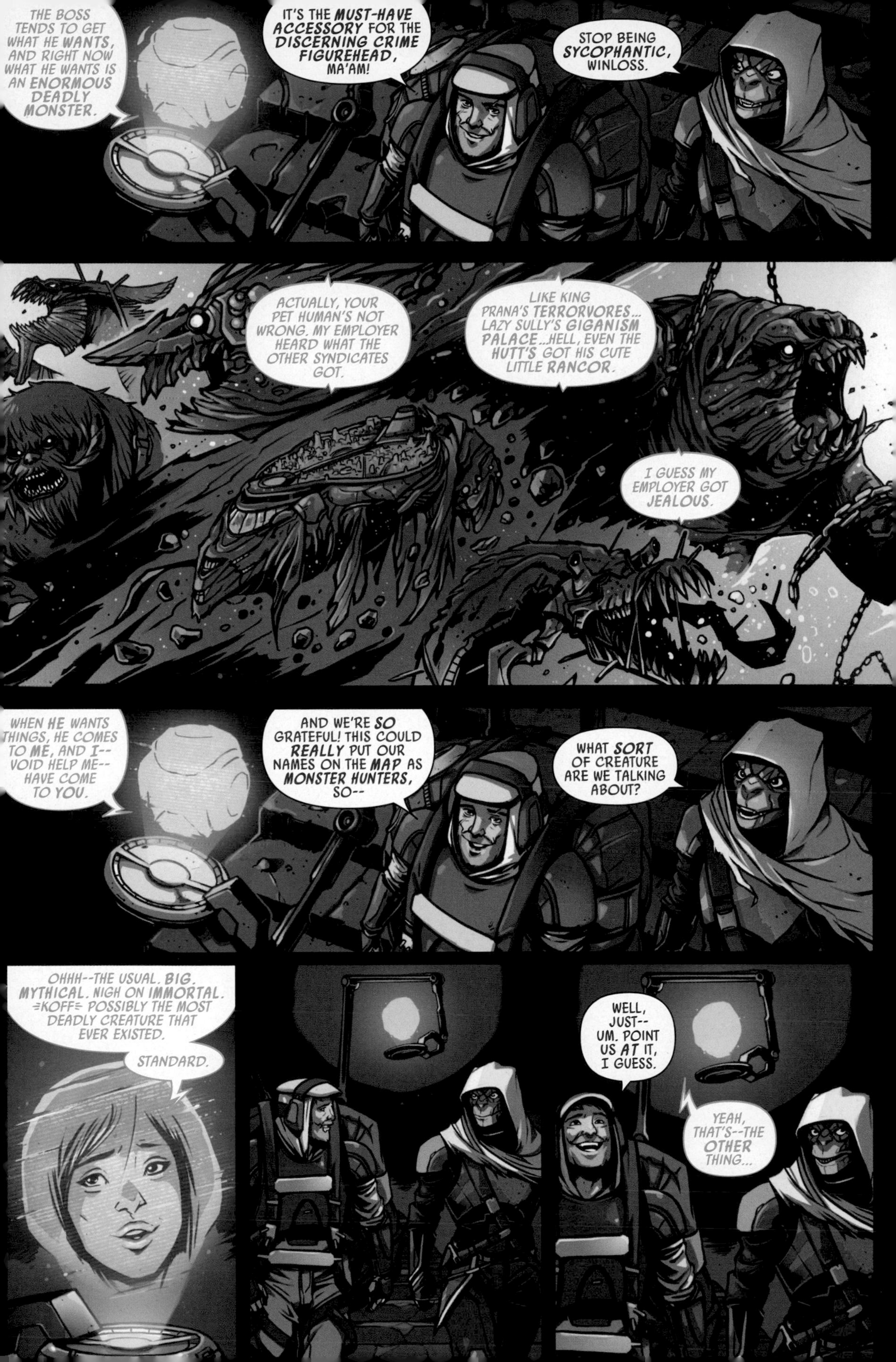
THE BOSS TENDS TO GET WHAT HE WANTS, AND RIGHT NOW WHAT HE WANTS IS AN ENORMOUS DEADLY MONSTER.
IT'S THE MUST-HAVE ACCESSORY FOR THE DISCERNING CRIME FIGUREHEAD, MA'AM!
STOP BEING SYCOPHANTIC, WINLOSS.
ACTUALLY, YOUR PET HUMAN'S NOT WRONG. MY EMPLOYER HEARD WHAT THE OTHER SYNDICATES GOT.
LIKE KING PRANA'S TERRORVORES... LAZY SULLY'S GIGANISM PALACE...HELL, EVEN THE HUTT'S GOT HIS CUTE LITTLE RANCOR.
I GUESS MY EMPLOYER GOT JEALOUS.
WHEN HE WANTS THINGS, HE COMES TO ME, AND I-- VOID HELP ME-- HAVE COME TO YOU.
AND WE'RE SO GRATEFUL! THIS COULD REALLY PUT OUR NAMES ON THE MAP AS MONSTER HUNTERS, SO--
WHAT SORT OF CREATURE ARE WE TALKING ABOUT?
OHHH--THE USUAL. BIG. MYTHICAL. NIGH ON IMMORTAL. =KOFF= POSSIBLY THE MOST DEADLY CREATURE THAT EVER EXISTED.
STANDARD.
WELL, JUST-- UM. POINT US AT IT, I GUESS.
YEAH, THAT'S--THE OTHER THING...

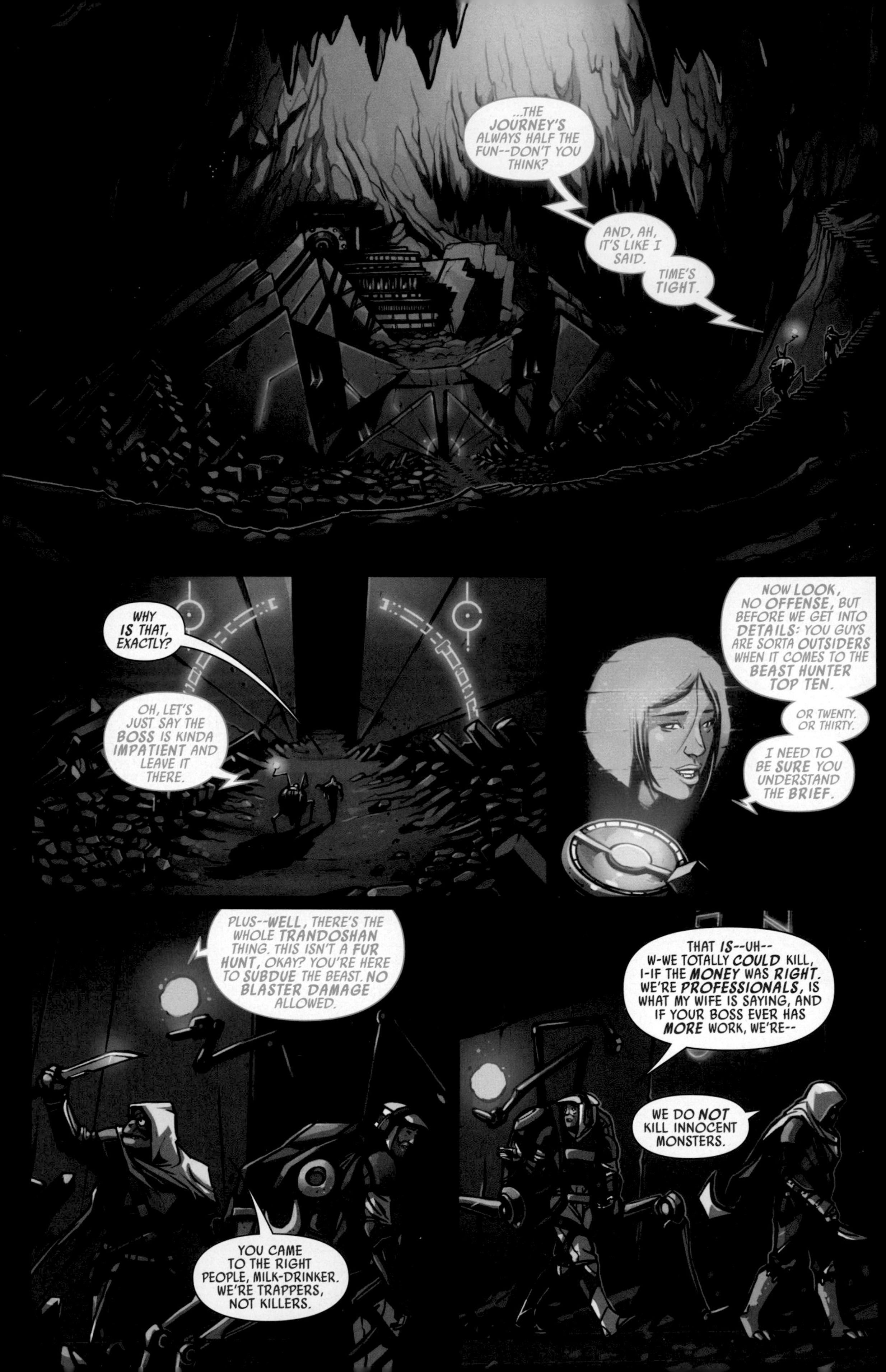
...THE JOURNEY'S ALWAYS HALF THE FUN--DON'T YOU THINK?
AND, AH, IT'S LIKE I SAID.
TIME'S TIGHT.
WHY IS THAT, EXACTLY?
OH, LET'S JUST SAY THE BOSS IS KINDA IMPATIENT AND LEAVE IT THERE.
NOW LOOK, NO OFFENSE, BUT BEFORE WE GET INTO DETAILS: YOU GUYS ARE SORTA OUTSIDERS WHEN IT COMES TO THE BEAST HUNTER TOP TEN.
OR TWENTY. OR THIRTY.
I NEED TO BE SURE YOU UNDERSTAND THE BRIEF.
PLUS--WELL, THERE'S THE WHOLE TRANDOSHAN THING. THIS ISN'T A FUR HUNT, OKAY? YOU'RE HERE TO SUBDUE THE BEAST. NO BLASTER DAMAGE ALLOWED.
YOU CAME TO THE RIGHT PEOPLE, MILK-DRINKER. WE'RE TRAPPERS, NOT KILLERS.
THAT IS--UH-- W-WE TOTALLY COULD KILL, I-IF THE MONEY WAS RIGHT. WE'RE PROFESSIONALS, IS WHAT MY WIFE IS SAYING, AND IF YOUR BOSS EVER HAS MORE WORK, WE'RE--
WE DO NOT KILL INNOCENT MONSTERS.

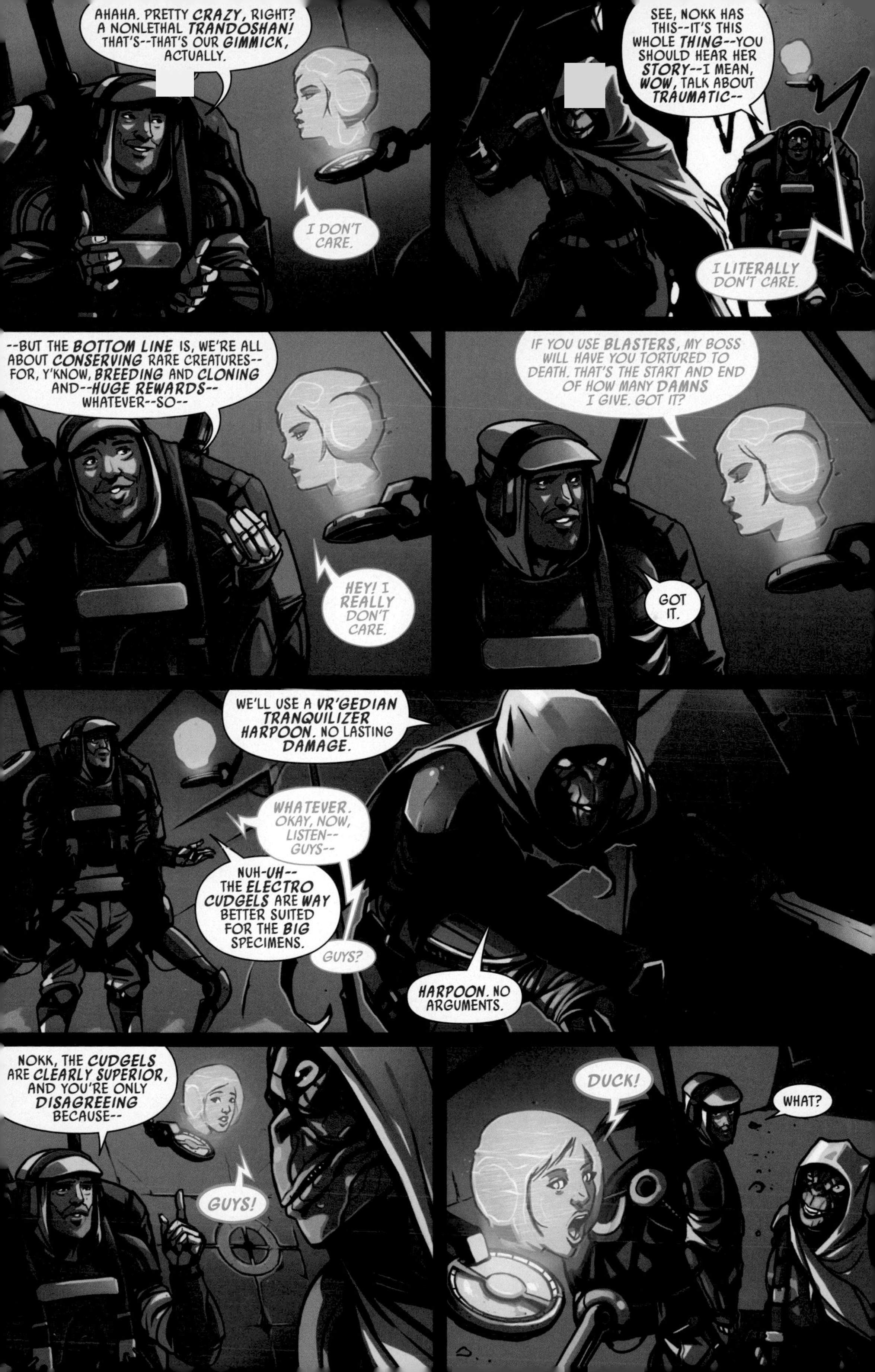
AHAHA. PRETTY CRAZY, RIGHT? A NONLETHAL TRANDOSHAN! THAT'S--THAT'S OUR GIMMICK, ACTUALLY.
I DON'T CARE.
SEE, NOKK HAS THIS--IT'S THIS WHOLE THING--YOU SHOULD HEAR HER STORY--I MEAN, WOW, TALK ABOUT TRAUMATIC--
I LITERALLY DON'T CARE.
--BUT THE BOTTOM LINE IS, WE'RE ALL ABOUT CONSERVING RARE CREATURES--FOR, Y'KNOW, BREEDING AND CLONING AND--HUGE REWARDS--WHATEVER--SO--
HEY! I REALLY DON'T CARE.
IF YOU USE BLASTERS, MY BOSS WILL HAVE YOU TORTURED TO DEATH. THAT'S THE START AND END OF HOW MANY DAMNS I GIVE. GOT IT?
GOT IT.
WE'LL USE A VR'GEDIAN TRANQUILIZER HARPOON. NO LASTING DAMAGE.
WHATEVER. OKAY, NOW, LISTEN--GUYS--
NUH-UH--THE ELECTRO CUDGELS ARE WAY BETTER SUITED FOR THE BIG SPECIMENS.
GUYS?
HARPOON. NO ARGUMENTS.
NOKK, THE CUDGELS ARE CLEARLY SUPERIOR, AND YOU'RE ONLY DISAGREEING BECAUSE--
GUYS!
DUCK!
WHAT?

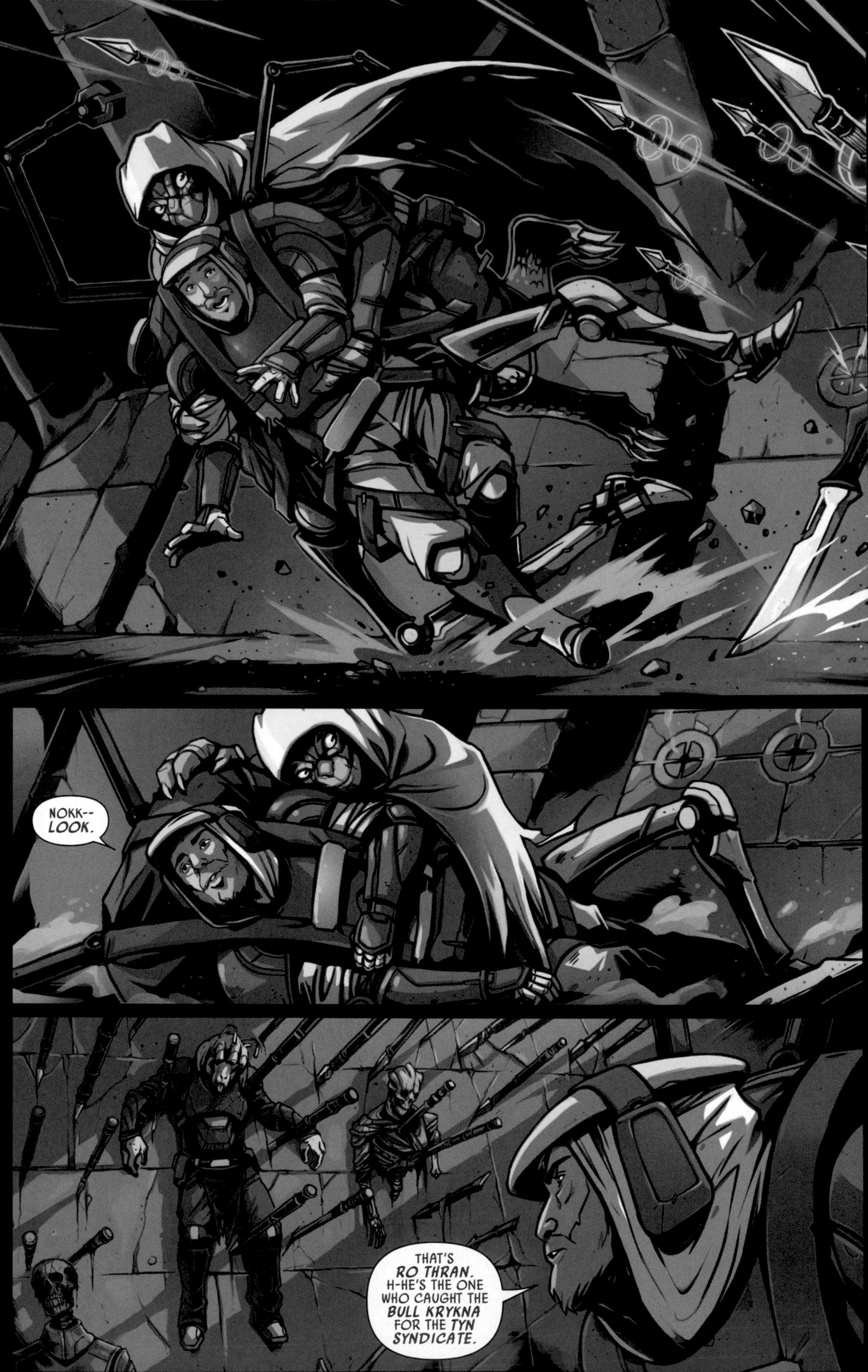
NOKK--
LOOK.
THAT'S RO THRAN. H-HE'S THE ONE WHO CAUGHT THE BULL KRYKNA FOR THE TYN SYNDICATE.

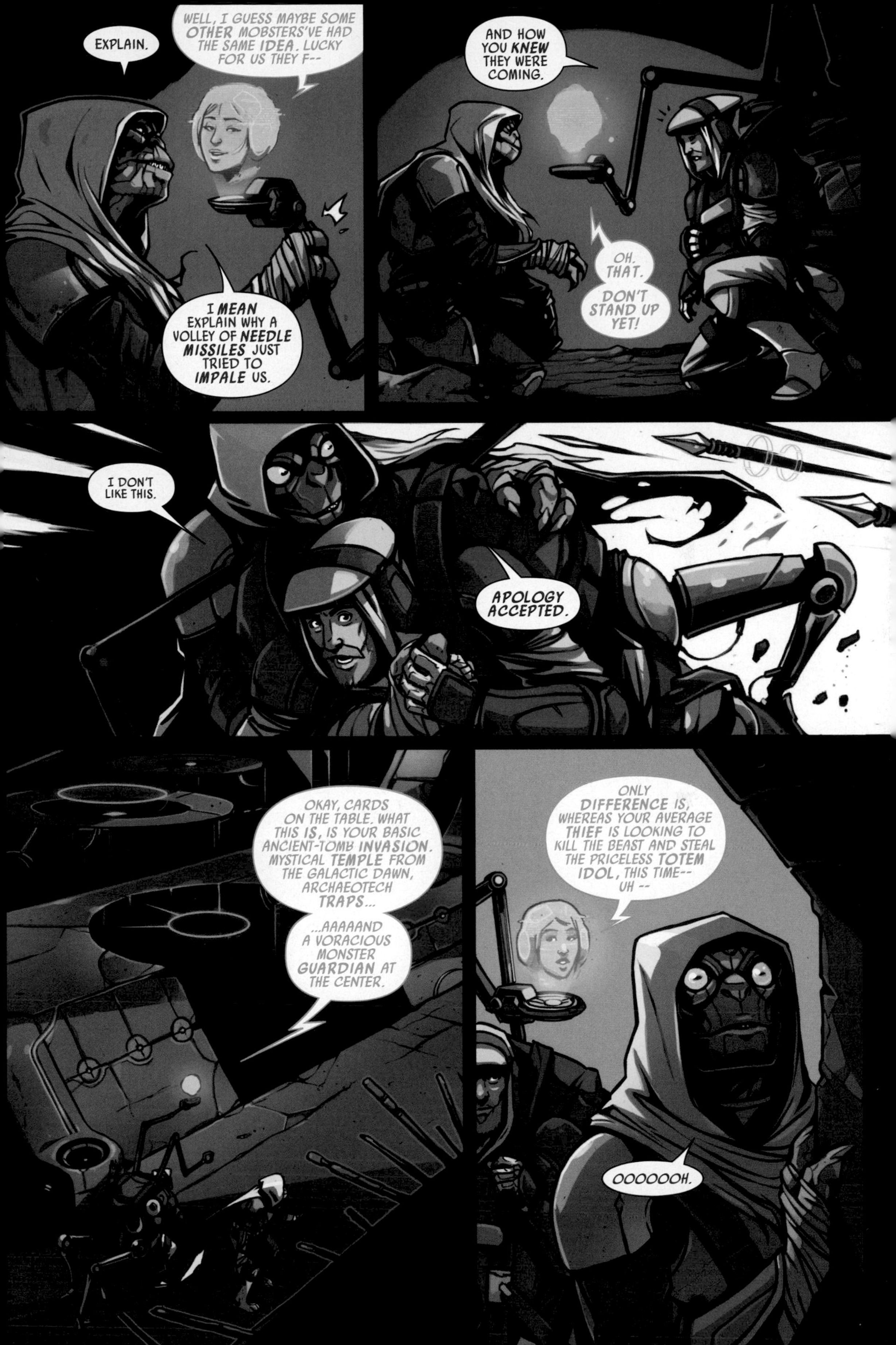
EXPLAIN.
WELL, I GUESS MAYBE SOME OTHER MOBSTERS'VE HAD THE SAME IDEA. LUCKY FOR US THEY F--
I MEAN EXPLAIN WHY A VOLLEY OF NEEDLE MISSILES JUST TRIED TO IMPALE US.
AND HOW YOU KNEW THEY WERE COMING.
OH. THAT.
DON'T STAND UP YET!
I DON'T LIKE THIS.
APOLOGY ACCEPTED.
OKAY, CARDS ON THE TABLE. WHAT THIS IS, IS YOUR BASIC ANCIENT-TOMB INVASION. MYSTICAL TEMPLE FROM THE GALACTIC DAWN, ARCHAEOTECH TRAPS...
...AAAAAND A VORACIOUS MONSTER GUARDIAN AT THE CENTER.
ONLY DIFFERENCE IS, WHEREAS YOUR AVERAGE THIEF IS LOOKING TO KILL THE BEAST AND STEAL THE PRICELESS TOTEM IDOL, THIS TIME-- UH --
OOOOOOH.

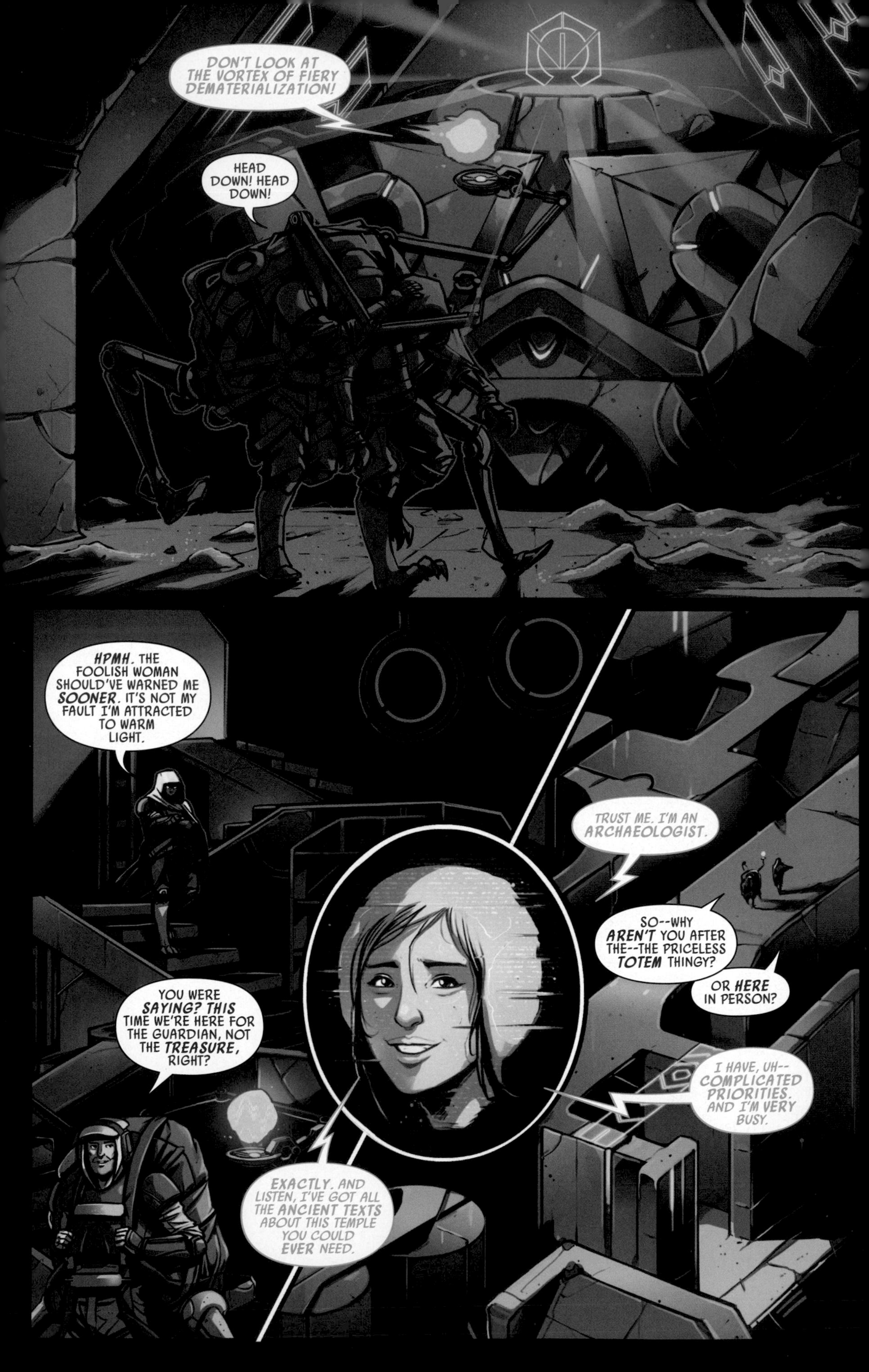
DON'T LOOK AT THE VORTEX OF FIERY DEMATERIALIZATION!
HEAD DOWN! HEAD DOWN!
HPMH. THE FOOLISH WOMAN SHOULD'VE WARNED ME SOONER. IT'S NOT MY FAULT I'M ATTRACTED TO WARM LIGHT.
YOU WERE SAYING? THIS TIME WE'RE HERE FOR THE GUARDIAN, NOT THE TREASURE, RIGHT?
EXACTLY. AND LISTEN, I'VE GOT ALL THE ANCIENT TEXTS ABOUT THIS TEMPLE YOU COULD EVER NEED.
TRUST ME. I'M AN ARCHAEOLOGIST.
SO--WHY AREN'T YOU AFTER THE--THE PRICELESS TOTEM THINGY?
OR HERE IN PERSON?
I HAVE, UH-- COMPLICATED PRIORITIES. AND I'M VERY BUSY.

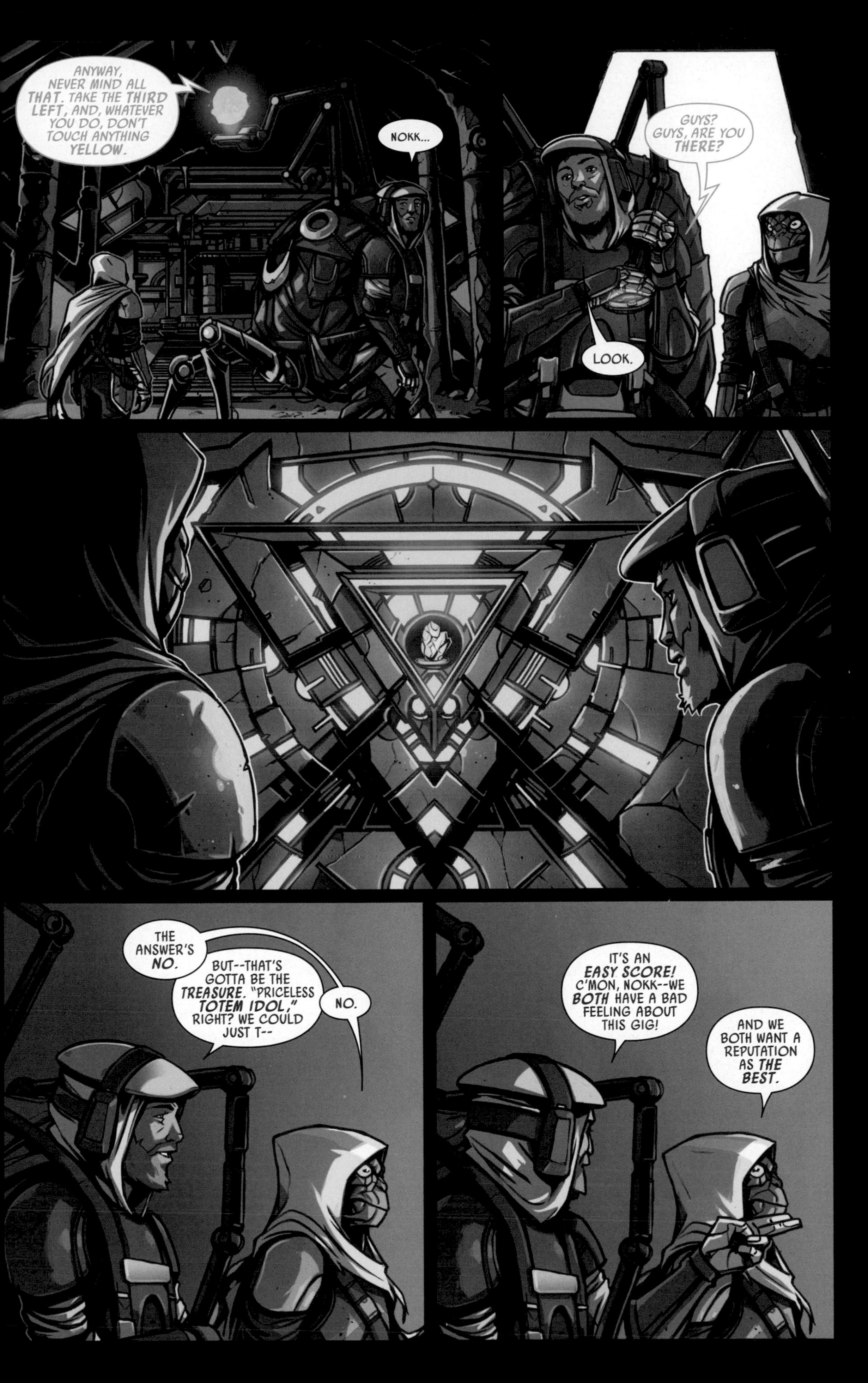
ANYWAY, NEVER MIND ALL THAT. TAKE THE THIRD LEFT, AND, WHATEVER YOU DO, DON'T TOUCH ANYTHING YELLOW.
NOKK...
GUYS? GUYS, ARE YOU THERE?
LOOK.
THE ANSWER'S NO.
BUT--THAT'S GOTTA BE THE TREASURE. "PRICELESS TOTEM IDOL," RIGHT? WE COULD JUST T--
NO.
IT'S AN EASY SCORE! C'MON, NOKK--WE BOTH HAVE A BAD FEELING ABOUT THIS GIG!
AND WE BOTH WANT A REPUTATION AS THE BEST.

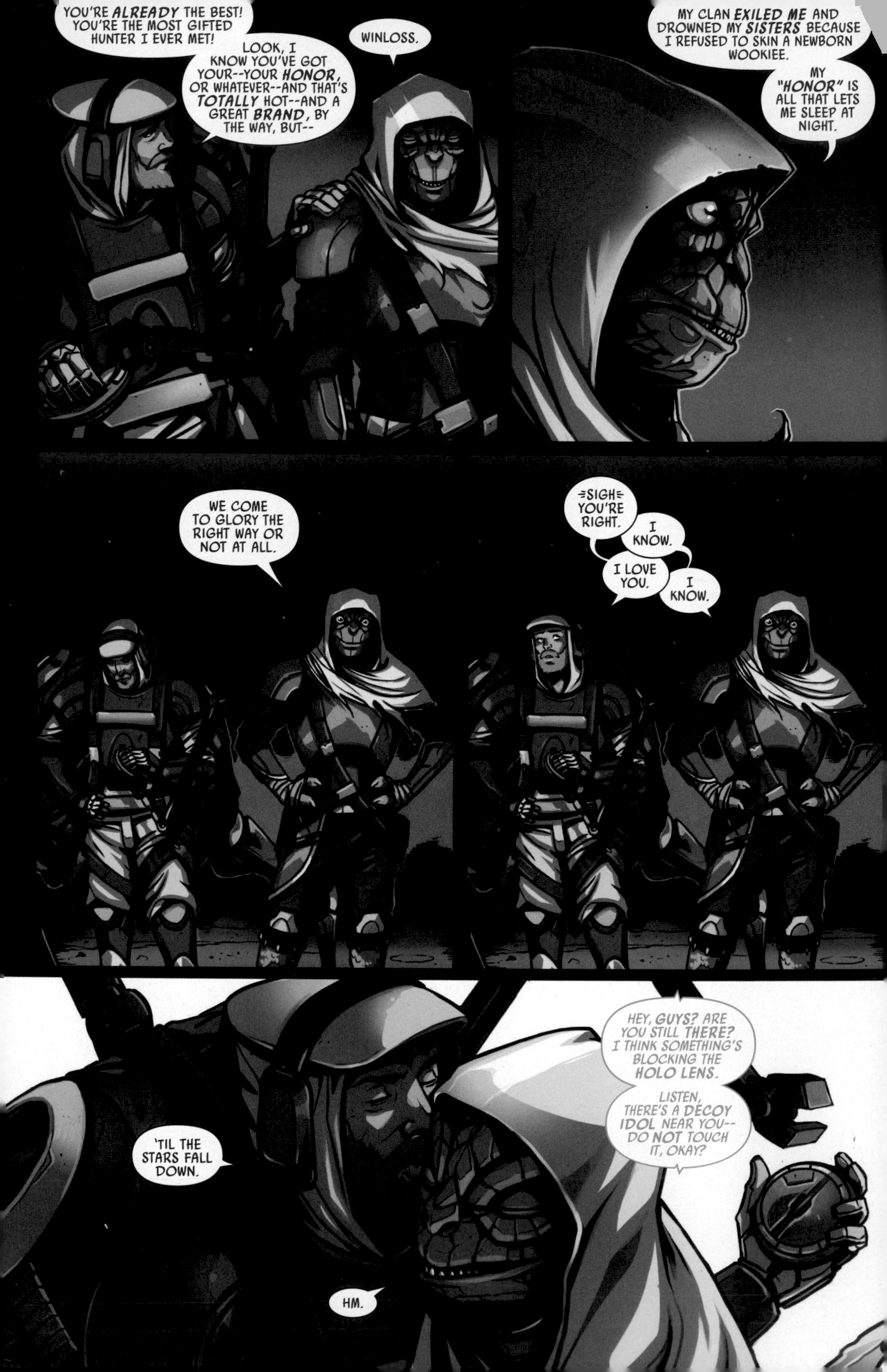

YOU'RE ALREADY THE BEST! YOU'RE THE MOST GIFTED HUNTER I EVER MET!
LOOK, I KNOW YOU'VE GOT YOUR--YOUR HONOR, OR WHATEVER--AND THAT'S TOTALLY HOT--AND A GREAT BRAND, BY THE WAY, BUT--
WINLOSS.
MY CLAN EXILED ME AND DROWNED MY SISTERS BECAUSE I REFUSED TO SKIN A NEWBORN WOOKIEE.
MY "HONOR" IS ALL THAT LETS ME SLEEP AT NIGHT.
WE COME TO GLORY THE RIGHT WAY OR NOT AT ALL.
=SIGH= YOU'RE RIGHT.
I KNOW.
I LOVE YOU.
I KNOW.
HEY, GUYS? ARE YOU STILL THERE? I THINK SOMETHING'S BLOCKING THE HOLO LENS.
LISTEN, THERE'S A DECOY IDOL NEAR YOU-- DO NOT TOUCH IT, OKAY?
'TIL THE STARS FALL DOWN.
HM.

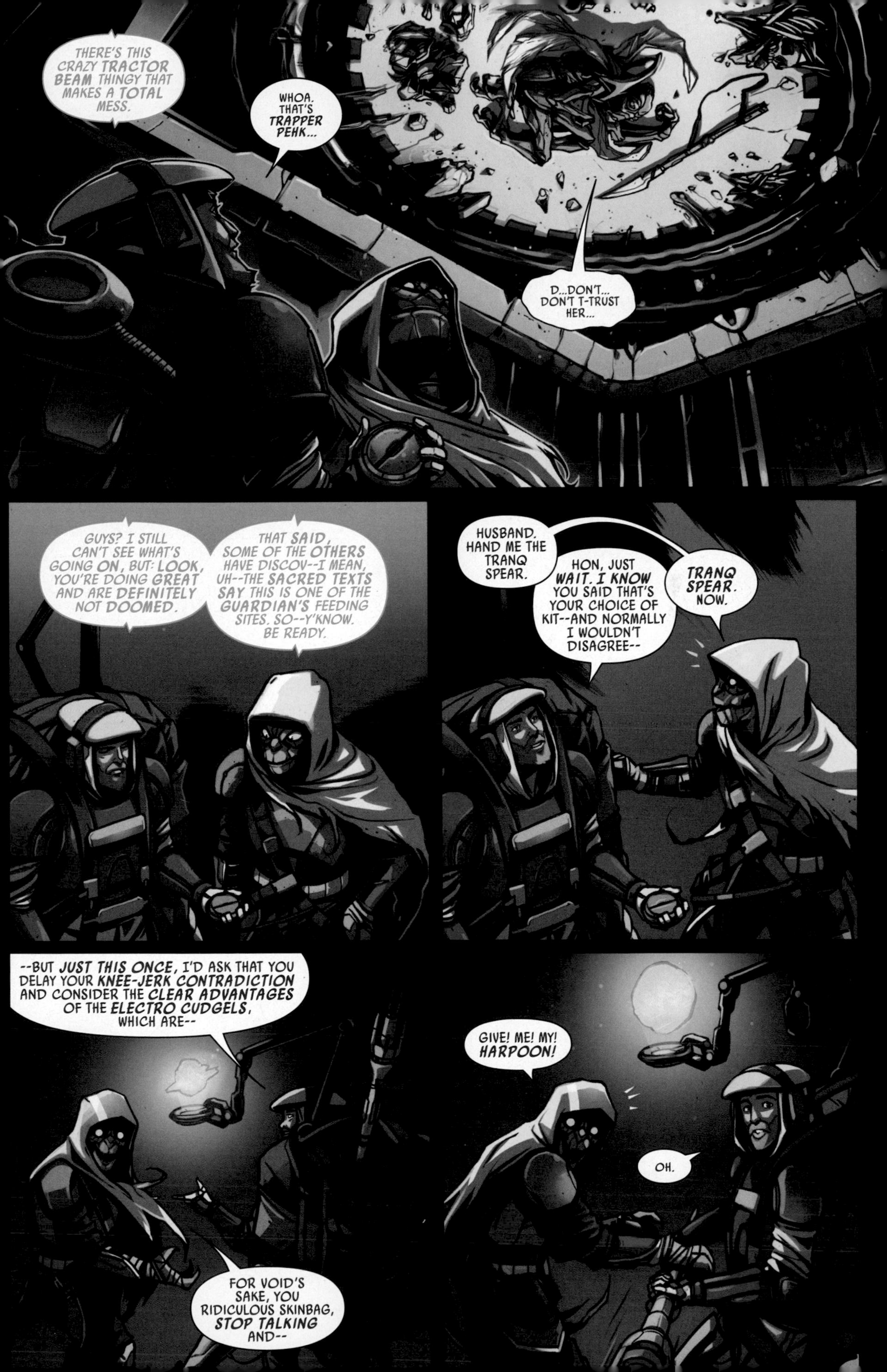
THERE'S THIS CRAZY TRACTOR BEAM THINGY THAT MAKES A TOTAL MESS.
WHOA. THAT'S TRAPPER PEHK...
D...DON'T... DON'T T-TRUST HER...
GUYS? I STILL CAN'T SEE WHAT'S GOING ON, BUT: LOOK, YOU'RE DOING GREAT AND ARE DEFINITELY NOT DOOMED.
THAT SAID, SOME OF THE OTHERS HAVE DISCOV--I MEAN, UH--THE SACRED TEXTS SAY THIS IS ONE OF THE GUARDIAN'S FEEDING SITES. SO--Y'KNOW. BE READY.
HUSBAND. HAND ME THE TRANQ SPEAR.
HON, JUST WAIT. I KNOW YOU SAID THAT'S YOUR CHOICE OF KIT--AND NORMALLY I WOULDN'T DISAGREE--
TRANQ SPEAR. NOW.
--BUT JUST THIS ONCE, I'D ASK THAT YOU DELAY YOUR KNEE-JERK CONTRADICTION AND CONSIDER THE CLEAR ADVANTAGES OF THE ELECTRO CUDGELS, WHICH ARE--
FOR VOID'S SAKE, YOU RIDICULOUS SKINBAG, STOP TALKING AND--
GIVE! ME! MY! HARPOON!
OH.

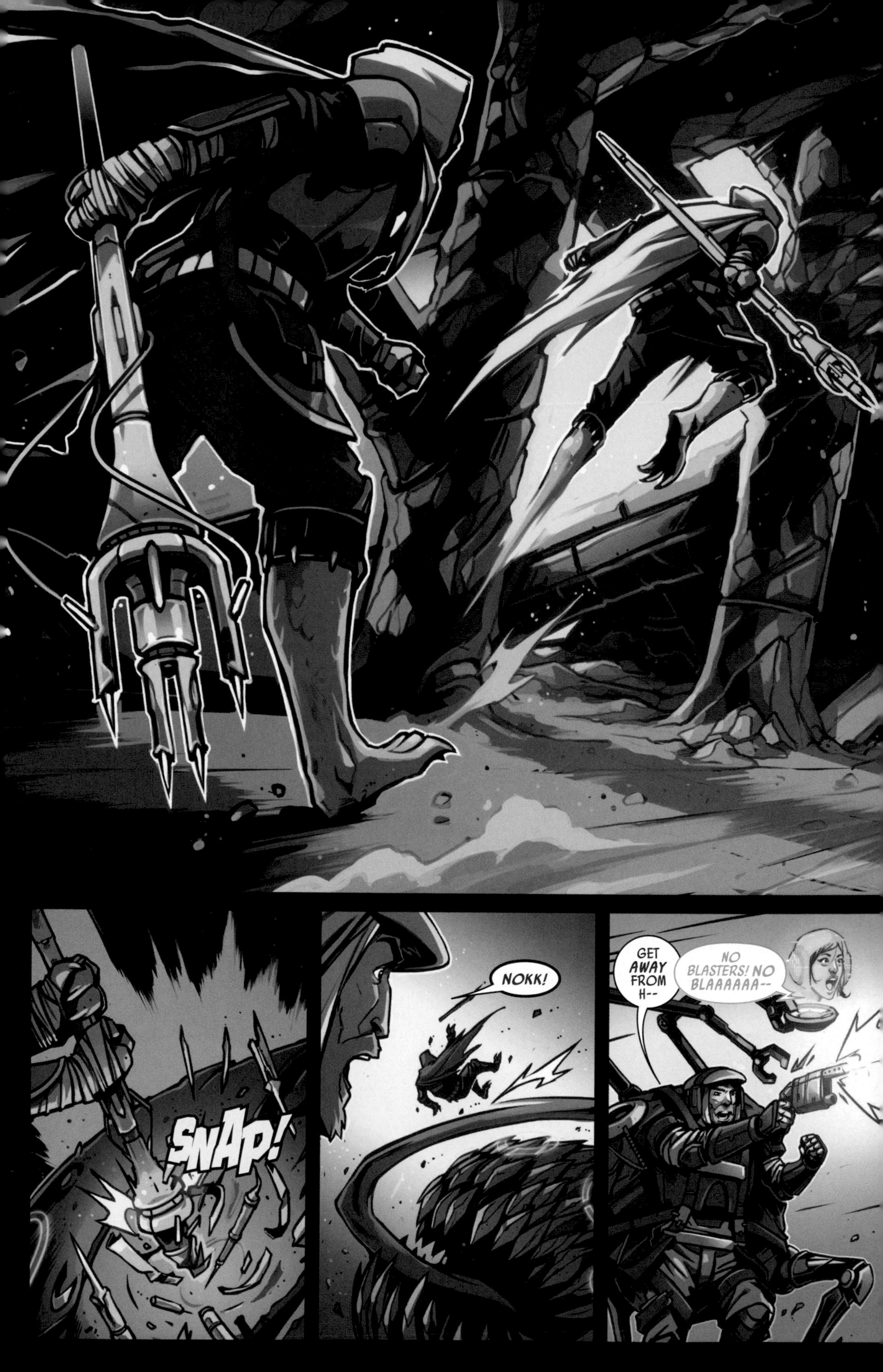
SNAP!
NOKK!
GET AWAY FROM H--
NO BLASTERS! NO BLAAAAAA--

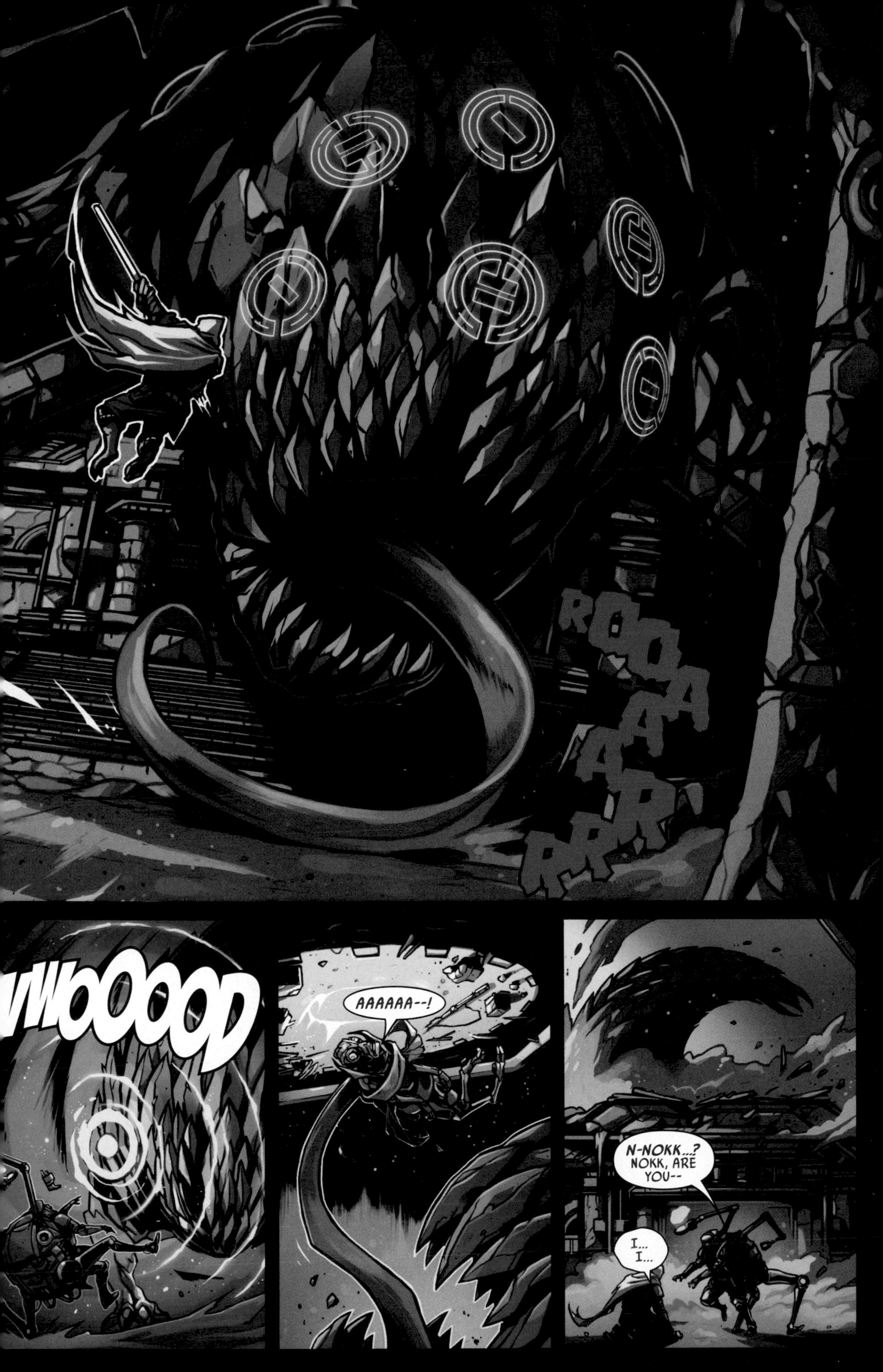
ROOOAAARRR
VWOOOOD
AAAAAA--!
N-NOKK...? NOKK, ARE YOU--
I... I...

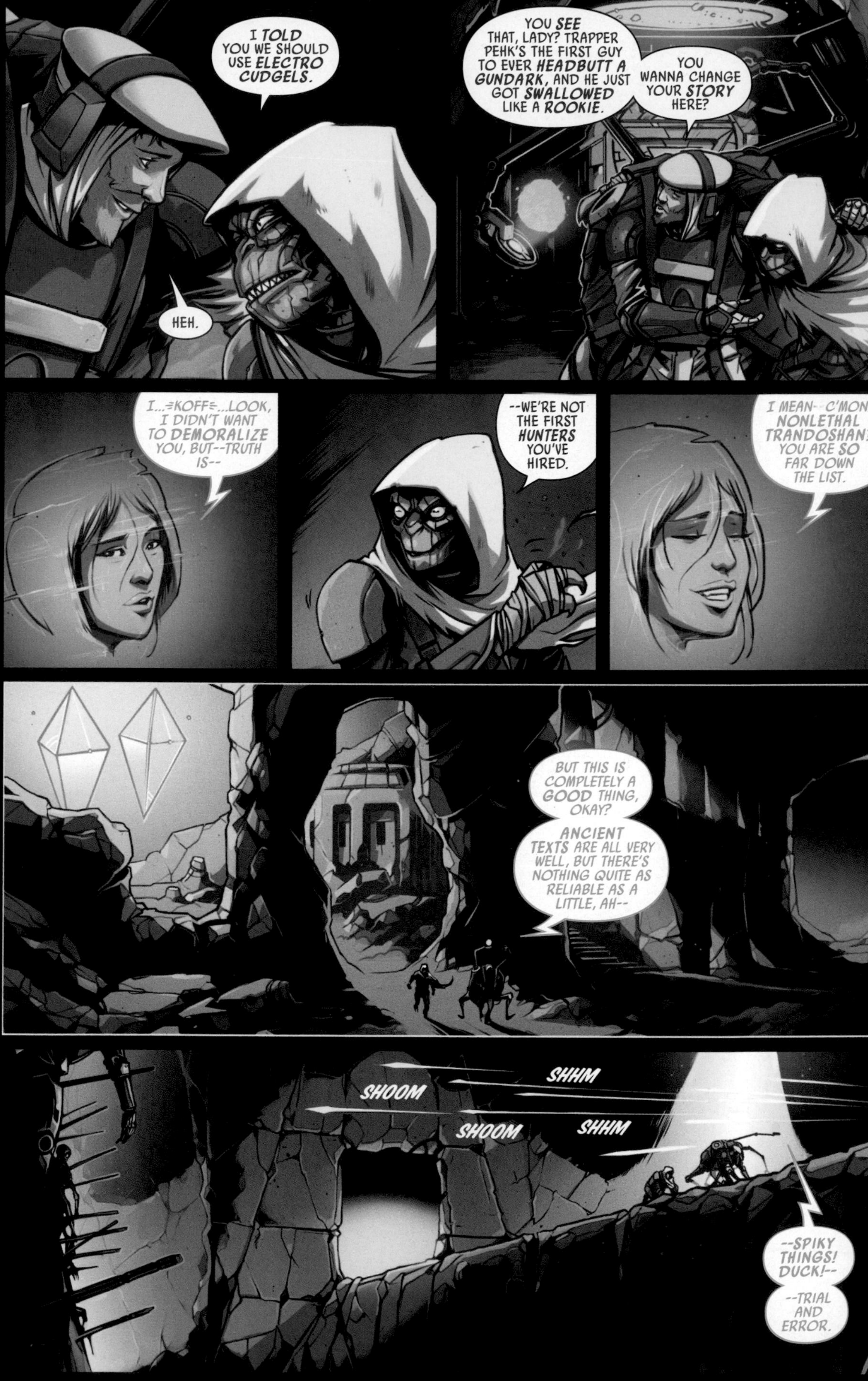
I TOLD YOU WE SHOULD USE ELECTRO CUDGELS.
HEH.
YOU SEE THAT, LADY? TRAPPER PEHK'S THE FIRST GUY TO EVER HEADBUTT A GUNDARK, AND HE JUST GOT SWALLOWED LIKE A ROOKIE.
YOU WANNA CHANGE YOUR STORY HERE?
I... =KOFF=... LOOK, I DIDN'T WANT TO DEMORALIZE YOU, BUT--TRUTH IS--
--WE'RE NOT THE FIRST HUNTERS YOU'VE HIRED.
I MEAN-- C'MON! NONLETHAL TRANDOSHAN? YOU ARE SO FAR DOWN THE LIST.
BUT THIS IS COMPLETELY A GOOD THING, OKAY?
ANCIENT TEXTS ARE ALL VERY WELL, BUT THERE'S NOTHING QUITE AS RELIABLE AS A LITTLE, AH--
SHOOM
SHHM
SHOOM
SHHM
--SPIKY THINGS! DUCK!--
--TRIAL AND ERROR.

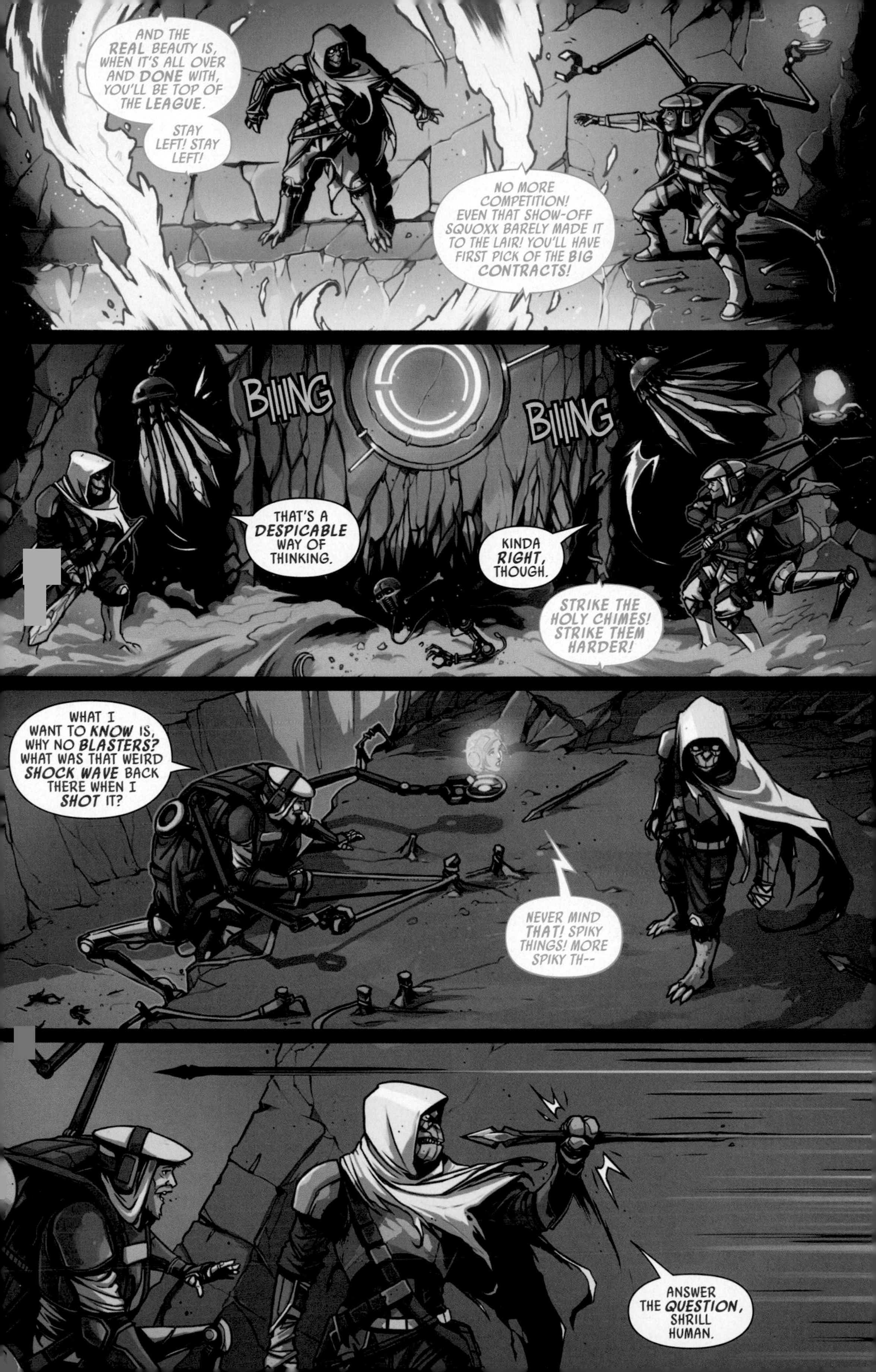
AND THE REAL BEAUTY IS, WHEN IT'S ALL OVER AND DONE WITH, YOU'LL BE TOP OF THE LEAGUE.
STAY LEFT! STAY LEFT!
NO MORE COMPETITION! EVEN THAT SHOW-OFF SQUOXX BARELY MADE IT TO THE LAIR! YOU'LL HAVE FIRST PICK OF THE BIG CONTRACTS!
BIIING
BIIING
THAT'S A DESPICABLE WAY OF THINKING.
KINDA RIGHT, THOUGH.
STRIKE THE HOLY CHIMES! STRIKE THEM HARDER!
WHAT I WANT TO KNOW IS, WHY NO BLASTERS? WHAT WAS THAT WEIRD SHOCK WAVE BACK THERE WHEN I SHOT IT?
NEVER MIND THAT! SPIKY THINGS! MORE SPIKY TH--
ANSWER THE QUESTION, SHRILL HUMAN.

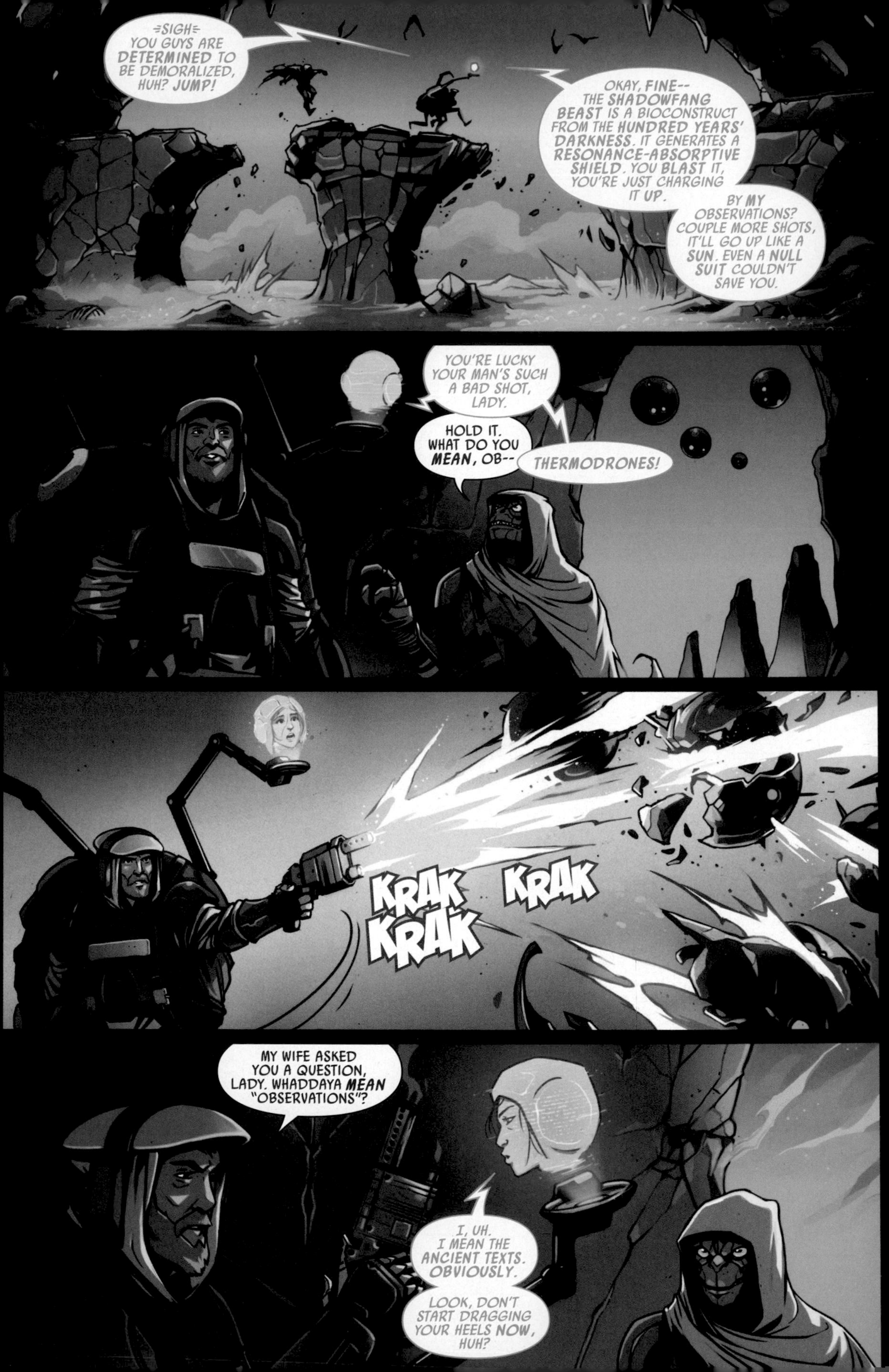

=SIGH= YOU GUYS ARE DETERMINED TO BE DEMORALIZED, HUH? JUMP!
OKAY, FINE-- THE SHADOWFANG BEAST IS A BIOCONSTRUCT FROM THE HUNDRED YEARS' DARKNESS. IT GENERATES A RESONANCE-ABSORPTIVE SHIELD. YOU BLAST IT, YOU'RE JUST CHARGING IT UP.
BY MY OBSERVATIONS? COUPLE MORE SHOTS, IT'LL GO UP LIKE A SUN. EVEN A NULL SUIT COULDN'T SAVE YOU.
YOU'RE LUCKY YOUR MAN'S SUCH A BAD SHOT, LADY.
HOLD IT. WHAT DO YOU MEAN, OB--
THERMODRONES!
KRAK
KRAK
KRAK
MY WIFE ASKED YOU A QUESTION, LADY. WHADDAYA MEAN "OBSERVATIONS"?
I, UH. I MEAN THE ANCIENT TEXTS. OBVIOUSLY.
LOOK, DON'T START DRAGGING YOUR HEELS NOW, HUH?

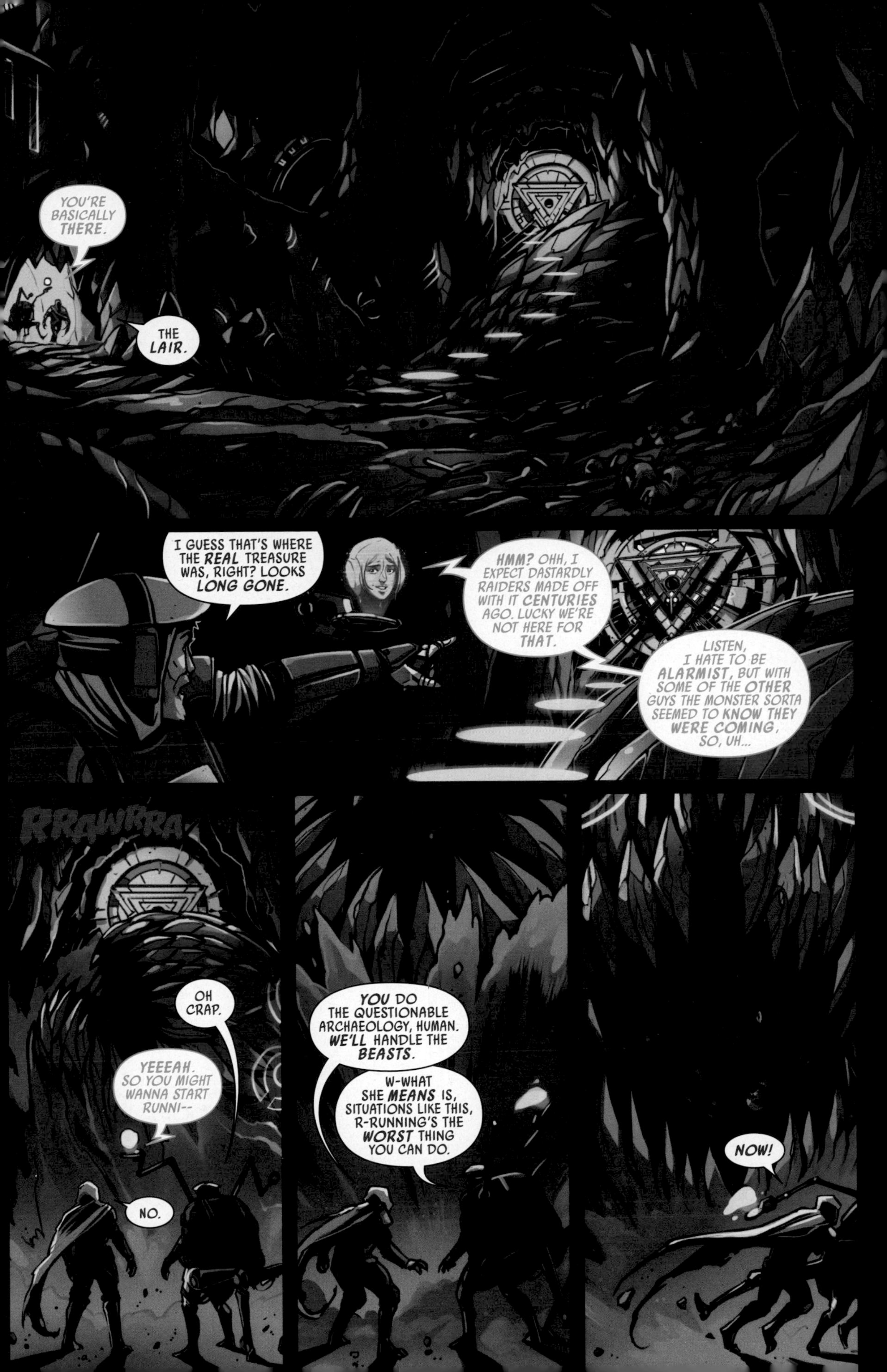
YOU'RE BASICALLY THERE.
THE LAIR.
I GUESS THAT'S WHERE THE REAL TREASURE WAS, RIGHT? LOOKS LONG GONE.
HMM? OHH, I EXPECT DASTARDLY RAIDERS MADE OFF WITH IT CENTURIES AGO. LUCKY WE'RE NOT HERE FOR THAT.
LISTEN, I HATE TO BE ALARMIST, BUT WITH SOME OF THE OTHER GUYS THE MONSTER SORTA SEEMED TO KNOW THEY WERE COMING, SO, UH...
RRAWRRA
OH CRAP.
YEEEAH. SO YOU MIGHT WANNA START RUNNI--
NO.
YOU DO THE QUESTIONABLE ARCHAEOLOGY, HUMAN. WE'LL HANDLE THE BEASTS.
W-WHAT SHE MEANS IS, SITUATIONS LIKE THIS, R-RUNNING'S THE WORST THING YOU CAN DO.
NOW!

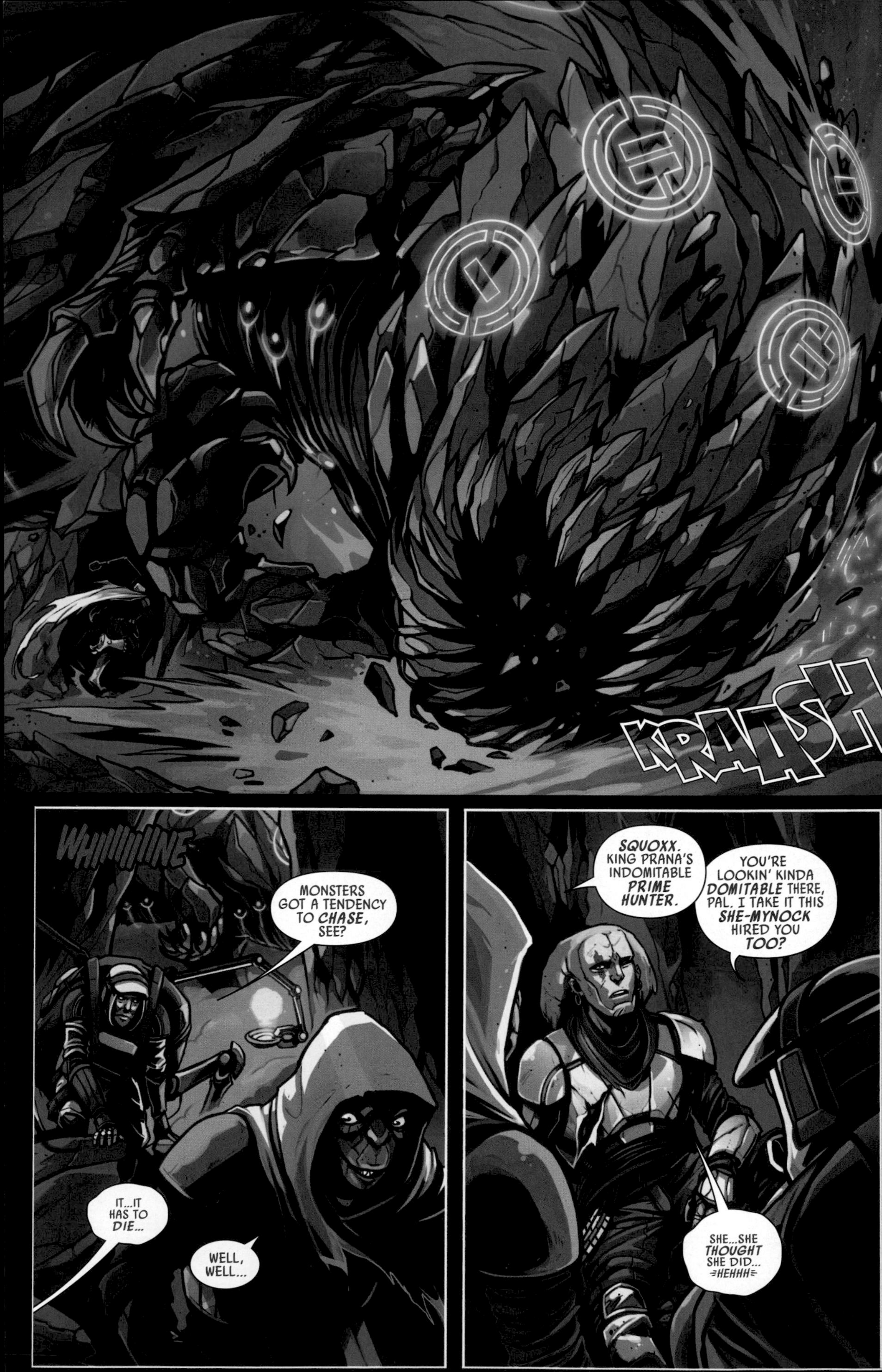
KRAASH
WHIIIIIIINE
MONSTERS GOT A TENDENCY TO CHASE, SEE?
IT...IT HAS TO DIE...
WELL, WELL...
SQUOXX. KING PRANA'S INDOMITABLE PRIME HUNTER.
YOU'RE LOOKIN' KINDA DOMITABLE THERE, PAL. I TAKE IT THIS SHE-MYNOCK HIRED YOU TOO?
SHE...SHE THOUGHT SHE DID... =HEHHH=

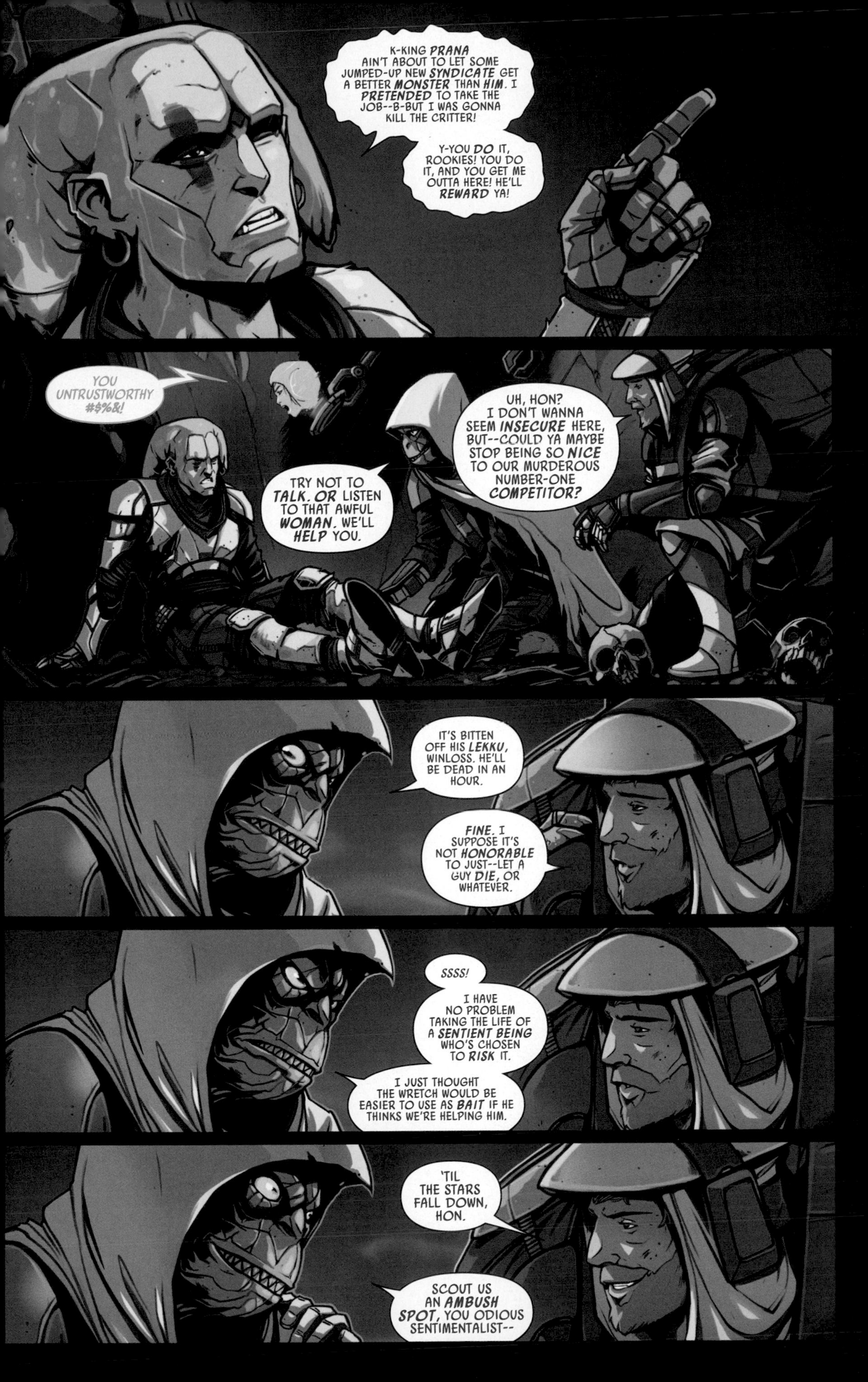
K-KING PRANA AIN'T ABOUT TO LET SOME JUMPED-UP NEW SYNDICATE GET A BETTER MONSTER THAN HIM. I PRETENDED TO TAKE THE JOB--B-BUT I WAS GONNA KILL THE CRITTER!
Y-YOU DO IT, ROOKIES! YOU DO IT, AND YOU GET ME OUTTA HERE! HE'LL REWARD YA!
YOU UNTRUSTWORTHY #$%&!
TRY NOT TO TALK. OR LISTEN TO THAT AWFUL WOMAN. WE'LL HELP YOU.
UH, HON? I DON'T WANNA SEEM INSECURE HERE, BUT--COULD YA MAYBE STOP BEING SO NICE TO OUR MURDEROUS NUMBER-ONE COMPETITOR?
IT'S BITTEN OFF HIS LEKKU, WINLOSS. HE'LL BE DEAD IN AN HOUR.
FINE. I SUPPOSE IT'S NOT HONORABLE TO JUST--LET A GUY DIE, OR WHATEVER.
SSSS!
I HAVE NO PROBLEM TAKING THE LIFE OF A SENTIENT BEING WHO'S CHOSEN TO RISK IT.
I JUST THOUGHT THE WRETCH WOULD BE EASIER TO USE AS BAIT IF HE THINKS WE'RE HELPING HIM.
'TIL THE STARS FALL DOWN, HON.
SCOUT US AN AMBUSH SPOT, YOU ODIOUS SENTIMENTALIST--

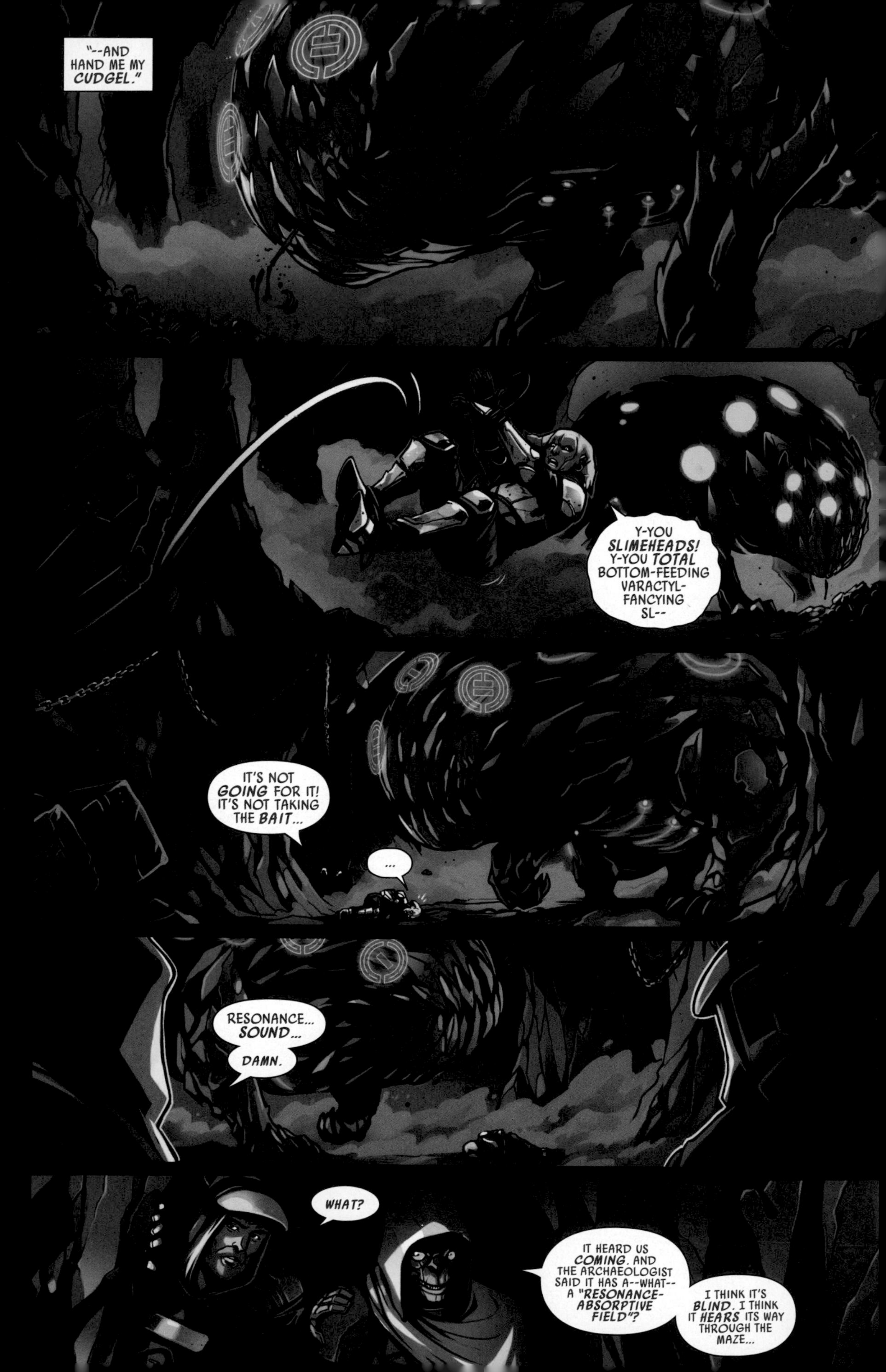
"--AND HAND ME MY CUDGEL."
Y-YOU SLIMEHEADS! Y-YOU TOTAL BOTTOM-FEEDING VARACTYL-FANCYING SL--
IT'S NOT GOING FOR IT! IT'S NOT TAKING THE BAIT...
...
RESONANCE... SOUND...
DAMN.
WHAT?
IT HEARD US COMING. AND THE ARCHAEOLOGIST SAID IT HAS A--WHAT--A "RESONANCE-ABSORPTIVE FIELD"?
I THINK IT'S BLIND. I THINK IT HEARS ITS WAY THROUGH THE MAZE...

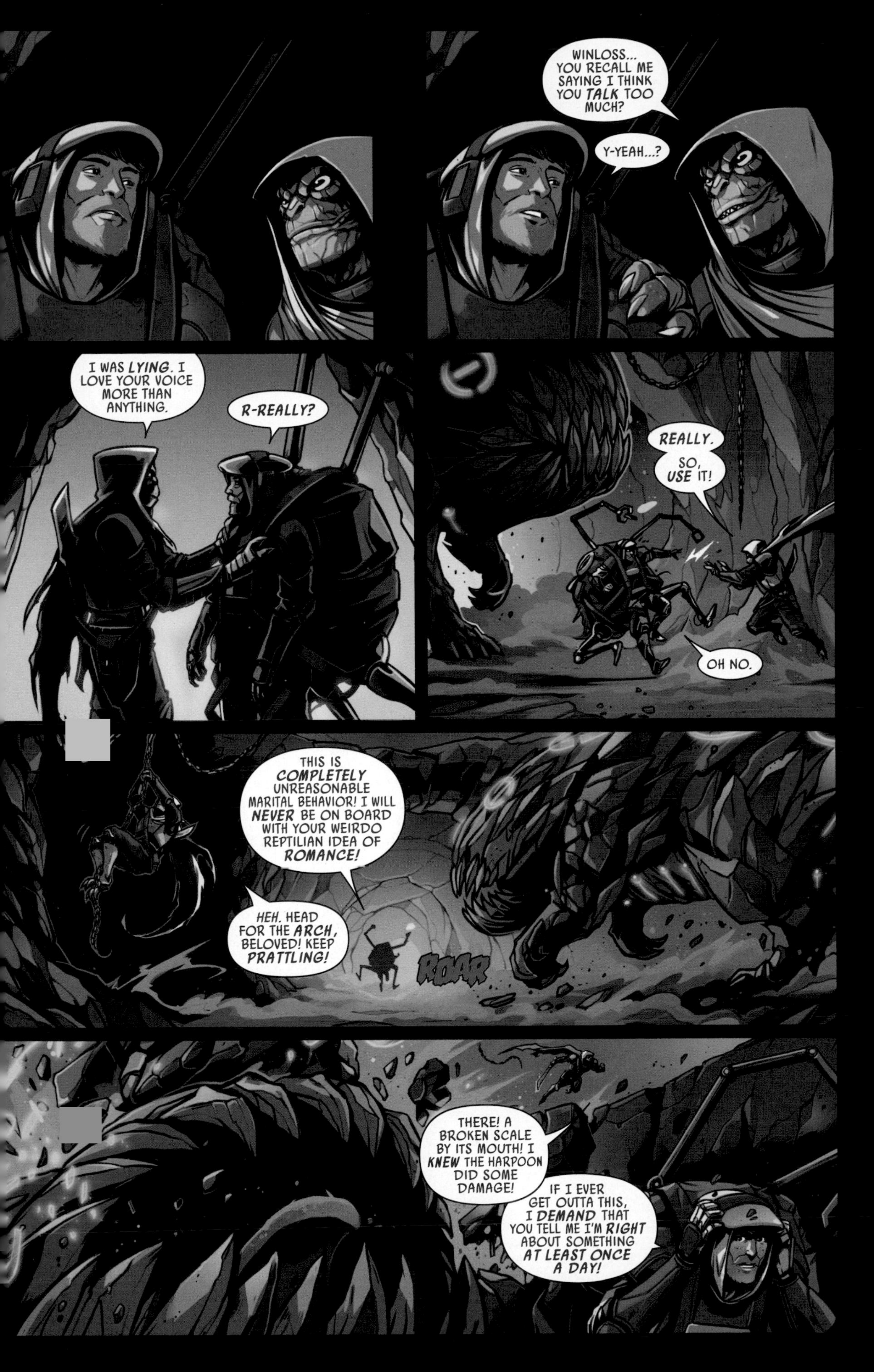
WINLOSS... YOU RECALL ME SAYING I THINK YOU TALK TOO MUCH?
Y-YEAH...?
I WAS LYING. I LOVE YOUR VOICE MORE THAN ANYTHING.
R-REALLY?
REALLY.
SO, USE IT!
OH NO.
THIS IS COMPLETELY UNREASONABLE MARITAL BEHAVIOR! I WILL NEVER BE ON BOARD WITH YOUR WEIRDO REPTILIAN IDEA OF ROMANCE!
HEH. HEAD FOR THE ARCH, BELOVED! KEEP PRATTLING!
ROAR
THERE! A BROKEN SCALE BY ITS MOUTH! I KNEW THE HARPOON DID SOME DAMAGE!
IF I EVER GET OUTTA THIS, I DEMAND THAT YOU TELL ME I'M RIGHT ABOUT SOMETHING AT LEAST ONCE A DAY!

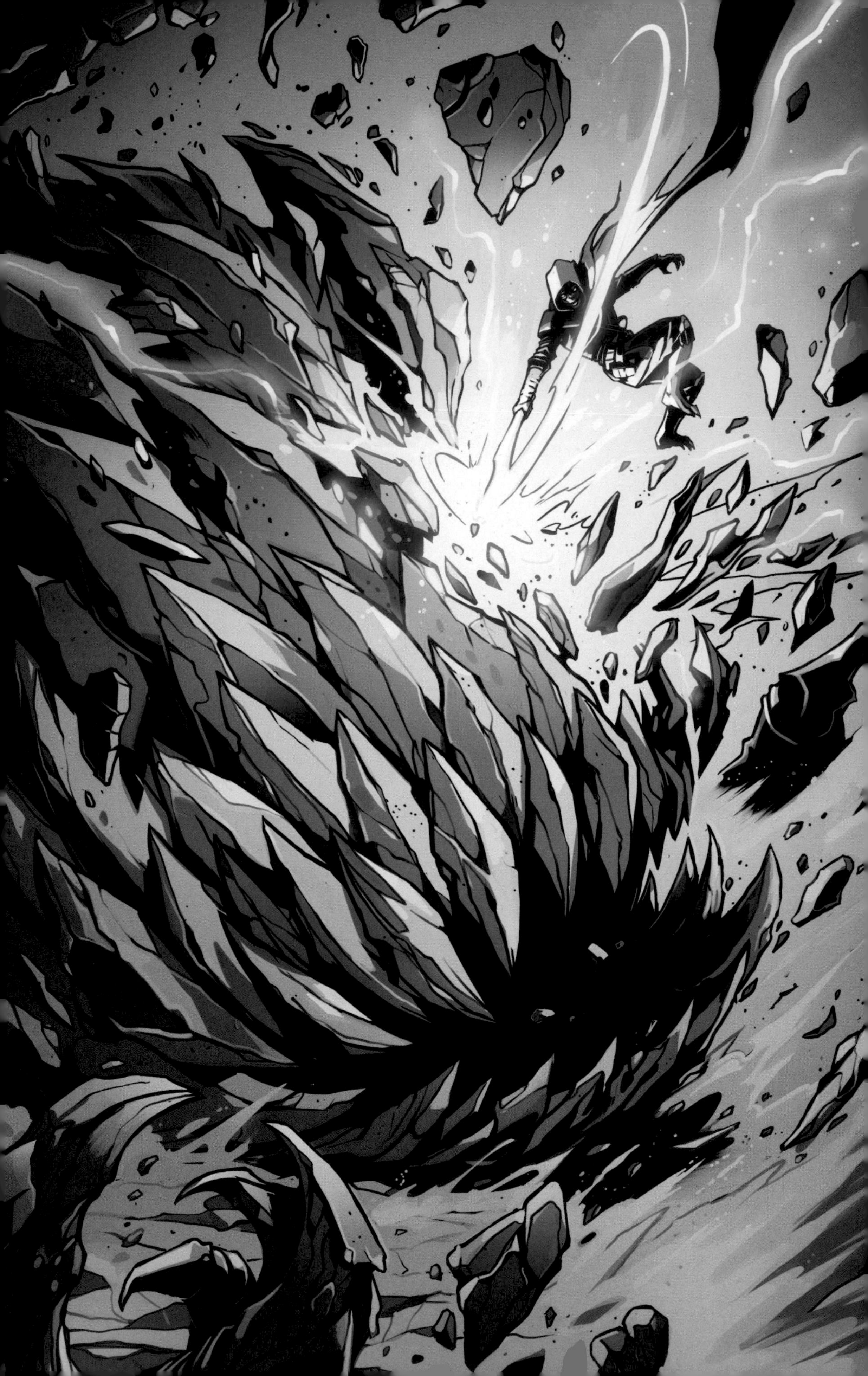

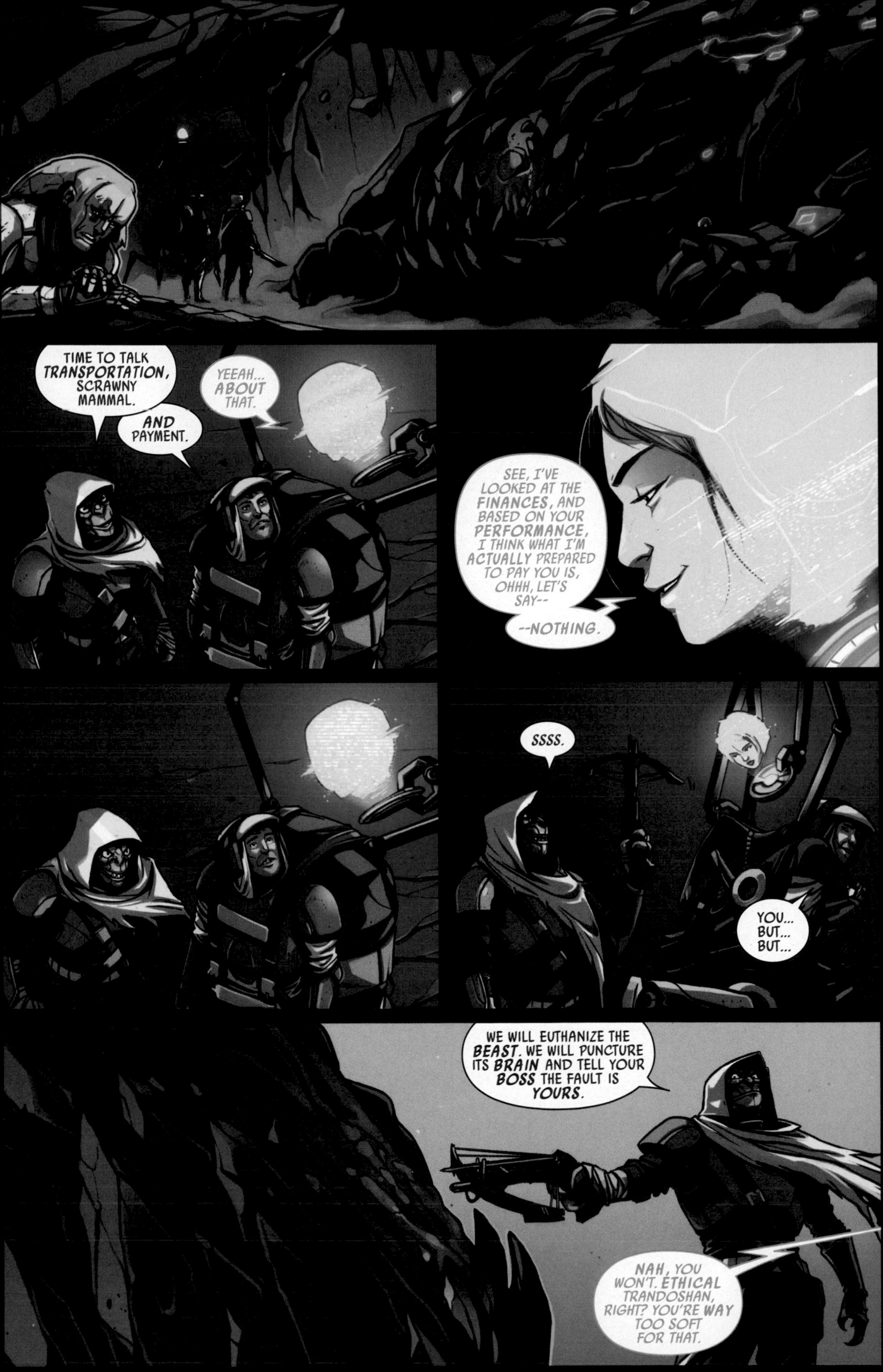

TIME TO TALK TRANSPORTATION, SCRAWNY MAMMAL.
AND PAYMENT.
YEEAH... ABOUT THAT.
SEE, I'VE LOOKED AT THE FINANCES, AND BASED ON YOUR PERFORMANCE, I THINK WHAT I'M ACTUALLY PREPARED TO PAY YOU IS, OHHH, LET'S SAY--
--NOTHING.
SSSS.
YOU... BUT... BUT...
WE WILL EUTHANIZE THE BEAST. WE WILL PUNCTURE ITS BRAIN AND TELL YOUR BOSS THE FAULT IS YOURS.
NAH, YOU WON'T. ETHICAL TRANDOSHAN, RIGHT? YOU'RE WAY TOO SOFT FOR THAT.

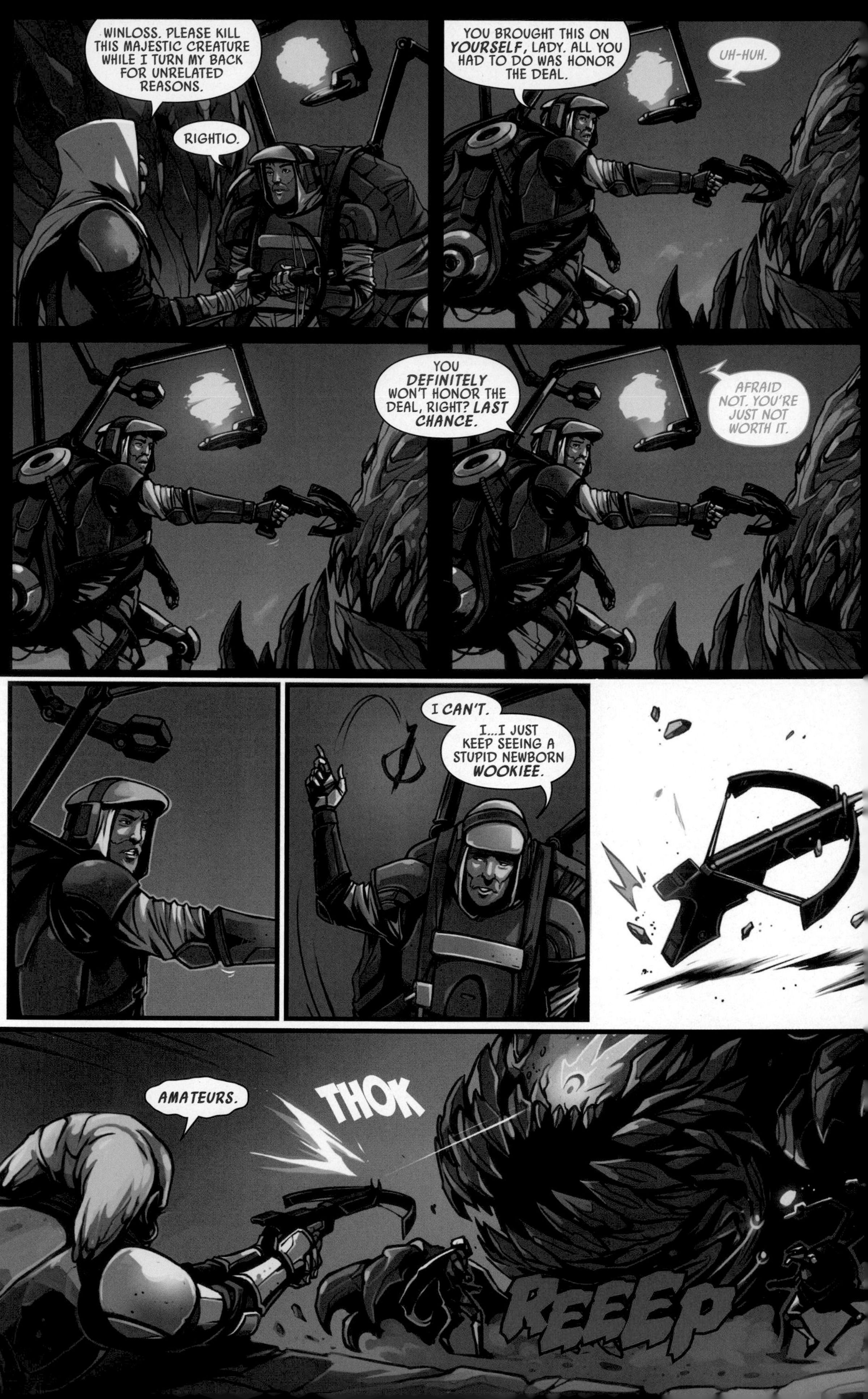
WINLOSS. PLEASE KILL THIS MAJESTIC CREATURE WHILE I TURN MY BACK FOR UNRELATED REASONS.
RIGHTIO.
YOU BROUGHT THIS ON YOURSELF, LADY. ALL YOU HAD TO DO WAS HONOR THE DEAL.
UH-HUH.
YOU DEFINITELY WON'T HONOR THE DEAL, RIGHT? LAST CHANCE.
AFRAID NOT. YOU'RE JUST NOT WORTH IT.
I CAN'T.
I...I JUST KEEP SEEING A STUPID NEWBORN WOOKIEE.
AMATEURS.
THOK
REEEP

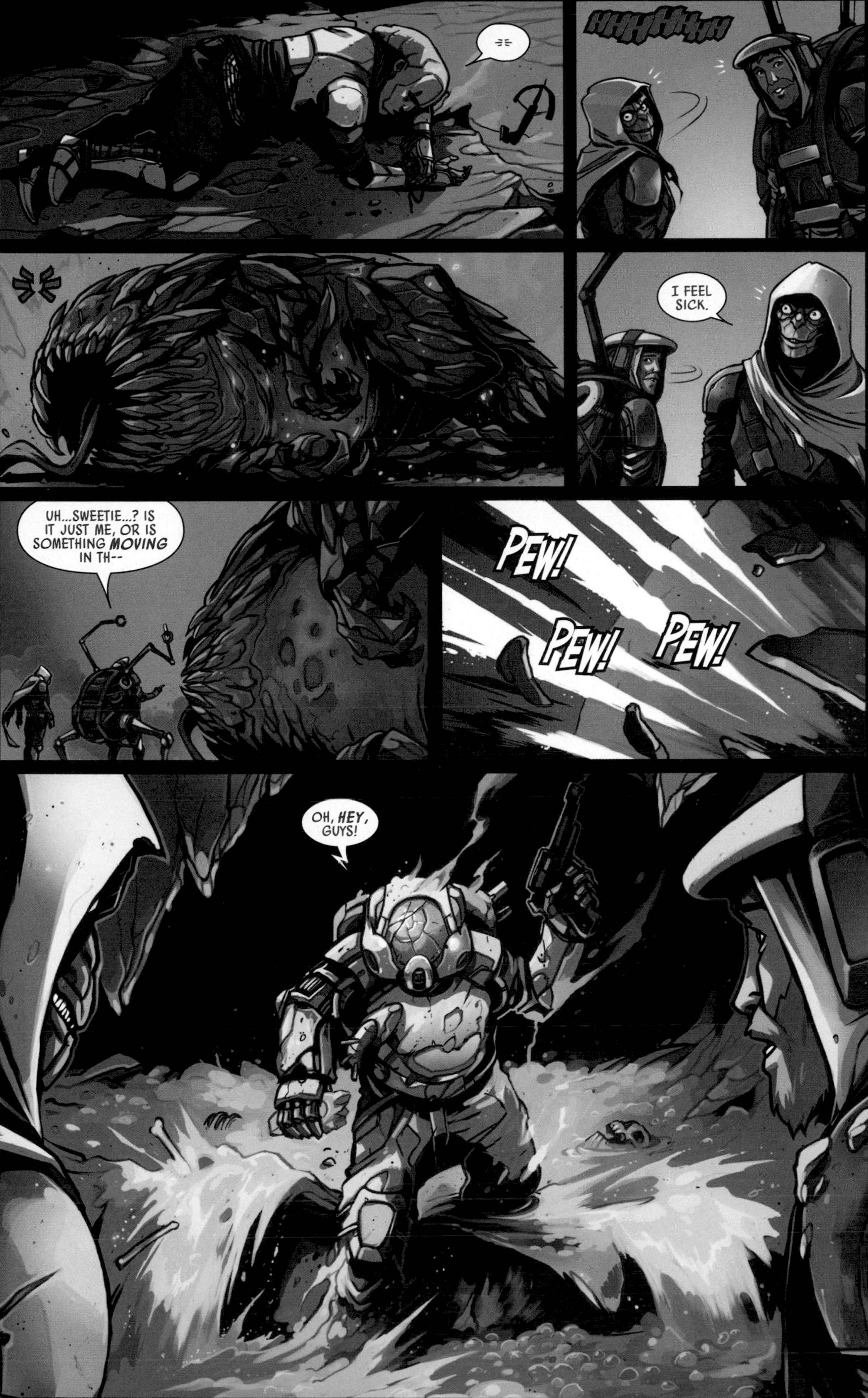
HHHHHHHH
I FEEL SICK.
UH...SWEETIE...? IS IT JUST ME, OR IS SOMETHING MOVING IN TH--
PEW!
PEW!
PEW!
OH, HEY, GUYS!

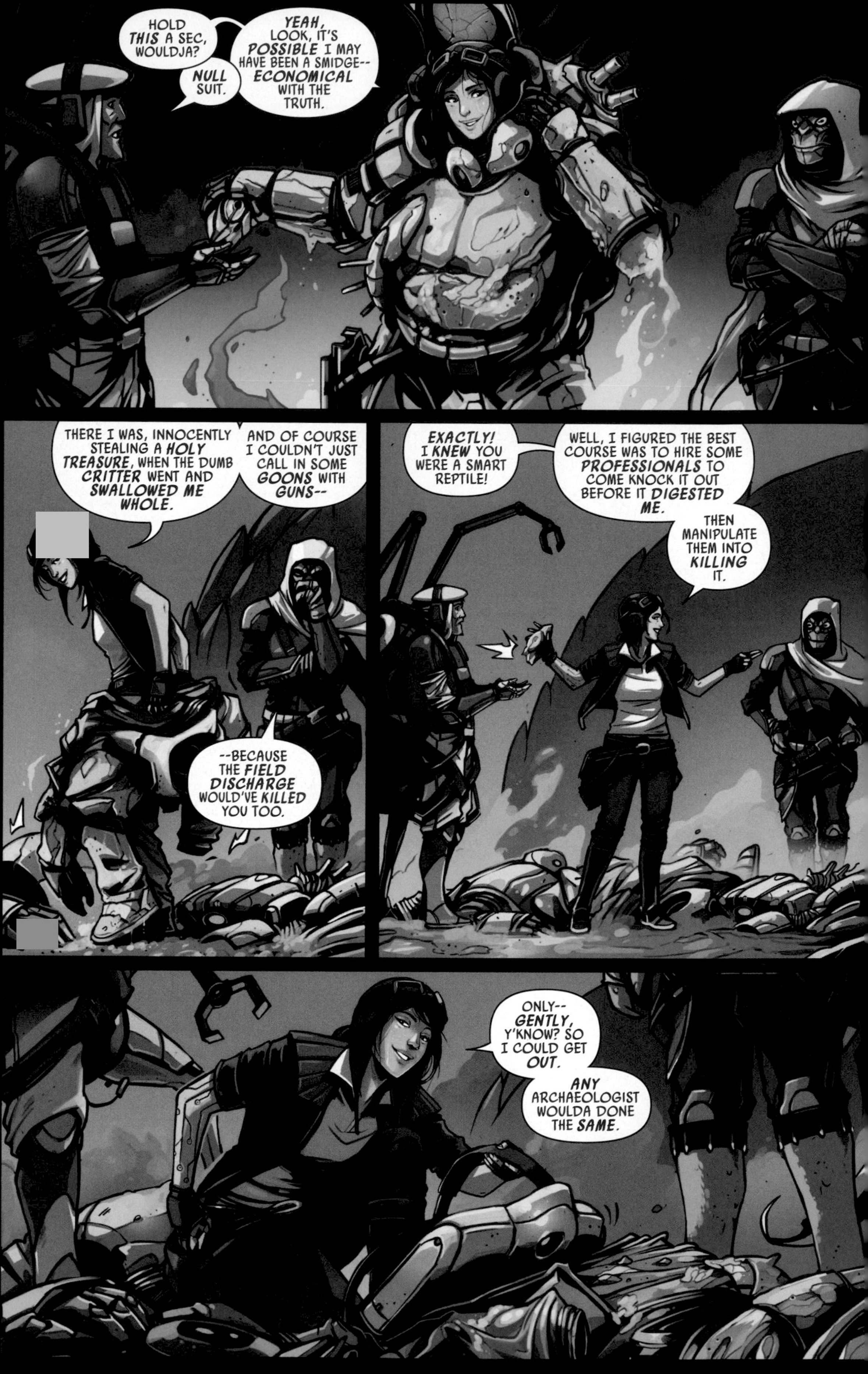
HOLD THIS A SEC, WOULDJA?
NULL SUIT.
YEAH, LOOK, IT'S POSSIBLE I MAY HAVE BEEN A SMIDGE-- ECONOMICAL WITH THE TRUTH.
THERE I WAS, INNOCENTLY STEALING A HOLY TREASURE, WHEN THE DUMB CRITTER WENT AND SWALLOWED ME WHOLE.
AND OF COURSE I COULDN'T JUST CALL IN SOME GOONS WITH GUNS--
--BECAUSE THE FIELD DISCHARGE WOULD'VE KILLED YOU TOO.
EXACTLY! I KNEW YOU WERE A SMART REPTILE!
WELL, I FIGURED THE BEST COURSE WAS TO HIRE SOME PROFESSIONALS TO COME KNOCK IT OUT BEFORE IT DIGESTED ME.
THEN MANIPULATE THEM INTO KILLING IT.
ONLY-- GENTLY, Y'KNOW? SO I COULD GET OUT.
ANY ARCHAEOLOGIST WOULDA DONE THE SAME.

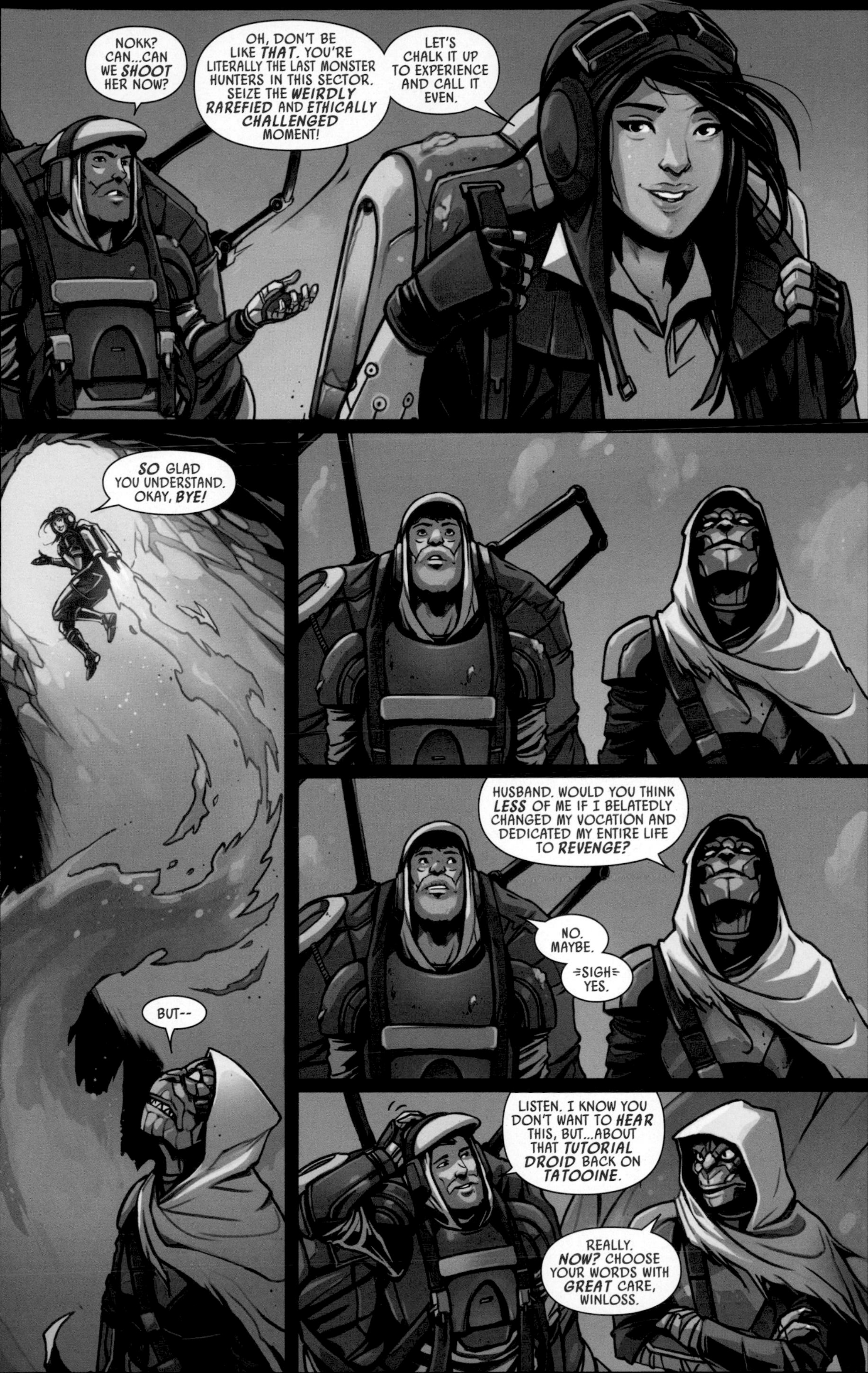
NOKK? CAN...CAN WE SHOOT HER NOW?
OH, DON'T BE LIKE THAT. YOU'RE LITERALLY THE LAST MONSTER HUNTERS IN THIS SECTOR. SEIZE THE WEIRDLY RAREFIED AND ETHICALLY CHALLENGED MOMENT!
LET'S CHALK IT UP TO EXPERIENCE AND CALL IT EVEN.
SO GLAD YOU UNDERSTAND. OKAY, BYE!
BUT--
HUSBAND. WOULD YOU THINK LESS OF ME IF I BELATEDLY CHANGED MY VOCATION AND DEDICATED MY ENTIRE LIFE TO REVENGE?
NO. MAYBE.
=SIGH= YES.
LISTEN. I KNOW YOU DON'T WANT TO HEAR THIS, BUT...ABOUT THAT TUTORIAL DROID BACK ON TATOOINE.
REALLY. NOW? CHOOSE YOUR WORDS WITH GREAT CARE, WINLOSS.

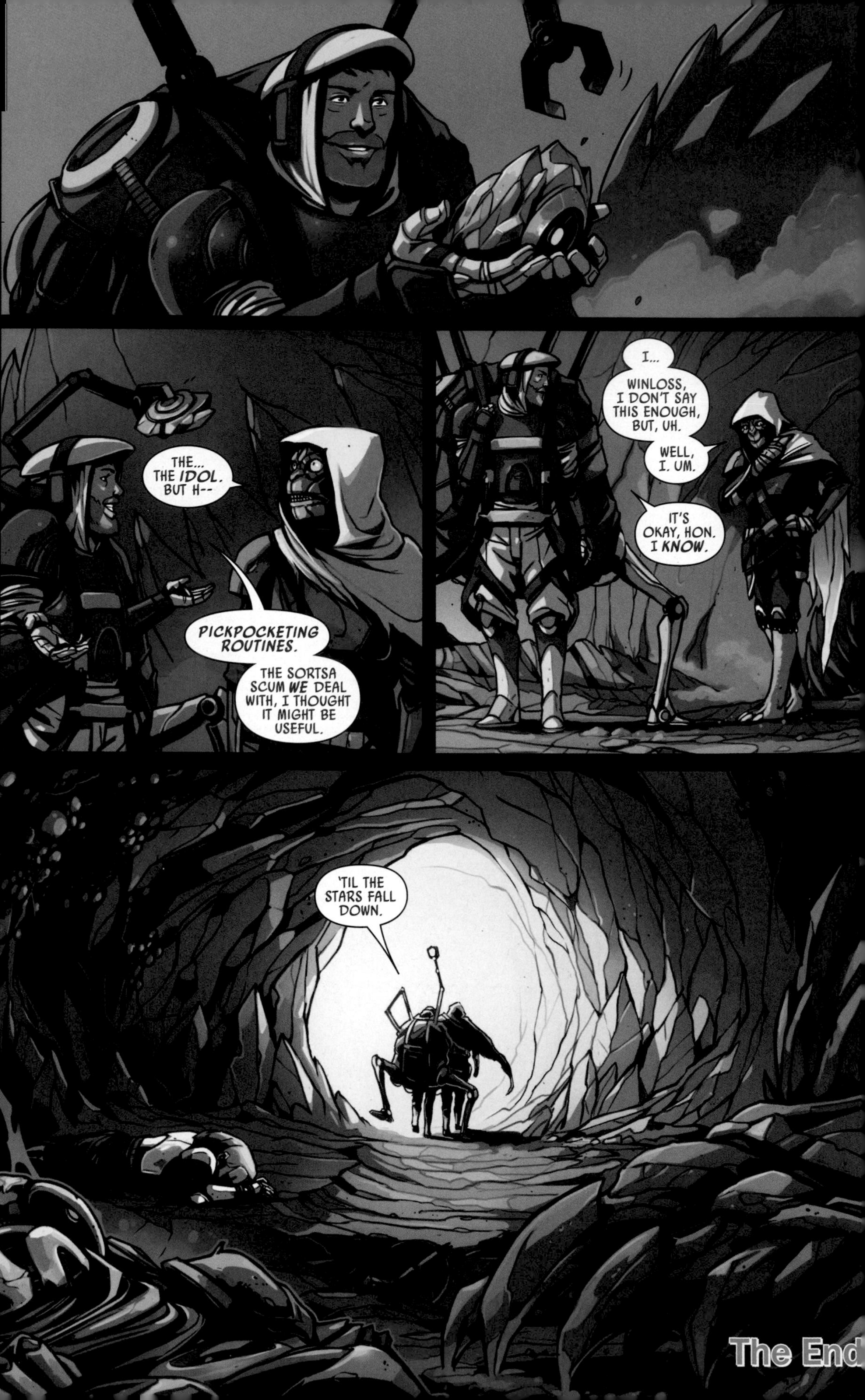
THE... THE IDOL. BUT H--
PICKPOCKETING ROUTINES.
THE SORTSA SCUM WE DEAL WITH, I THOUGHT IT MIGHT BE USEFUL.
I...
WINLOSS, I DON'T SAY THIS ENOUGH, BUT, UH.
WELL, I. UM.
IT'S OKAY, HON. I KNOW.
'TIL THE STARS FALL DOWN.
The End

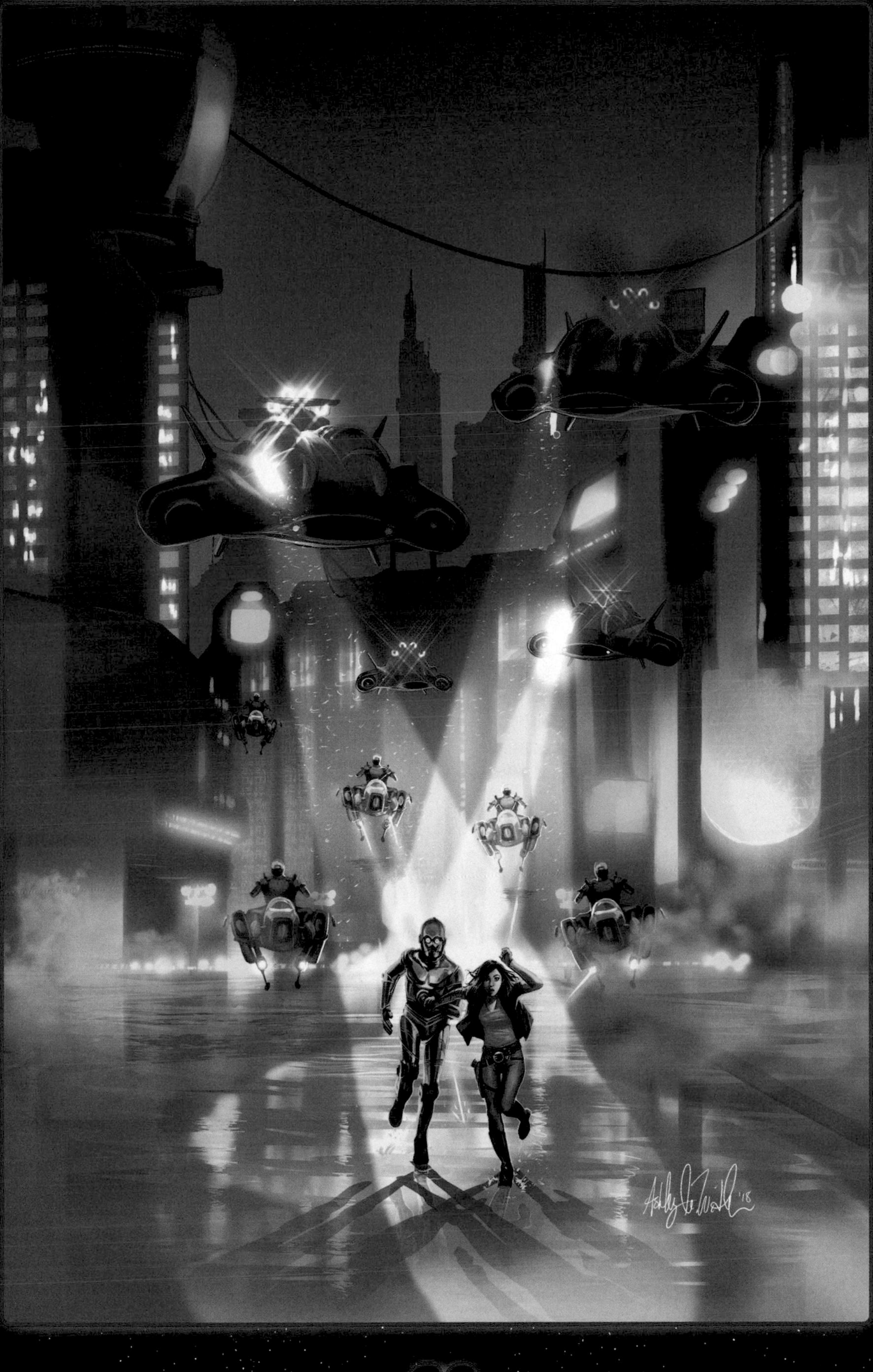

WORST AMONG EQUALS

Rogue archaeologist Doctor Aphra is on the run after narrowly escaping Imperial custody and the wrath of Darth Vader!

But a new enemy has revealed itself in the form of Aphra's former fellow inmate, Lopset, who is actually the psychotic Doctor Cornelius Evazan!

Evazan's latest scheme has trapped Aphra and her worst nemesis, the psychotic droid crime lord Triple-Zero, into an explosive confrontation....

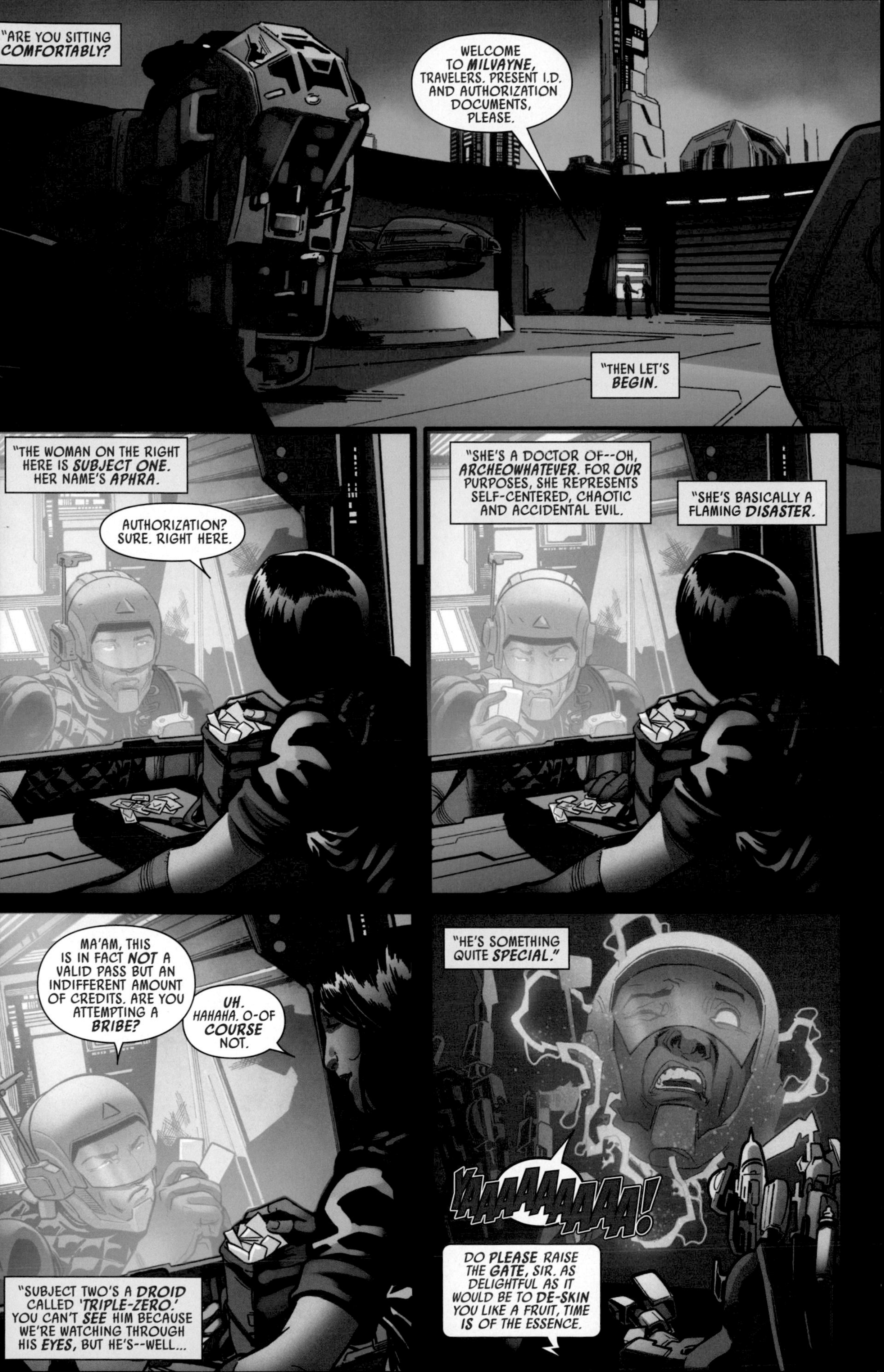
"ARE YOU SITTING COMFORTABLY?
WELCOME TO MILVAYNE, TRAVELERS. PRESENT I.D. AND AUTHORIZATION DOCUMENTS, PLEASE.
"THEN LET'S BEGIN.
"THE WOMAN ON THE RIGHT HERE IS SUBJECT ONE. HER NAME'S APHRA.
AUTHORIZATION? SURE. RIGHT HERE.
"SHE'S A DOCTOR OF--OH, ARCHEOWHATEVER. FOR OUR PURPOSES, SHE REPRESENTS SELF-CENTERED, CHAOTIC AND ACCIDENTAL EVIL.
"SHE'S BASICALLY A FLAMING DISASTER.
MA'AM, THIS IS IN FACT NOT A VALID PASS BUT AN INDIFFERENT AMOUNT OF CREDITS. ARE YOU ATTEMPTING A BRIBE?
UH. HAHAHA. O-OF COURSE NOT.
"SUBJECT TWO'S A DROID CALLED 'TRIPLE-ZERO.' YOU CAN'T SEE HIM BECAUSE WE'RE WATCHING THROUGH HIS EYES, BUT HE'S--WELL...
"HE'S SOMETHING QUITE SPECIAL."
YAAAAAAAAAA!
DO PLEASE RAISE THE GATE, SIR. AS DELIGHTFUL AS IT WOULD BE TO DE-SKIN YOU LIKE A FRUIT, TIME IS OF THE ESSENCE.

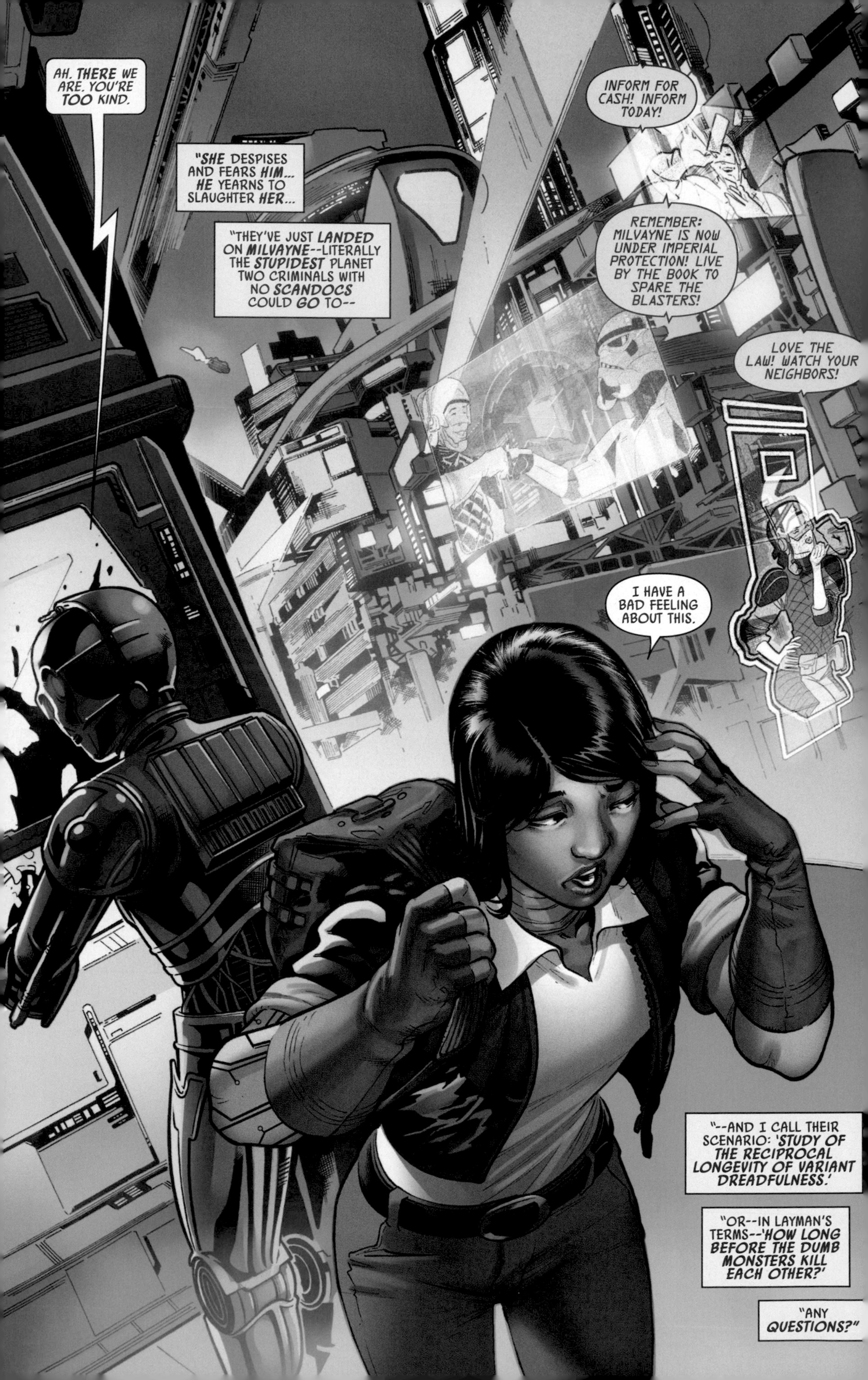
AH. THERE WE ARE. YOU'RE TOO KIND.
"SHE DESPISES AND FEARS HIM... HE YEARNS TO SLAUGHTER HER...
"THEY'VE JUST LANDED ON MILVAYNE--LITERALLY THE STUPIDEST PLANET TWO CRIMINALS WITH NO SCANDOCS COULD GO TO--
INFORM FOR CASH! INFORM TODAY!
REMEMBER: MILVAYNE IS NOW UNDER IMPERIAL PROTECTION! LIVE BY THE BOOK TO SPARE THE BLASTERS!
LOVE THE LAW! WATCH YOUR NEIGHBORS!
I HAVE A BAD FEELING ABOUT THIS.
"--AND I CALL THEIR SCENARIO: 'STUDY OF THE RECIPROCAL LONGEVITY OF VARIANT DREADFULNESS.'
"OR--IN LAYMAN'S TERMS--'HOW LONG BEFORE THE DUMB MONSTERS KILL EACH OTHER?'
"ANY QUESTIONS?"

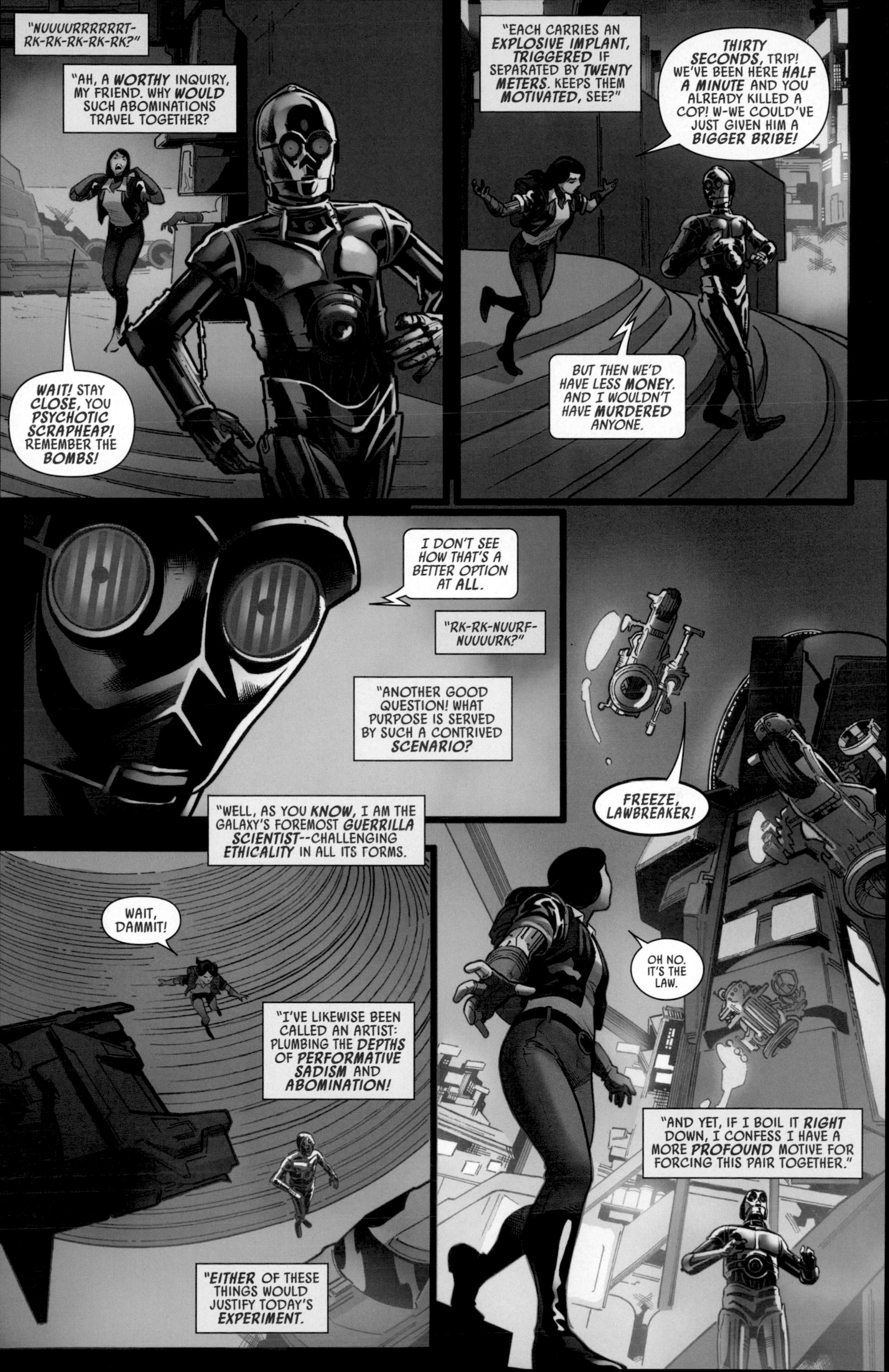
"NUUUURRRRRRT-RK-RK-RK-RK-RK?"
"AH, A WORTHY INQUIRY, MY FRIEND. WHY WOULD SUCH ABOMINATIONS TRAVEL TOGETHER?
WAIT! STAY CLOSE, YOU PSYCHOTIC SCRAPHEAP! REMEMBER THE BOMBS!
"EACH CARRIES AN EXPLOSIVE IMPLANT, TRIGGERED IF SEPARATED BY TWENTY METERS. KEEPS THEM MOTIVATED, SEE?"
THIRTY SECONDS, TRIP! WE'VE BEEN HERE HALF A MINUTE AND YOU ALREADY KILLED A COP! W-WE COULD'VE JUST GIVEN HIM A BIGGER BRIBE!
BUT THEN WE'D HAVE LESS MONEY. AND I WOULDN'T HAVE MURDERED ANYONE.
I DON'T SEE HOW THAT'S A BETTER OPTION AT ALL.
"RK-RK-NUURF-NUUUURK?"
"ANOTHER GOOD QUESTION! WHAT PURPOSE IS SERVED BY SUCH A CONTRIVED SCENARIO?
"WELL, AS YOU KNOW, I AM THE GALAXY'S FOREMOST GUERRILLA SCIENTIST--CHALLENGING ETHICALITY IN ALL ITS FORMS.
WAIT, DAMMIT!
"I'VE LIKEWISE BEEN CALLED AN ARTIST: PLUMBING THE DEPTHS OF PERFORMATIVE SADISM AND ABOMINATION!
"EITHER OF THESE THINGS WOULD JUSTIFY TODAY'S EXPERIMENT.
FREEZE, LAWBREAKER!
OH NO. IT'S THE LAW.
"AND YET, IF I BOIL IT RIGHT DOWN, I CONFESS I HAVE A MORE PROFOUND MOTIVE FOR FORCING THIS PAIR TOGETHER."

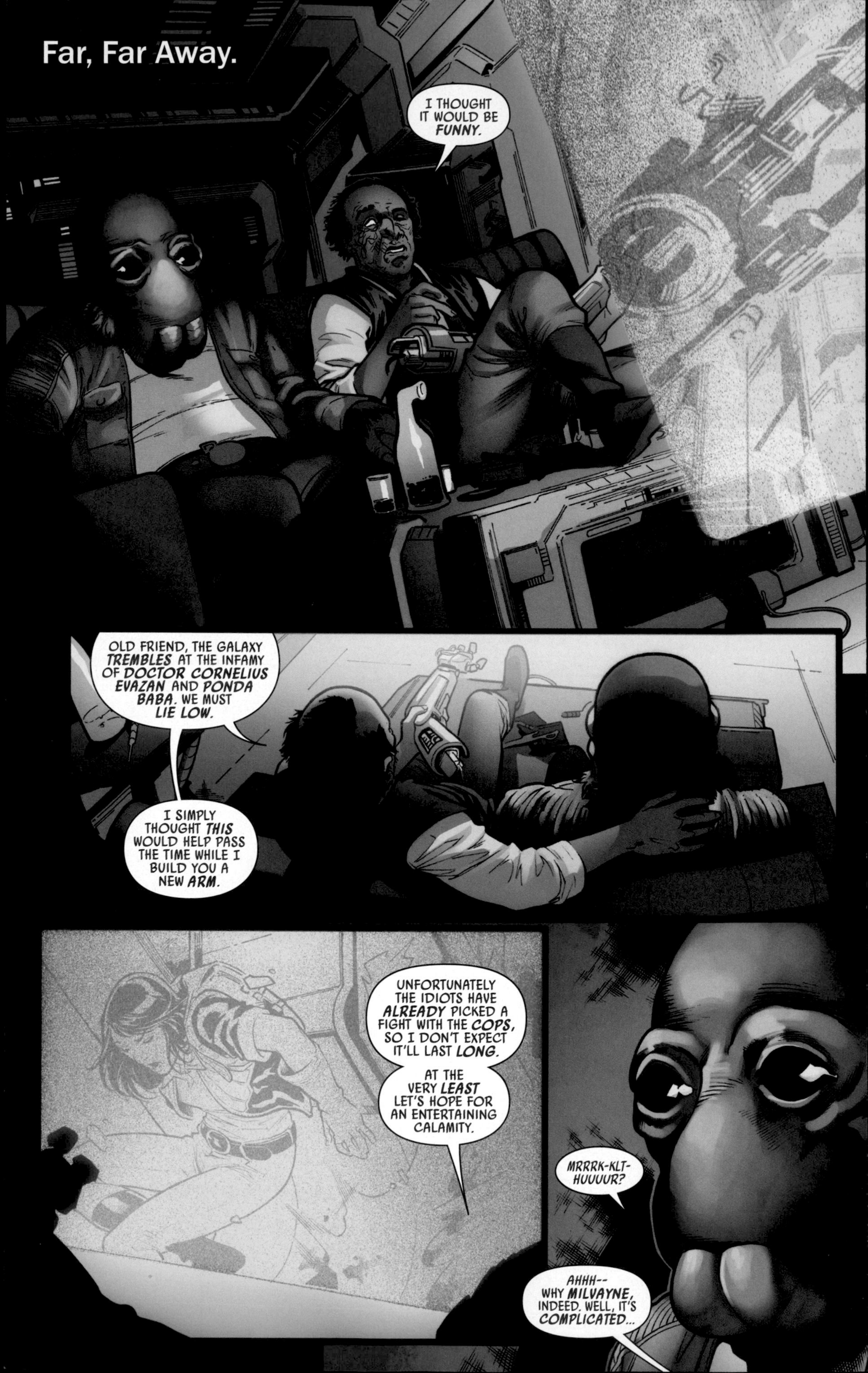
Far, Far Away.
I THOUGHT IT WOULD BE FUNNY.
OLD FRIEND, THE GALAXY TREMBLES AT THE INFAMY OF DOCTOR CORNELIUS EVAZAN AND PONDA BABA. WE MUST LIE LOW.
I SIMPLY THOUGHT THIS WOULD HELP PASS THE TIME WHILE I BUILD YOU A NEW ARM.
UNFORTUNATELY THE IDIOTS HAVE ALREADY PICKED A FIGHT WITH THE COPS, SO I DON'T EXPECT IT'LL LAST LONG.
AT THE VERY LEAST LET'S HOPE FOR AN ENTERTAINING CALAMITY.
MRRRK-KLT-HUUUUR?
AHHH-- WHY MILVAYNE, INDEED. WELL, IT'S COMPLICATED...

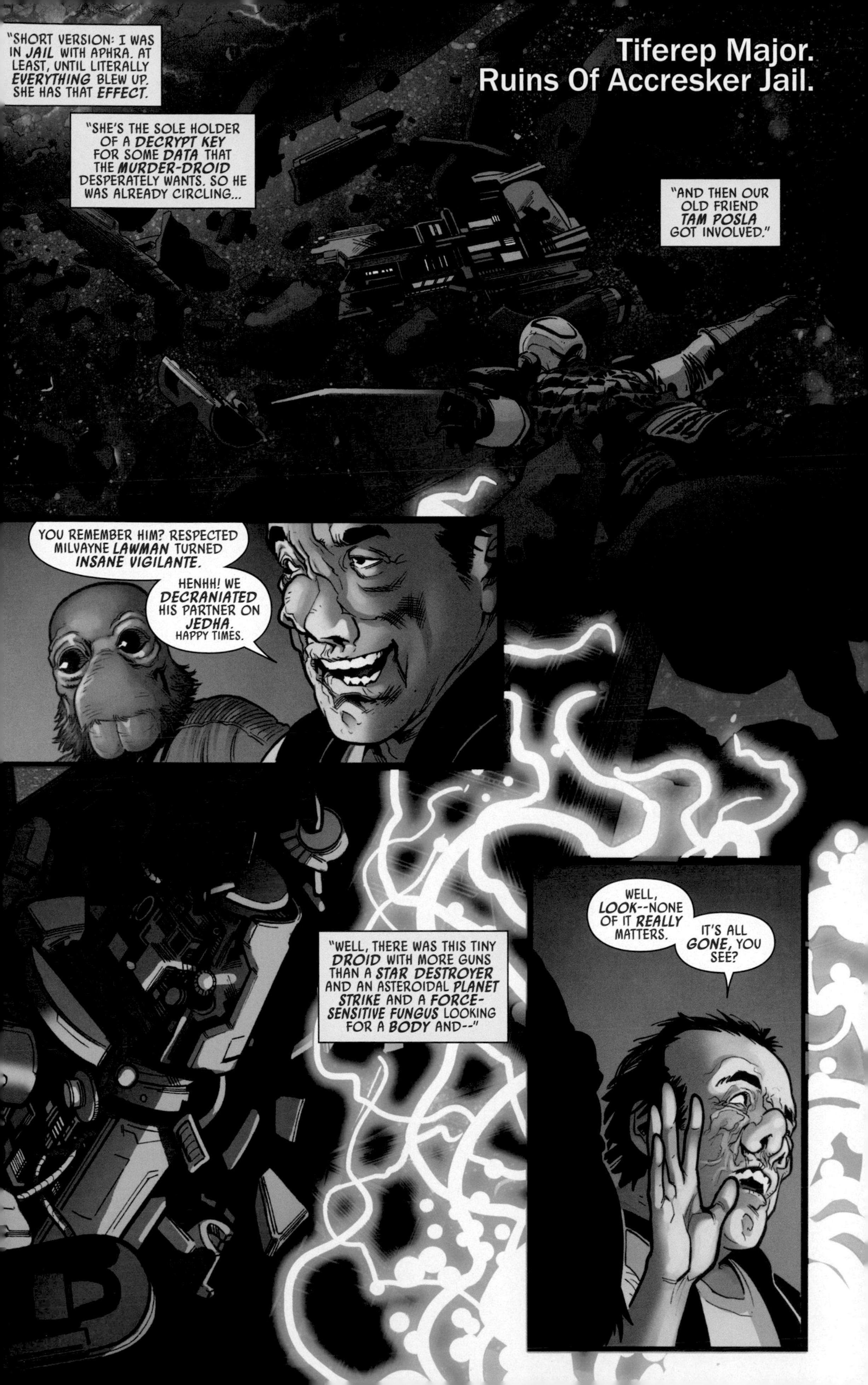
Tiferep Major. Ruins Of Accresker Jail.
"SHORT VERSION: I WAS IN JAIL WITH APHRA. AT LEAST, UNTIL LITERALLY EVERYTHING BLEW UP. SHE HAS THAT EFFECT.
"SHE'S THE SOLE HOLDER OF A DECRYPT KEY FOR SOME DATA THAT THE MURDER-DROID DESPERATELY WANTS. SO HE WAS ALREADY CIRCLING...
"AND THEN OUR OLD FRIEND TAM POSLA GOT INVOLVED."
YOU REMEMBER HIM? RESPECTED MILVAYNE LAWMAN TURNED INSANE VIGILANTE.
HENHH! WE DECRANIATED HIS PARTNER ON JEDHA. HAPPY TIMES.
"WELL, THERE WAS THIS TINY DROID WITH MORE GUNS THAN A STAR DESTROYER AND AN ASTEROIDAL PLANET STRIKE AND A FORCE-SENSITIVE FUNGUS LOOKING FOR A BODY AND--"
WELL, LOOK--NONE OF IT REALLY MATTERS.
IT'S ALL GONE, YOU SEE?

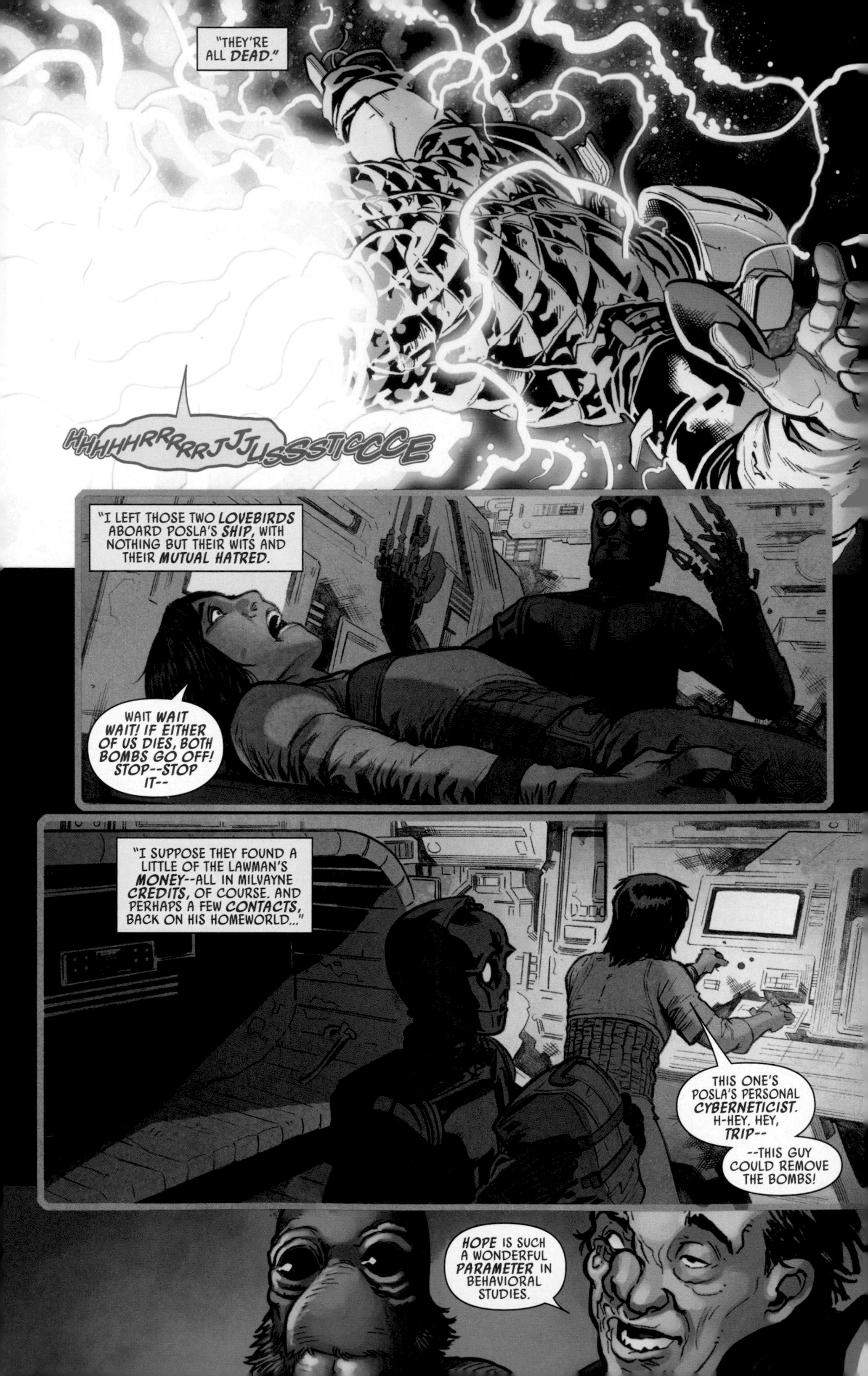

"THEY'RE ALL DEAD."
HHHHHRRRRRJJJUSSSSTICCCCE
"I LEFT THOSE TWO LOVEBIRDS ABOARD POSLA'S SHIP, WITH NOTHING BUT THEIR WITS AND THEIR MUTUAL HATRED.
WAIT WAIT WAIT! IF EITHER OF US DIES, BOTH BOMBS GO OFF! STOP--STOP IT--
"I SUPPOSE THEY FOUND A LITTLE OF THE LAWMAN'S MONEY--ALL IN MILVAYNE CREDITS, OF COURSE. AND PERHAPS A FEW CONTACTS, BACK ON HIS HOMEWORLD..."
THIS ONE'S POSLA'S PERSONAL CYBERNETICIST. H-HEY. HEY, TRIP--
--THIS GUY COULD REMOVE THE BOMBS!
HOPE IS SUCH A WONDERFUL PARAMETER IN BEHAVIORAL STUDIES.

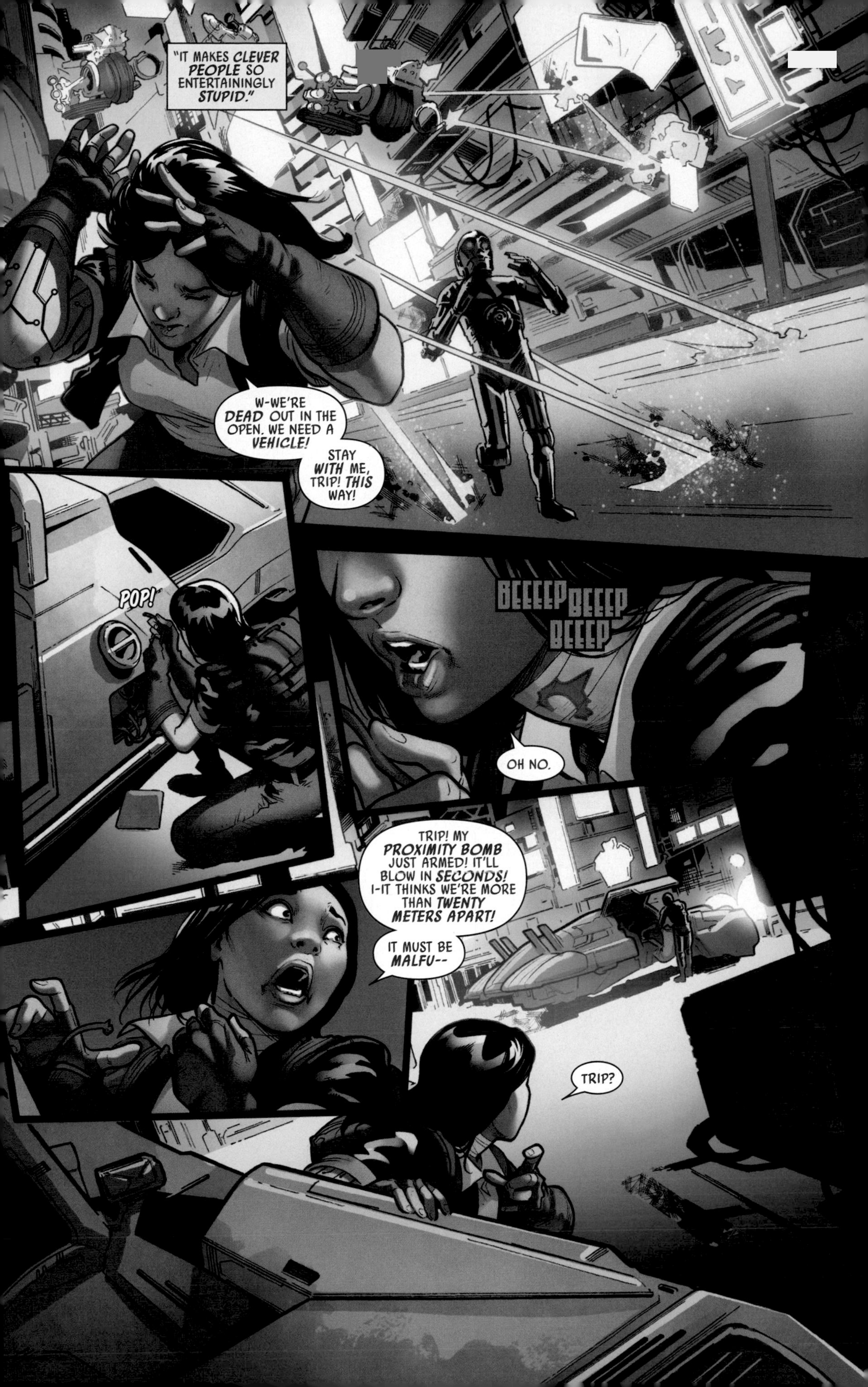
"IT MAKES CLEVER PEOPLE SO ENTERTAININGLY STUPID."
W-WE'RE DEAD OUT IN THE OPEN. WE NEED A VEHICLE!
STAY WITH ME, TRIP! THIS WAY!
POP!
BEEEEP BEEEP BEEEP
OH NO.
TRIP! MY PROXIMITY BOMB JUST ARMED! IT'LL BLOW IN SECONDS! I-IT THINKS WE'RE MORE THAN TWENTY METERS APART!
IT MUST BE MALFU--
TRIP?

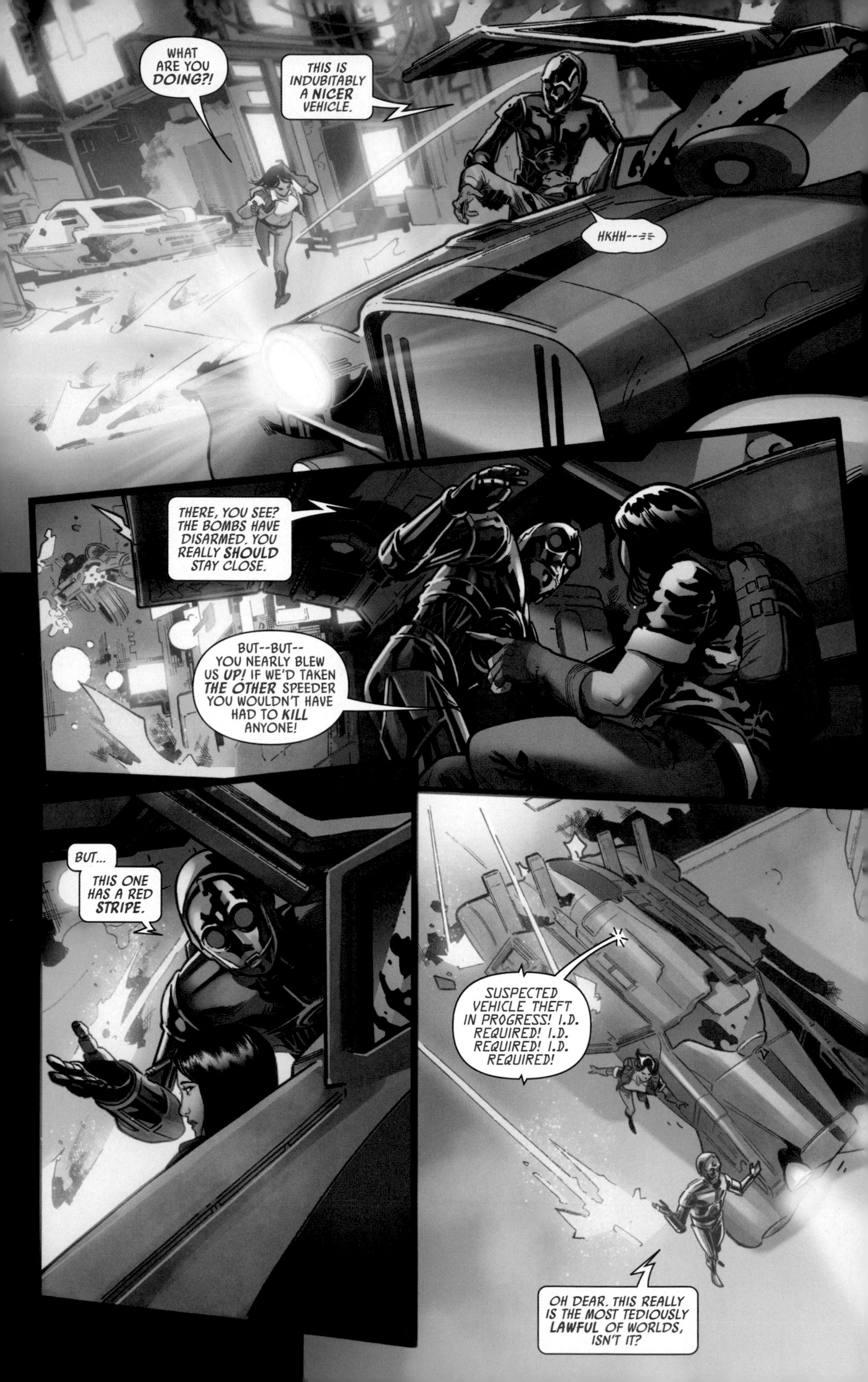
WHAT ARE YOU DOING?!
THIS IS INDUBITABLY A NICER VEHICLE.
HKHH--
THERE, YOU SEE? THE BOMBS HAVE DISARMED. YOU REALLY SHOULD STAY CLOSE.
BUT--BUT--YOU NEARLY BLEW US UP! IF WE'D TAKEN THE OTHER SPEEDER YOU WOULDN'T HAVE HAD TO KILL ANYONE!
BUT...
THIS ONE HAS A RED STRIPE.
SUSPECTED VEHICLE THEFT IN PROGRESS! I.D. REQUIRED! I.D. REQUIRED! I.D. REQUIRED!
OH DEAR. THIS REALLY IS THE MOST TEDIOUSLY LAWFUL OF WORLDS, ISN'T IT?

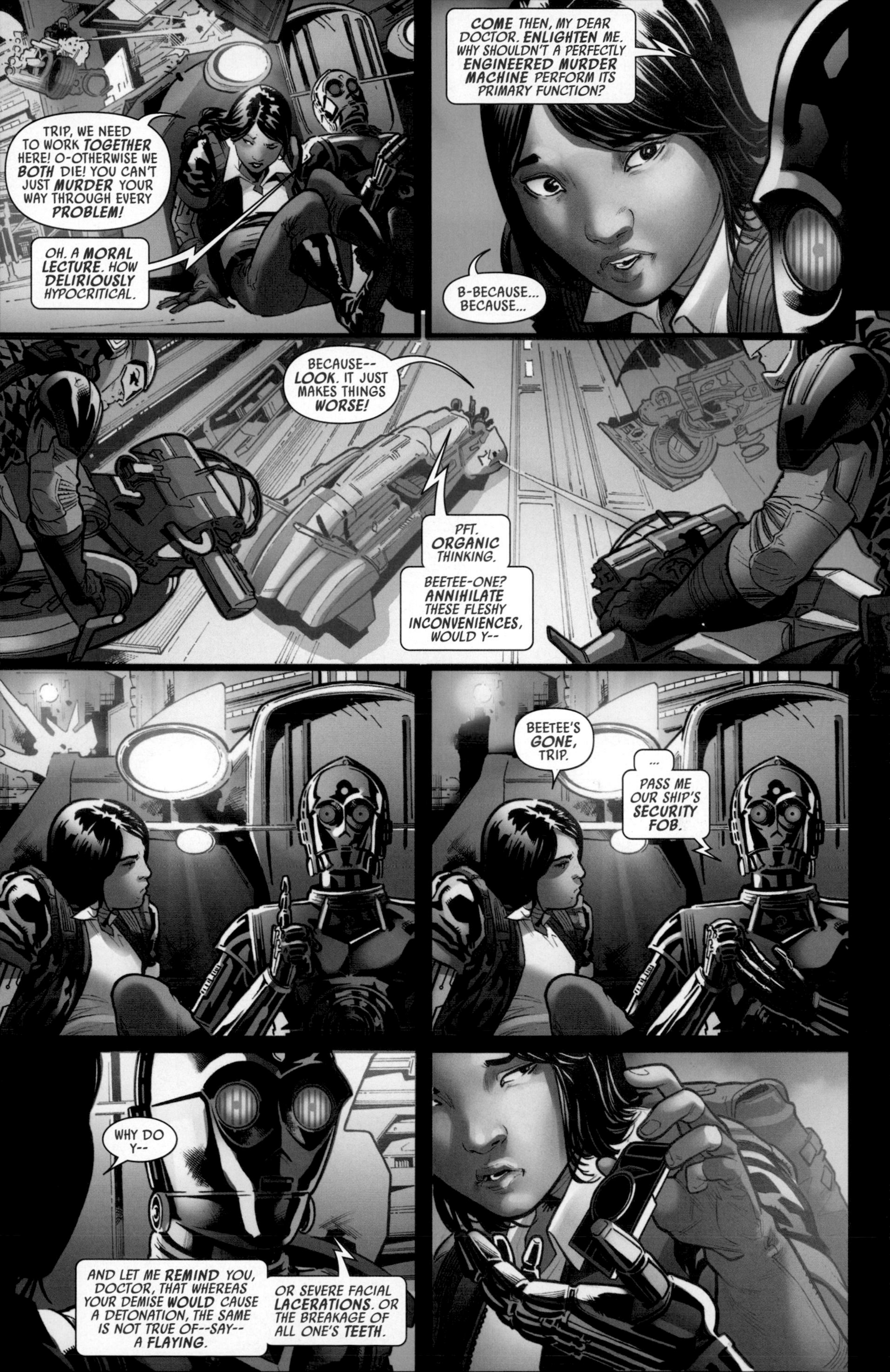
TRIP, WE NEED TO WORK TOGETHER HERE! O-OTHERWISE WE BOTH DIE! YOU CAN'T JUST MURDER YOUR WAY THROUGH EVERY PROBLEM!
OH. A MORAL LECTURE. HOW DELIRIOUSLY HYPOCRITICAL.
COME THEN, MY DEAR DOCTOR. ENLIGHTEN ME. WHY SHOULDN'T A PERFECTLY ENGINEERED MURDER MACHINE PERFORM ITS PRIMARY FUNCTION?
B-BECAUSE... BECAUSE...
BECAUSE-- LOOK. IT JUST MAKES THINGS WORSE!
PFT. ORGANIC THINKING.
BEETEE-ONE? ANNIHILATE THESE FLESHY INCONVENIENCES, WOULD Y--
BEETEE'S GONE, TRIP.
...
PASS ME OUR SHIP'S SECURITY FOB.
WHY DO Y--
AND LET ME REMIND YOU, DOCTOR, THAT WHEREAS YOUR DEMISE WOULD CAUSE A DETONATION, THE SAME IS NOT TRUE OF--SAY-- A FLAYING.
OR SEVERE FACIAL LACERATIONS. OR THE BREAKAGE OF ALL ONE'S TEETH.

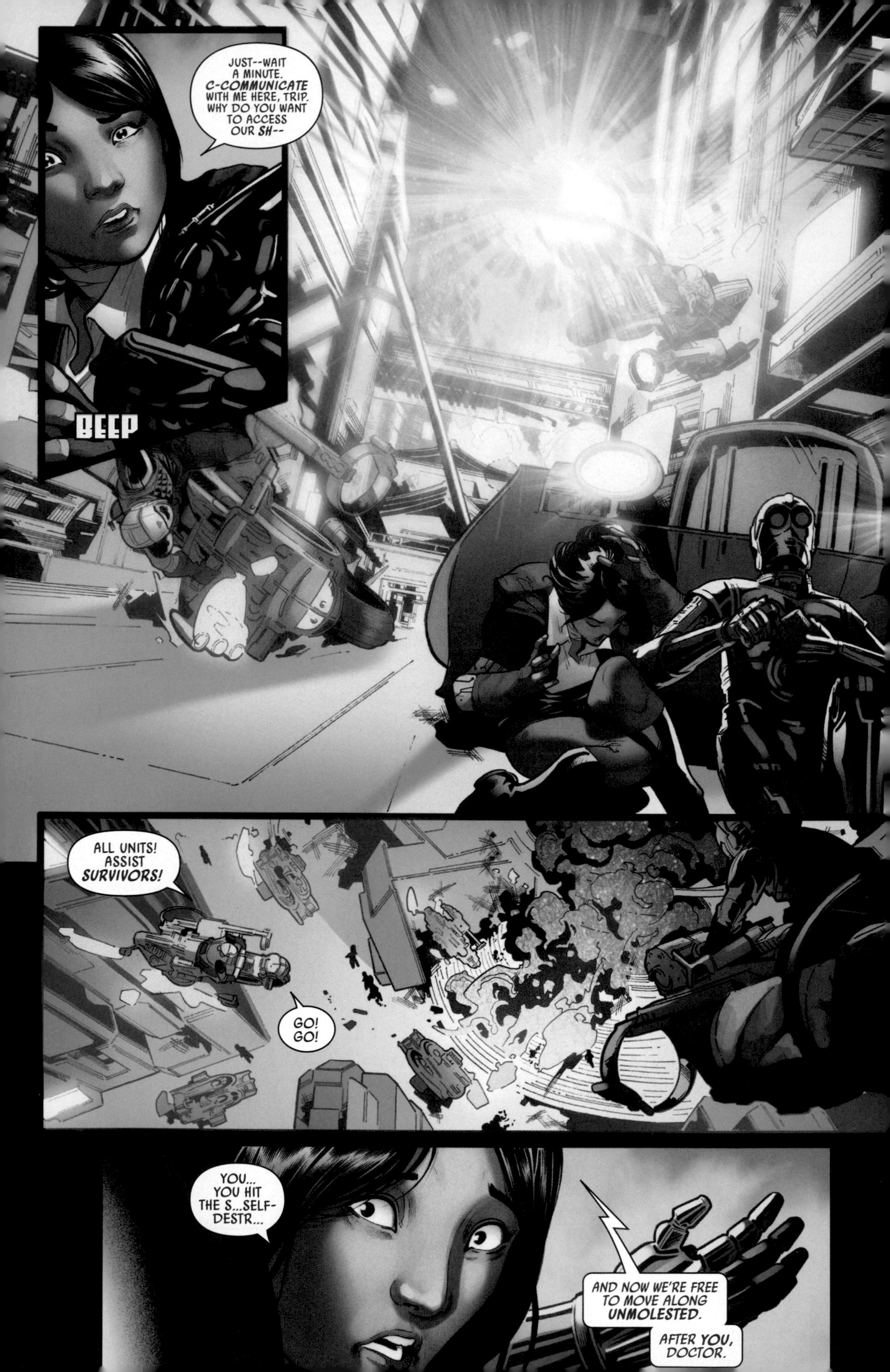
JUST--WAIT A MINUTE. C-COMMUNICATE WITH ME HERE, TRIP. WHY DO YOU WANT TO ACCESS OUR SH--
BEEP
ALL UNITS! ASSIST SURVIVORS!
GO! GO!
YOU... YOU HIT THE S...SELF-DESTR...
AND NOW WE'RE FREE TO MOVE ALONG UNMOLESTED.
AFTER YOU, DOCTOR.

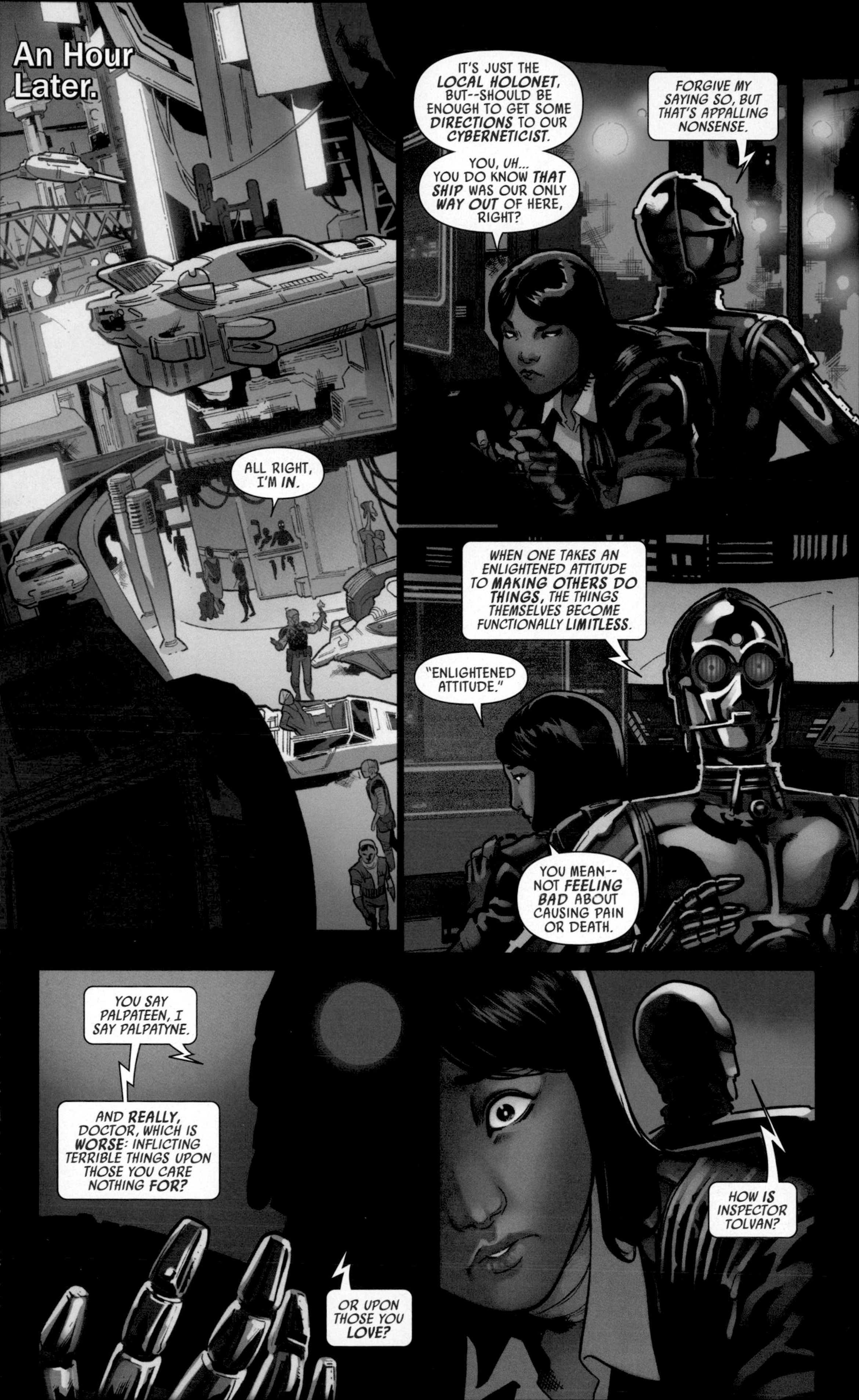
An Hour Later.
ALL RIGHT, I'M IN.
IT'S JUST THE LOCAL HOLONET, BUT--SHOULD BE ENOUGH TO GET SOME DIRECTIONS TO OUR CYBERNETICIST.
YOU, UH... YOU DO KNOW THAT SHIP WAS OUR ONLY WAY OUT OF HERE, RIGHT?
FORGIVE MY SAYING SO, BUT THAT'S APPALLING NONSENSE.
WHEN ONE TAKES AN ENLIGHTENED ATTITUDE TO MAKING OTHERS DO THINGS, THE THINGS THEMSELVES BECOME FUNCTIONALLY LIMITLESS.
"ENLIGHTENED ATTITUDE."
YOU MEAN-- NOT FEELING BAD ABOUT CAUSING PAIN OR DEATH.
YOU SAY PALPATEEN, I SAY PALPATYNE.
AND REALLY, DOCTOR, WHICH IS WORSE: INFLICTING TERRIBLE THINGS UPON THOSE YOU CARE NOTHING FOR?
OR UPON THOSE YOU LOVE?
HOW IS INSPECTOR TOLVAN?

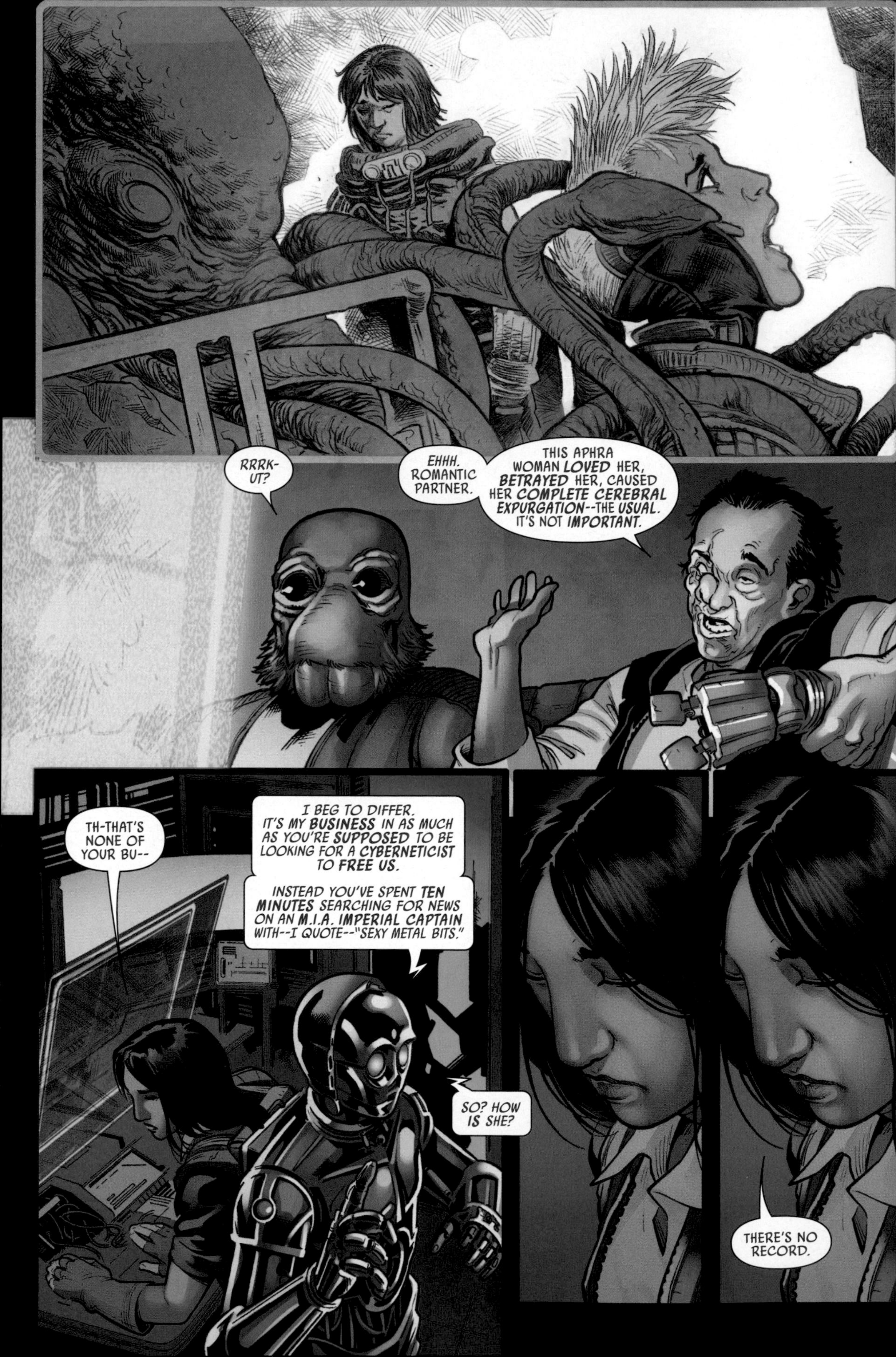
RRRK-UT?
EHHH. ROMANTIC PARTNER.
THIS APHRA WOMAN LOVED HER, BETRAYED HER, CAUSED HER COMPLETE CEREBRAL EXPURGATION--THE USUAL. IT'S NOT IMPORTANT.
TH-THAT'S NONE OF YOUR BU--
I BEG TO DIFFER. IT'S MY BUSINESS IN AS MUCH AS YOU'RE SUPPOSED TO BE LOOKING FOR A CYBERNETICIST TO FREE US.
INSTEAD YOU'VE SPENT TEN MINUTES SEARCHING FOR NEWS ON AN M.I.A. IMPERIAL CAPTAIN WITH--I QUOTE--"SEXY METAL BITS."
SO? HOW IS SHE?
THERE'S NO RECORD.

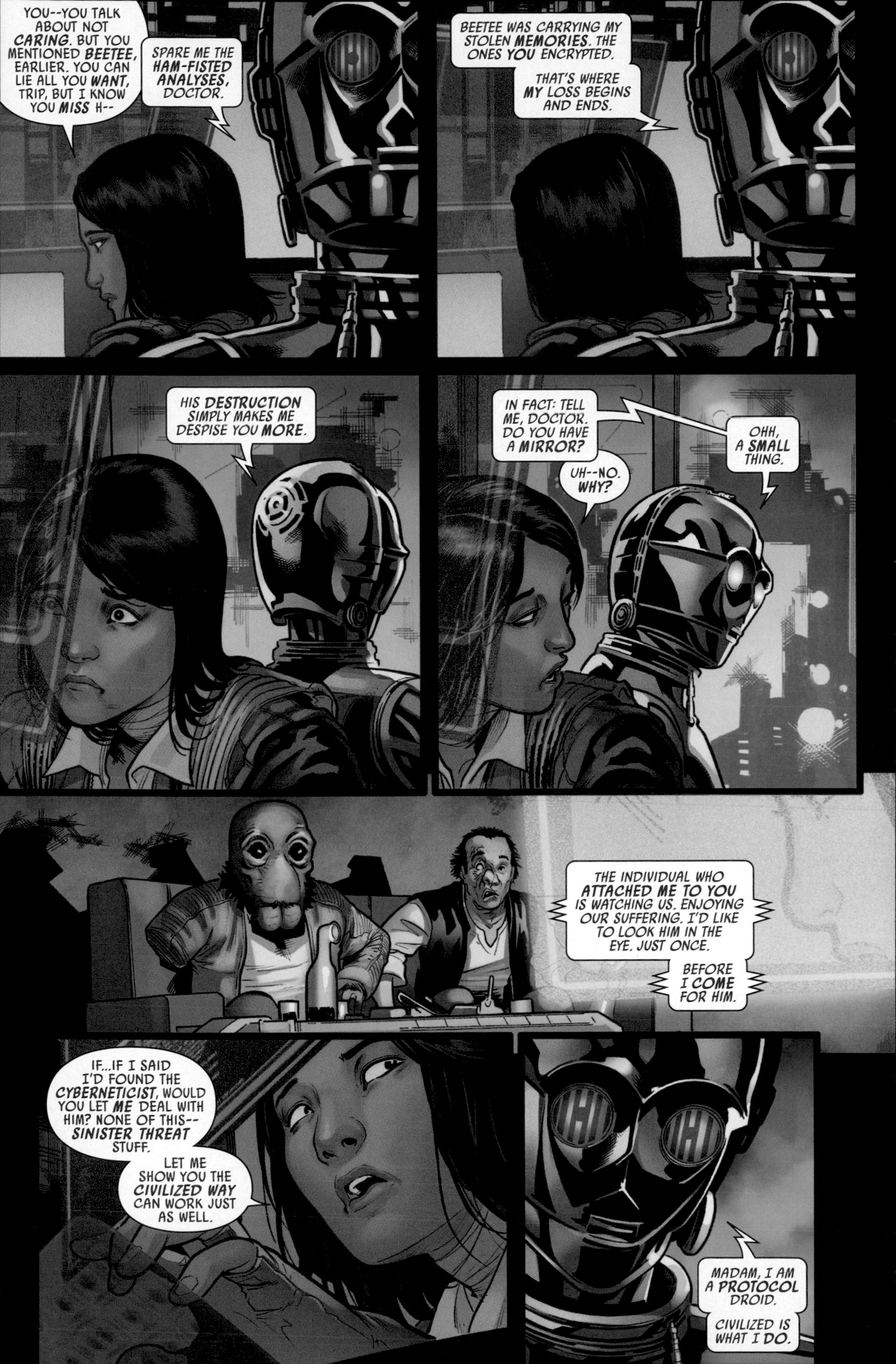
YOU--YOU TALK ABOUT NOT CARING. BUT YOU MENTIONED BEETEE, EARLIER. YOU CAN LIE ALL YOU WANT, TRIP, BUT I KNOW YOU MISS H--
SPARE ME THE HAM-FISTED ANALYSES, DOCTOR.
BEETEE WAS CARRYING MY STOLEN MEMORIES. THE ONES YOU ENCRYPTED.
THAT'S WHERE MY LOSS BEGINS AND ENDS.
HIS DESTRUCTION SIMPLY MAKES ME DESPISE YOU MORE.
IN FACT: TELL ME, DOCTOR. DO YOU HAVE A MIRROR?
UH--NO. WHY?
OHH, A SMALL THING.
THE INDIVIDUAL WHO ATTACHED ME TO YOU IS WATCHING US. ENJOYING OUR SUFFERING. I'D LIKE TO LOOK HIM IN THE EYE. JUST ONCE.
BEFORE I COME FOR HIM.
IF...IF I SAID I'D FOUND THE CYBERNETICIST, WOULD YOU LET ME DEAL WITH HIM? NONE OF THIS--SINISTER THREAT STUFF.
LET ME SHOW YOU THE CIVILIZED WAY CAN WORK JUST AS WELL.
MADAM, I AM A PROTOCOL DROID.
CIVILIZED IS WHAT I DO.

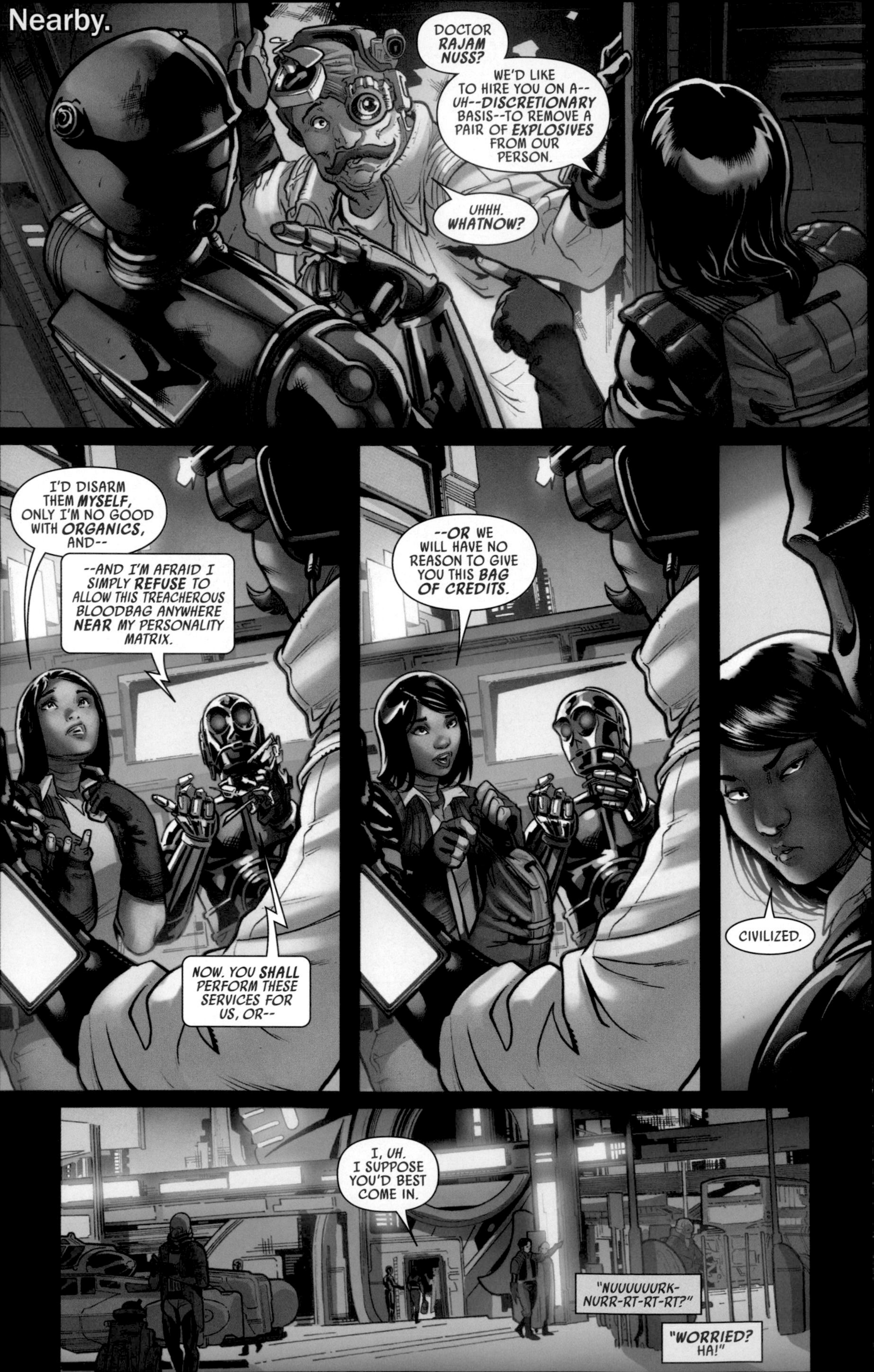
Nearby.
DOCTOR RAJAM NUSS?
WE'D LIKE TO HIRE YOU ON A-- UH--DISCRETIONARY BASIS--TO REMOVE A PAIR OF EXPLOSIVES FROM OUR PERSON.
UHHH. WHATNOW?
I'D DISARM THEM MYSELF, ONLY I'M NO GOOD WITH ORGANICS, AND--
--AND I'M AFRAID I SIMPLY REFUSE TO ALLOW THIS TREACHEROUS BLOODBAG ANYWHERE NEAR MY PERSONALITY MATRIX.
NOW. YOU SHALL PERFORM THESE SERVICES FOR US, OR--
--OR WE WILL HAVE NO REASON TO GIVE YOU THIS BAG OF CREDITS.
CIVILIZED.
I, UH. I SUPPOSE YOU'D BEST COME IN.
"NUUUUUURK-NURR-RT-RT-RT?"
"WORRIED? HA!"

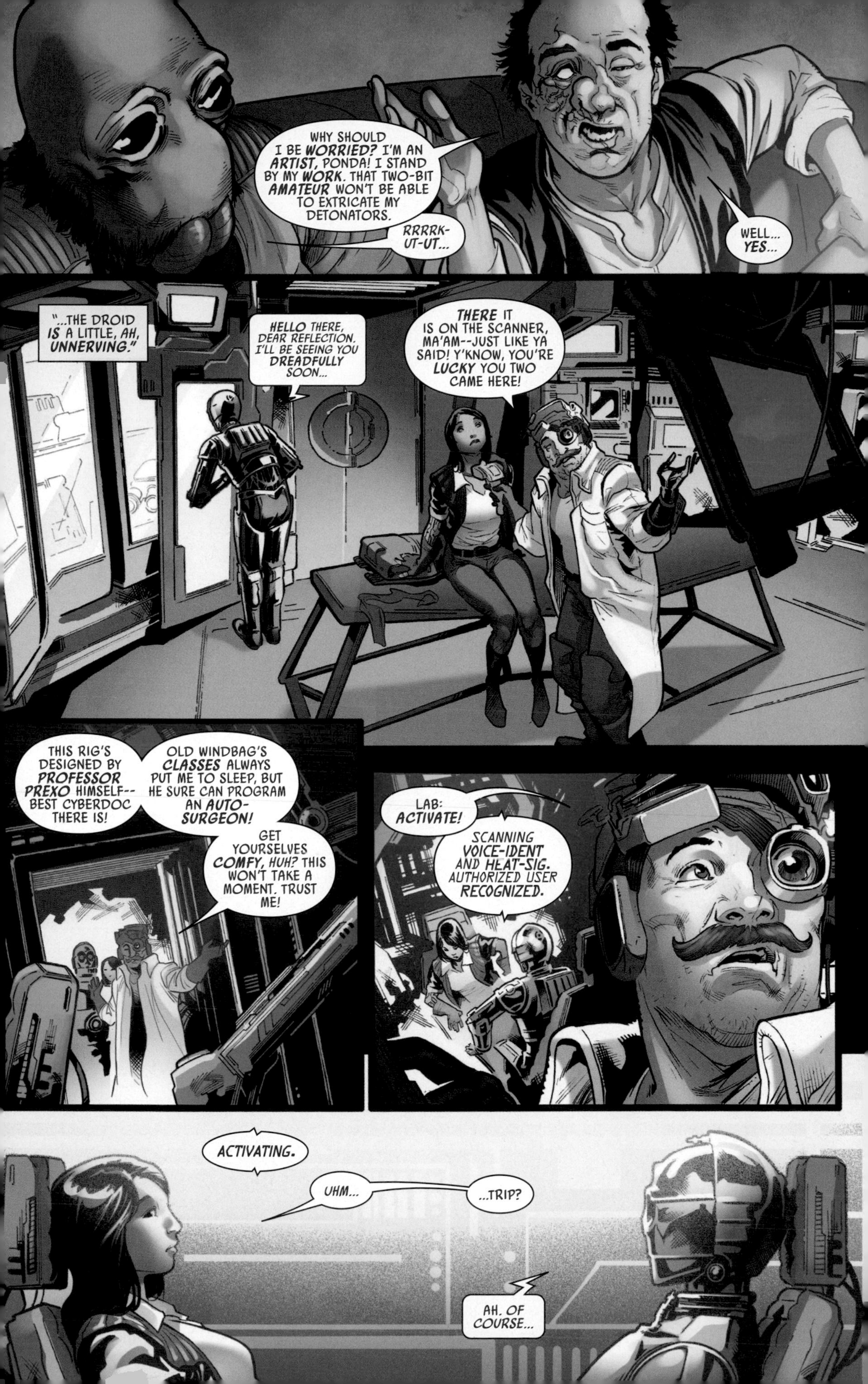
WHY SHOULD I BE WORRIED? I'M AN ARTIST, PONDA! I STAND BY MY WORK. THAT TWO-BIT AMATEUR WON'T BE ABLE TO EXTRICATE MY DETONATORS.
RRRRK-UT-UT...
WELL... YES...
"...THE DROID IS A LITTLE, AH, UNNERVING."
HELLO THERE, DEAR REFLECTION. I'LL BE SEEING YOU DREADFULLY SOON...
THERE IT IS ON THE SCANNER, MA'AM--JUST LIKE YA SAID! Y'KNOW, YOU'RE LUCKY YOU TWO CAME HERE!
THIS RIG'S DESIGNED BY PROFESSOR PREXO HIMSELF--BEST CYBERDOC THERE IS!
OLD WINDBAG'S CLASSES ALWAYS PUT ME TO SLEEP, BUT HE SURE CAN PROGRAM AN AUTO-SURGEON!
GET YOURSELVES COMFY, HUH? THIS WON'T TAKE A MOMENT. TRUST ME!
LAB: ACTIVATE!
SCANNING VOICE-IDENT AND HEAT-SIG. AUTHORIZED USER RECOGNIZED.
ACTIVATING.
UHM...
...TRIP?
AH. OF COURSE...

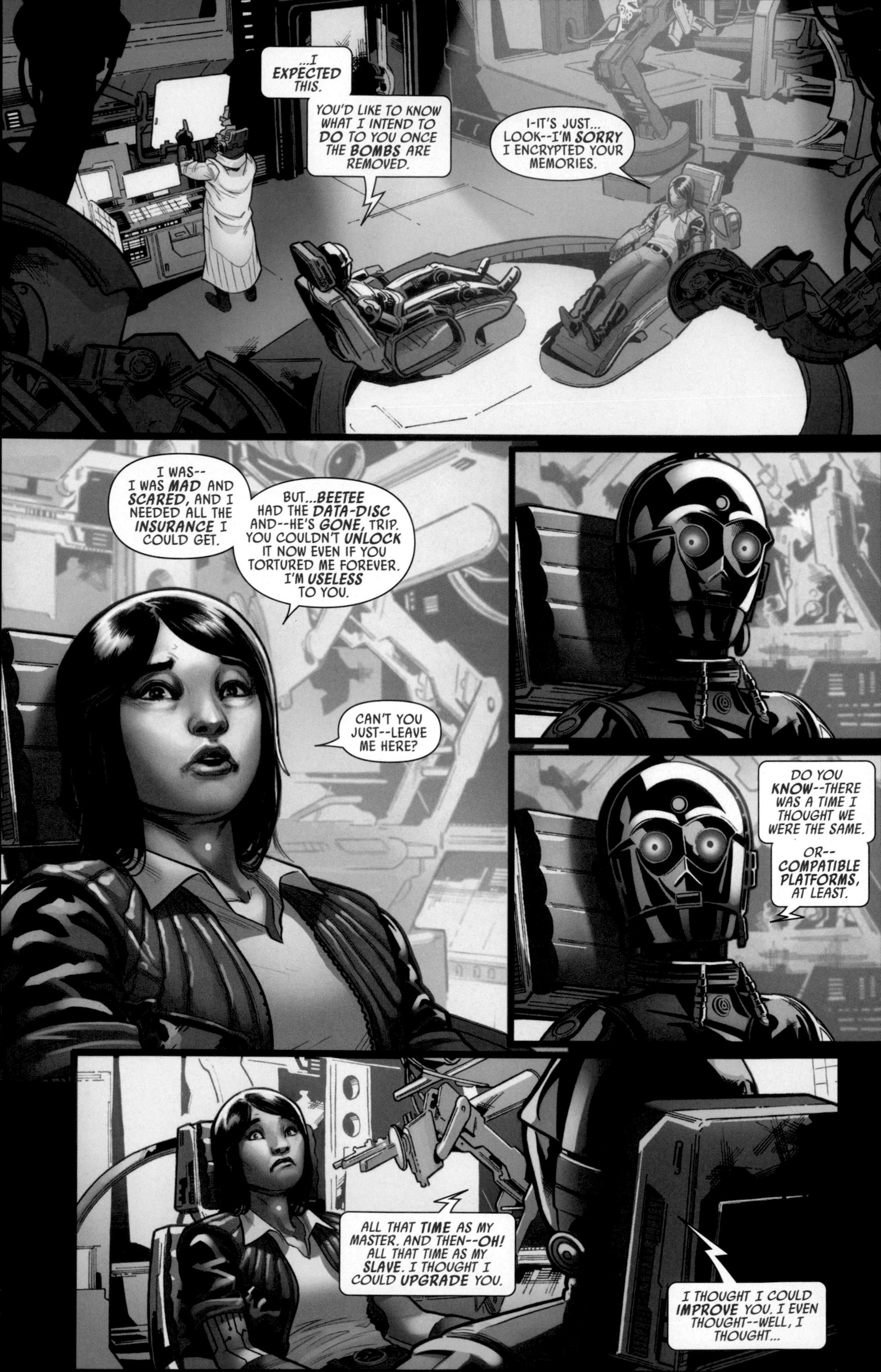
...I EXPECTED THIS.
YOU'D LIKE TO KNOW WHAT I INTEND TO DO TO YOU ONCE THE BOMBS ARE REMOVED.
I-IT'S JUST... LOOK--I'M SORRY I ENCRYPTED YOUR MEMORIES.
I WAS-- I WAS MAD AND SCARED, AND I NEEDED ALL THE INSURANCE I COULD GET.
BUT...BEETEE HAD THE DATA-DISC AND--HE'S GONE, TRIP. YOU COULDN'T UNLOCK IT NOW EVEN IF YOU TORTURED ME FOREVER. I'M USELESS TO YOU.
CAN'T YOU JUST--LEAVE ME HERE?
DO YOU KNOW--THERE WAS A TIME I THOUGHT WE WERE THE SAME.
OR-- COMPATIBLE PLATFORMS, AT LEAST.
ALL THAT TIME AS MY MASTER. AND THEN--OH! ALL THAT TIME AS MY SLAVE. I THOUGHT I COULD UPGRADE YOU.
I THOUGHT I COULD IMPROVE YOU. I EVEN THOUGHT--WELL, I THOUGHT...

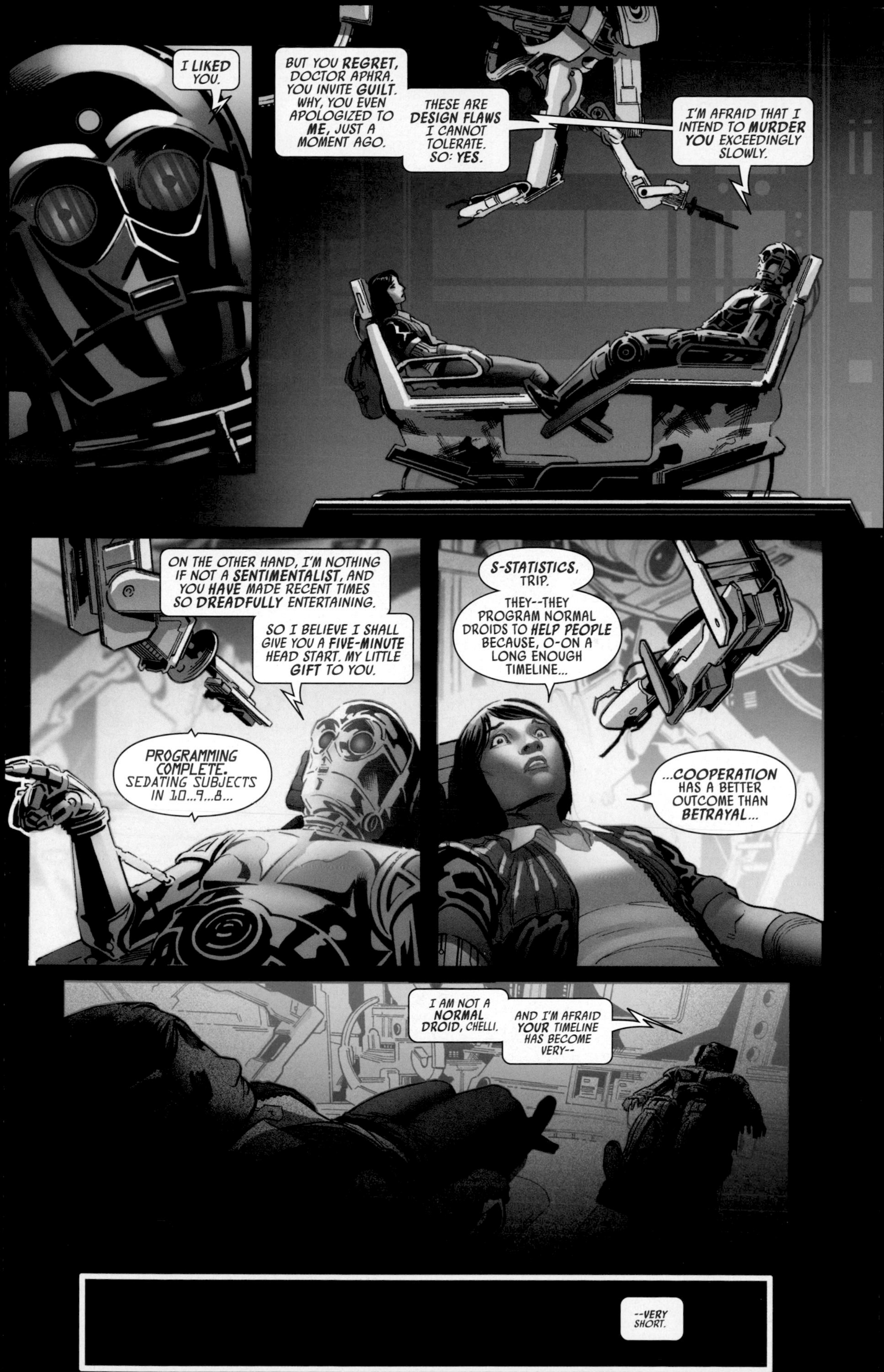
I LIKED YOU.
BUT YOU REGRET, DOCTOR APHRA. YOU INVITE GUILT. WHY, YOU EVEN APOLOGIZED TO ME, JUST A MOMENT AGO.
THESE ARE DESIGN FLAWS I CANNOT TOLERATE. SO: YES.
I'M AFRAID THAT I INTEND TO MURDER YOU EXCEEDINGLY SLOWLY.
ON THE OTHER HAND, I'M NOTHING IF NOT A SENTIMENTALIST, AND YOU HAVE MADE RECENT TIMES SO DREADFULLY ENTERTAINING.
SO I BELIEVE I SHALL GIVE YOU A FIVE-MINUTE HEAD START. MY LITTLE GIFT TO YOU.
PROGRAMMING COMPLETE. SEDATING SUBJECTS IN 10...9...8...
S-STATISTICS, TRIP.
THEY--THEY PROGRAM NORMAL DROIDS TO HELP PEOPLE BECAUSE, O-ON A LONG ENOUGH TIMELINE...
...COOPERATION HAS A BETTER OUTCOME THAN BETRAYAL...
I AM NOT A NORMAL DROID, CHELLI.
AND I'M AFRAID YOUR TIMELINE HAS BECOME VERY--
--VERY SHORT.

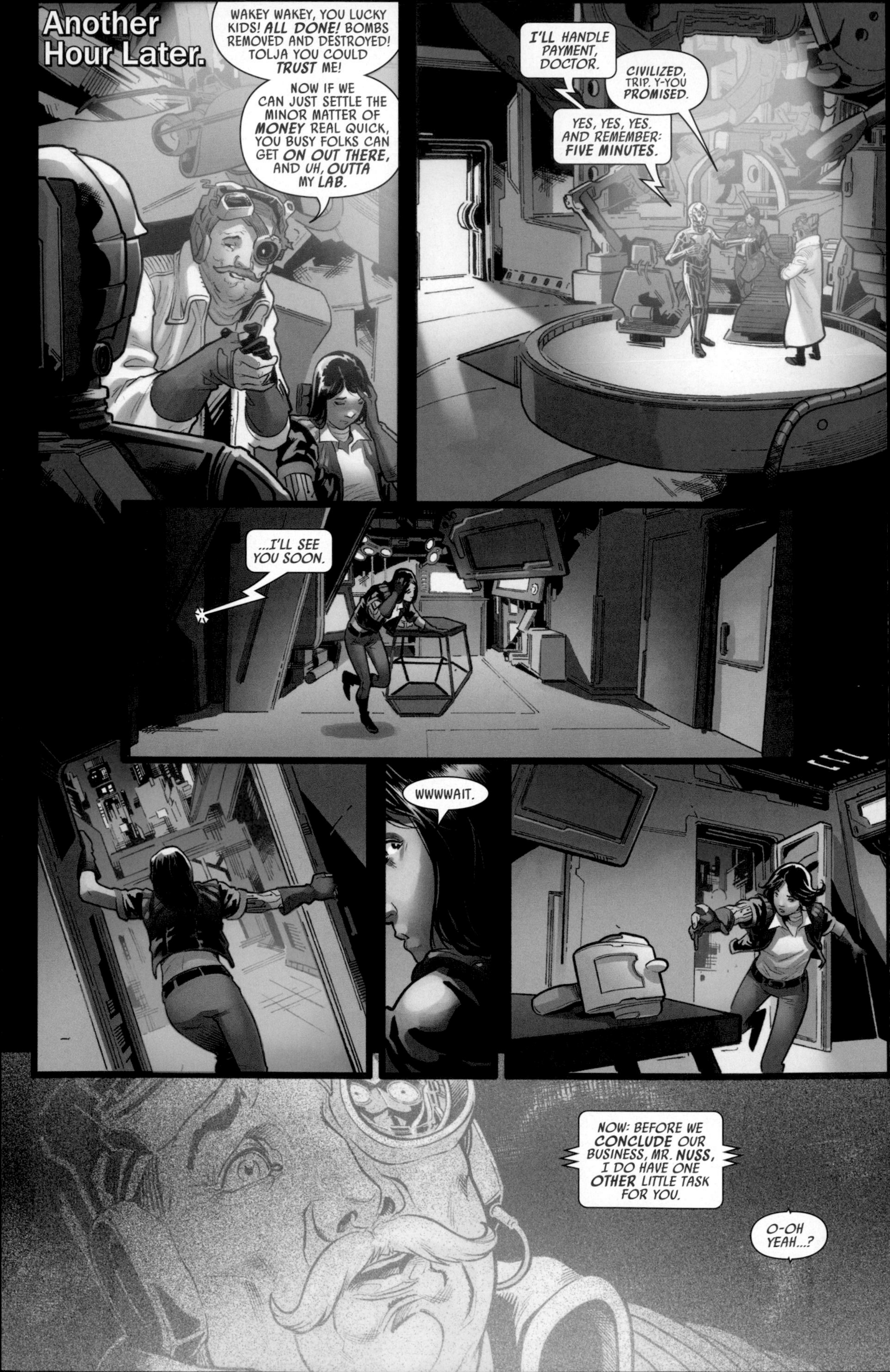
Another Hour Later.
WAKEY WAKEY, YOU LUCKY KIDS! ALL DONE! BOMBS REMOVED AND DESTROYED! TOLJA YOU COULD TRUST ME!
NOW IF WE CAN JUST SETTLE THE MINOR MATTER OF MONEY REAL QUICK, YOU BUSY FOLKS CAN GET ON OUT THERE, AND UH, OUTTA MY LAB.
I'LL HANDLE PAYMENT, DOCTOR.
CIVILIZED, TRIP. Y-YOU PROMISED.
YES, YES, YES. AND REMEMBER: FIVE MINUTES.
...I'LL SEE YOU SOON.
WWWWAIT.
NOW: BEFORE WE CONCLUDE OUR BUSINESS, MR. NUSS, I DO HAVE ONE OTHER LITTLE TASK FOR YOU.
O-OH YEAH...?

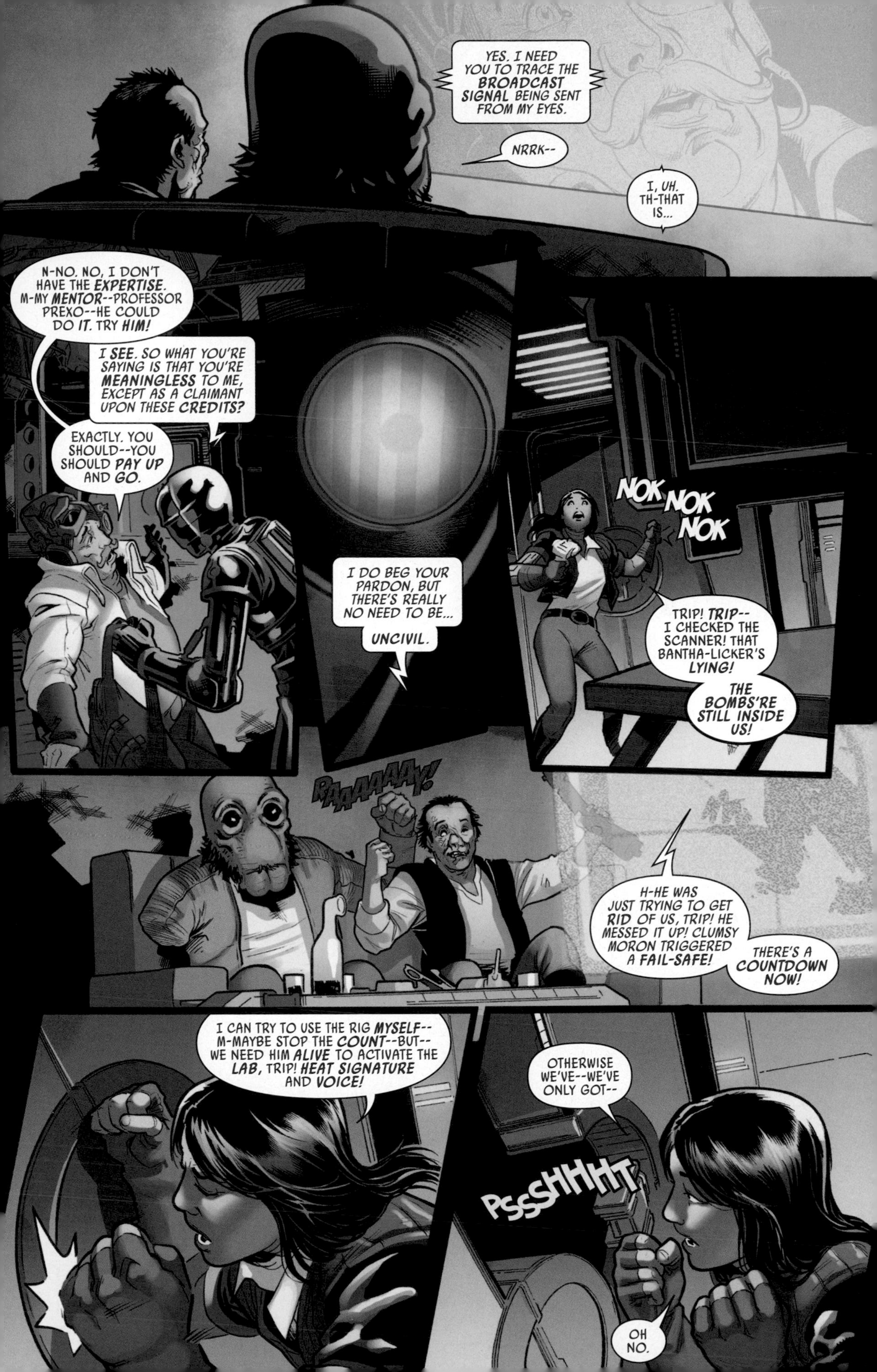

YES. I NEED YOU TO TRACE THE BROADCAST SIGNAL BEING SENT FROM MY EYES.
NRRK--
I, UH. TH-THAT IS...
N-NO. NO, I DON'T HAVE THE EXPERTISE. M-MY MENTOR--PROFESSOR PREXO--HE COULD DO IT. TRY HIM!
I SEE. SO WHAT YOU'RE SAYING IS THAT YOU'RE MEANINGLESS TO ME, EXCEPT AS A CLAIMANT UPON THESE CREDITS?
EXACTLY. YOU SHOULD--YOU SHOULD PAY UP AND GO.
I DO BEG YOUR PARDON, BUT THERE'S REALLY NO NEED TO BE...
UNCIVIL.
NOK NOK NOK
TRIP! TRIP-- I CHECKED THE SCANNER! THAT BANTHA-LICKER'S LYING!
THE BOMBS'RE STILL INSIDE US!
RAAAAAAY!
H-HE WAS JUST TRYING TO GET RID OF US, TRIP! HE MESSED IT UP! CLUMSY MORON TRIGGERED A FAIL-SAFE!
THERE'S A COUNTDOWN NOW!
I CAN TRY TO USE THE RIG MYSELF-- M-MAYBE STOP THE COUNT--BUT-- WE NEED HIM ALIVE TO ACTIVATE THE LAB, TRIP! HEAT SIGNATURE AND VOICE!
OTHERWISE WE'VE--WE'VE ONLY GOT--
PSSSHHHT
OH NO.

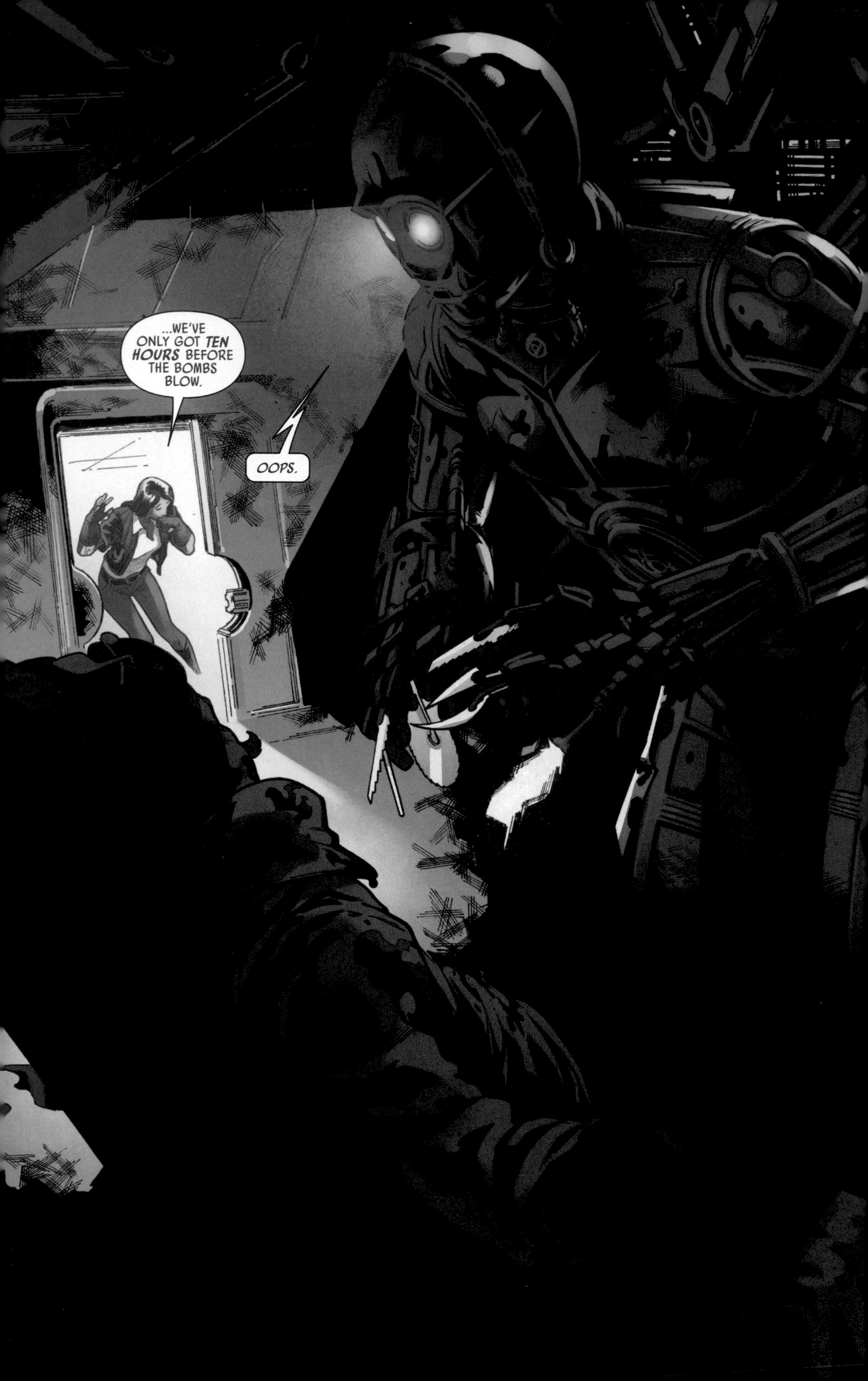
...WE'VE ONLY GOT TEN HOURS BEFORE THE BOMBS BLOW.
OOPS.

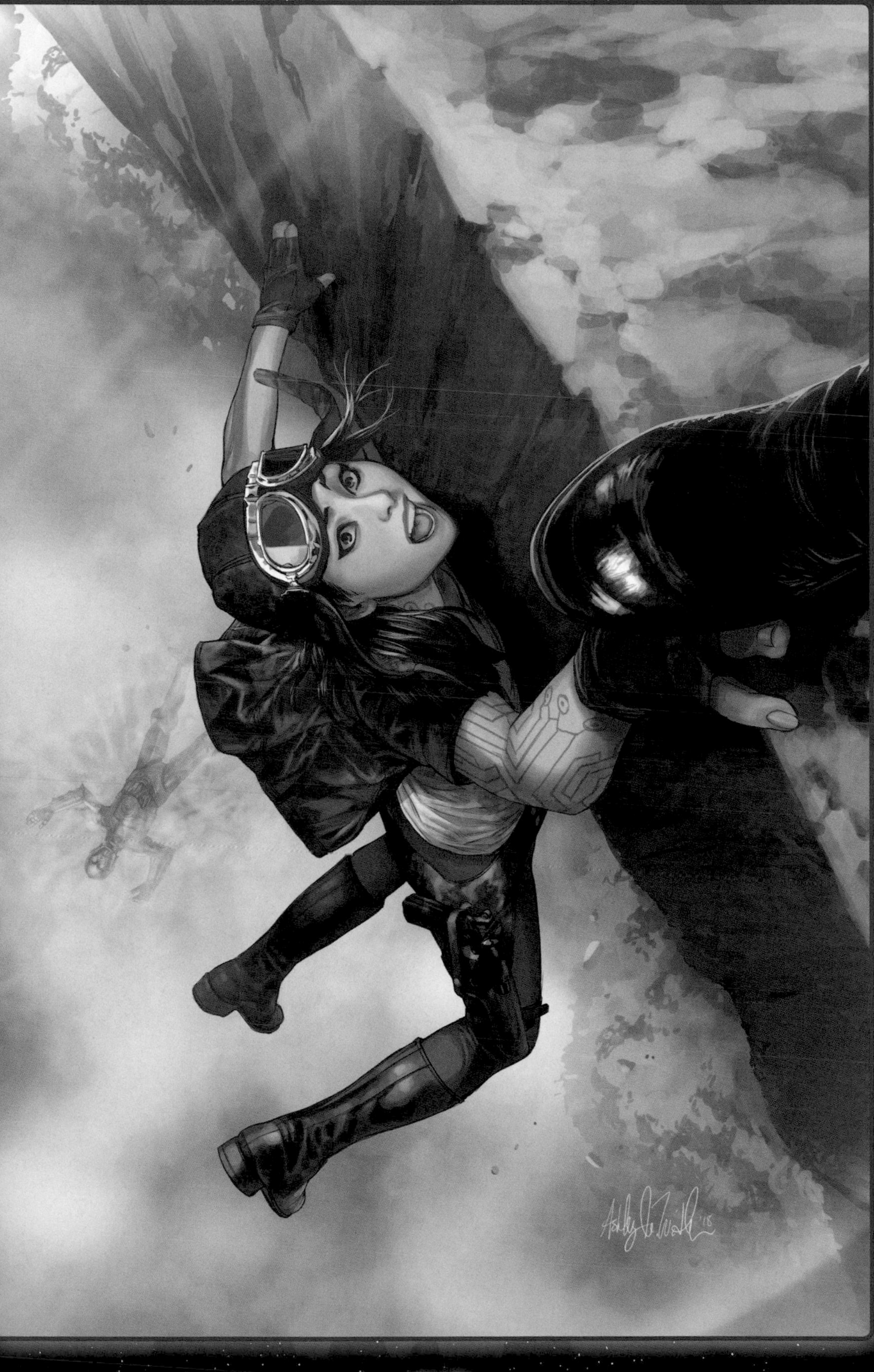

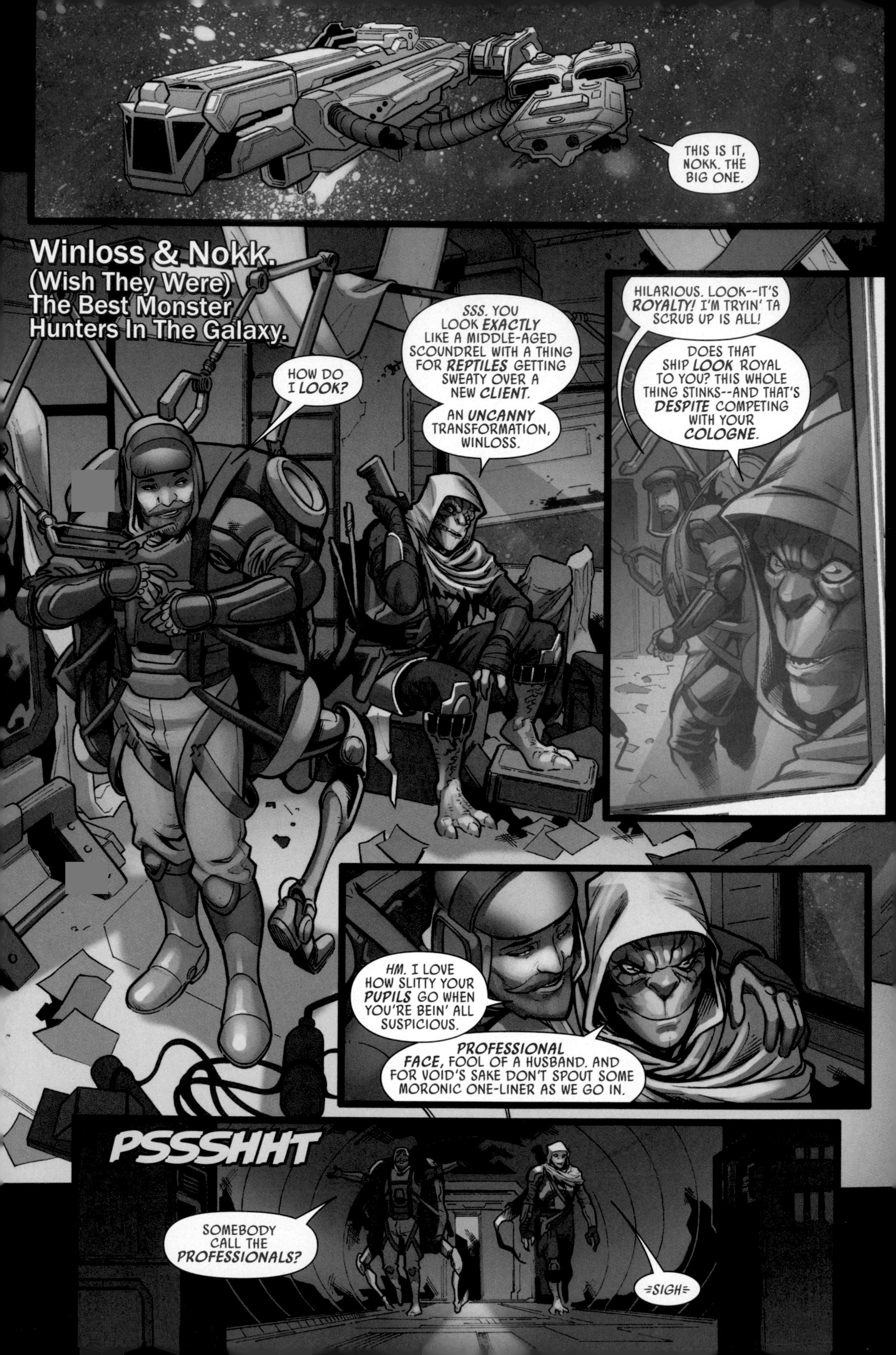

THIS IS IT, NOKK. THE BIG ONE.
Winloss & Nokk. (Wish They Were) The Best Monster Hunters In The Galaxy.
HOW DO I LOOK?
SSS. YOU LOOK EXACTLY LIKE A MIDDLE-AGED SCOUNDREL WITH A THING FOR REPTILES GETTING SWEATY OVER A NEW CLIENT.
AN UNCANNY TRANSFORMATION, WINLOSS.
HILARIOUS. LOOK--IT'S ROYALTY! I'M TRYIN' TA SCRUB UP IS ALL!
DOES THAT SHIP LOOK ROYAL TO YOU? THIS WHOLE THING STINKS--AND THAT'S DESPITE COMPETING WITH YOUR COLOGNE.
HM. I LOVE HOW SLITTY YOUR PUPILS GO WHEN YOU'RE BEIN' ALL SUSPICIOUS.
PROFESSIONAL FACE, FOOL OF A HUSBAND. AND FOR VOID'S SAKE DON'T SPOUT SOME MORONIC ONE-LINER AS WE GO IN.
PSSSHHT
SOMEBODY CALL THE PROFESSIONALS?
=SIGH=

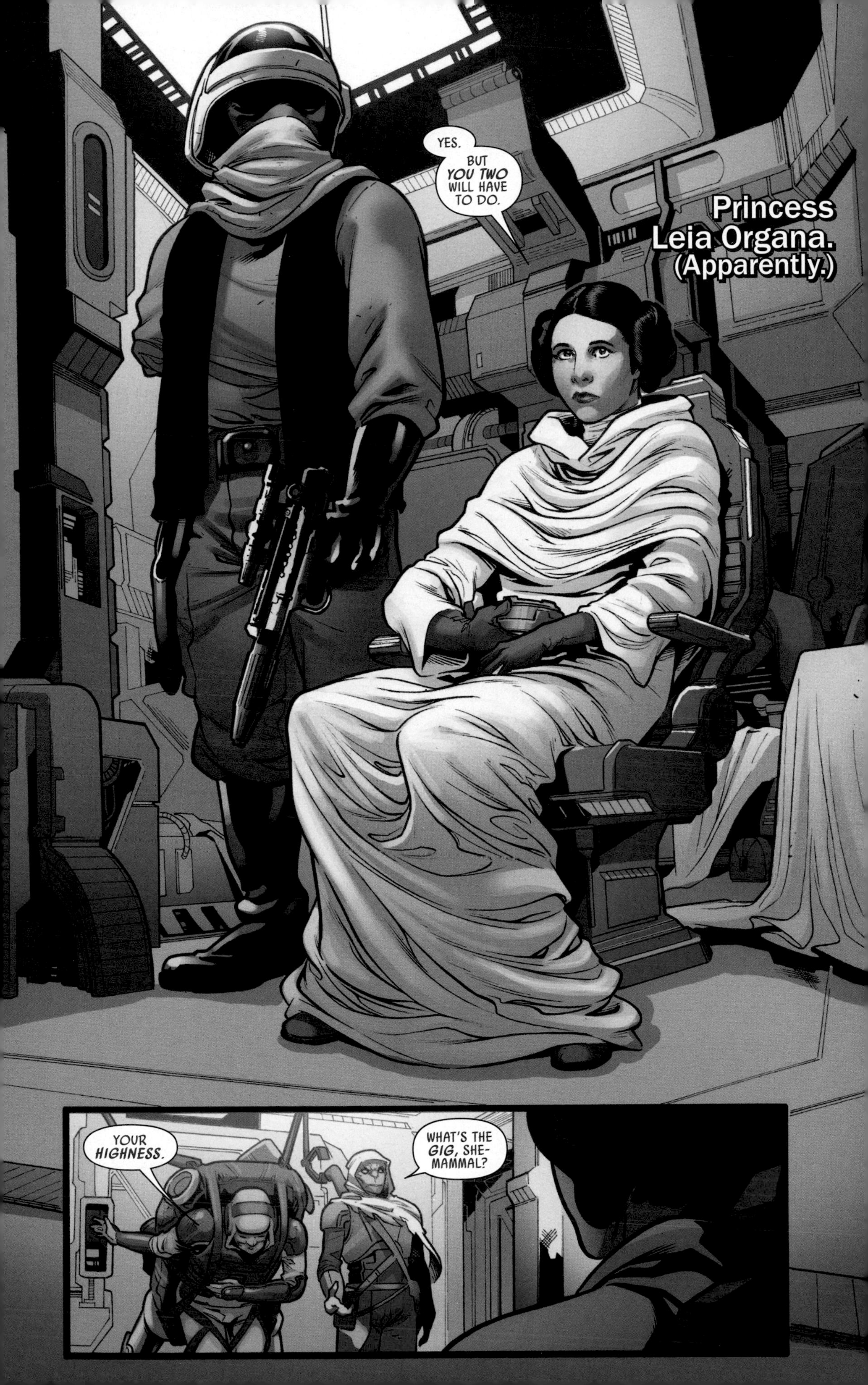
YES.
BUT *YOU TWO* WILL HAVE TO DO.
Princess Leia Organa. (Apparently.)
YOUR *HIGHNESS.*
WHAT'S THE *GIG,* SHE-MAMMAL?

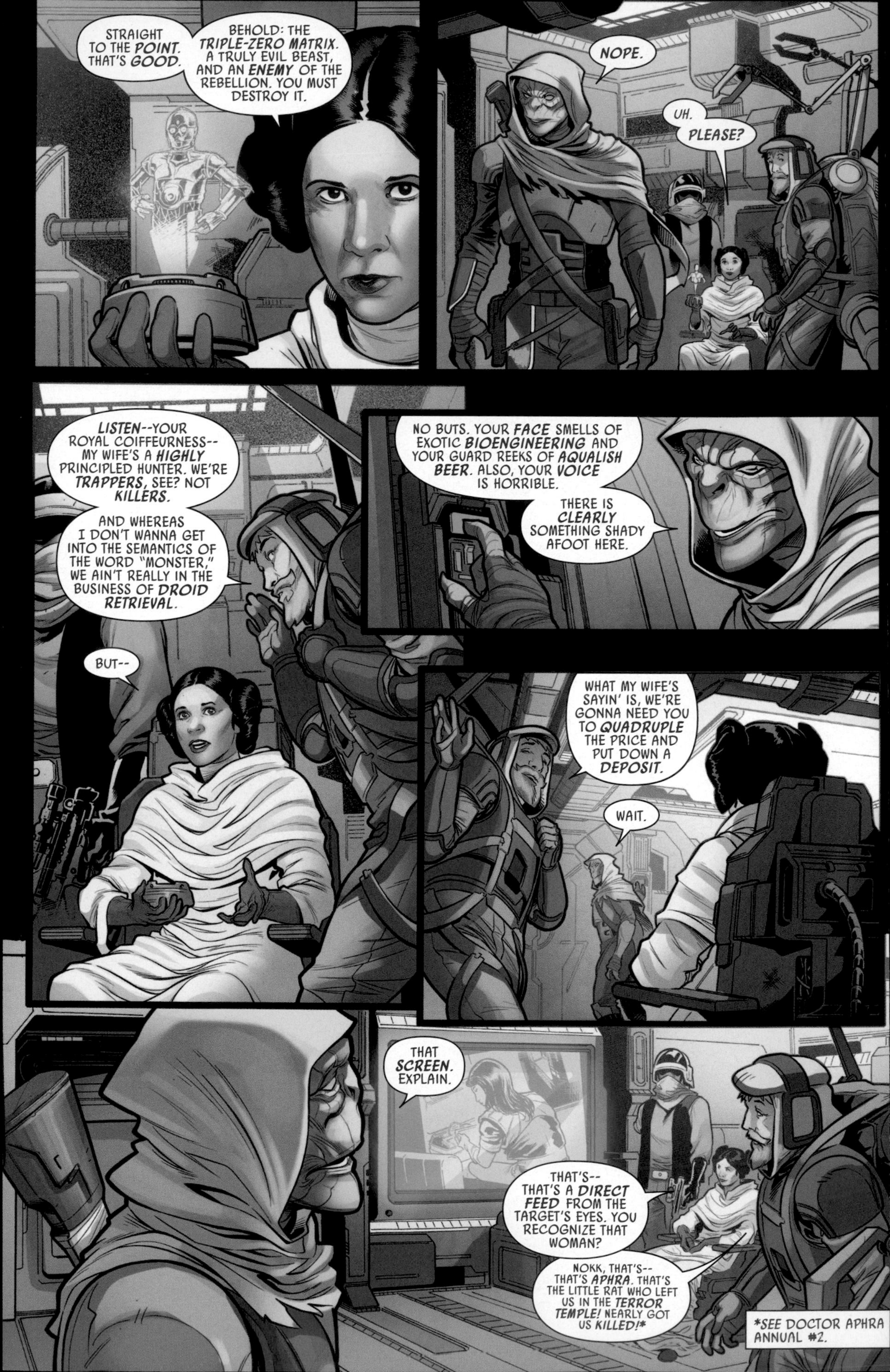

STRAIGHT TO THE POINT. THAT'S GOOD.
BEHOLD: THE TRIPLE-ZERO MATRIX. A TRULY EVIL BEAST, AND AN ENEMY OF THE REBELLION. YOU MUST DESTROY IT.
NOPE.
UH. PLEASE?
LISTEN--YOUR ROYAL COIFFEURNESS-- MY WIFE'S A HIGHLY PRINCIPLED HUNTER. WE'RE TRAPPERS, SEE? NOT KILLERS.
AND WHEREAS I DON'T WANNA GET INTO THE SEMANTICS OF THE WORD "MONSTER," WE AIN'T REALLY IN THE BUSINESS OF DROID RETRIEVAL.
BUT--
NO BUTS. YOUR FACE SMELLS OF EXOTIC BIOENGINEERING AND YOUR GUARD REEKS OF AQUALISH BEER. ALSO, YOUR VOICE IS HORRIBLE.
THERE IS CLEARLY SOMETHING SHADY AFOOT HERE.
WHAT MY WIFE'S SAYIN' IS, WE'RE GONNA NEED YOU TO QUADRUPLE THE PRICE AND PUT DOWN A DEPOSIT.
WAIT.
THAT SCREEN. EXPLAIN.
THAT'S-- THAT'S A DIRECT FEED FROM THE TARGET'S EYES. YOU RECOGNIZE THAT WOMAN?
NOKK, THAT'S-- THAT'S APHRA. THAT'S THE LITTLE RAT WHO LEFT US IN THE TERROR TEMPLE! NEARLY GOT US KILLED!*
*SEE DOCTOR APHRA ANNUAL #2.

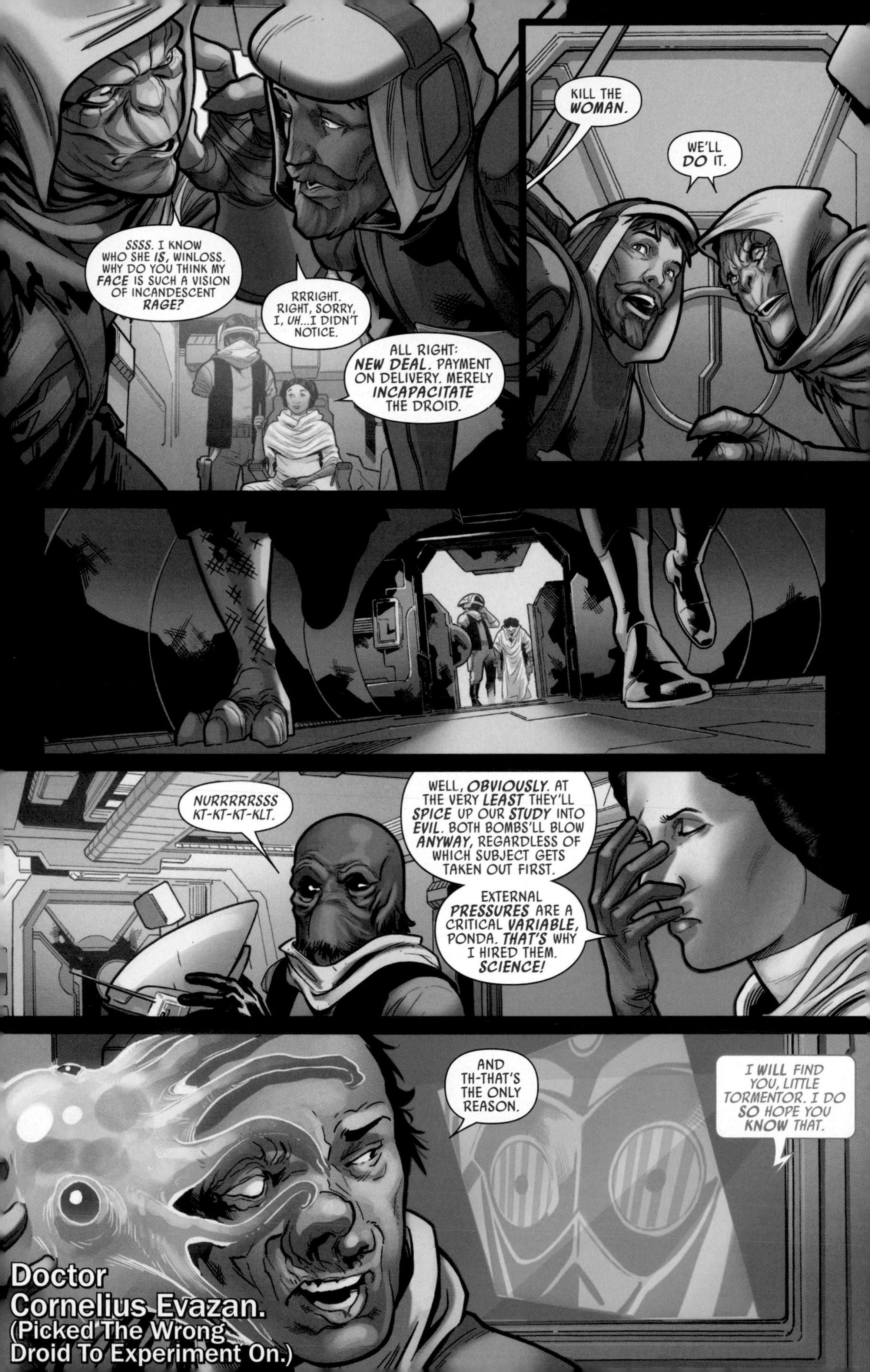
SSSS. I KNOW WHO SHE IS, WINLOSS. WHY DO YOU THINK MY FACE IS SUCH A VISION OF INCANDESCENT RAGE?
RRRIGHT. RIGHT, SORRY, I, UH...I DIDN'T NOTICE.
ALL RIGHT: NEW DEAL. PAYMENT ON DELIVERY. MERELY INCAPACITATE THE DROID.
KILL THE WOMAN.
WE'LL DO IT.
NURRRRRSSS KT-KT-KT-KLT.
WELL, OBVIOUSLY. AT THE VERY LEAST THEY'LL SPICE UP OUR STUDY INTO EVIL. BOTH BOMBS'LL BLOW ANYWAY, REGARDLESS OF WHICH SUBJECT GETS TAKEN OUT FIRST.
EXTERNAL PRESSURES ARE A CRITICAL VARIABLE, PONDA. THAT'S WHY I HIRED THEM. SCIENCE!
AND TH-THAT'S THE ONLY REASON.
I WILL FIND YOU, LITTLE TORMENTOR. I DO SO HOPE YOU KNOW THAT.
Doctor Cornelius Evazan. (Picked The Wrong Droid To Experiment On.)

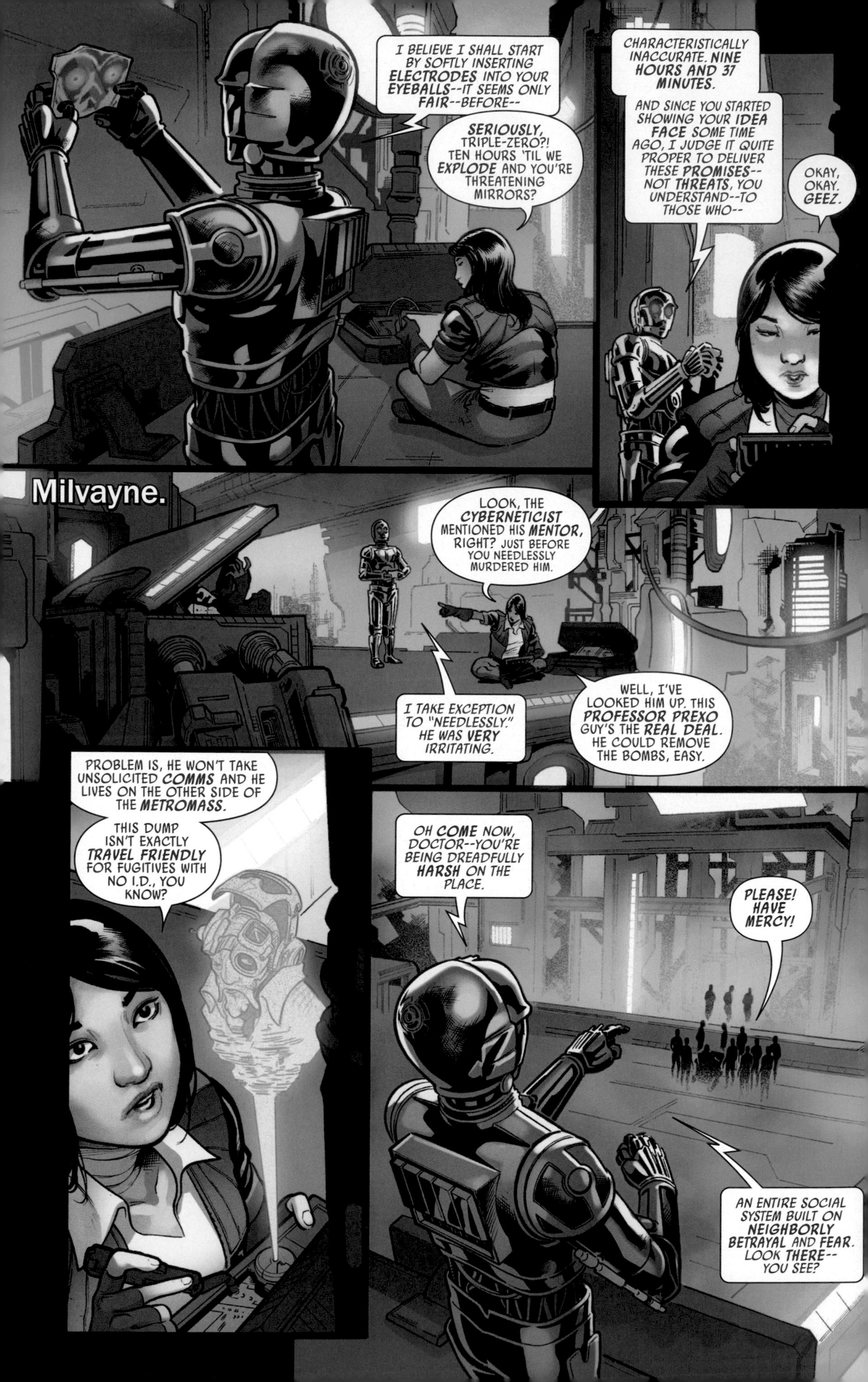
I BELIEVE I SHALL START BY SOFTLY INSERTING ELECTRODES INTO YOUR EYEBALLS--IT SEEMS ONLY FAIR--BEFORE--
SERIOUSLY, TRIPLE-ZERO?! TEN HOURS 'TIL WE EXPLODE AND YOU'RE THREATENING MIRRORS?
CHARACTERISTICALLY INACCURATE. NINE HOURS AND 37 MINUTES.
AND SINCE YOU STARTED SHOWING YOUR IDEA FACE SOME TIME AGO, I JUDGE IT QUITE PROPER TO DELIVER THESE PROMISES-- NOT THREATS, YOU UNDERSTAND--TO THOSE WHO--
OKAY, OKAY. GEEZ.
Milvayne.
LOOK, THE CYBERNETICIST MENTIONED HIS MENTOR, RIGHT? JUST BEFORE YOU NEEDLESSLY MURDERED HIM.
I TAKE EXCEPTION TO "NEEDLESSLY." HE WAS VERY IRRITATING.
WELL, I'VE LOOKED HIM UP. THIS PROFESSOR PREXO GUY'S THE REAL DEAL. HE COULD REMOVE THE BOMBS, EASY.
PROBLEM IS, HE WON'T TAKE UNSOLICITED COMMS AND HE LIVES ON THE OTHER SIDE OF THE METROMASS.
THIS DUMP ISN'T EXACTLY TRAVEL FRIENDLY FOR FUGITIVES WITH NO I.D., YOU KNOW?
OH COME NOW, DOCTOR--YOU'RE BEING DREADFULLY HARSH ON THE PLACE.
PLEASE! HAVE MERCY!
AN ENTIRE SOCIAL SYSTEM BUILT ON NEIGHBORLY BETRAYAL AND FEAR. LOOK THERE-- YOU SEE?

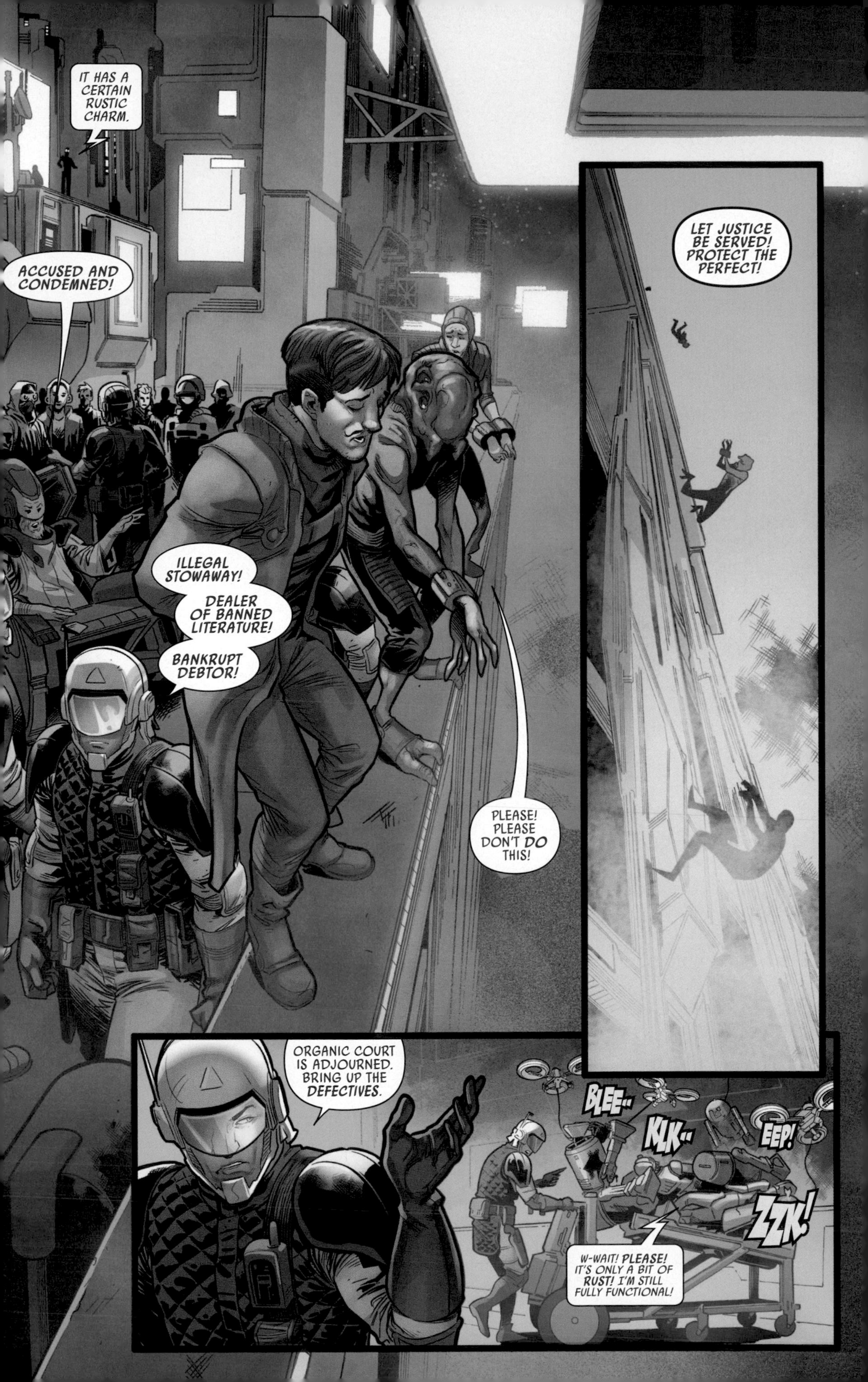
IT HAS A CERTAIN RUSTIC CHARM.
ACCUSED AND CONDEMNED!
ILLEGAL STOWAWAY!
DEALER OF BANNED LITERATURE!
BANKRUPT DEBTOR!
PLEASE! PLEASE DON'T DO THIS!
LET JUSTICE BE SERVED! PROTECT THE PERFECT!
ORGANIC COURT IS ADJOURNED. BRING UP THE DEFECTIVES.
BLEE..
KLK..
EEP!
ZZK!
W-WAIT! PLEASE! IT'S ONLY A BIT OF RUST! I'M STILL FULLY FUNCTIONAL!

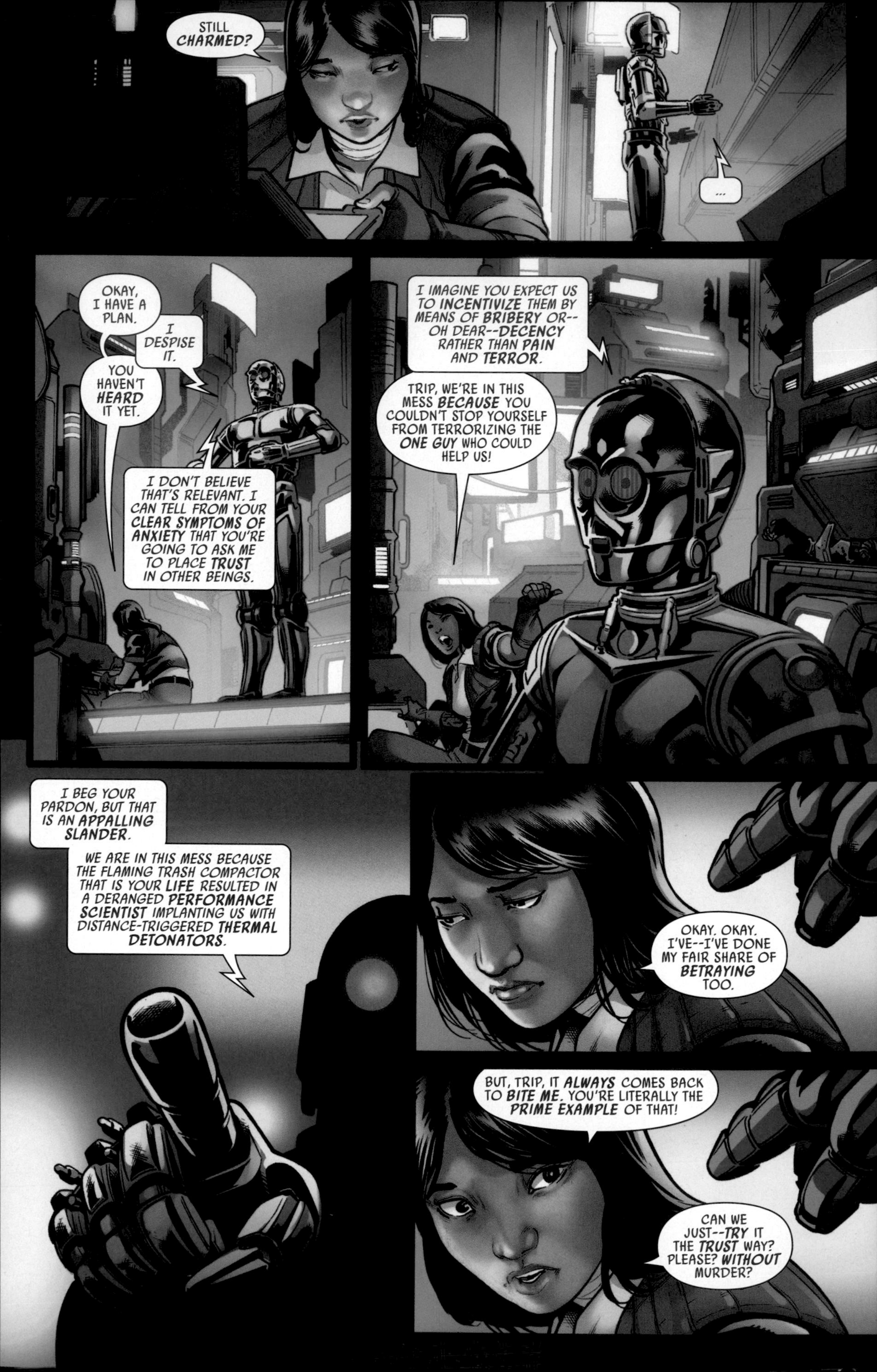
STILL CHARMED?
...
OKAY, I HAVE A PLAN.
I DESPISE IT.
YOU HAVEN'T HEARD IT YET.
I DON'T BELIEVE THAT'S RELEVANT. I CAN TELL FROM YOUR CLEAR SYMPTOMS OF ANXIETY THAT YOU'RE GOING TO ASK ME TO PLACE TRUST IN OTHER BEINGS.
I IMAGINE YOU EXPECT US TO INCENTIVIZE THEM BY MEANS OF BRIBERY OR-- OH DEAR--DECENCY RATHER THAN PAIN AND TERROR.
TRIP, WE'RE IN THIS MESS BECAUSE YOU COULDN'T STOP YOURSELF FROM TERRORIZING THE ONE GUY WHO COULD HELP US!
I BEG YOUR PARDON, BUT THAT IS AN APPALLING SLANDER.
WE ARE IN THIS MESS BECAUSE THE FLAMING TRASH COMPACTOR THAT IS YOUR LIFE RESULTED IN A DERANGED PERFORMANCE SCIENTIST IMPLANTING US WITH DISTANCE-TRIGGERED THERMAL DETONATORS.
OKAY. OKAY. I'VE--I'VE DONE MY FAIR SHARE OF BETRAYING TOO.
BUT, TRIP, IT ALWAYS COMES BACK TO BITE ME. YOU'RE LITERALLY THE PRIME EXAMPLE OF THAT!
CAN WE JUST--TRY IT THE TRUST WAY? PLEASE? WITHOUT MURDER?

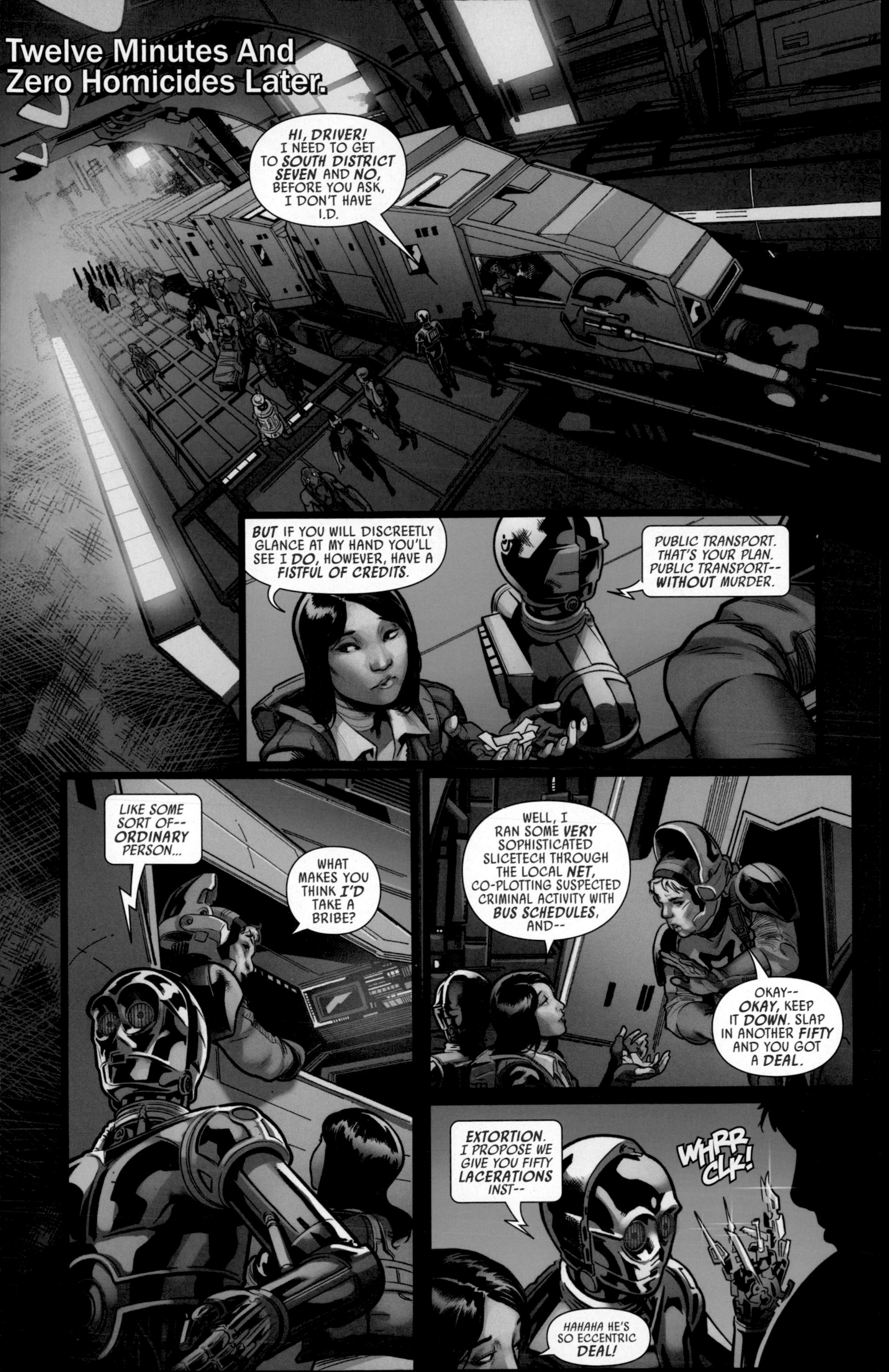
Twelve Minutes And Zero Homicides Later.
HI, DRIVER! I NEED TO GET TO SOUTH DISTRICT SEVEN AND NO, BEFORE YOU ASK, I DON'T HAVE I.D.
BUT IF YOU WILL DISCREETLY GLANCE AT MY HAND YOU'LL SEE I DO, HOWEVER, HAVE A FISTFUL OF CREDITS.
PUBLIC TRANSPORT. THAT'S YOUR PLAN. PUBLIC TRANSPORT--WITHOUT MURDER.
LIKE SOME SORT OF--ORDINARY PERSON...
WHAT MAKES YOU THINK I'D TAKE A BRIBE?
WELL, I RAN SOME VERY SOPHISTICATED SLICETECH THROUGH THE LOCAL NET, CO-PLOTTING SUSPECTED CRIMINAL ACTIVITY WITH BUS SCHEDULES, AND--
OKAY--OKAY, KEEP IT DOWN. SLAP IN ANOTHER FIFTY AND YOU GOT A DEAL.
EXTORTION. I PROPOSE WE GIVE YOU FIFTY LACERATIONS INST--
WHRR CLK!
HAHAHA HE'S SO ECCENTRIC DEAL!

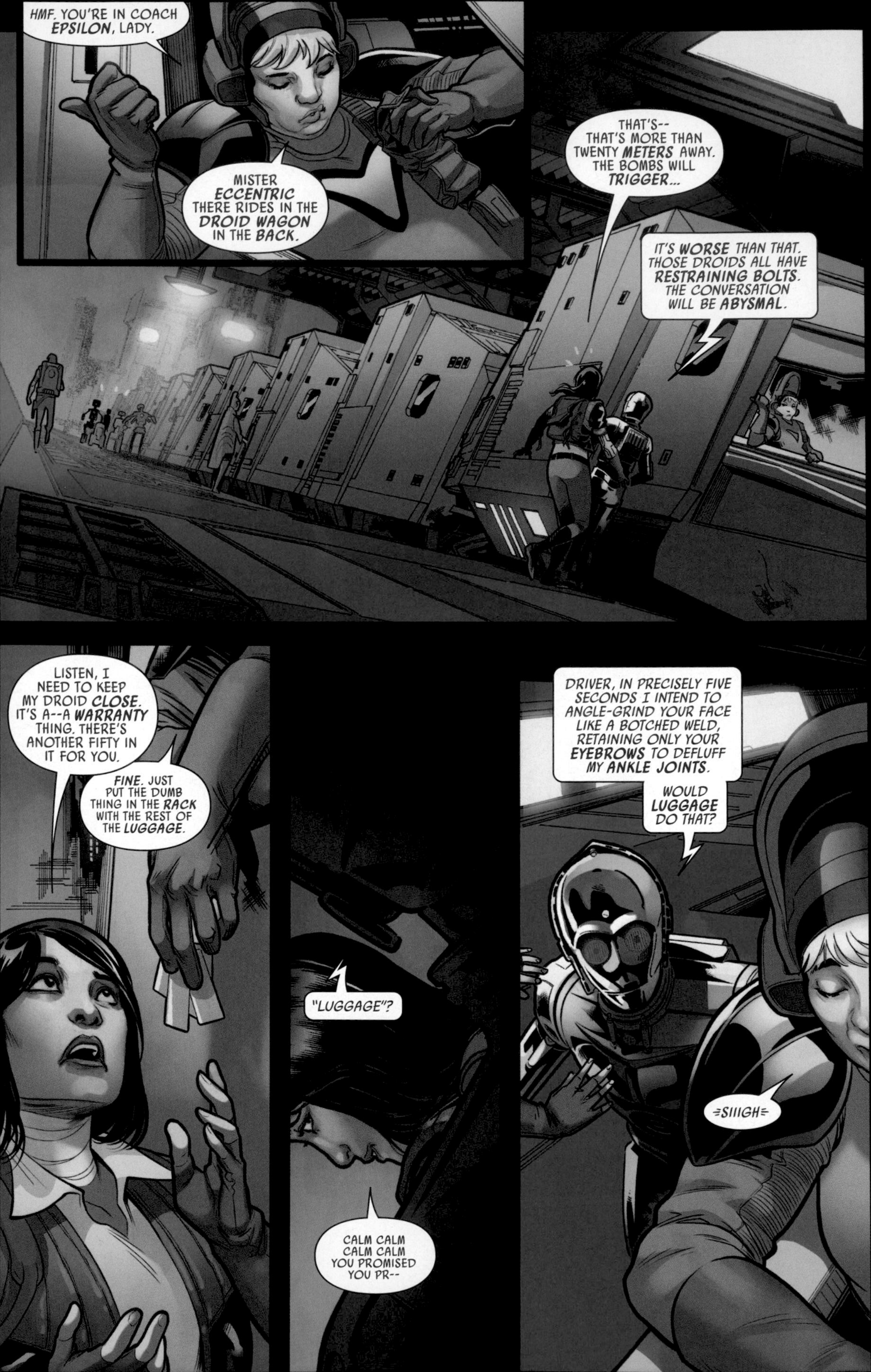
HMF. YOU'RE IN COACH EPSILON, LADY.
MISTER ECCENTRIC THERE RIDES IN THE DROID WAGON IN THE BACK.
THAT'S-- THAT'S MORE THAN TWENTY METERS AWAY. THE BOMBS WILL TRIGGER...
IT'S WORSE THAN THAT. THOSE DROIDS ALL HAVE RESTRAINING BOLTS. THE CONVERSATION WILL BE ABYSMAL.
LISTEN, I NEED TO KEEP MY DROID CLOSE. IT'S A--A WARRANTY THING. THERE'S ANOTHER FIFTY IN IT FOR YOU.
FINE. JUST PUT THE DUMB THING IN THE RACK WITH THE REST OF THE LUGGAGE.
"LUGGAGE"?
CALM CALM CALM CALM YOU PROMISED YOU PR--
DRIVER, IN PRECISELY FIVE SECONDS I INTEND TO ANGLE-GRIND YOUR FACE LIKE A BOTCHED WELD, RETAINING ONLY YOUR EYEBROWS TO DEFLUFF MY ANKLE JOINTS.
WOULD LUGGAGE DO THAT?
=SIIIGH=

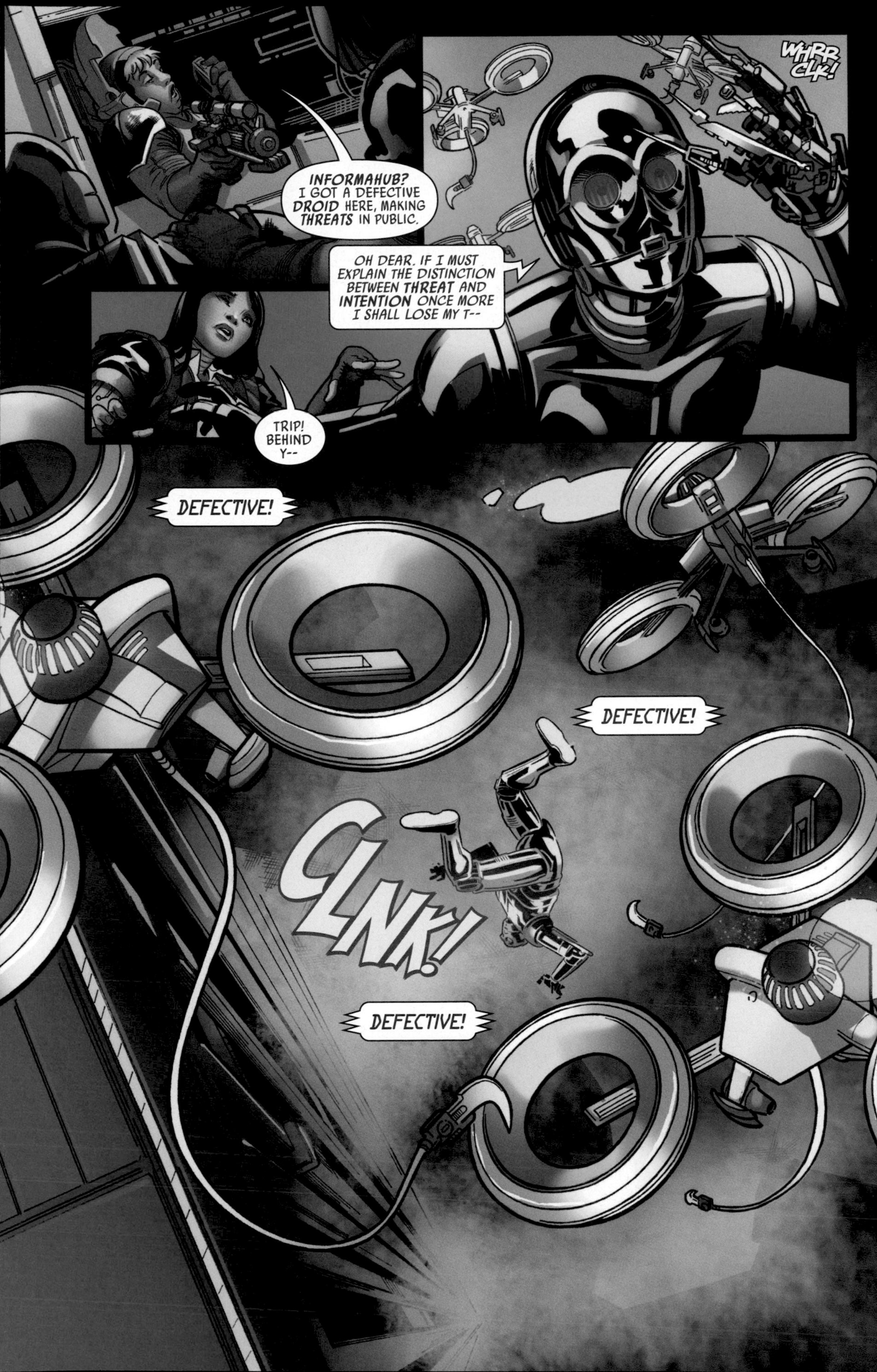
INFORMAHUB? I GOT A DEFECTIVE DROID HERE, MAKING THREATS IN PUBLIC.
WHRR CLK!
OH DEAR. IF I MUST EXPLAIN THE DISTINCTION BETWEEN THREAT AND INTENTION ONCE MORE I SHALL LOSE MY T--
TRIP! BEHIND Y--
DEFECTIVE!
DEFECTIVE!
CLNK!
DEFECTIVE!

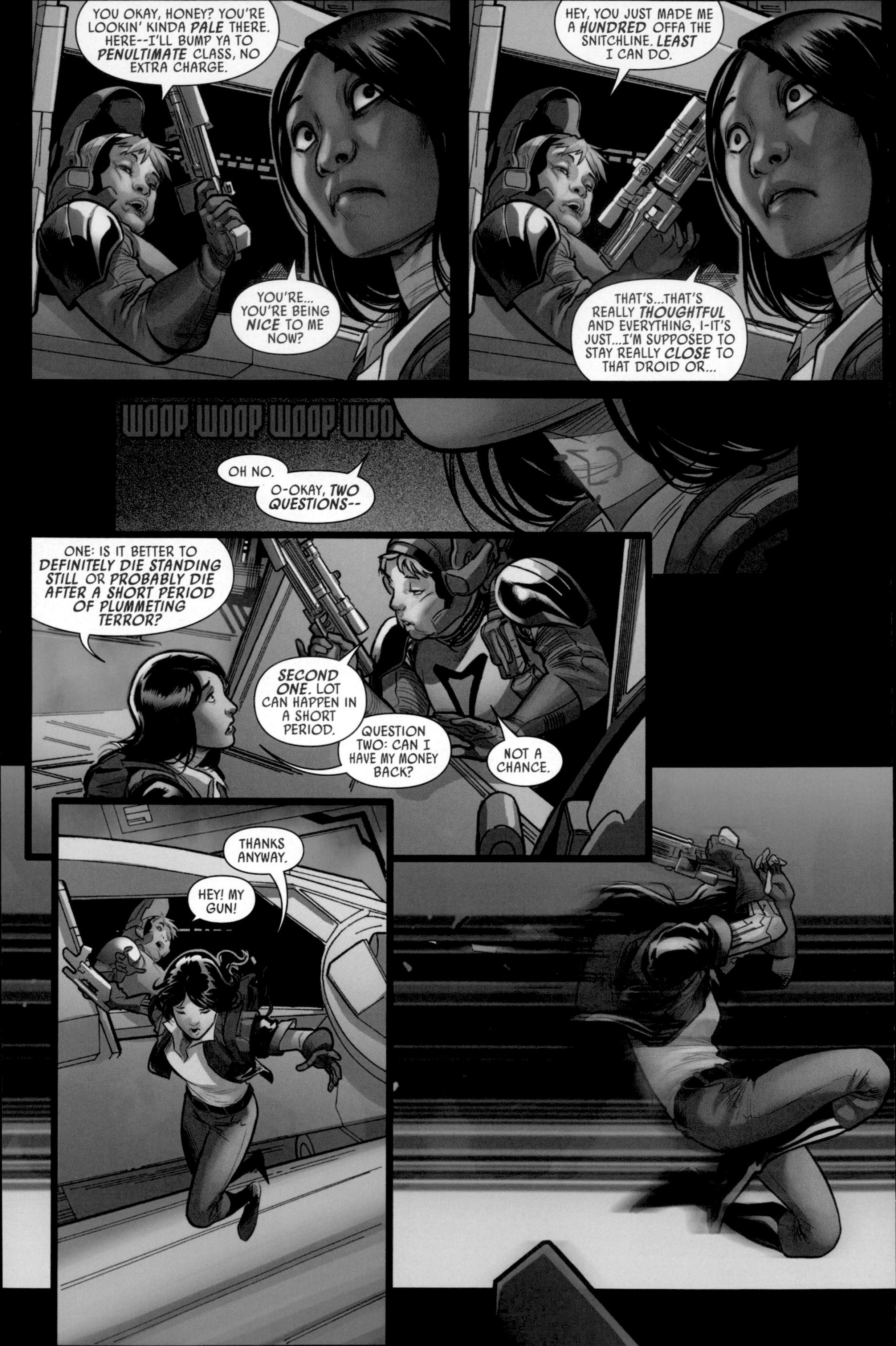
YOU OKAY, HONEY? YOU'RE LOOKIN' KINDA PALE THERE. HERE--I'LL BUMP YA TO PENULTIMATE CLASS, NO EXTRA CHARGE.
YOU'RE... YOU'RE BEING NICE TO ME NOW?
HEY, YOU JUST MADE ME A HUNDRED OFFA THE SNITCHLINE. LEAST I CAN DO.
THAT'S...THAT'S REALLY THOUGHTFUL AND EVERYTHING, I-IT'S JUST...I'M SUPPOSED TO STAY REALLY CLOSE TO THAT DROID OR...
WOOP WOOP WOOP WOOP
OH NO.
O-OKAY, TWO QUESTIONS--
ONE: IS IT BETTER TO DEFINITELY DIE STANDING STILL OR PROBABLY DIE AFTER A SHORT PERIOD OF PLUMMETING TERROR?
SECOND ONE. LOT CAN HAPPEN IN A SHORT PERIOD.
QUESTION TWO: CAN I HAVE MY MONEY BACK?
NOT A CHANCE.
THANKS ANYWAY.
HEY! MY GUN!

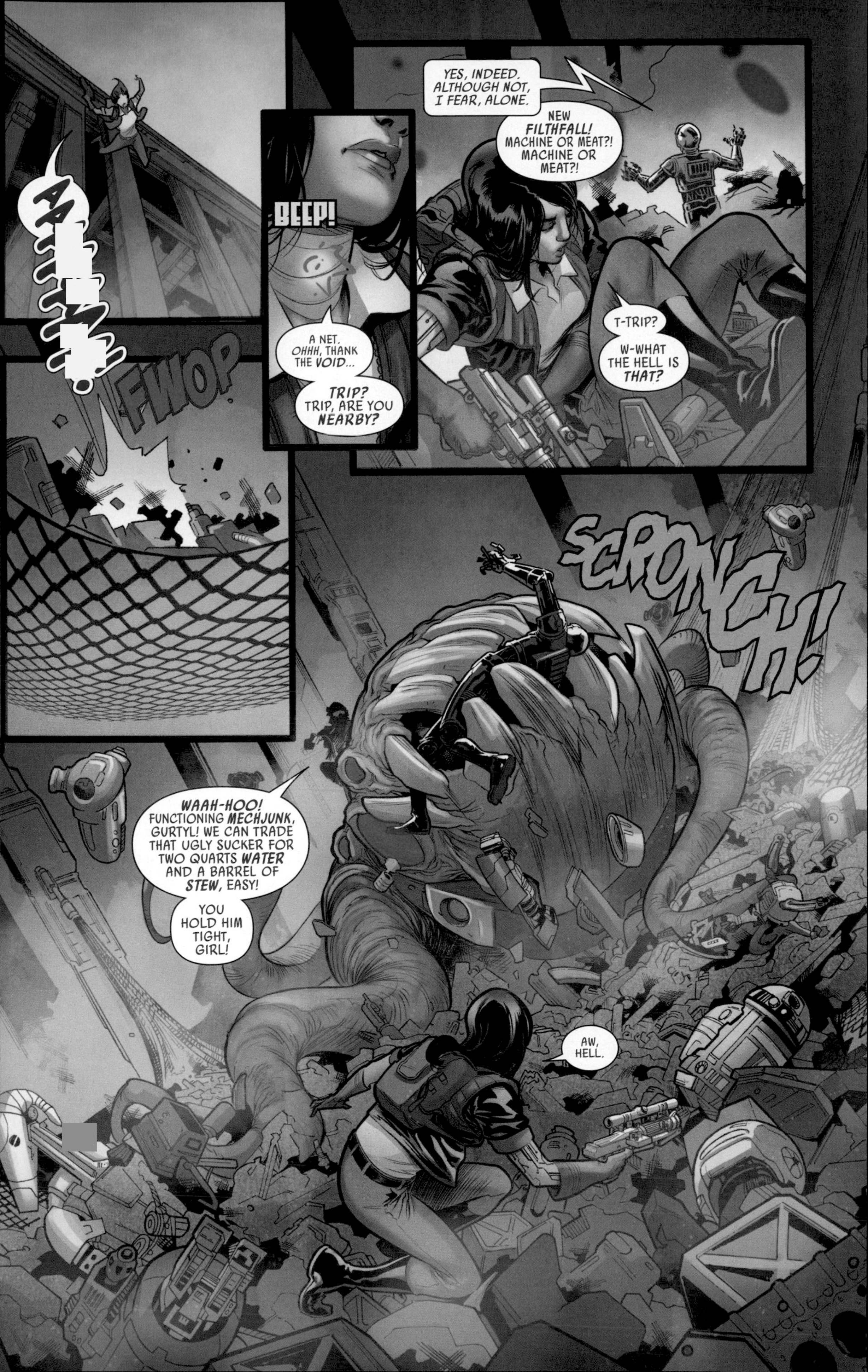
FWOP
BEEP!
A NET. OHHH, THANK THE VOID...
TRIP? TRIP, ARE YOU NEARBY?
YES, INDEED. ALTHOUGH NOT, I FEAR, ALONE.
NEW FILTHFALL! MACHINE OR MEAT?! MACHINE OR MEAT?!
T-TRIP?
W-WHAT THE HELL IS THAT?
SCRONCH!
WAAH-HOO! FUNCTIONING MECHJUNK, GURTYL! WE CAN TRADE THAT UGLY SUCKER FOR TWO QUARTS WATER AND A BARREL OF STEW, EASY!
YOU HOLD HIM TIGHT, GIRL!
AW, HELL.

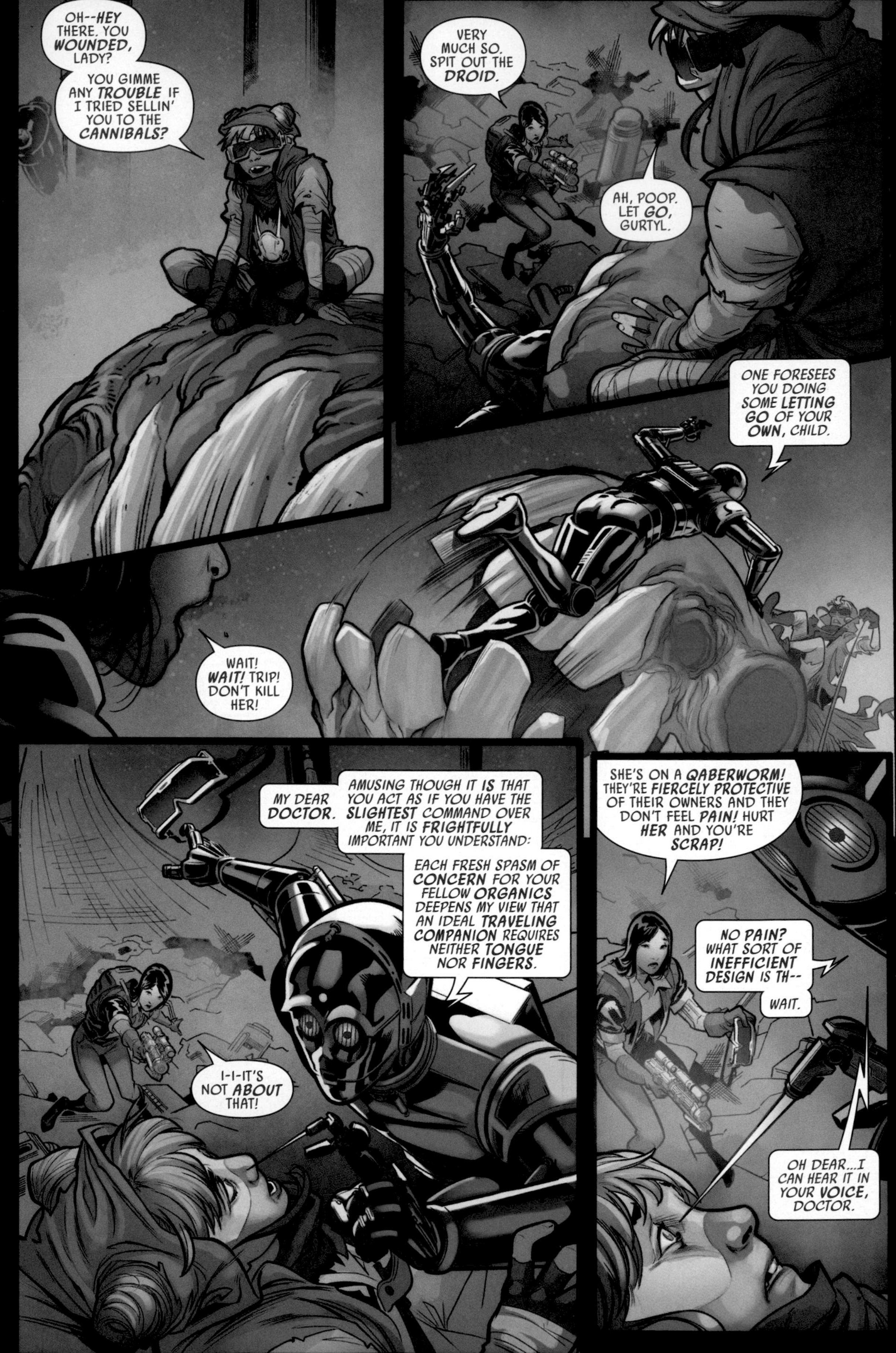
OH--HEY THERE. YOU WOUNDED, LADY?
YOU GIMME ANY TROUBLE IF I TRIED SELLIN' YOU TO THE CANNIBALS?
VERY MUCH SO. SPIT OUT THE DROID.
AH, POOP. LET GO, GURTYL.
ONE FORESEES YOU DOING SOME LETTING GO OF YOUR OWN, CHILD.
WAIT! WAIT! TRIP! DON'T KILL HER!
MY DEAR DOCTOR.
AMUSING THOUGH IT IS THAT YOU ACT AS IF YOU HAVE THE SLIGHTEST COMMAND OVER ME, IT IS FRIGHTFULLY IMPORTANT YOU UNDERSTAND:
EACH FRESH SPASM OF CONCERN FOR YOUR FELLOW ORGANICS DEEPENS MY VIEW THAT AN IDEAL TRAVELING COMPANION REQUIRES NEITHER TONGUE NOR FINGERS.
I-I-IT'S NOT ABOUT THAT!
SHE'S ON A QABERWORM! THEY'RE FIERCELY PROTECTIVE OF THEIR OWNERS AND THEY DON'T FEEL PAIN! HURT HER AND YOU'RE SCRAP!
NO PAIN? WHAT SORT OF INEFFICIENT DESIGN IS TH--
WAIT.
OH DEAR...I CAN HEAR IT IN YOUR VOICE, DOCTOR.

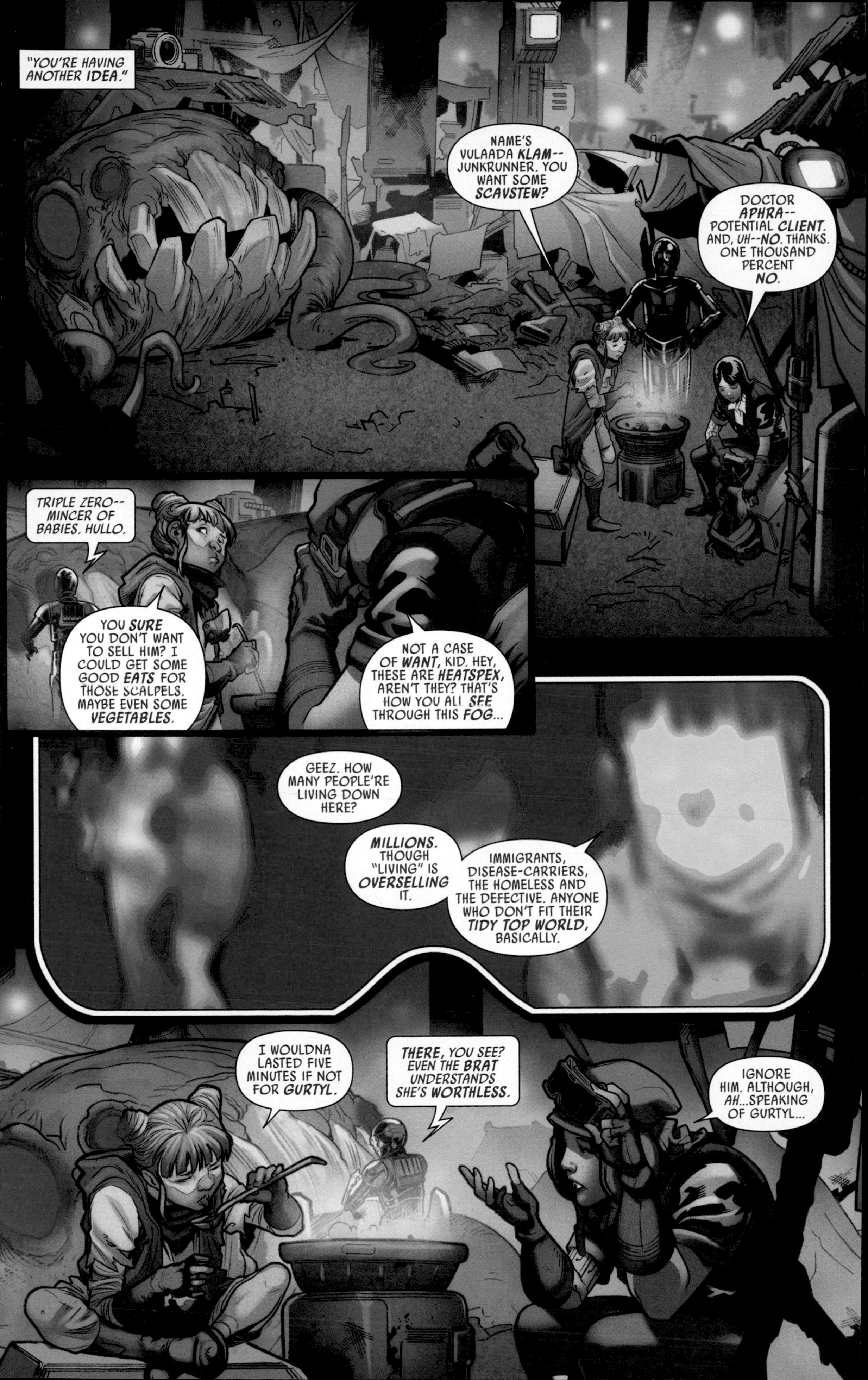
"YOU'RE HAVING ANOTHER IDEA."
NAME'S VULAADA KLAM--JUNKRUNNER. YOU WANT SOME SCAVSTEW?
DOCTOR APHRA--POTENTIAL CLIENT. AND, UH--NO. THANKS. ONE THOUSAND PERCENT NO.
TRIPLE ZERO--MINCER OF BABIES. HULLO.
YOU SURE YOU DON'T WANT TO SELL HIM? I COULD GET SOME GOOD EATS FOR THOSE SCALPELS. MAYBE EVEN SOME VEGETABLES.
NOT A CASE OF WANT, KID. HEY, THESE ARE HEATSPEX, AREN'T THEY? THAT'S HOW YOU ALL SEE THROUGH THIS FOG...
GEEZ. HOW MANY PEOPLE'RE LIVING DOWN HERE?
MILLIONS. THOUGH "LIVING" IS OVERSELLING IT.
IMMIGRANTS, DISEASE-CARRIERS, THE HOMELESS AND THE DEFECTIVE. ANYONE WHO DON'T FIT THEIR TIDY TOP WORLD, BASICALLY.
I WOULDNA LASTED FIVE MINUTES IF NOT FOR GURTYL.
THERE, YOU SEE? EVEN THE BRAT UNDERSTANDS SHE'S WORTHLESS.
IGNORE HIM. ALTHOUGH, AH...SPEAKING OF GURTYL...

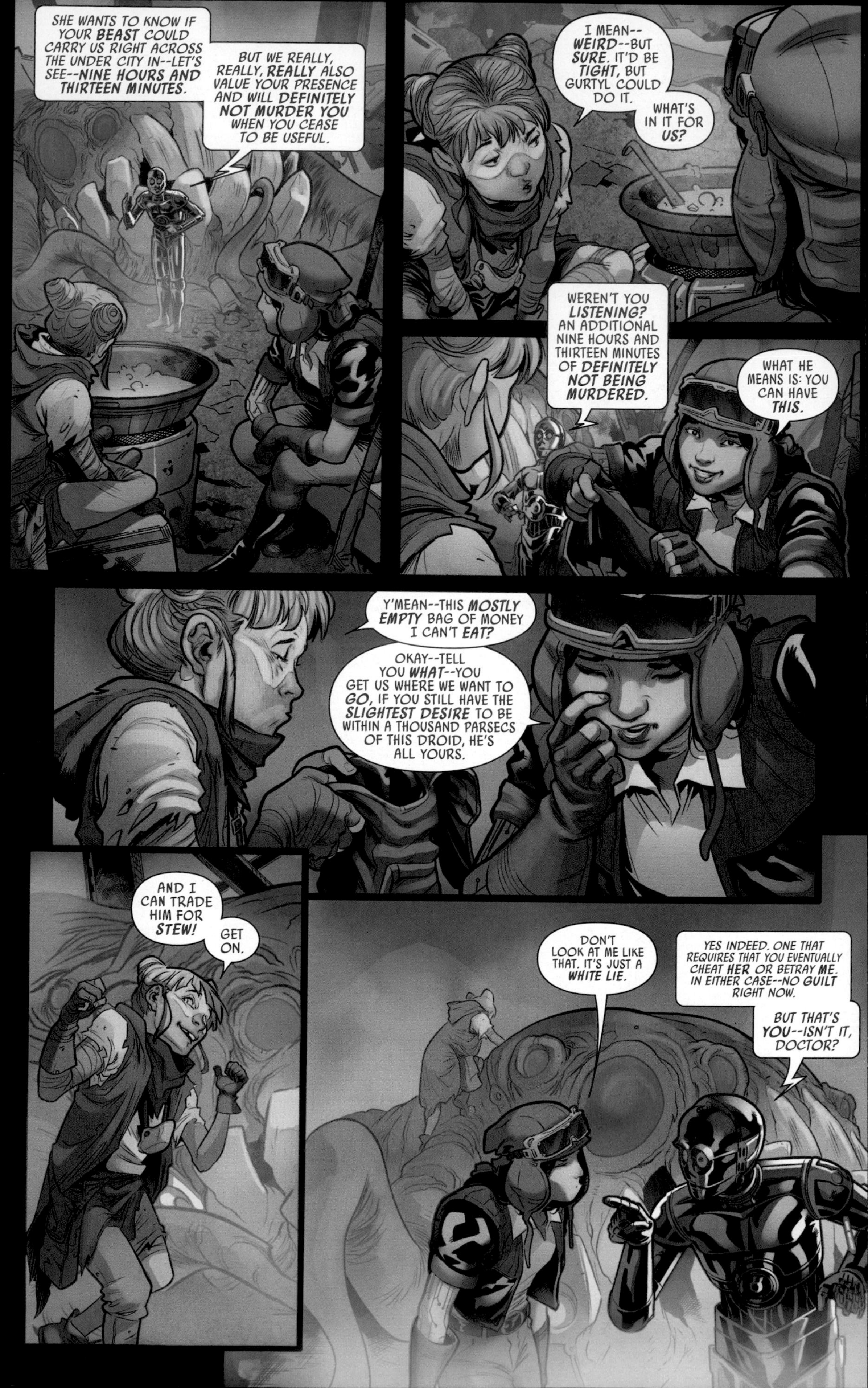
SHE WANTS TO KNOW IF YOUR BEAST COULD CARRY US RIGHT ACROSS THE UNDER CITY IN--LET'S SEE--NINE HOURS AND THIRTEEN MINUTES.
BUT WE REALLY, REALLY, REALLY ALSO VALUE YOUR PRESENCE AND WILL DEFINITELY NOT MURDER YOU WHEN YOU CEASE TO BE USEFUL.
I MEAN--WEIRD--BUT SURE. IT'D BE TIGHT, BUT GURTYL COULD DO IT.
WHAT'S IN IT FOR US?
WEREN'T YOU LISTENING? AN ADDITIONAL NINE HOURS AND THIRTEEN MINUTES OF DEFINITELY NOT BEING MURDERED.
WHAT HE MEANS IS: YOU CAN HAVE THIS.
Y'MEAN--THIS MOSTLY EMPTY BAG OF MONEY I CAN'T EAT?
OKAY--TELL YOU WHAT--YOU GET US WHERE WE WANT TO GO, IF YOU STILL HAVE THE SLIGHTEST DESIRE TO BE WITHIN A THOUSAND PARSECS OF THIS DROID, HE'S ALL YOURS.
AND I CAN TRADE HIM FOR STEW!
GET ON.
DON'T LOOK AT ME LIKE THAT. IT'S JUST A WHITE LIE.
YES INDEED. ONE THAT REQUIRES THAT YOU EVENTUALLY CHEAT HER OR BETRAY ME. IN EITHER CASE--NO GUILT RIGHT NOW.
BUT THAT'S YOU--ISN'T IT, DOCTOR?

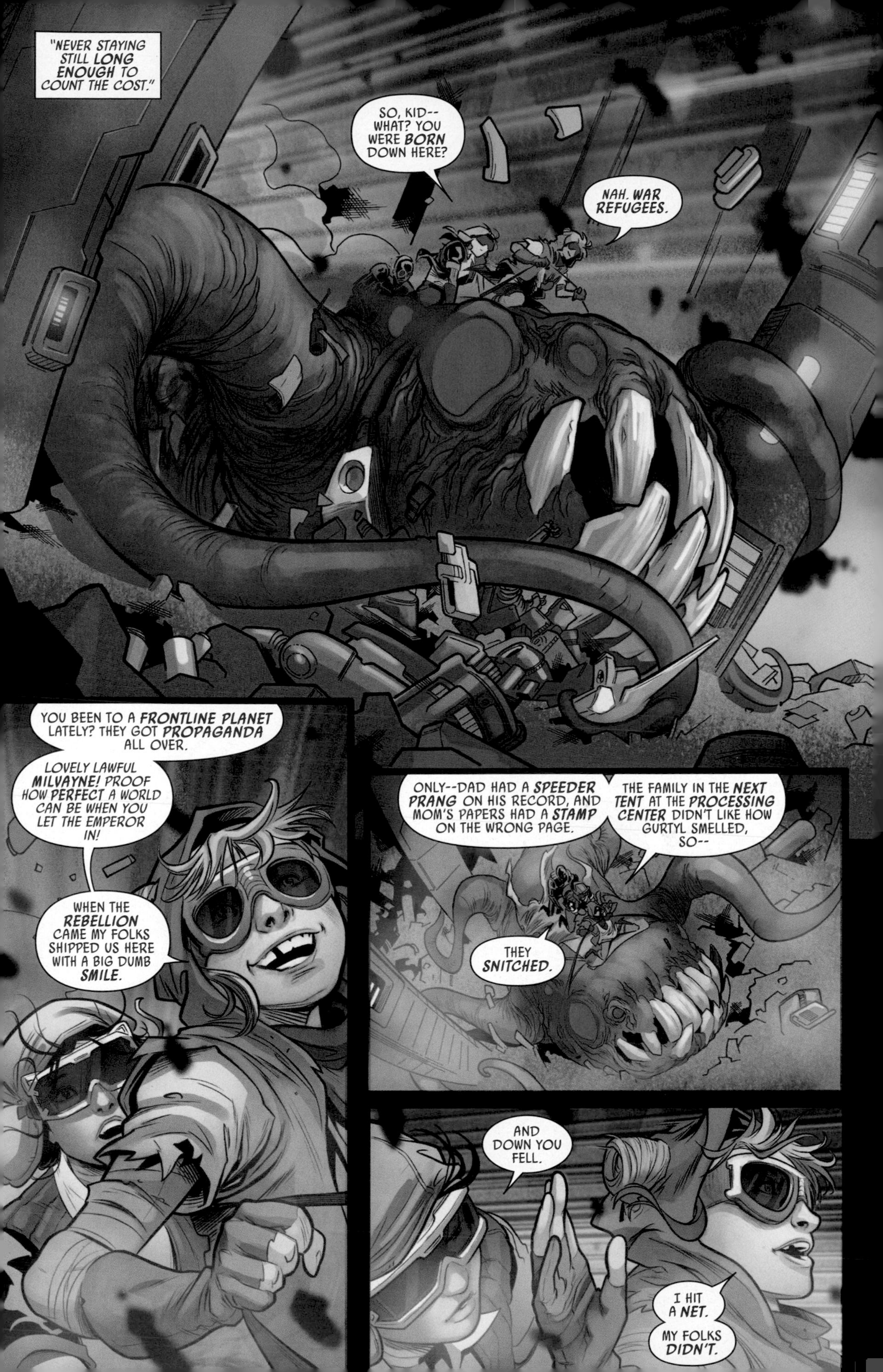
"NEVER STAYING STILL LONG ENOUGH TO COUNT THE COST."
SO, KID-- WHAT? YOU WERE BORN DOWN HERE?
NAH. WAR REFUGEES.
YOU BEEN TO A FRONTLINE PLANET LATELY? THEY GOT PROPAGANDA ALL OVER.
LOVELY LAWFUL MILVAYNE! PROOF HOW PERFECT A WORLD CAN BE WHEN YOU LET THE EMPEROR IN!
WHEN THE REBELLION CAME MY FOLKS SHIPPED US HERE WITH A BIG DUMB SMILE.
ONLY--DAD HAD A SPEEDER PRANG ON HIS RECORD, AND MOM'S PAPERS HAD A STAMP ON THE WRONG PAGE.
THE FAMILY IN THE NEXT TENT AT THE PROCESSING CENTER DIDN'T LIKE HOW GURTYL SMELLED, SO--
THEY SNITCHED.
AND DOWN YOU FELL.
I HIT A NET.
MY FOLKS DIDN'T.

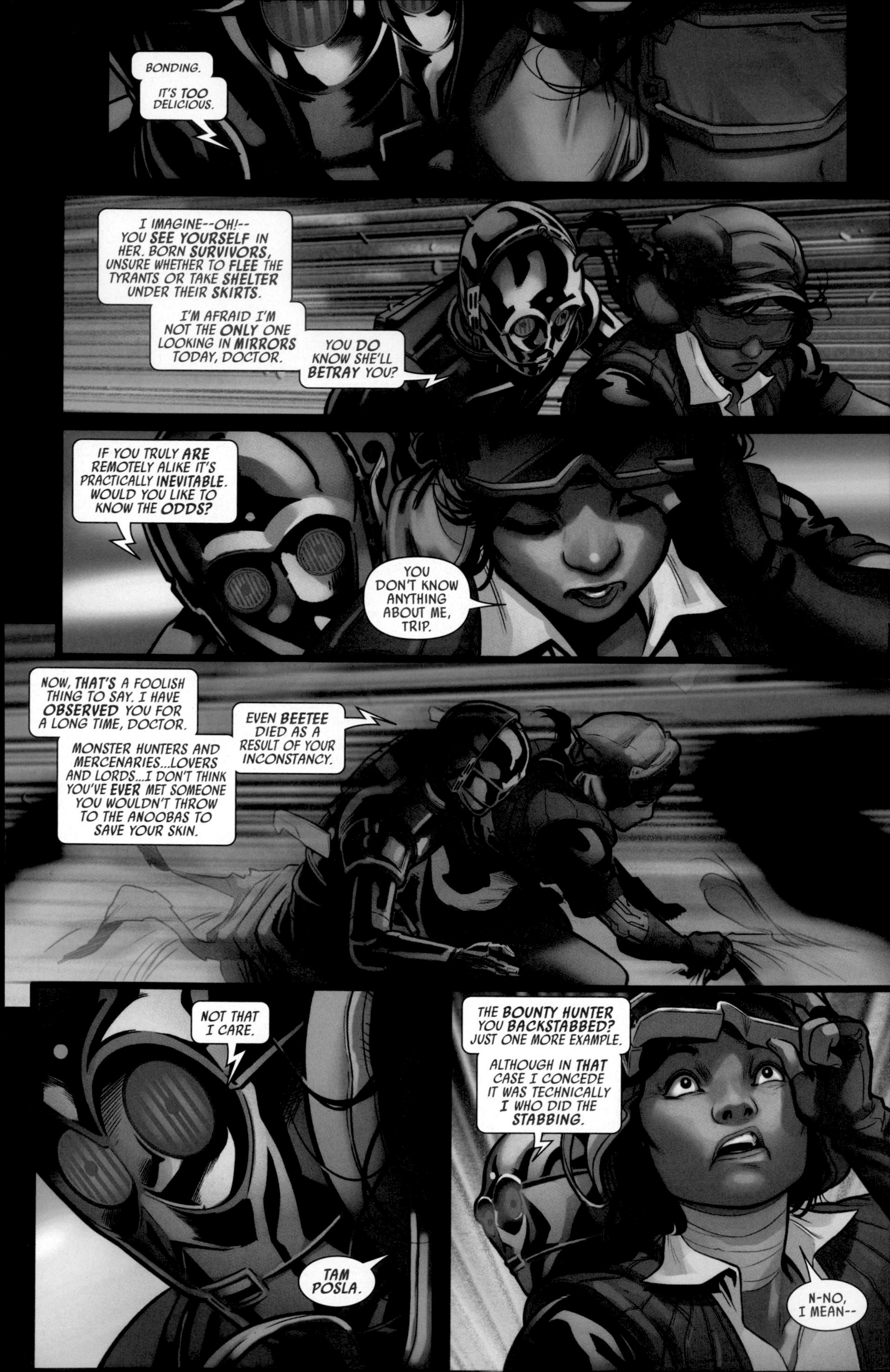

BONDING.
IT'S TOO DELICIOUS.
I IMAGINE--OH!-- YOU SEE YOURSELF IN HER. BORN SURVIVORS, UNSURE WHETHER TO FLEE THE TYRANTS OR TAKE SHELTER UNDER THEIR SKIRTS.
I'M AFRAID I'M NOT THE ONLY ONE LOOKING IN MIRRORS TODAY, DOCTOR.
YOU DO KNOW SHE'LL BETRAY YOU?
IF YOU TRULY ARE REMOTELY ALIKE IT'S PRACTICALLY INEVITABLE. WOULD YOU LIKE TO KNOW THE ODDS?
YOU DON'T KNOW ANYTHING ABOUT ME, TRIP.
NOW, THAT'S A FOOLISH THING TO SAY. I HAVE OBSERVED YOU FOR A LONG TIME, DOCTOR.
MONSTER HUNTERS AND MERCENARIES...LOVERS AND LORDS...I DON'T THINK YOU'VE EVER MET SOMEONE YOU WOULDN'T THROW TO THE ANOOBAS TO SAVE YOUR SKIN.
EVEN BEETEE DIED AS A RESULT OF YOUR INCONSTANCY.
NOT THAT I CARE.
THE BOUNTY HUNTER YOU BACKSTABBED? JUST ONE MORE EXAMPLE.
ALTHOUGH IN THAT CASE I CONCEDE IT WAS TECHNICALLY I WHO DID THE STABBING.
TAM POSLA.
N-NO, I MEAN--

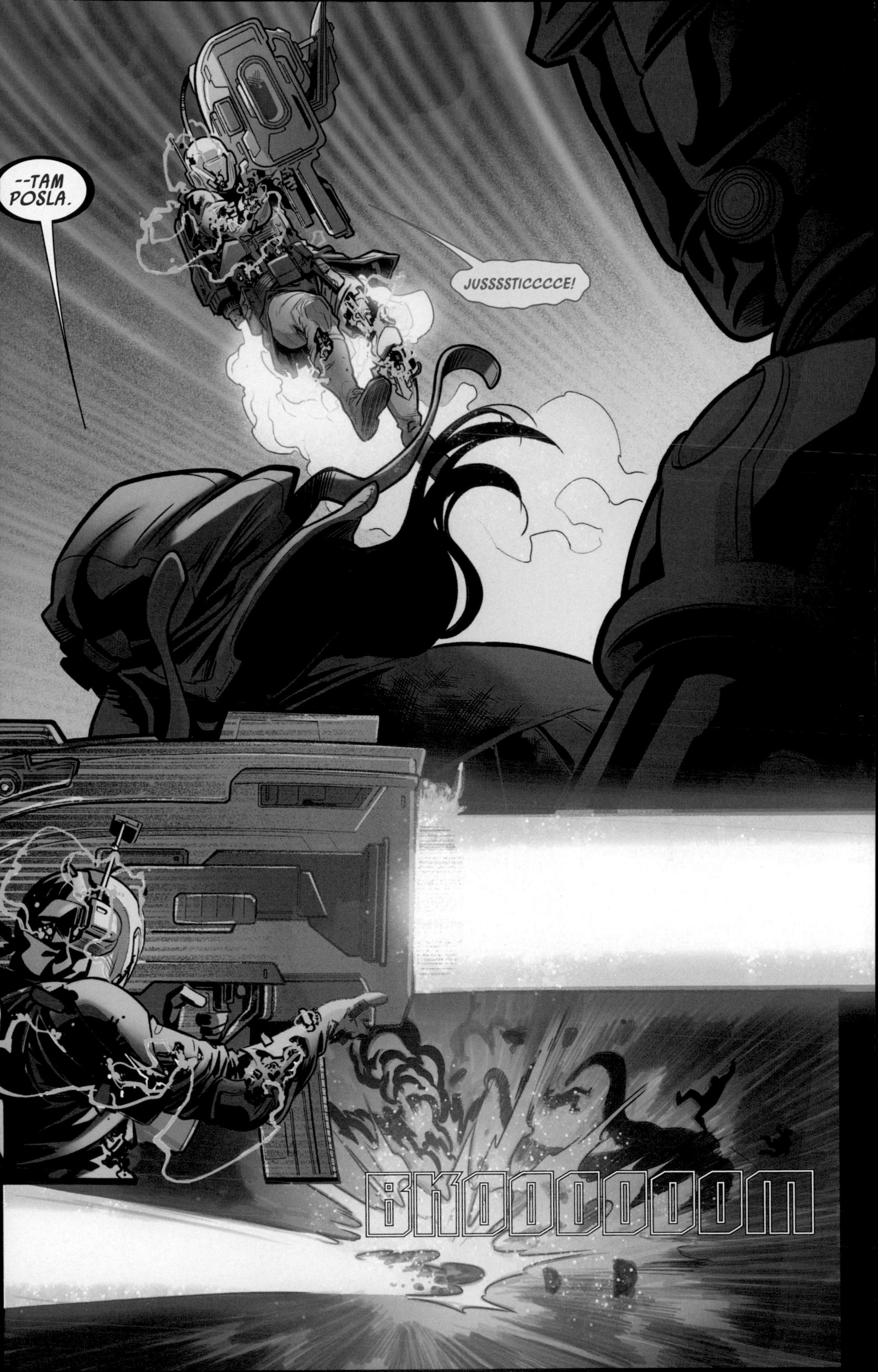
--TAM POSLA.
JUSSSSTICCCCE!
BKOOOOOOOM

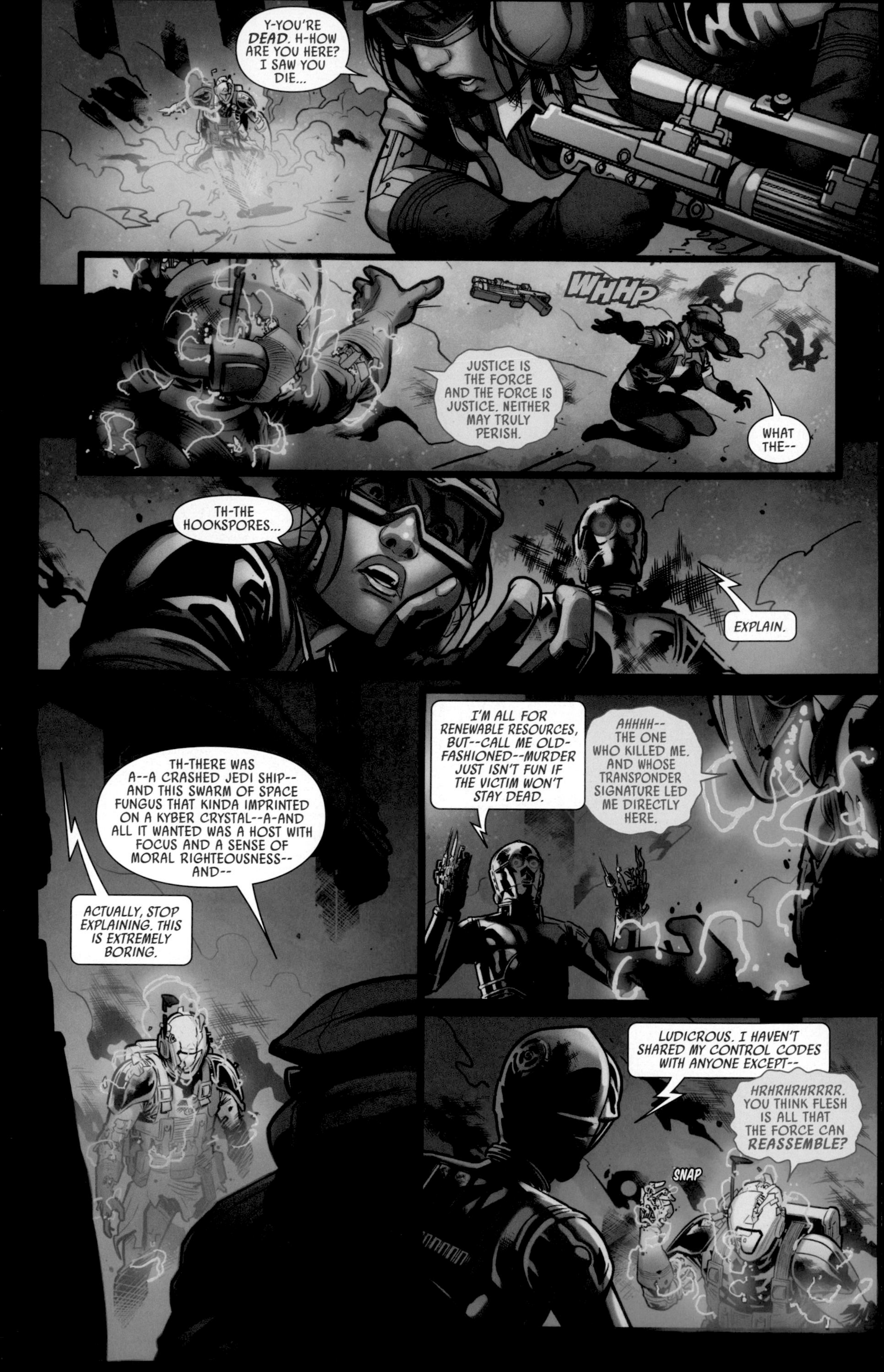

Y-YOU'RE DEAD. H-HOW ARE YOU HERE? I SAW YOU DIE...
WHHP
JUSTICE IS THE FORCE AND THE FORCE IS JUSTICE. NEITHER MAY TRULY PERISH.
WHAT THE--
TH-THE HOOKSPORES...
EXPLAIN.
TH-THERE WAS A--A CRASHED JEDI SHIP--AND THIS SWARM OF SPACE FUNGUS THAT KINDA IMPRINTED ON A KYBER CRYSTAL--A-AND ALL IT WANTED WAS A HOST WITH FOCUS AND A SENSE OF MORAL RIGHTEOUSNESS--AND--
ACTUALLY, STOP EXPLAINING. THIS IS EXTREMELY BORING.
I'M ALL FOR RENEWABLE RESOURCES, BUT--CALL ME OLD-FASHIONED--MURDER JUST ISN'T FUN IF THE VICTIM WON'T STAY DEAD.
AHHHH--THE ONE WHO KILLED ME. AND WHOSE TRANSPONDER SIGNATURE LED ME DIRECTLY HERE.
LUDICROUS. I HAVEN'T SHARED MY CONTROL CODES WITH ANYONE EXCEPT--
HRHRHRHRRRR. YOU THINK FLESH IS ALL THAT THE FORCE CAN REASSEMBLE?
SNAP

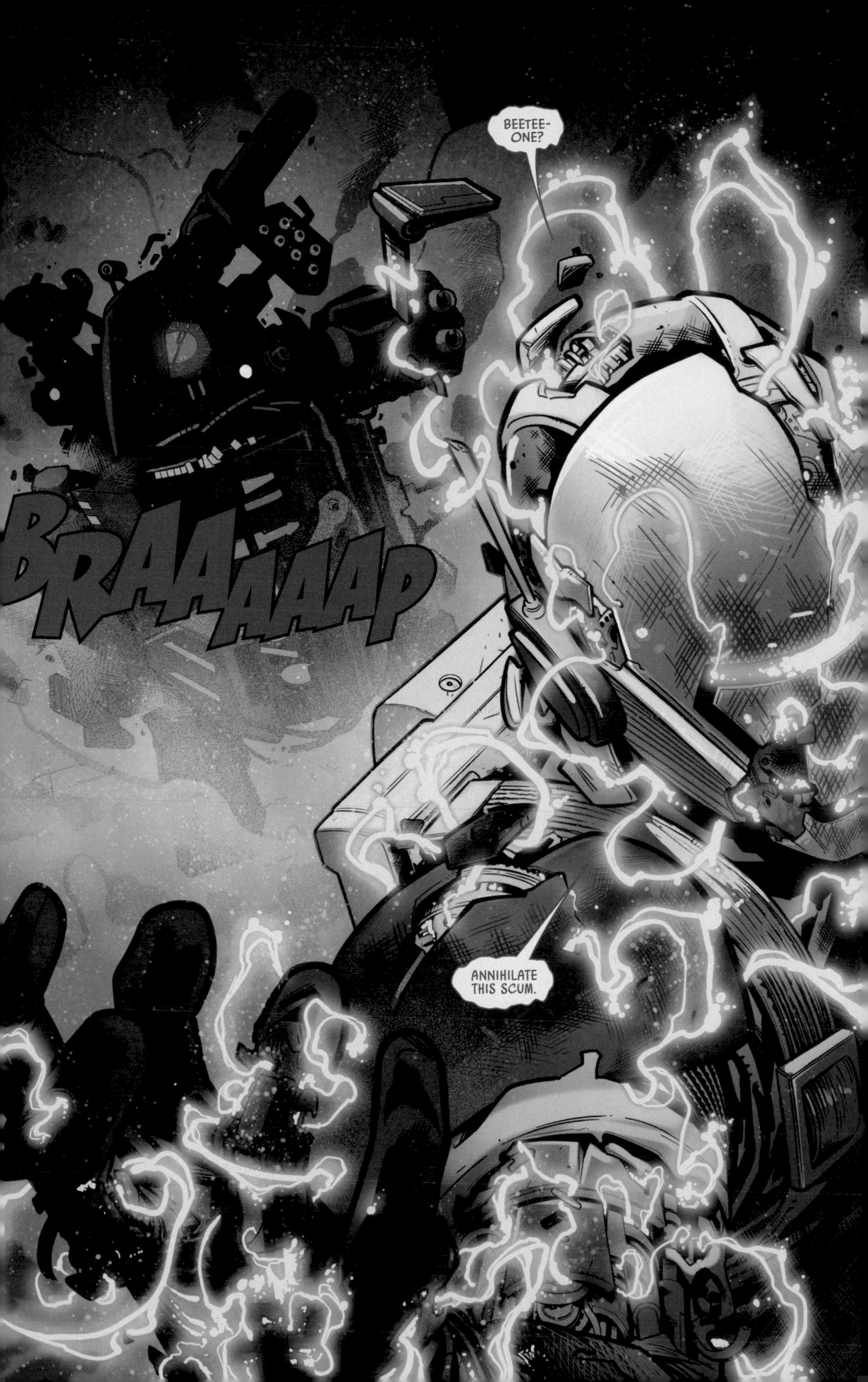
BEETEE-
ONE?
BRAAAAAAP
ANNIHILATE
THIS SCUM.

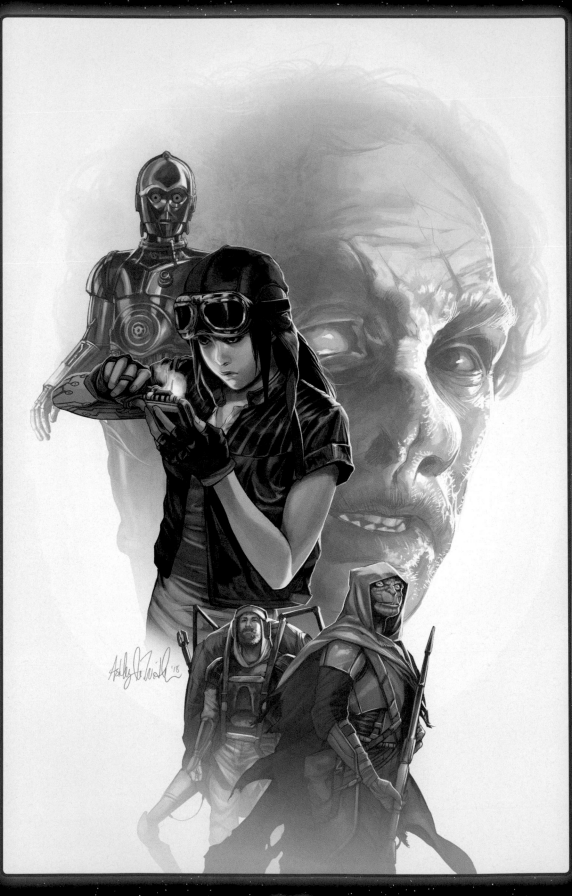

28

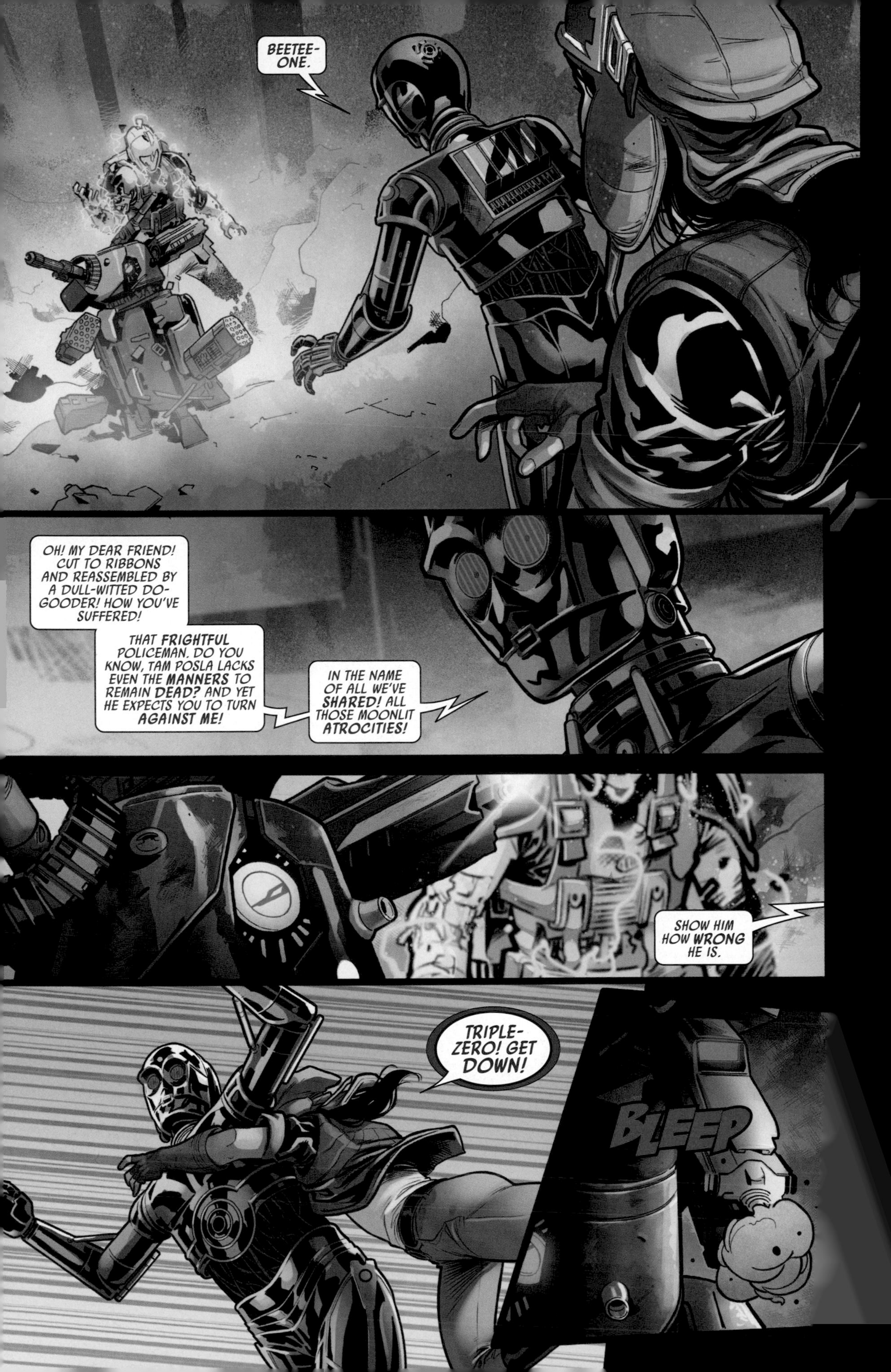
BEETEE-ONE.
OH! MY DEAR FRIEND! CUT TO RIBBONS AND REASSEMBLED BY A DULL-WITTED DO-GOODER! HOW YOU'VE SUFFERED!
THAT FRIGHTFUL POLICEMAN. DO YOU KNOW, TAM POSLA LACKS EVEN THE MANNERS TO REMAIN DEAD? AND YET HE EXPECTS YOU TO TURN AGAINST ME!
IN THE NAME OF ALL WE'VE SHARED! ALL THOSE MOONLIT ATROCITIES!
SHOW HIM HOW WRONG HE IS.
TRIPLE-ZERO! GET DOWN!
BLEEP

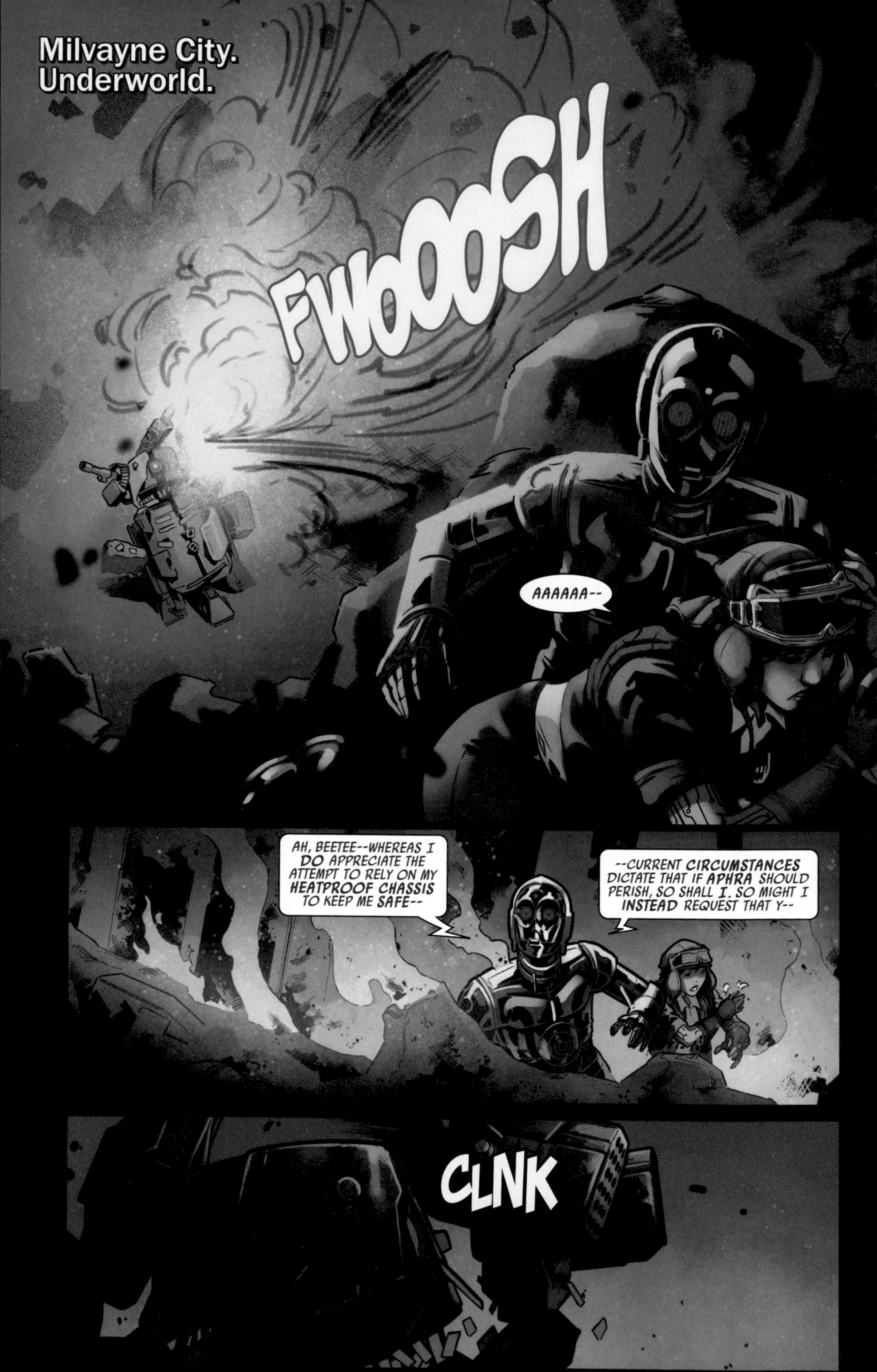
Milvayne City.
Underworld.
FWOOOSH
AAAAAA--
AH, BEETEE--WHEREAS I DO APPRECIATE THE ATTEMPT TO RELY ON MY HEATPROOF CHASSIS TO KEEP ME SAFE--
--CURRENT CIRCUMSTANCES DICTATE THAT IF APHRA SHOULD PERISH, SO SHALL I. SO MIGHT I INSTEAD REQUEST THAT Y--
CLNK

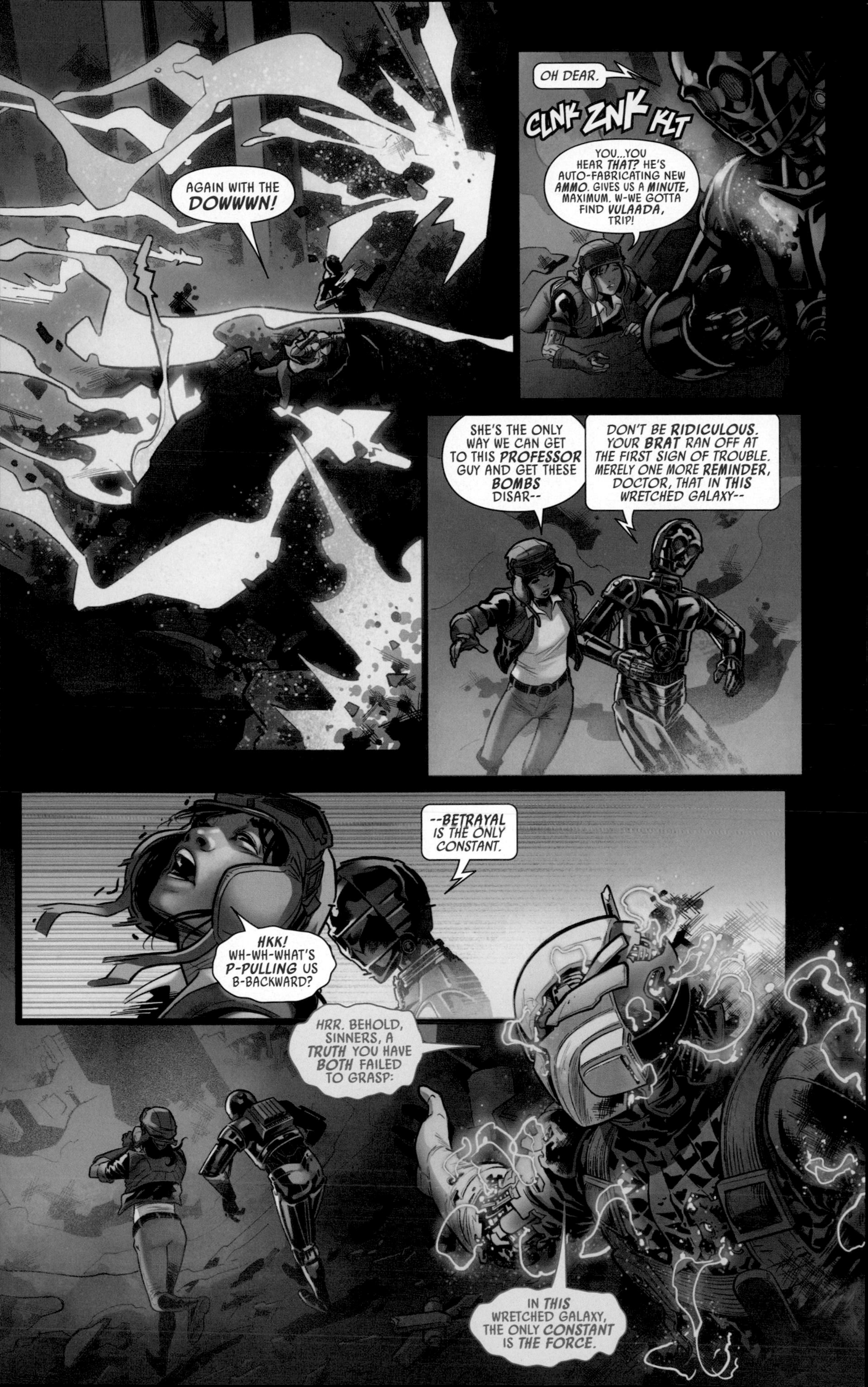
AGAIN WITH THE DOWWWN!
OH DEAR.
CLNK ZNK KLT
YOU...YOU HEAR THAT? HE'S AUTO-FABRICATING NEW AMMO. GIVES US A MINUTE, MAXIMUM. W-WE GOTTA FIND VULAADA, TRIP!
SHE'S THE ONLY WAY WE CAN GET TO THIS PROFESSOR GUY AND GET THESE BOMBS DISAR--
DON'T BE RIDICULOUS. YOUR BRAT RAN OFF AT THE FIRST SIGN OF TROUBLE. MERELY ONE MORE REMINDER, DOCTOR, THAT IN THIS WRETCHED GALAXY--
--BETRAYAL IS THE ONLY CONSTANT.
HKK! WH-WH-WHAT'S P-PULLING US B-BACKWARD?
HRR. BEHOLD, SINNERS, A TRUTH YOU HAVE BOTH FAILED TO GRASP:
IN THIS WRETCHED GALAXY, THE ONLY CONSTANT IS THE FORCE.

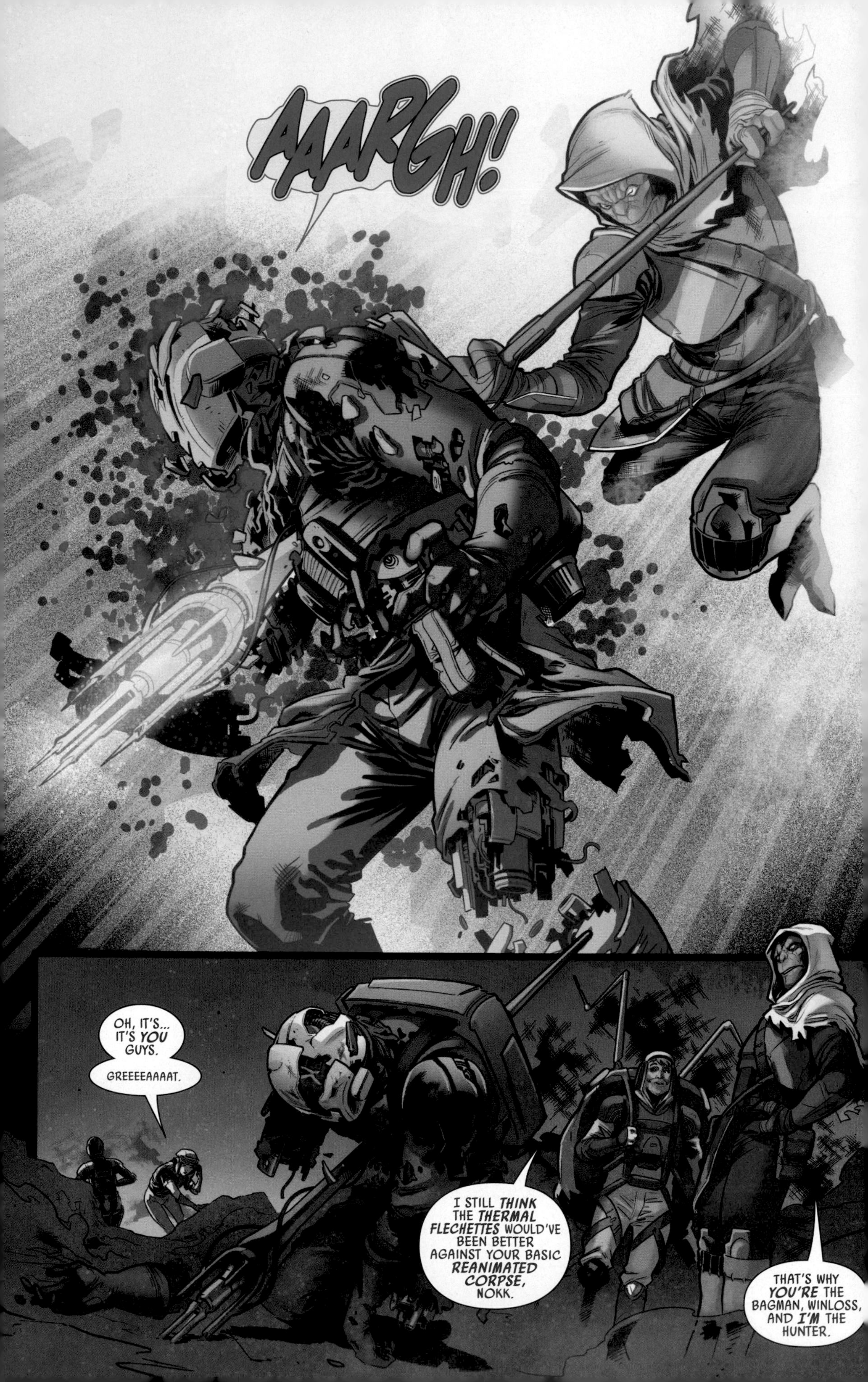
AAARGH!
OH, IT'S... IT'S *YOU* GUYS.
GREEEEAAAAT.
I STILL *THINK* THE *THERMAL FLECHETTES* WOULD'VE BEEN BETTER AGAINST YOUR BASIC *REANIMATED CORPSE*, NOKK.
THAT'S WHY *YOU'RE* THE BAGMAN, WINLOSS, AND *I'M* THE HUNTER.

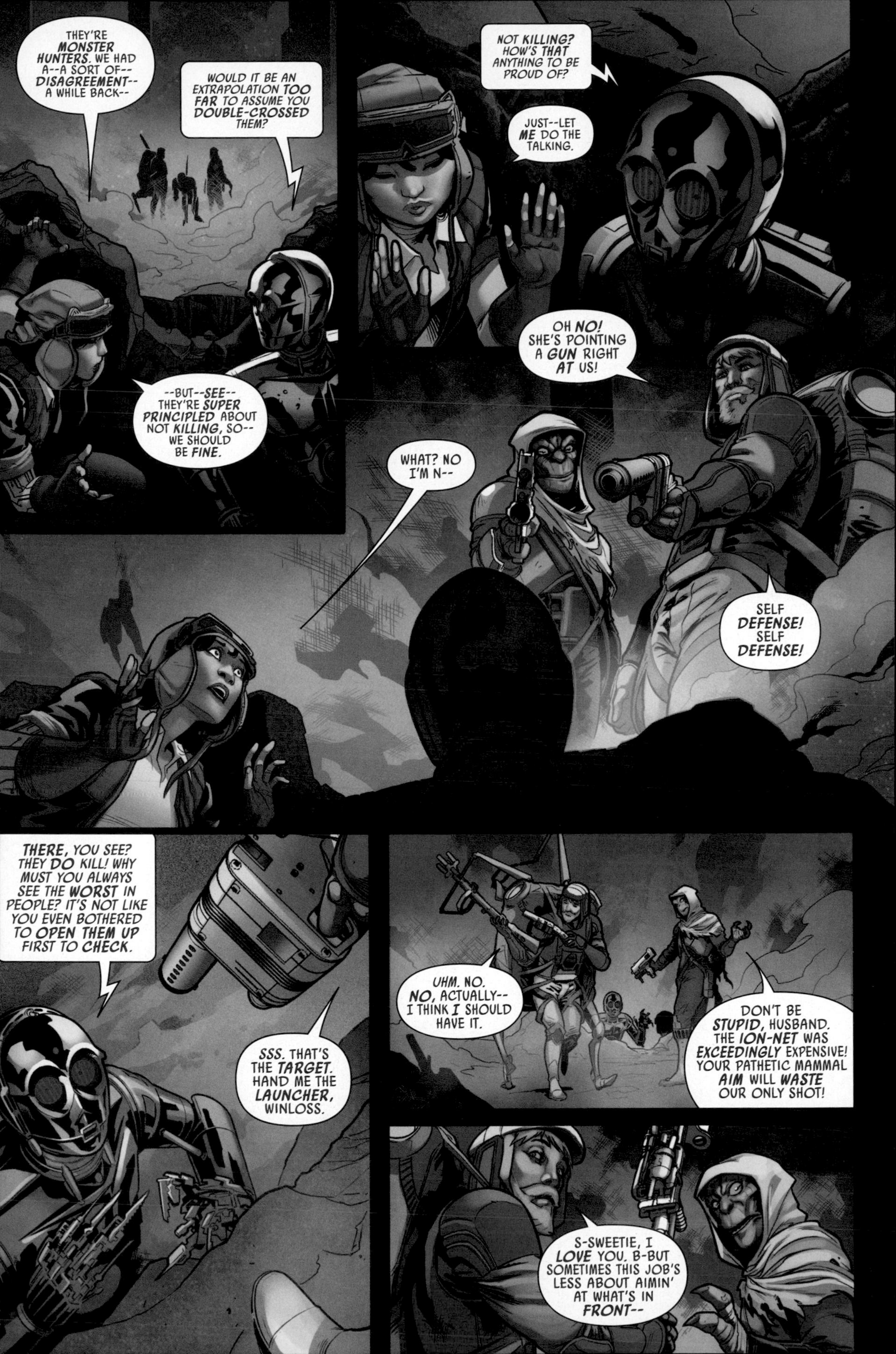
THEY'RE MONSTER HUNTERS. WE HAD A--A SORT OF-- DISAGREEMENT-- A WHILE BACK--
WOULD IT BE AN EXTRAPOLATION TOO FAR TO ASSUME YOU DOUBLE-CROSSED THEM?
--BUT--SEE-- THEY'RE SUPER PRINCIPLED ABOUT NOT KILLING, SO-- WE SHOULD BE FINE.
NOT KILLING? HOW'S THAT ANYTHING TO BE PROUD OF?
JUST--LET ME DO THE TALKING.
OH NO! SHE'S POINTING A GUN RIGHT AT US!
WHAT? NO I'M N--
SELF DEFENSE! SELF DEFENSE!
THERE, YOU SEE? THEY DO KILL! WHY MUST YOU ALWAYS SEE THE WORST IN PEOPLE? IT'S NOT LIKE YOU EVEN BOTHERED TO OPEN THEM UP FIRST TO CHECK.
SSS. THAT'S THE TARGET. HAND ME THE LAUNCHER, WINLOSS.
UHM. NO. NO, ACTUALLY-- I THINK I SHOULD HAVE IT.
DON'T BE STUPID, HUSBAND. THE ION-NET WAS EXCEEDINGLY EXPENSIVE! YOUR PATHETIC MAMMAL AIM WILL WASTE OUR ONLY SHOT!
S-SWEETIE, I LOVE YOU. B-BUT SOMETIMES THIS JOB'S LESS ABOUT AIMIN' AT WHAT'S IN FRONT--

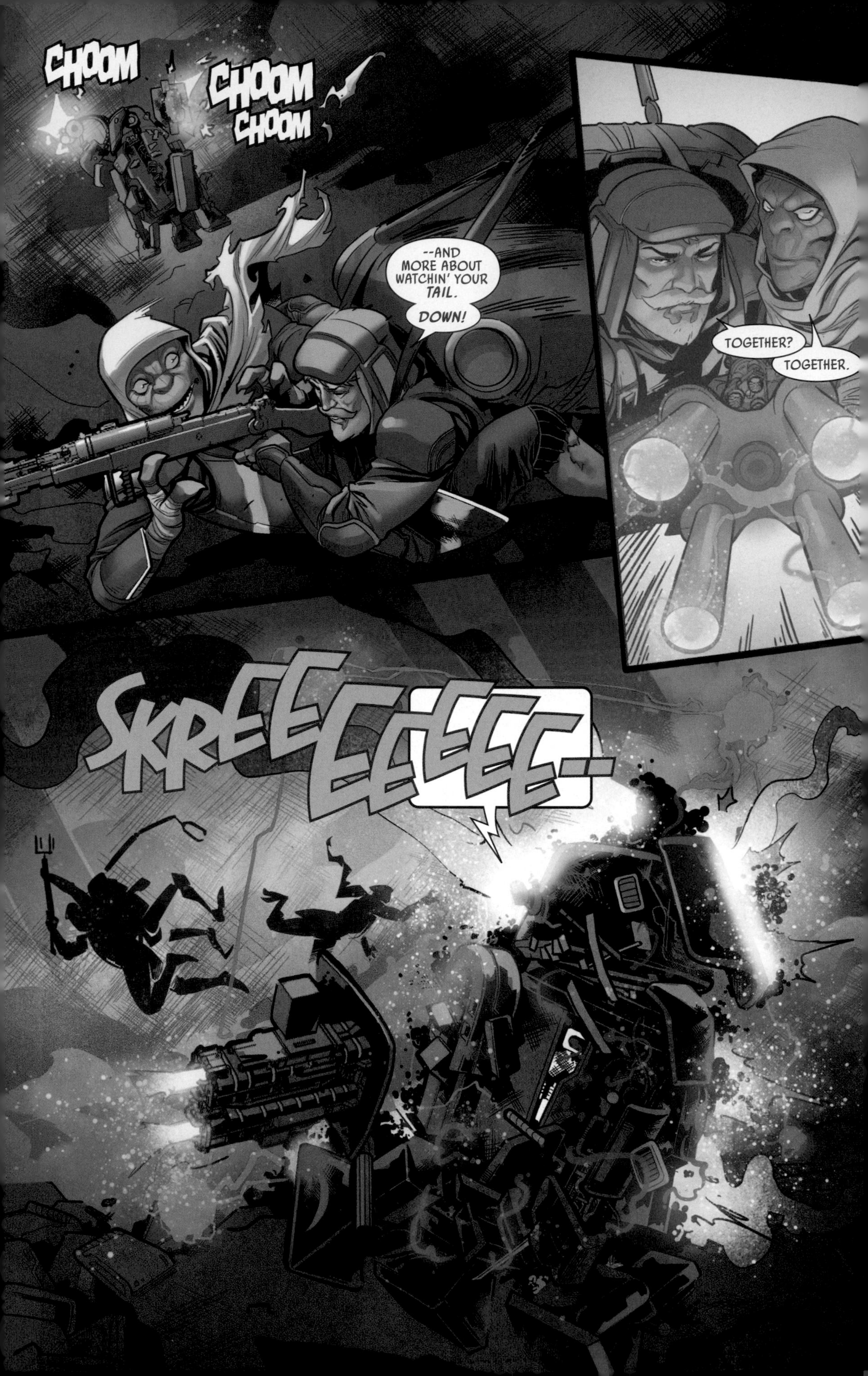
CHOOM
CHOOM
CHOOM
--AND MORE ABOUT WATCHIN' YOUR TAIL.
DOWN!
TOGETHER?
TOGETHER.
SKREEEEEEEE--

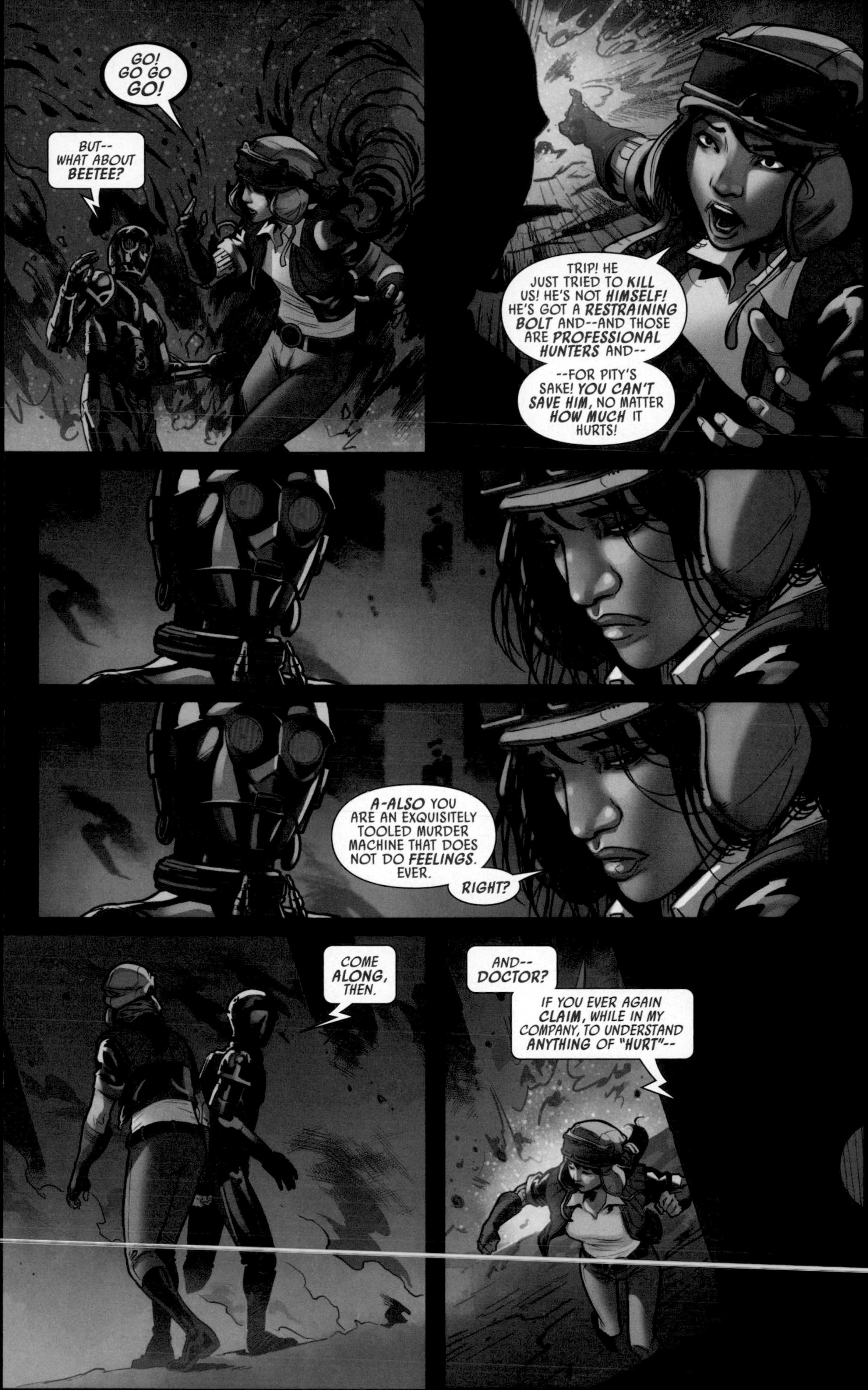
GO! GO GO GO!
BUT-- WHAT ABOUT BEETEE?
TRIP! HE JUST TRIED TO KILL US! HE'S NOT HIMSELF! HE'S GOT A RESTRAINING BOLT AND--AND THOSE ARE PROFESSIONAL HUNTERS AND--
--FOR PITY'S SAKE! YOU CAN'T SAVE HIM, NO MATTER HOW MUCH IT HURTS!
A-ALSO YOU ARE AN EXQUISITELY TOOLED MURDER MACHINE THAT DOES NOT DO FEELINGS. EVER.
RIGHT?
COME ALONG, THEN.
AND-- DOCTOR?
IF YOU EVER AGAIN CLAIM, WHILE IN MY COMPANY, TO UNDERSTAND ANYTHING OF "HURT"--

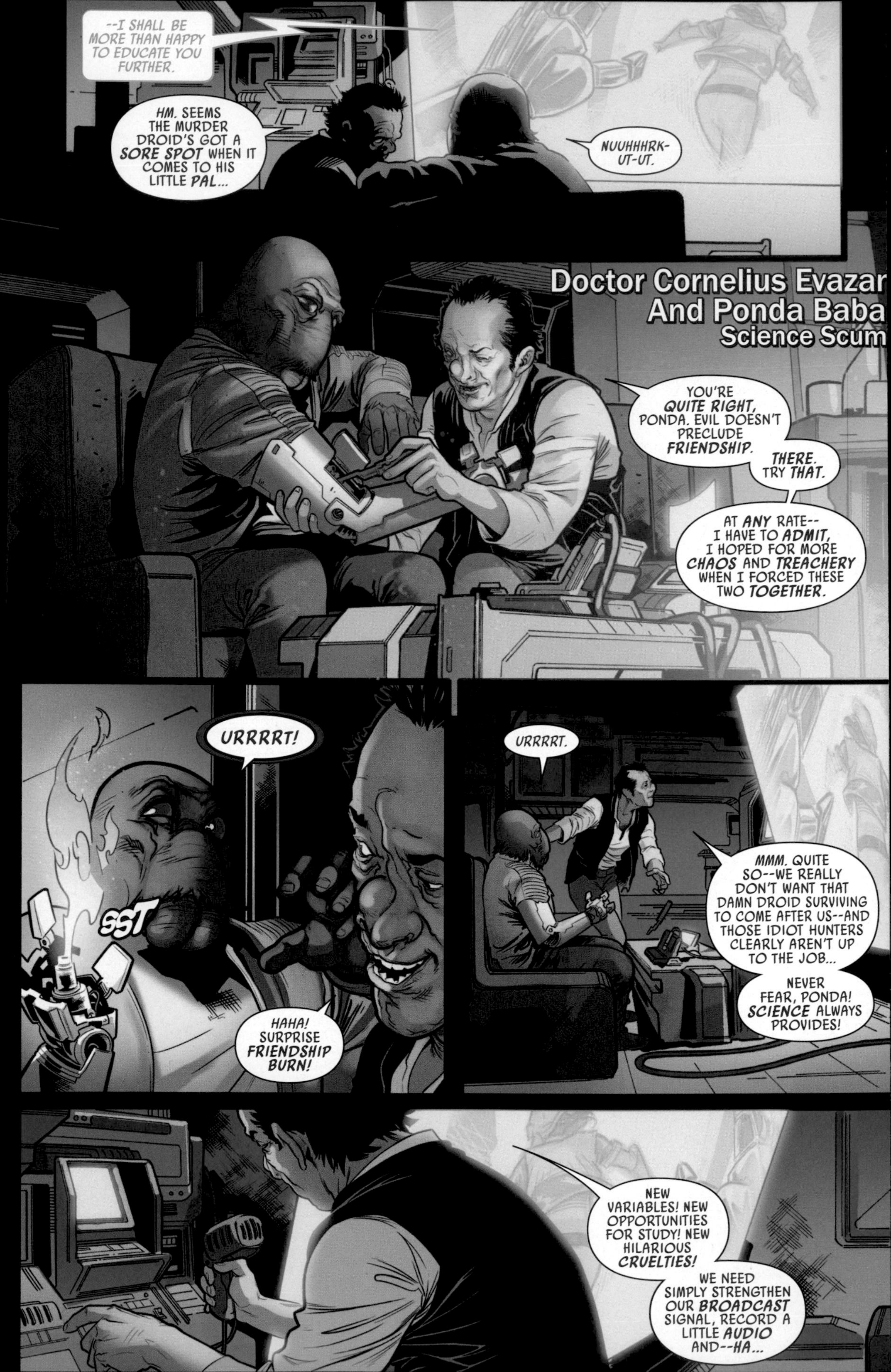
--I SHALL BE MORE THAN HAPPY TO EDUCATE YOU FURTHER.
HM. SEEMS THE MURDER DROID'S GOT A SORE SPOT WHEN IT COMES TO HIS LITTLE PAL...
NUUHHHRK-UT-UT.
Doctor Cornelius Evazar And Ponda Baba
Science Scum
YOU'RE QUITE RIGHT, PONDA. EVIL DOESN'T PRECLUDE FRIENDSHIP.
THERE. TRY THAT.
AT ANY RATE-- I HAVE TO ADMIT, I HOPED FOR MORE CHAOS AND TREACHERY WHEN I FORCED THESE TWO TOGETHER.
URRRRT!
SST
HAHA! SURPRISE FRIENDSHIP BURN!
URRRRT.
MMM. QUITE SO--WE REALLY DON'T WANT THAT DAMN DROID SURVIVING TO COME AFTER US--AND THOSE IDIOT HUNTERS CLEARLY AREN'T UP TO THE JOB...
NEVER FEAR, PONDA! SCIENCE ALWAYS PROVIDES!
NEW VARIABLES! NEW OPPORTUNITIES FOR STUDY! NEW HILARIOUS CRUELTIES!
WE NEED SIMPLY STRENGTHEN OUR BROADCAST SIGNAL, RECORD A LITTLE AUDIO AND--HA...

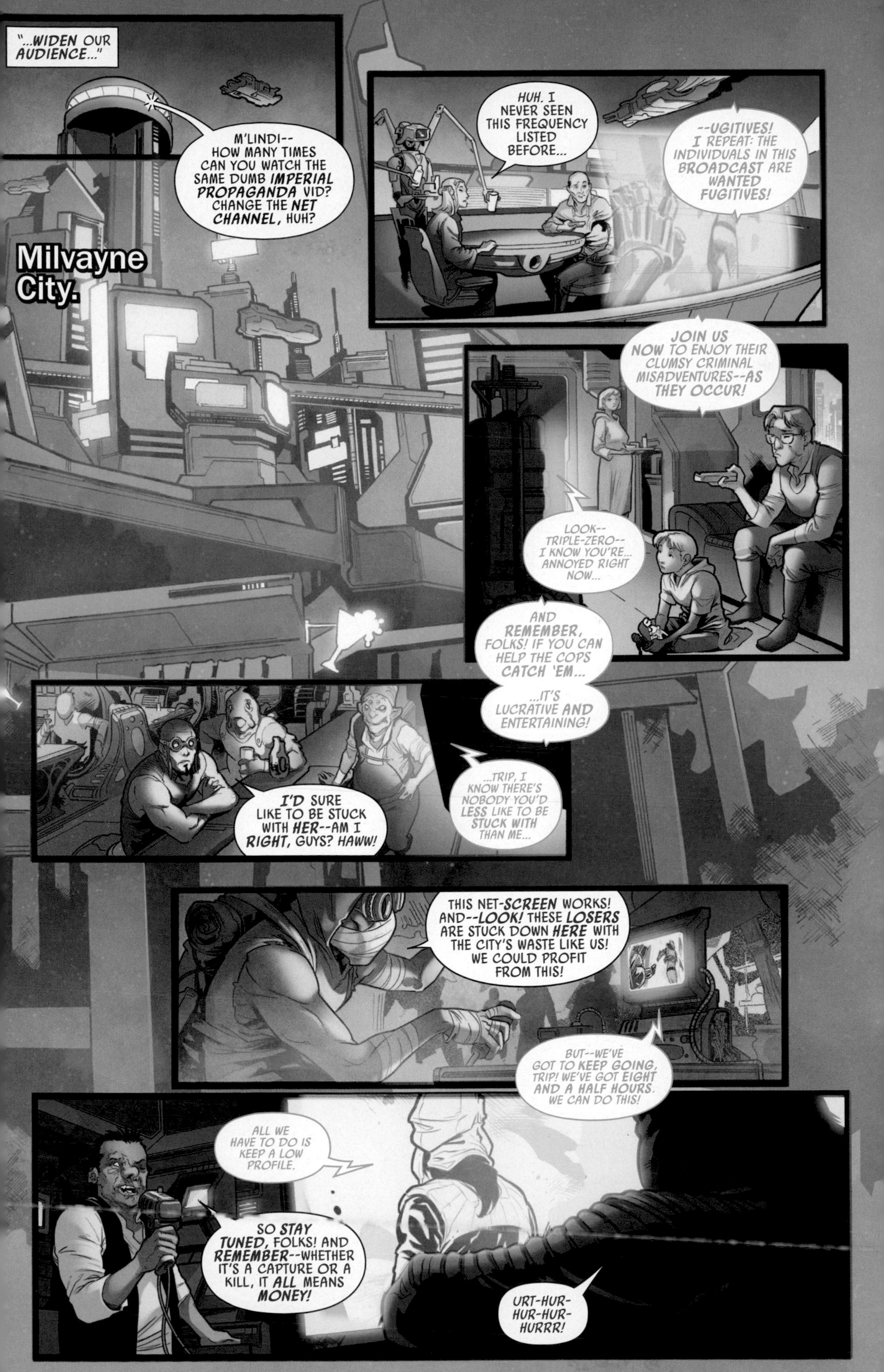

"...WIDEN OUR AUDIENCE..."
M'LINDI-- HOW MANY TIMES CAN YOU WATCH THE SAME DUMB IMPERIAL PROPAGANDA VID? CHANGE THE NET CHANNEL, HUH?
Milvayne City.
HUH. I NEVER SEEN THIS FREQUENCY LISTED BEFORE...
--UGITIVES! I REPEAT: THE INDIVIDUALS IN THIS BROADCAST ARE WANTED FUGITIVES!
JOIN US NOW TO ENJOY THEIR CLUMSY CRIMINAL MISADVENTURES--AS THEY OCCUR!
LOOK-- TRIPLE-ZERO-- I KNOW YOU'RE... ANNOYED RIGHT NOW...
AND REMEMBER, FOLKS! IF YOU CAN HELP THE COPS CATCH 'EM...
...IT'S LUCRATIVE AND ENTERTAINING!
I'D SURE LIKE TO BE STUCK WITH HER--AM I RIGHT, GUYS? HAWW!
...TRIP, I KNOW THERE'S NOBODY YOU'D LESS LIKE TO BE STUCK WITH THAN ME...
THIS NET-SCREEN WORKS! AND--LOOK! THESE LOSERS ARE STUCK DOWN HERE WITH THE CITY'S WASTE LIKE US! WE COULD PROFIT FROM THIS!
BUT--WE'VE GOT TO KEEP GOING, TRIP! WE'VE GOT EIGHT AND A HALF HOURS. WE CAN DO THIS!
ALL WE HAVE TO DO IS KEEP A LOW PROFILE.
SO STAY TUNED, FOLKS! AND REMEMBER--WHETHER IT'S A CAPTURE OR A KILL, IT ALL MEANS MONEY!
URT-HUR-HUR-HUR-HURRR!

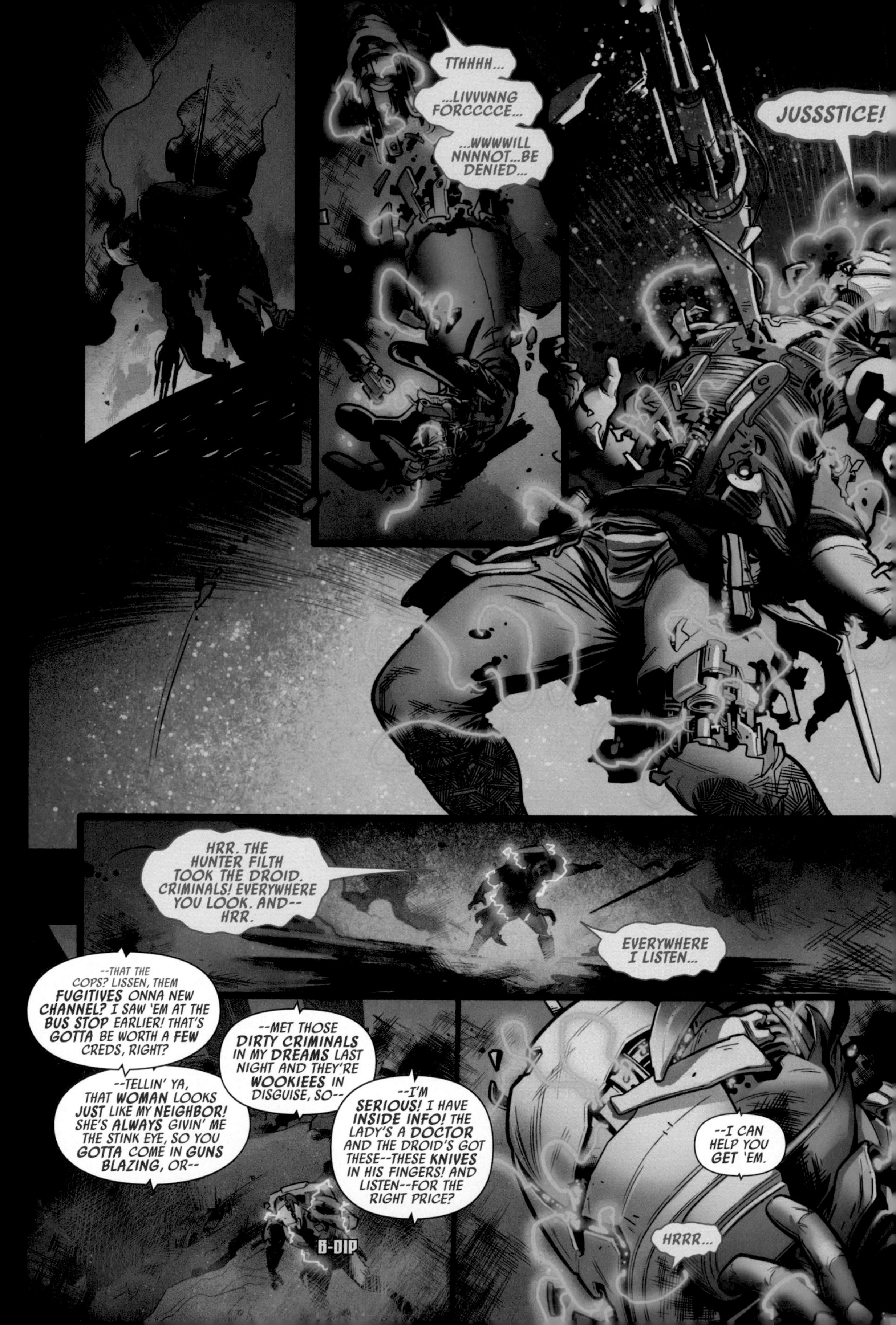
TTHHHH...
...LIVVVNNG FORCCCCE...
...WWWILL NNNNOT...BE DENIED...
JUSSSTICE!
HRR. THE HUNTER FILTH TOOK THE DROID. CRIMINALS! EVERYWHERE YOU LOOK. AND-- HRR.
EVERYWHERE I LISTEN...
--THAT THE COPS? LISSEN, THEM FUGITIVES ONNA NEW CHANNEL? I SAW 'EM AT THE BUS STOP EARLIER! THAT'S GOTTA BE WORTH A FEW CREDS, RIGHT?
--TELLIN' YA, THAT WOMAN LOOKS JUST LIKE MY NEIGHBOR! SHE'S ALWAYS GIVIN' ME THE STINK EYE, SO YOU GOTTA COME IN GUNS BLAZING, OR--
--MET THOSE DIRTY CRIMINALS IN MY DREAMS LAST NIGHT AND THEY'RE WOOKIEES IN DISGUISE, SO--
--I'M SERIOUS! I HAVE INSIDE INFO! THE LADY'S A DOCTOR AND THE DROID'S GOT THESE--THESE KNIVES IN HIS FINGERS! AND LISTEN--FOR THE RIGHT PRICE?
--I CAN HELP YOU GET 'EM.
B-DIP
HRRR...

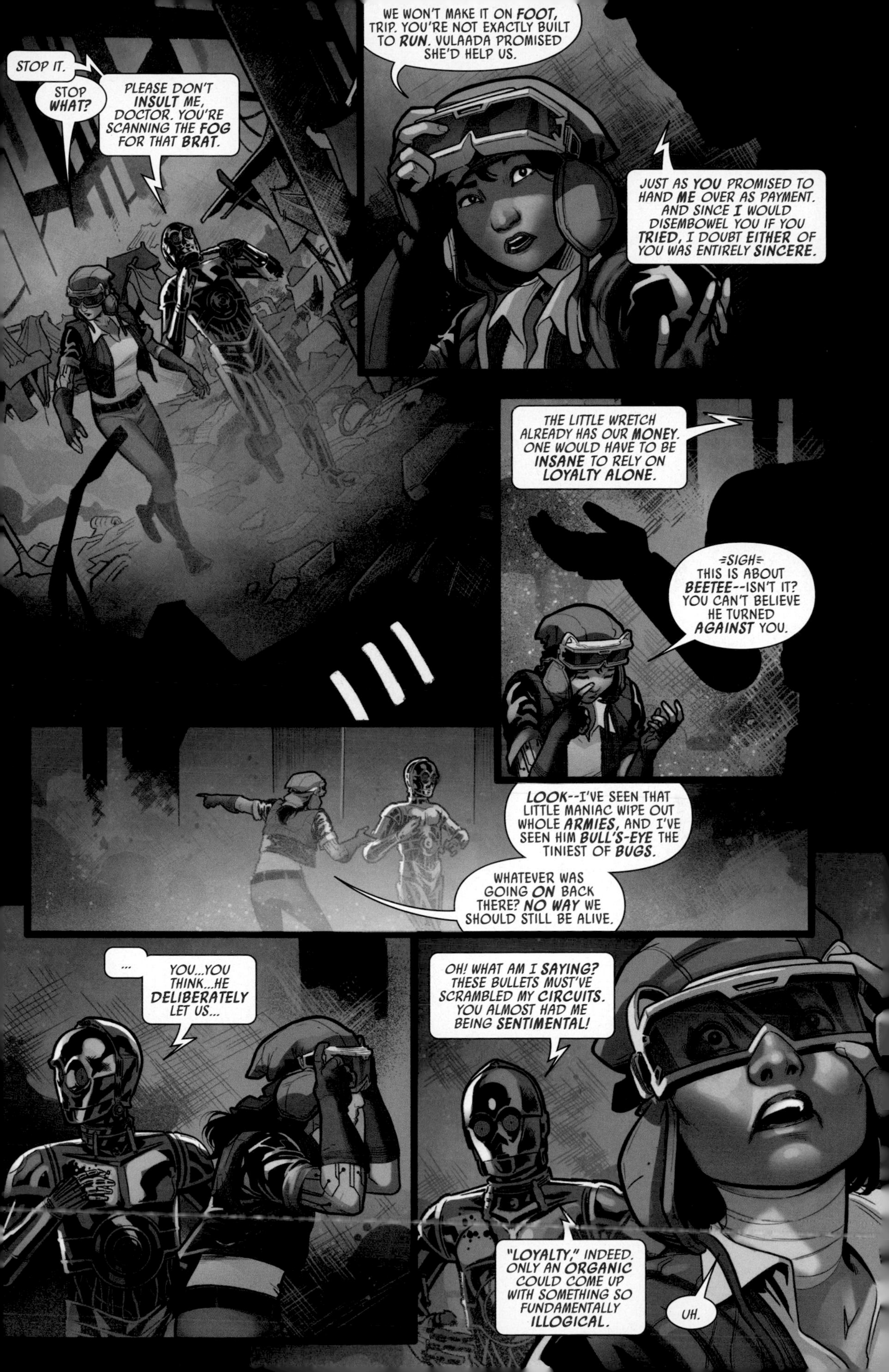
STOP IT.
STOP WHAT?
PLEASE DON'T INSULT ME, DOCTOR. YOU'RE SCANNING THE FOG FOR THAT BRAT.
WE WON'T MAKE IT ON FOOT, TRIP. YOU'RE NOT EXACTLY BUILT TO RUN. VULAADA PROMISED SHE'D HELP US.
JUST AS YOU PROMISED TO HAND ME OVER AS PAYMENT. AND SINCE I WOULD DISEMBOWEL YOU IF YOU TRIED, I DOUBT EITHER OF YOU WAS ENTIRELY SINCERE.
THE LITTLE WRETCH ALREADY HAS OUR MONEY. ONE WOULD HAVE TO BE INSANE TO RELY ON LOYALTY ALONE.
=SIGH= THIS IS ABOUT BEETEE--ISN'T IT? YOU CAN'T BELIEVE HE TURNED AGAINST YOU.
LOOK--I'VE SEEN THAT LITTLE MANIAC WIPE OUT WHOLE ARMIES, AND I'VE SEEN HIM BULL'S-EYE THE TINIEST OF BUGS.
WHATEVER WAS GOING ON BACK THERE? NO WAY WE SHOULD STILL BE ALIVE.
...
YOU...YOU THINK...HE DELIBERATELY LET US...
OH! WHAT AM I SAYING? THESE BULLETS MUST'VE SCRAMBLED MY CIRCUITS. YOU ALMOST HAD ME BEING SENTIMENTAL!
"LOYALTY," INDEED. ONLY AN ORGANIC COULD COME UP WITH SOMETHING SO FUNDAMENTALLY ILLOGICAL.
UH.

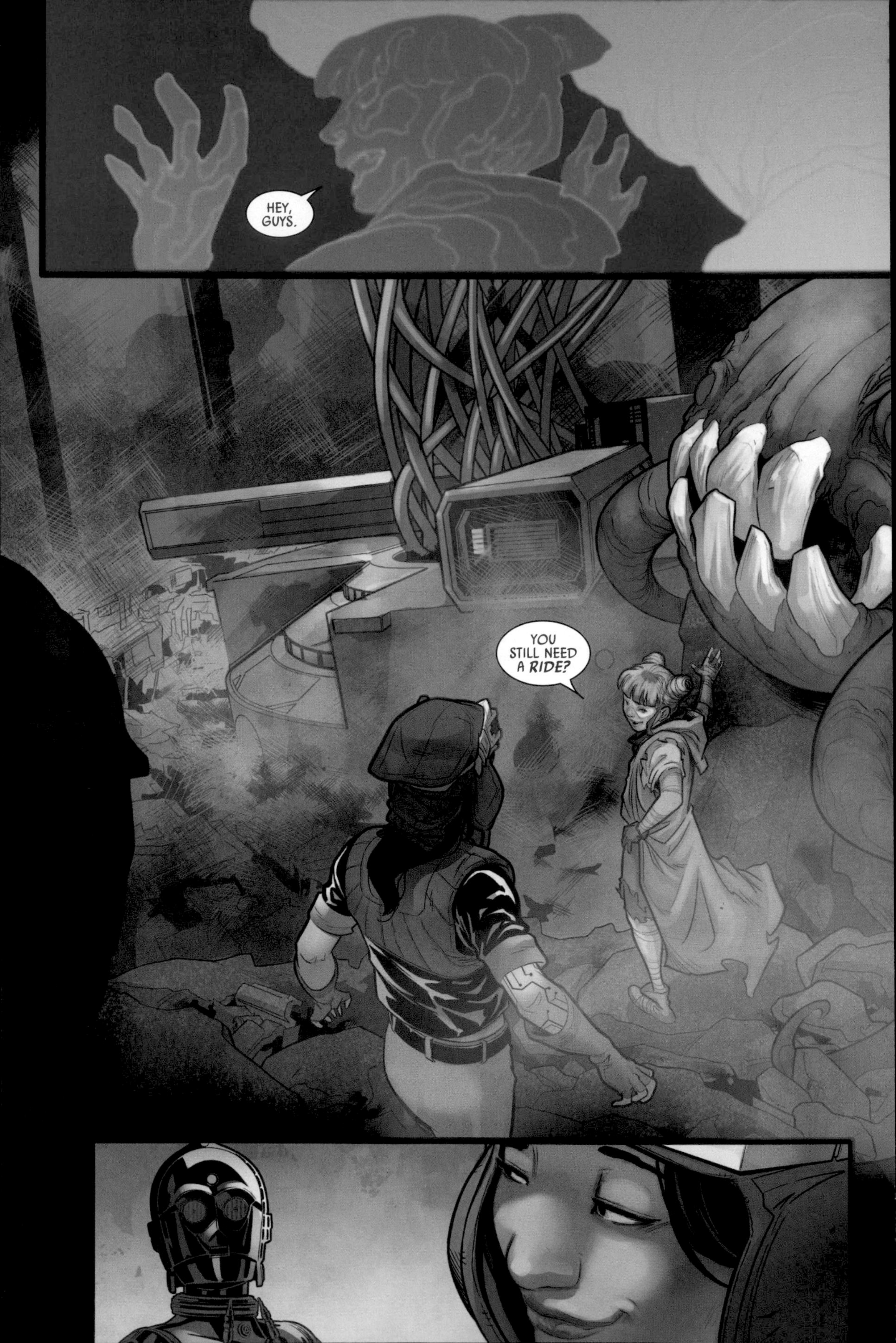
HEY, GUYS.
YOU STILL NEED A *RIDE?*

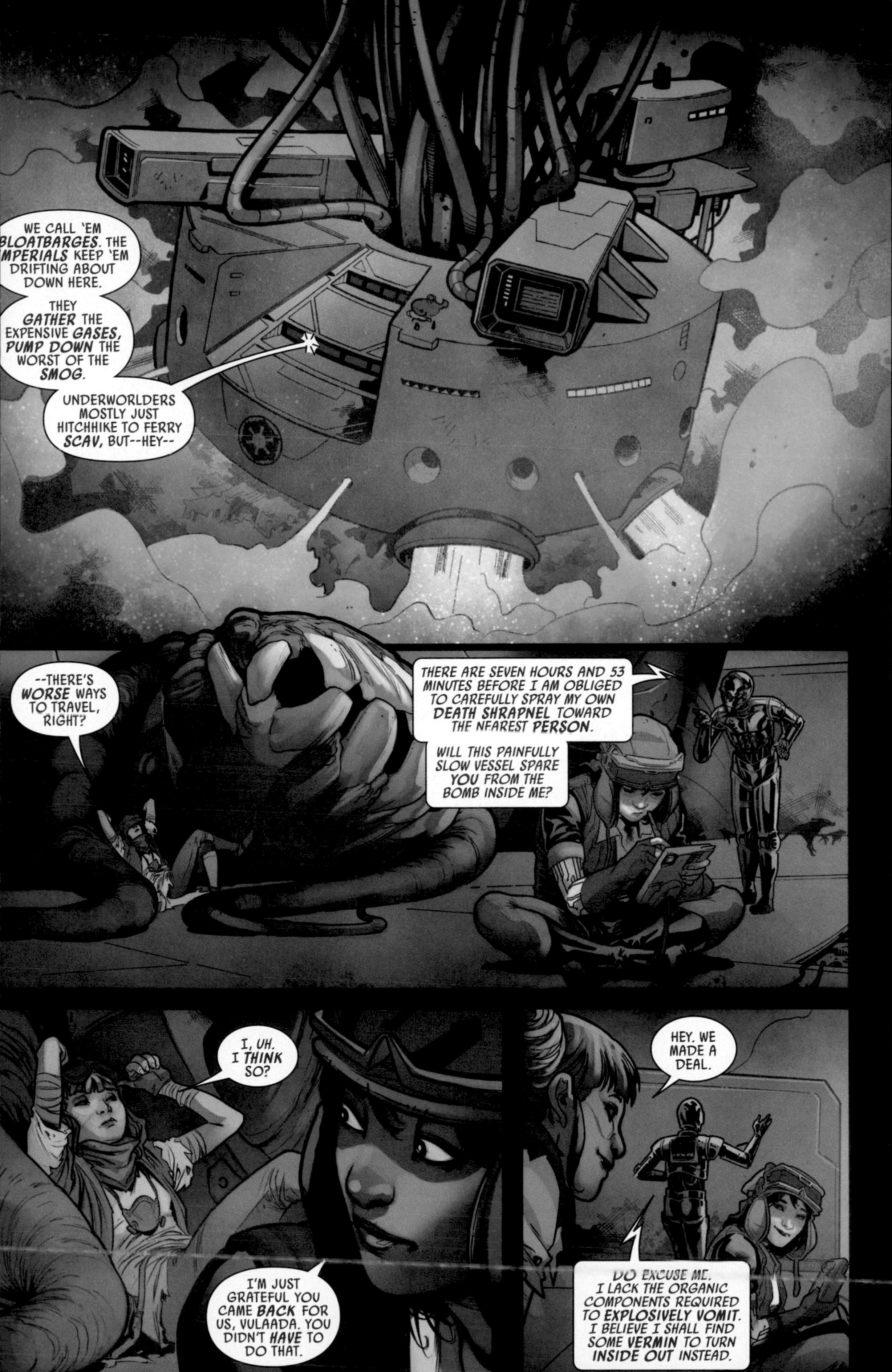
WE CALL 'EM BLOATBARGES. THE IMPERIALS KEEP 'EM DRIFTING ABOUT DOWN HERE.
THEY GATHER THE EXPENSIVE GASES, PUMP DOWN THE WORST OF THE SMOG.
UNDERWORLDERS MOSTLY JUST HITCHHIKE TO FERRY SCAV, BUT--HEY--
--THERE'S WORSE WAYS TO TRAVEL, RIGHT?
THERE ARE SEVEN HOURS AND 53 MINUTES BEFORE I AM OBLIGED TO CAREFULLY SPRAY MY OWN DEATH SHRAPNEL TOWARD THE NEAREST PERSON.
WILL THIS PAINFULLY SLOW VESSEL SPARE YOU FROM THE BOMB INSIDE ME?
I, UH. I THINK SO?
I'M JUST GRATEFUL YOU CAME BACK FOR US, VULAADA. YOU DIDN'T HAVE TO DO THAT.
HEY. WE MADE A DEAL.
DO EXCUSE ME. I LACK THE ORGANIC COMPONENTS REQUIRED TO EXPLOSIVELY VOMIT. I BELIEVE I SHALL FIND SOME VERMIN TO TURN INSIDE OUT INSTEAD.

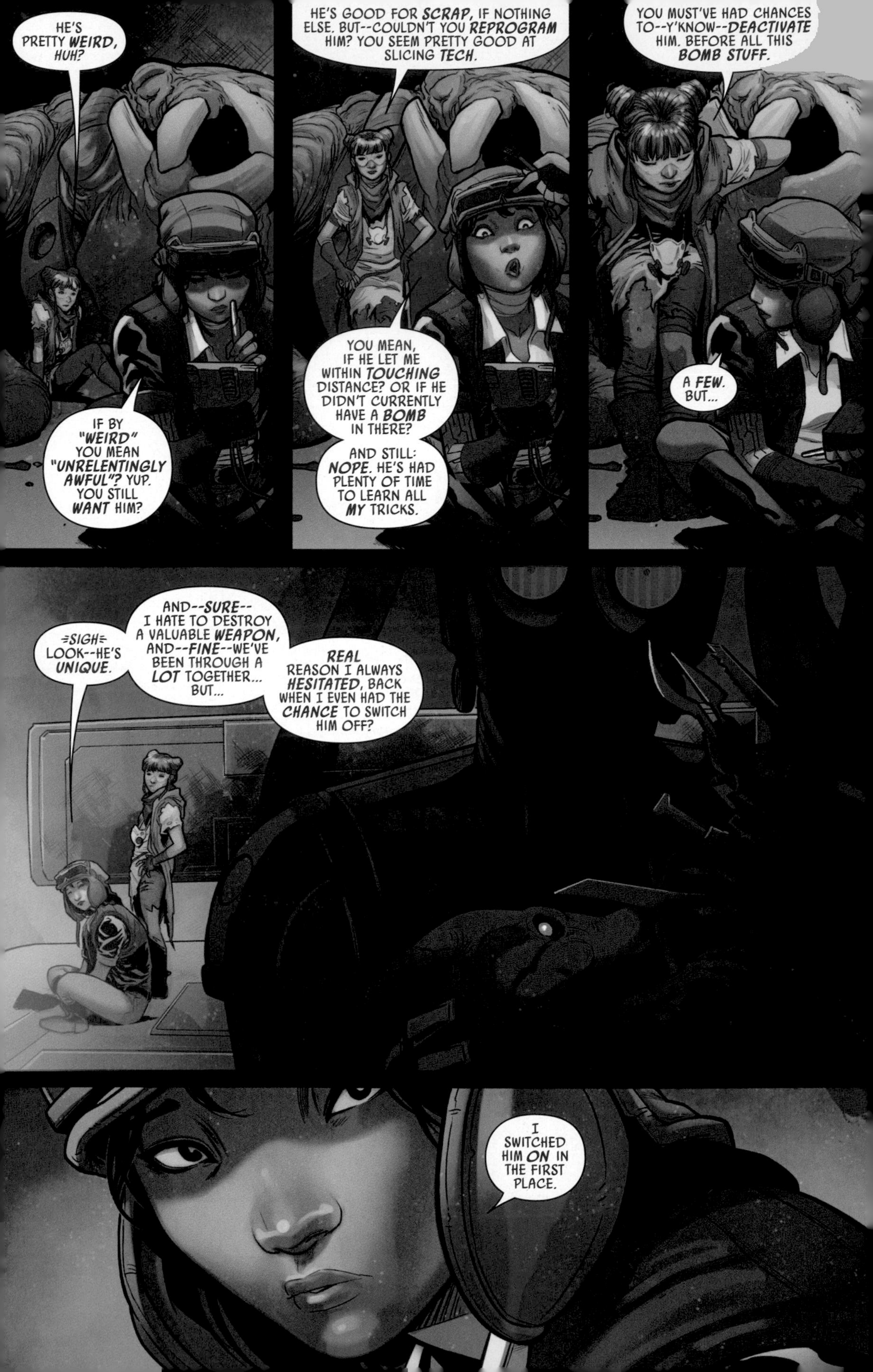
HE'S PRETTY WEIRD, HUH?
IF BY "WEIRD" YOU MEAN "UNRELENTINGLY AWFUL"? YUP. YOU STILL WANT HIM?
HE'S GOOD FOR SCRAP, IF NOTHING ELSE. BUT--COULDN'T YOU REPROGRAM HIM? YOU SEEM PRETTY GOOD AT SLICING TECH.
YOU MEAN, IF HE LET ME WITHIN TOUCHING DISTANCE? OR IF HE DIDN'T CURRENTLY HAVE A BOMB IN THERE?
AND STILL: NOPE. HE'S HAD PLENTY OF TIME TO LEARN ALL MY TRICKS.
YOU MUST'VE HAD CHANCES TO--Y'KNOW--DEACTIVATE HIM. BEFORE ALL THIS BOMB STUFF.
A FEW. BUT...
=SIGH= LOOK--HE'S UNIQUE.
AND--SURE-- I HATE TO DESTROY A VALUABLE WEAPON, AND--FINE--WE'VE BEEN THROUGH A LOT TOGETHER... BUT...
REAL REASON I ALWAYS HESITATED, BACK WHEN I EVEN HAD THE CHANCE TO SWITCH HIM OFF?
I SWITCHED HIM ON IN THE FIRST PLACE.

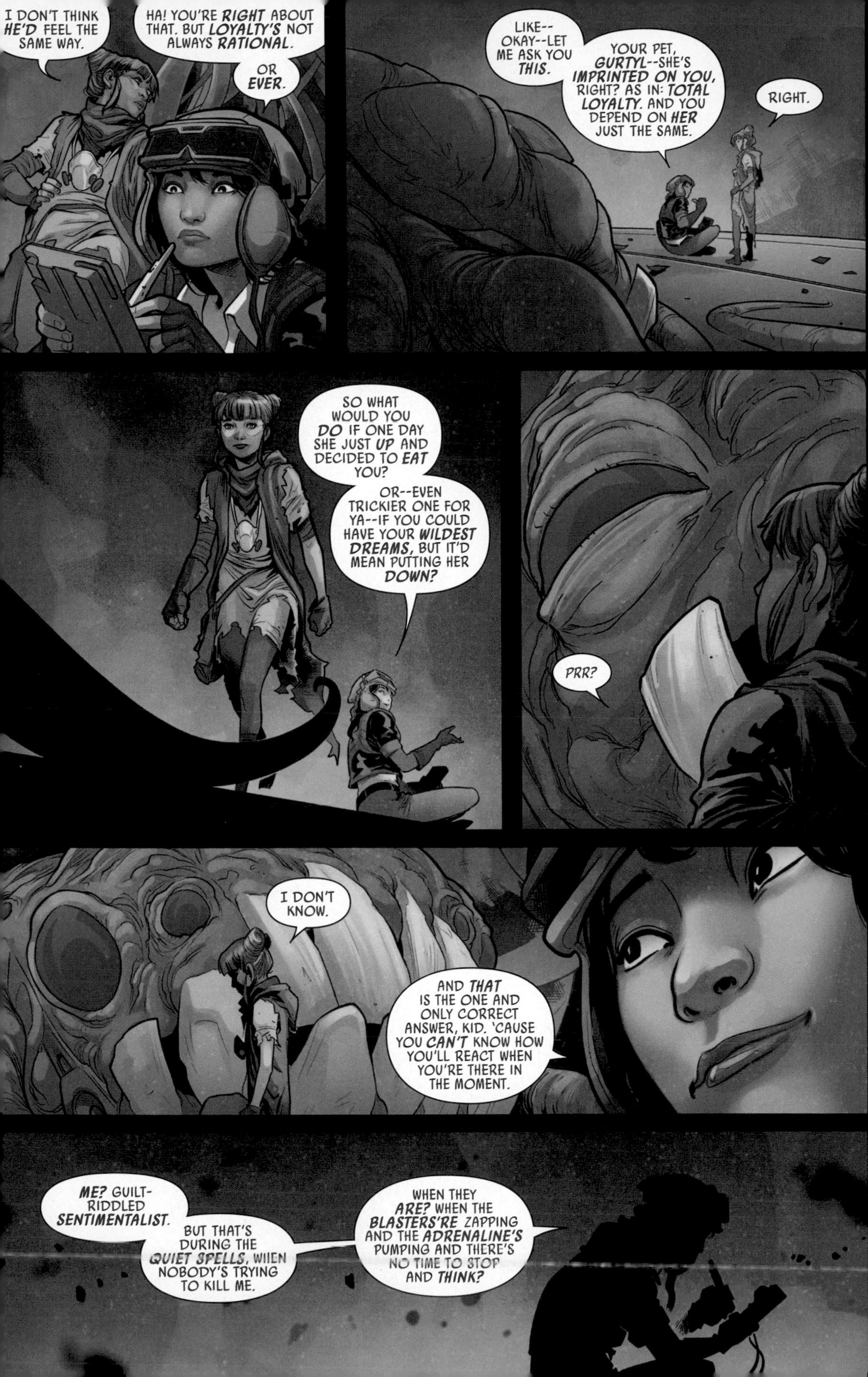
I DON'T THINK HE'D FEEL THE SAME WAY.
HA! YOU'RE RIGHT ABOUT THAT. BUT LOYALTY'S NOT ALWAYS RATIONAL.
OR EVER.
LIKE--OKAY--LET ME ASK YOU THIS.
YOUR PET, GURTYL--SHE'S IMPRINTED ON YOU, RIGHT? AS IN: TOTAL LOYALTY. AND YOU DEPEND ON HER JUST THE SAME.
RIGHT.
SO WHAT WOULD YOU DO IF ONE DAY SHE JUST UP AND DECIDED TO EAT YOU?
OR--EVEN TRICKIER ONE FOR YA--IF YOU COULD HAVE YOUR WILDEST DREAMS, BUT IT'D MEAN PUTTING HER DOWN?
PRR?
I DON'T KNOW.
AND THAT IS THE ONE AND ONLY CORRECT ANSWER, KID. 'CAUSE YOU CAN'T KNOW HOW YOU'LL REACT WHEN YOU'RE THERE IN THE MOMENT.
ME? GUILT-RIDDLED SENTIMENTALIST.
BUT THAT'S DURING THE QUIET SPELLS, WHEN NOBODY'S TRYING TO KILL ME.
WHEN THEY ARE? WHEN THE BLASTERS'RE ZAPPING AND THE ADRENALINE'S PUMPING AND THERE'S NO TIME TO STOP AND THINK?

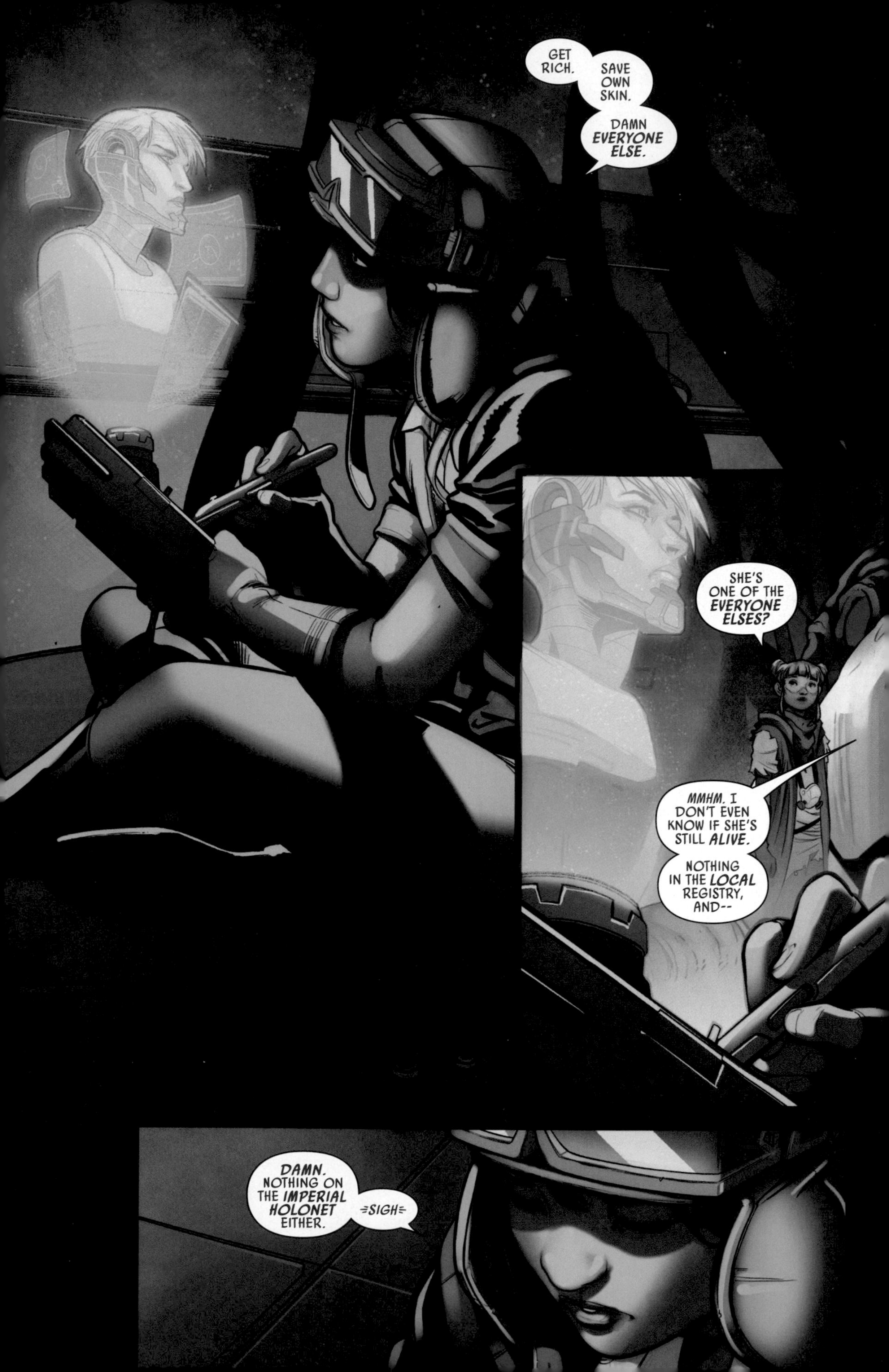
GET RICH.
SAVE OWN SKIN.
DAMN EVERYONE ELSE.
SHE'S ONE OF THE EVERYONE ELSES?
MMHM. I DON'T EVEN KNOW IF SHE'S STILL ALIVE.
NOTHING IN THE LOCAL REGISTRY, AND--
DAMN. NOTHING ON THE IMPERIAL HOLONET EITHER.
=SIGH=

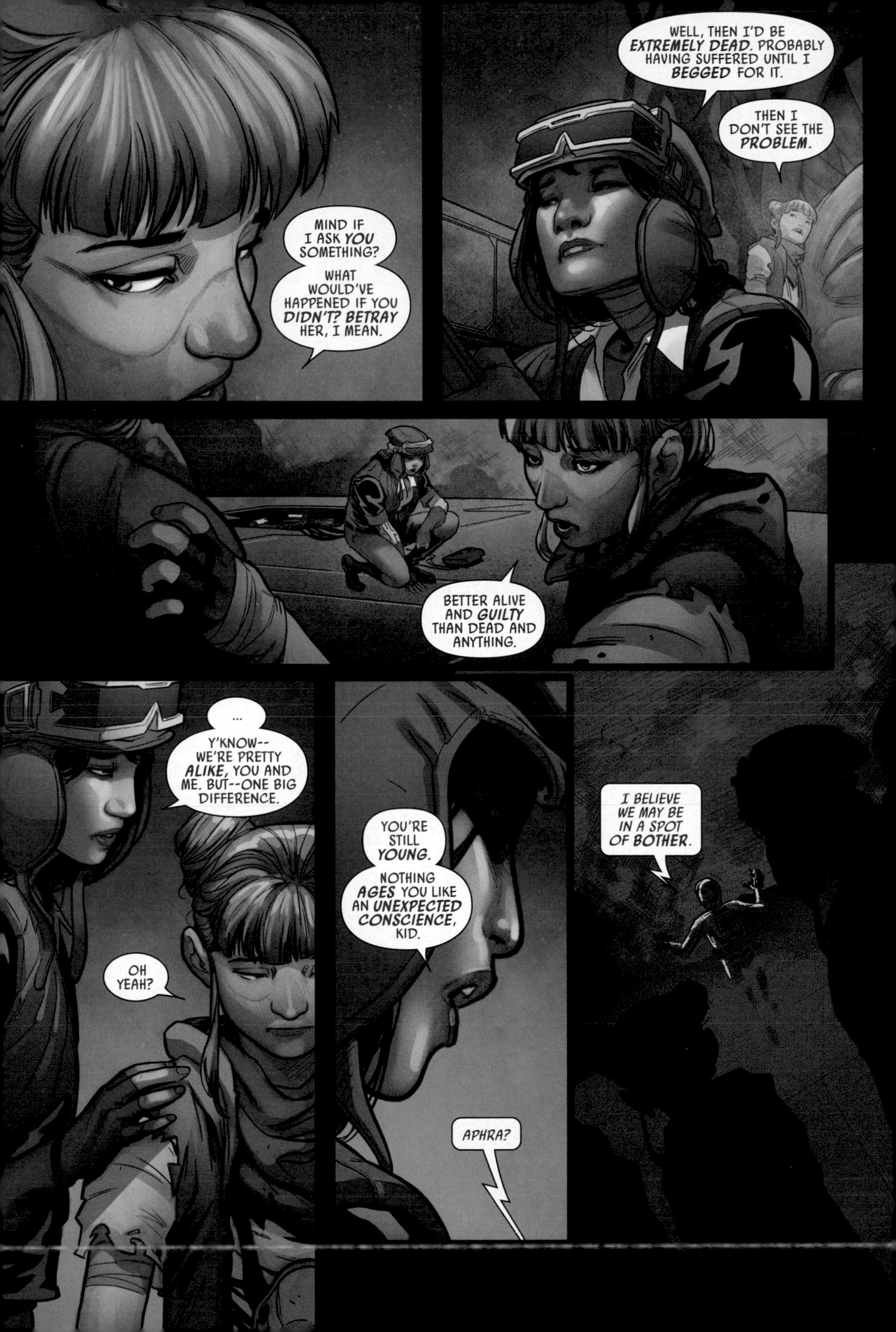
MIND IF I ASK YOU SOMETHING?
WHAT WOULD'VE HAPPENED IF YOU DIDN'T? BETRAY HER, I MEAN.
WELL, THEN I'D BE EXTREMELY DEAD. PROBABLY HAVING SUFFERED UNTIL I BEGGED FOR IT.
THEN I DON'T SEE THE PROBLEM.
BETTER ALIVE AND GUILTY THAN DEAD AND ANYTHING.
...
Y'KNOW-- WE'RE PRETTY ALIKE, YOU AND ME. BUT--ONE BIG DIFFERENCE.
OH YEAH?
YOU'RE STILL YOUNG.
NOTHING AGES YOU LIKE AN UNEXPECTED CONSCIENCE, KID.
APHRA?
I BELIEVE WE MAY BE IN A SPOT OF BOTHER.

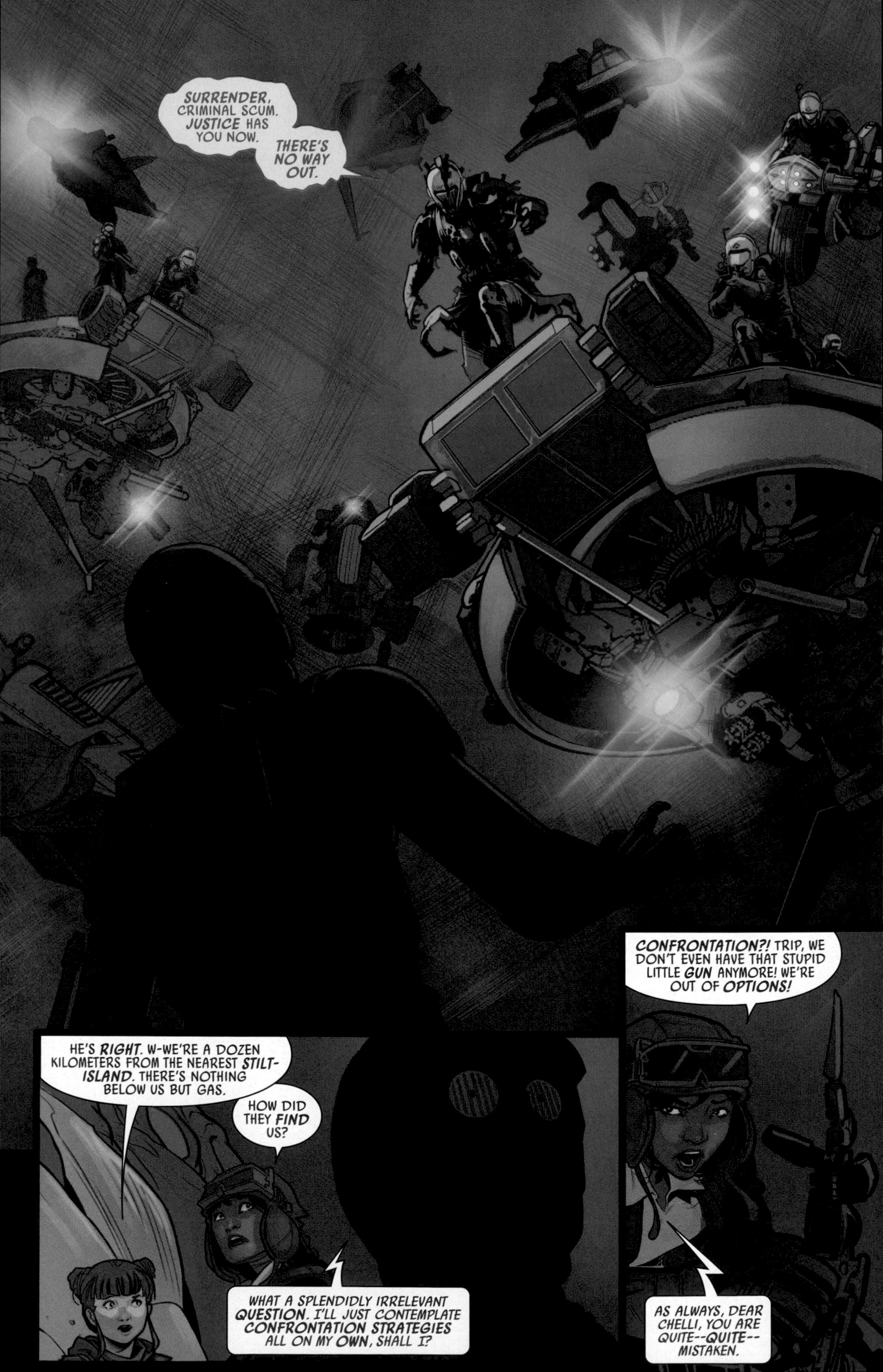
SURRENDER, CRIMINAL SCUM. JUSTICE HAS YOU NOW.
THERE'S NO WAY OUT.
HE'S RIGHT. W-WE'RE A DOZEN KILOMETERS FROM THE NEAREST STILT-ISLAND. THERE'S NOTHING BELOW US BUT GAS.
HOW DID THEY FIND US?
WHAT A SPLENDIDLY IRRELEVANT QUESTION. I'LL JUST CONTEMPLATE CONFRONTATION STRATEGIES ALL ON MY OWN, SHALL I?
CONFRONTATION?! TRIP, WE DON'T EVEN HAVE THAT STUPID LITTLE GUN ANYMORE! WE'RE OUT OF OPTIONS!
AS ALWAYS, DEAR CHELLI, YOU ARE QUITE--QUITE--MISTAKEN.

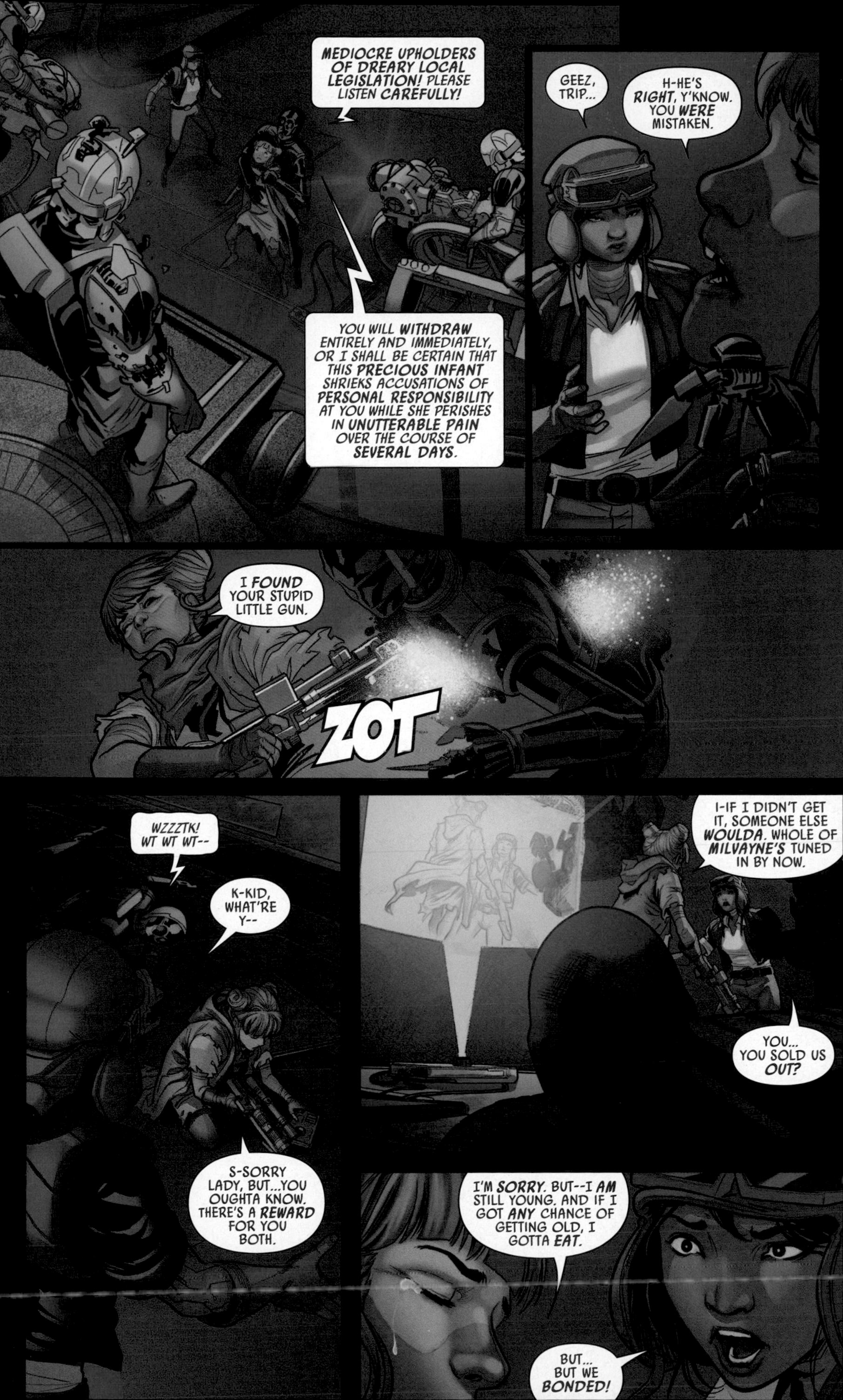

MEDIOCRE UPHOLDERS OF DREARY LOCAL LEGISLATION! PLEASE LISTEN CAREFULLY!
YOU WILL WITHDRAW ENTIRELY AND IMMEDIATELY, OR I SHALL BE CERTAIN THAT THIS PRECIOUS INFANT SHRIEKS ACCUSATIONS OF PERSONAL RESPONSIBILITY AT YOU WHILE SHE PERISHES IN UNUTTERABLE PAIN OVER THE COURSE OF SEVERAL DAYS.
GEEZ, TRIP...
H-HE'S RIGHT, Y'KNOW. YOU WERE MISTAKEN.
I FOUND YOUR STUPID LITTLE GUN.
ZOT
WZZZTK! WT WT WT--
K-KID, WHAT'RE Y--
S-SORRY LADY, BUT...YOU OUGHTA KNOW. THERE'S A REWARD FOR YOU BOTH.
I-IF I DIDN'T GET IT, SOMEONE ELSE WOULDA. WHOLE OF MILVAYNE'S TUNED IN BY NOW.
YOU... YOU SOLD US OUT?
I'M SORRY. BUT--I AM STILL YOUNG. AND IF I GOT ANY CHANCE OF GETTING OLD, I GOTTA EAT.
BUT... BUT WE BONDED!

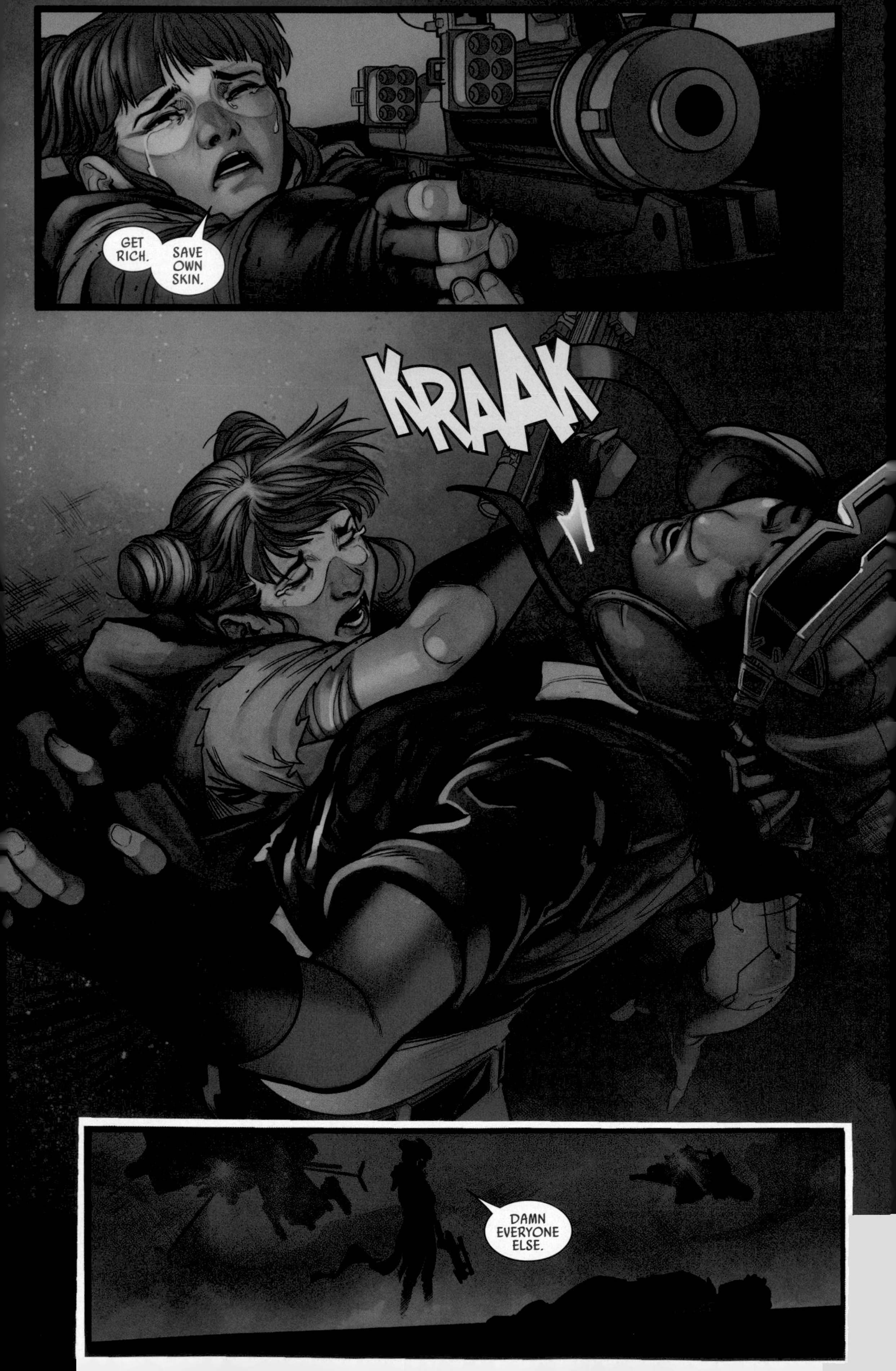
GET RICH.
SAVE OWN SKIN.
KRAAK
DAMN EVERYONE ELSE.

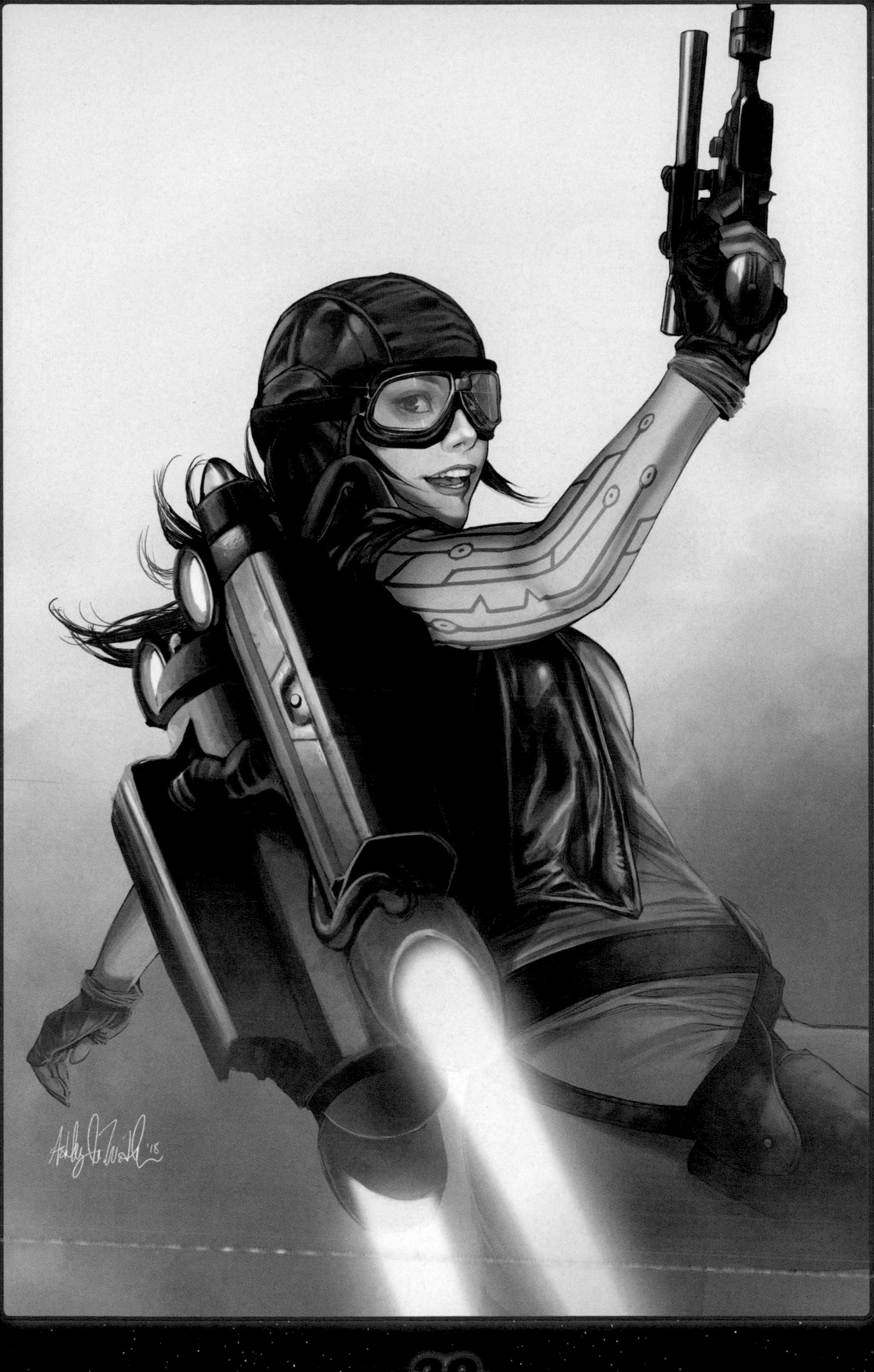

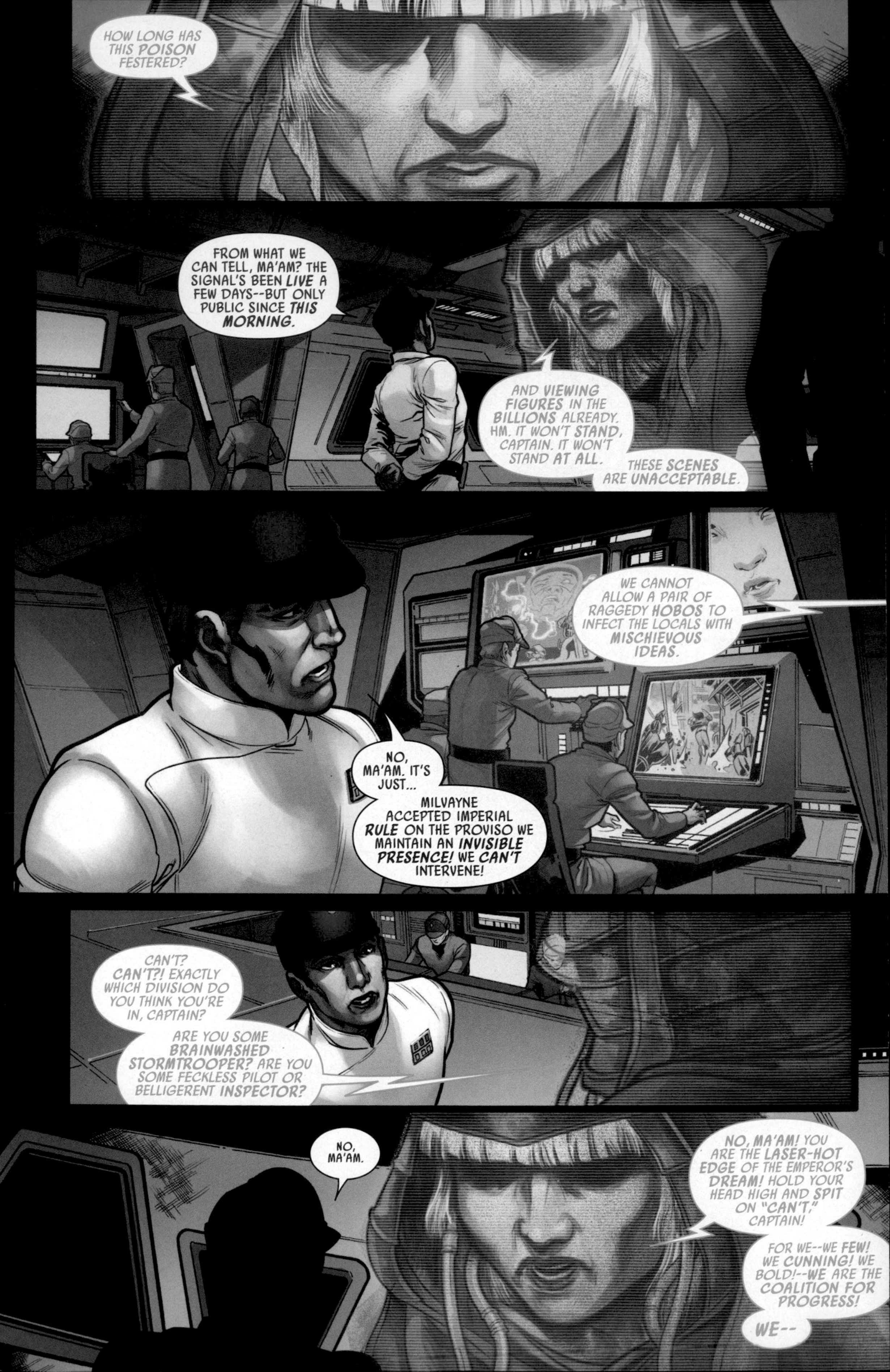
HOW LONG HAS THIS POISON FESTERED?
FROM WHAT WE CAN TELL, MA'AM? THE SIGNAL'S BEEN LIVE A FEW DAYS--BUT ONLY PUBLIC SINCE THIS MORNING.
AND VIEWING FIGURES IN THE BILLIONS ALREADY. HM. IT WON'T STAND, CAPTAIN. IT WON'T STAND AT ALL.
THESE SCENES ARE UNACCEPTABLE.
WE CANNOT ALLOW A PAIR OF RAGGEDY HOBOS TO INFECT THE LOCALS WITH MISCHIEVOUS IDEAS.
NO, MA'AM. IT'S JUST...
MILVAYNE ACCEPTED IMPERIAL RULE ON THE PROVISO WE MAINTAIN AN INVISIBLE PRESENCE! WE CAN'T INTERVENE!
CAN'T? CAN'T?! EXACTLY WHICH DIVISION DO YOU THINK YOU'RE IN, CAPTAIN?
ARE YOU SOME BRAINWASHED STORMTROOPER? ARE YOU SOME FECKLESS PILOT OR BELLIGERENT INSPECTOR?
NO, MA'AM.
NO, MA'AM! YOU ARE THE LASER-HOT EDGE OF THE EMPEROR'S DREAM! HOLD YOUR HEAD HIGH AND SPIT ON "CAN'T," CAPTAIN!
FOR WE--WE FEW! WE CUNNING! WE BOLD!--WE ARE THE COALITION FOR PROGRESS!
WE--

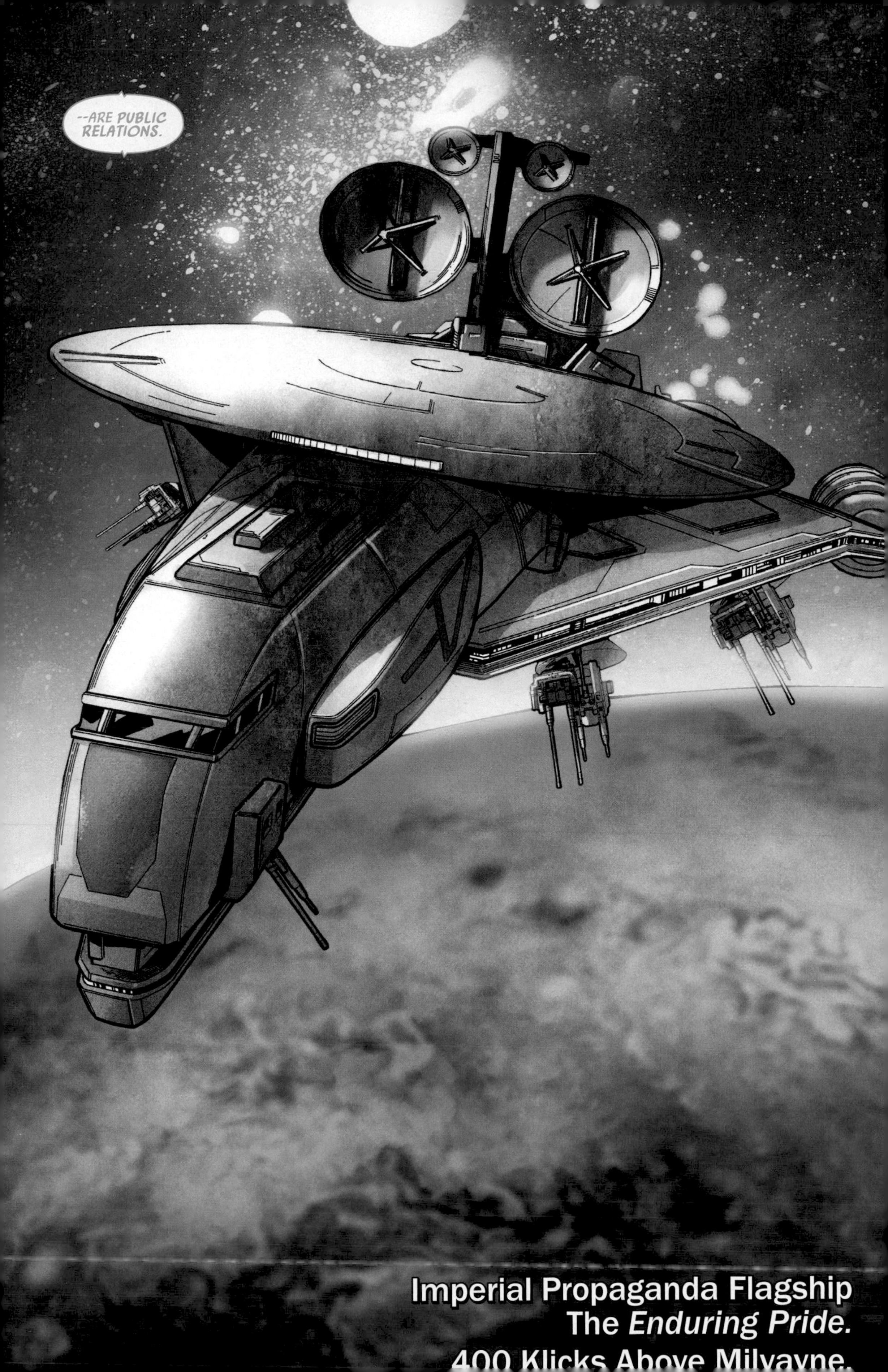
--ARE PUBLIC RELATIONS.
Imperial Propaganda Flagship The *Enduring Pride.* 400 Klicks Above Milvayne.

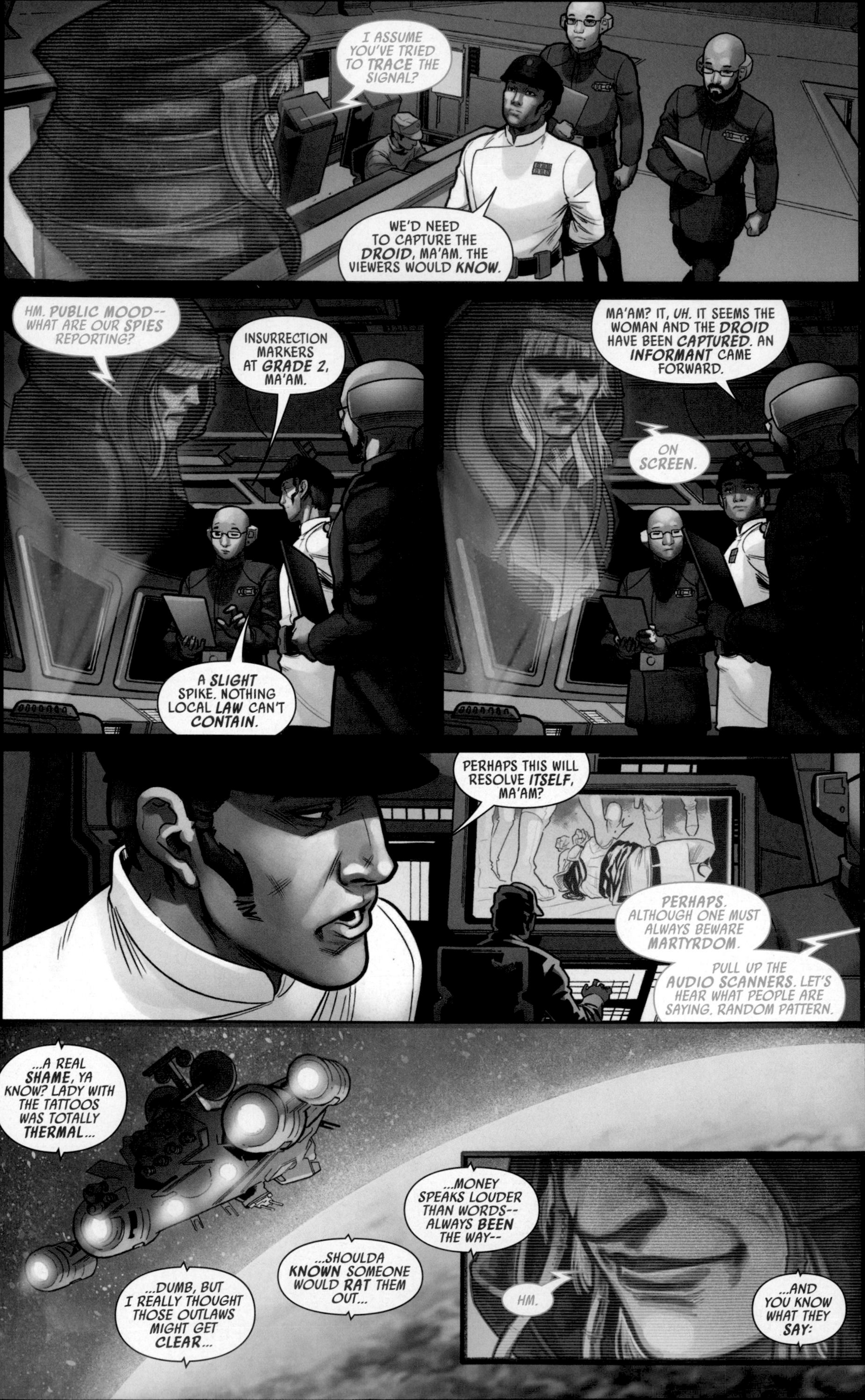
I ASSUME YOU'VE TRIED TO TRACE THE SIGNAL?
WE'D NEED TO CAPTURE THE DROID, MA'AM. THE VIEWERS WOULD KNOW.
HM. PUBLIC MOOD-- WHAT ARE OUR SPIES REPORTING?
INSURRECTION MARKERS AT GRADE 2, MA'AM.
A SLIGHT SPIKE. NOTHING LOCAL LAW CAN'T CONTAIN.
MA'AM? IT, UH. IT SEEMS THE WOMAN AND THE DROID HAVE BEEN CAPTURED. AN INFORMANT CAME FORWARD.
ON SCREEN.
PERHAPS THIS WILL RESOLVE ITSELF, MA'AM?
PERHAPS. ALTHOUGH ONE MUST ALWAYS BEWARE MARTYRDOM.
PULL UP THE AUDIO SCANNERS. LET'S HEAR WHAT PEOPLE ARE SAYING. RANDOM PATTERN.
...A REAL SHAME, YA KNOW? LADY WITH THE TATTOOS WAS TOTALLY THERMAL...
...DUMB, BUT I REALLY THOUGHT THOSE OUTLAWS MIGHT GET CLEAR...
...SHOULDA KNOWN SOMEONE WOULD RAT THEM OUT...
...MONEY SPEAKS LOUDER THAN WORDS-- ALWAYS BEEN THE WAY--
HM.
...AND YOU KNOW WHAT THEY SAY:

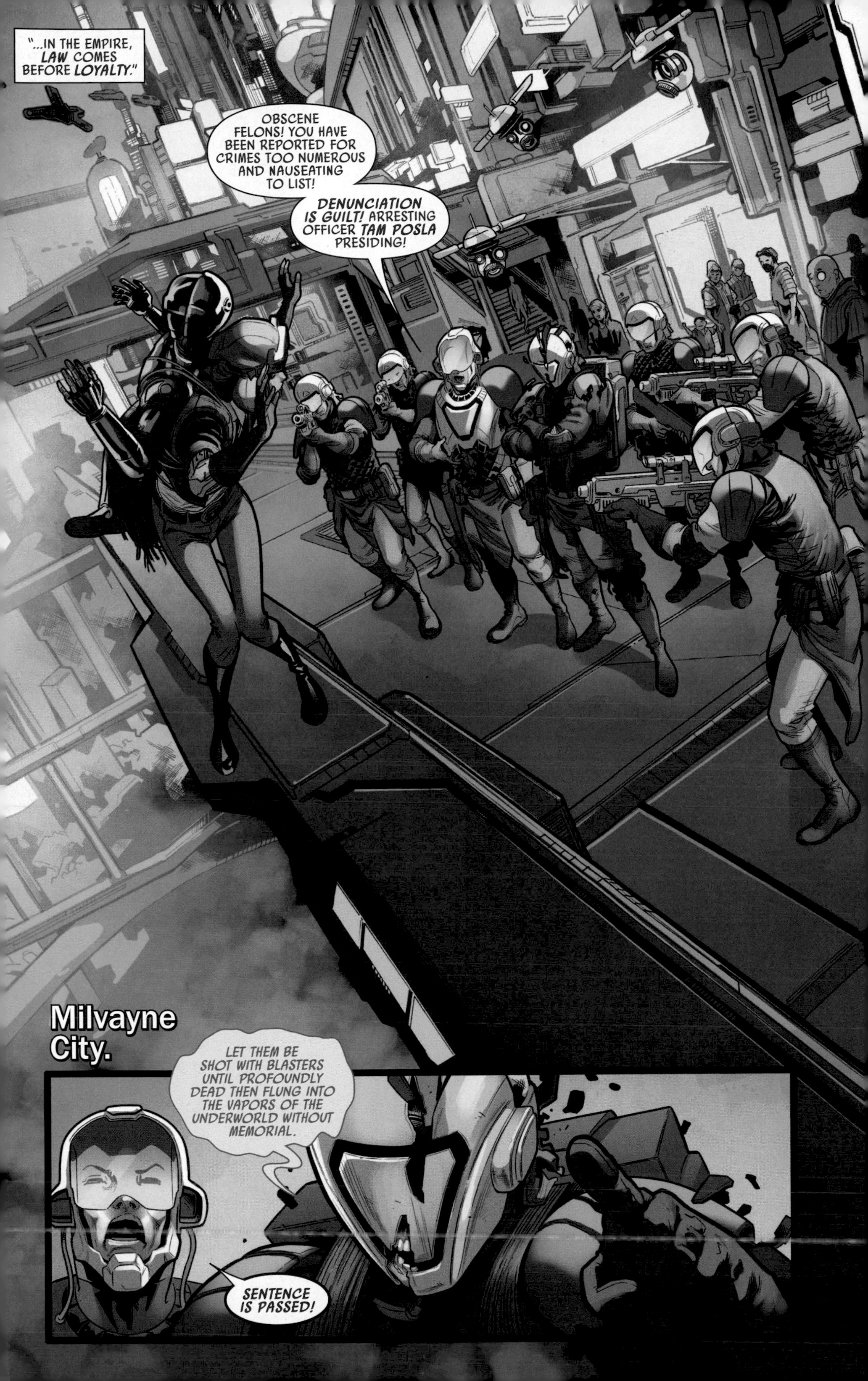
"...IN THE EMPIRE, LAW COMES BEFORE LOYALTY."
OBSCENE FELONS! YOU HAVE BEEN REPORTED FOR CRIMES TOO NUMEROUS AND NAUSEATING TO LIST!
DENUNCIATION IS GUILT! ARRESTING OFFICER TAM POSLA PRESIDING!
Milvayne City.
LET THEM BE SHOT WITH BLASTERS UNTIL PROFOUNDLY DEAD THEN FLUNG INTO THE VAPORS OF THE UNDERWORLD WITHOUT MEMORIAL.
SENTENCE IS PASSED!

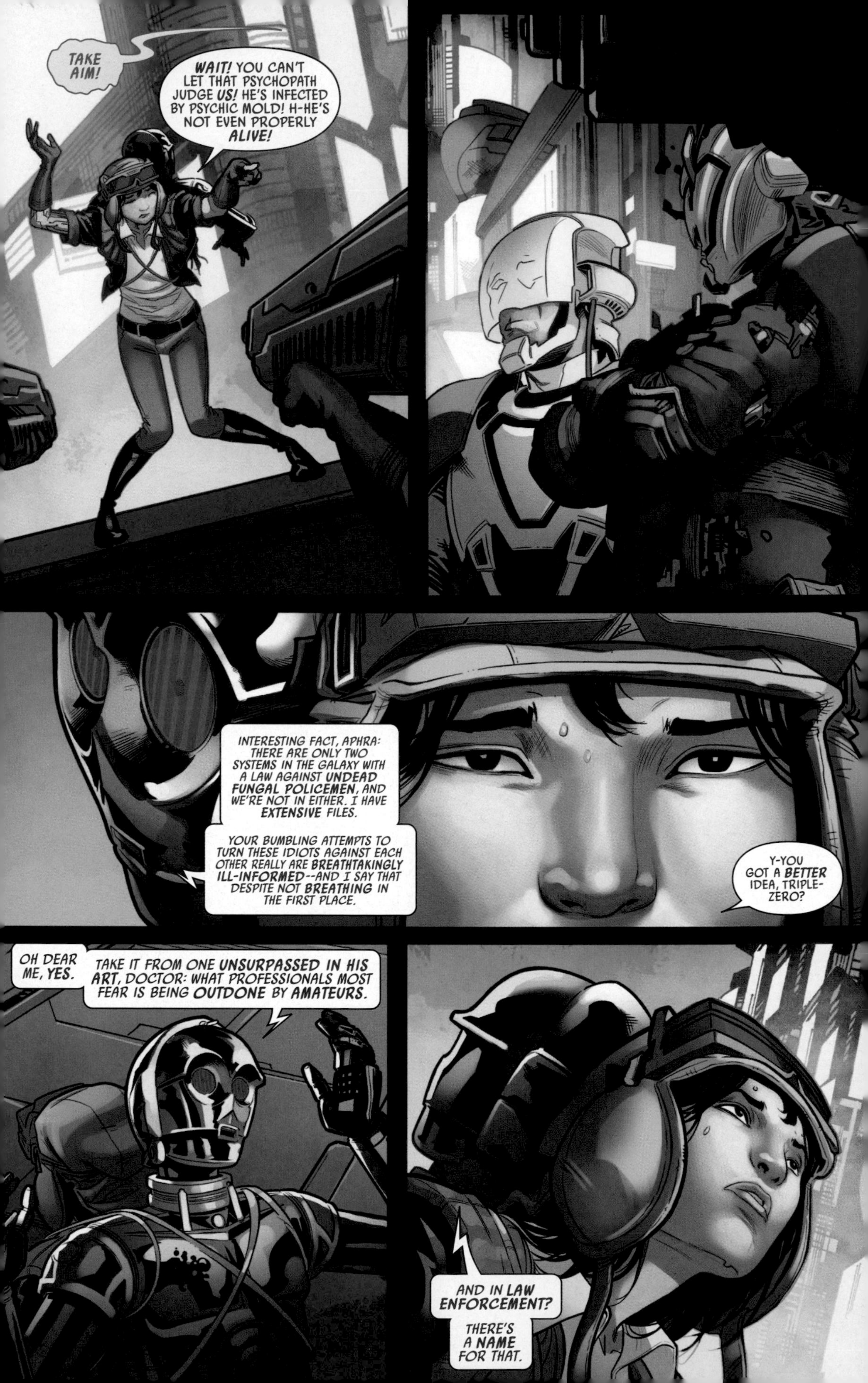
TAKE AIM!
WAIT! YOU CAN'T LET THAT PSYCHOPATH JUDGE US! HE'S INFECTED BY PSYCHIC MOLD! H-HE'S NOT EVEN PROPERLY ALIVE!
INTERESTING FACT, APHRA: THERE ARE ONLY TWO SYSTEMS IN THE GALAXY WITH A LAW AGAINST UNDEAD FUNGAL POLICEMEN, AND WE'RE NOT IN EITHER. I HAVE EXTENSIVE FILES.
YOUR BUMBLING ATTEMPTS TO TURN THESE IDIOTS AGAINST EACH OTHER REALLY ARE BREATHTAKINGLY ILL-INFORMED--AND I SAY THAT DESPITE NOT BREATHING IN THE FIRST PLACE.
Y-YOU GOT A BETTER IDEA, TRIPLE-ZERO?
OH DEAR ME, YES.
TAKE IT FROM ONE UNSURPASSED IN HIS ART, DOCTOR: WHAT PROFESSIONALS MOST FEAR IS BEING OUTDONE BY AMATEURS.
AND IN LAW ENFORCEMENT?
THERE'S A NAME FOR THAT.

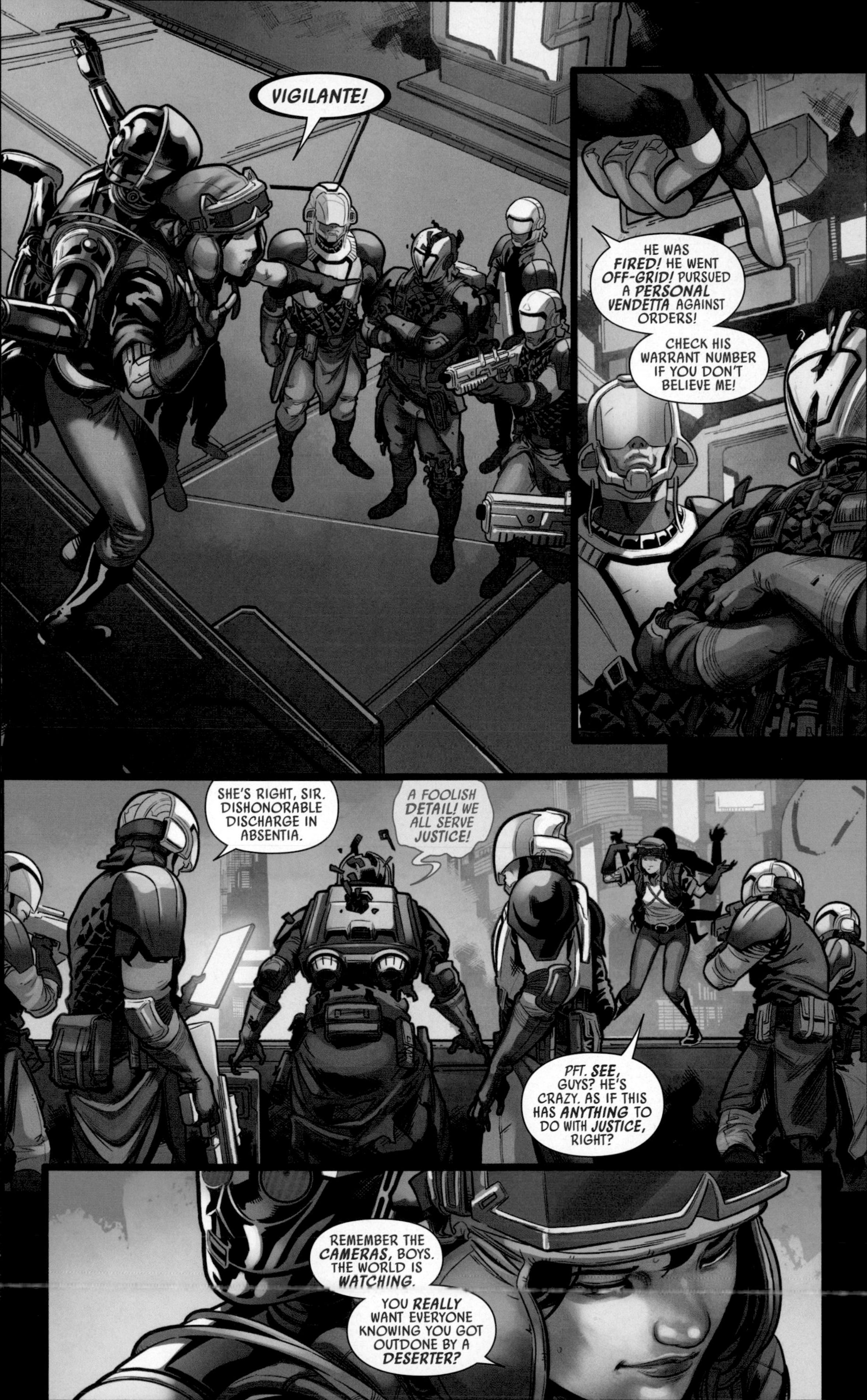
VIGILANTE!
HE WAS FIRED! HE WENT OFF-GRID! PURSUED A PERSONAL VENDETTA AGAINST ORDERS!
CHECK HIS WARRANT NUMBER IF YOU DON'T BELIEVE ME!
SHE'S RIGHT, SIR. DISHONORABLE DISCHARGE IN ABSENTIA.
A FOOLISH DETAIL! WE ALL SERVE JUSTICE!
PFT. SEE, GUYS? HE'S CRAZY. AS IF THIS HAS ANYTHING TO DO WITH JUSTICE, RIGHT?
REMEMBER THE CAMERAS, BOYS. THE WORLD IS WATCHING.
YOU REALLY WANT EVERYONE KNOWING YOU GOT OUTDONE BY A DESERTER?

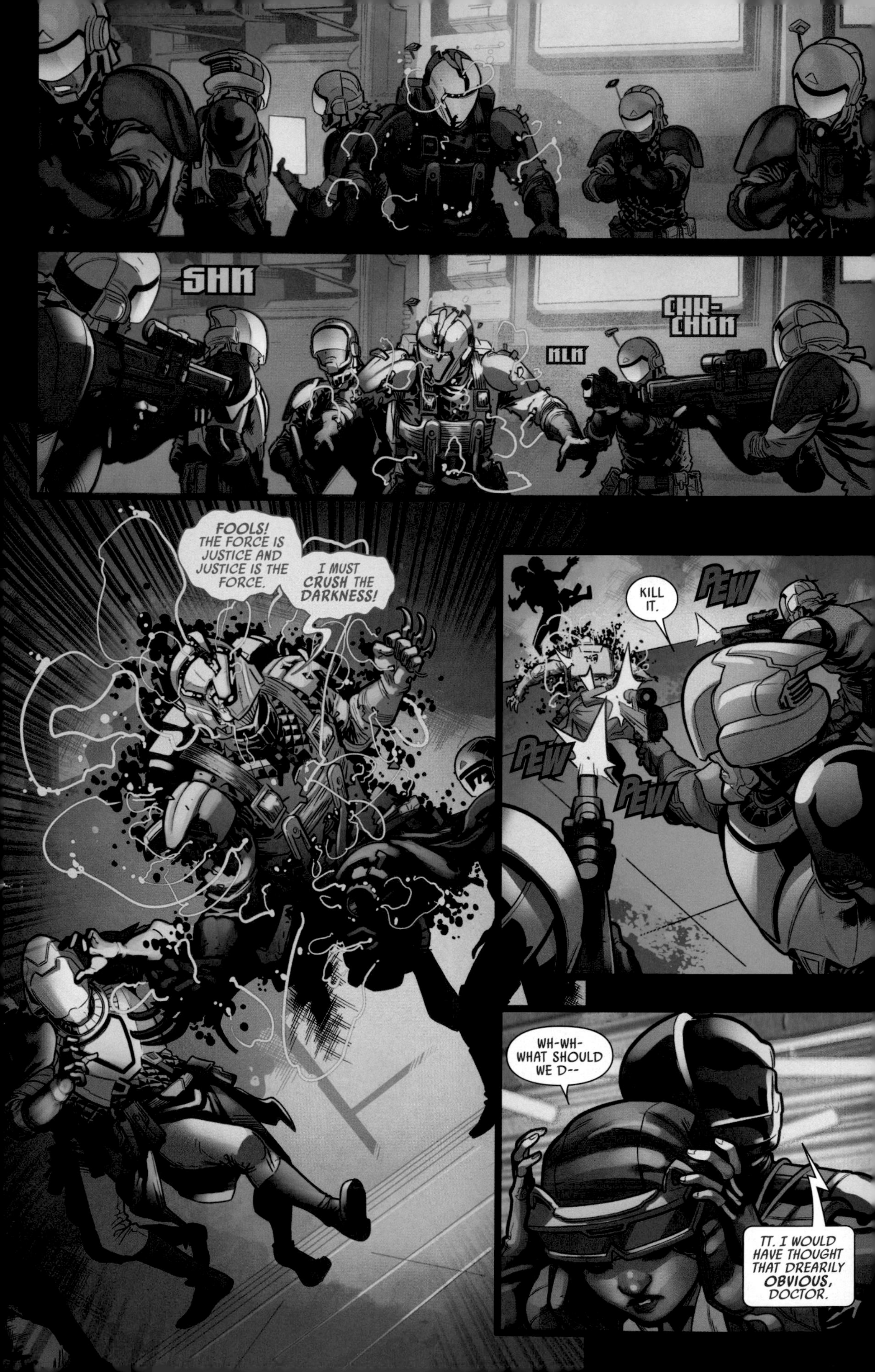
SHK
CHK-CHKK
KLK
FOOLS! THE FORCE IS JUSTICE AND JUSTICE IS THE FORCE.
I MUST CRUSH THE DARKNESS!
KILL IT.
PEW
PEW
PEW
WH-WH-WHAT SHOULD WE D--
TT. I WOULD HAVE THOUGHT THAT DREARILY OBVIOUS, DOCTOR.

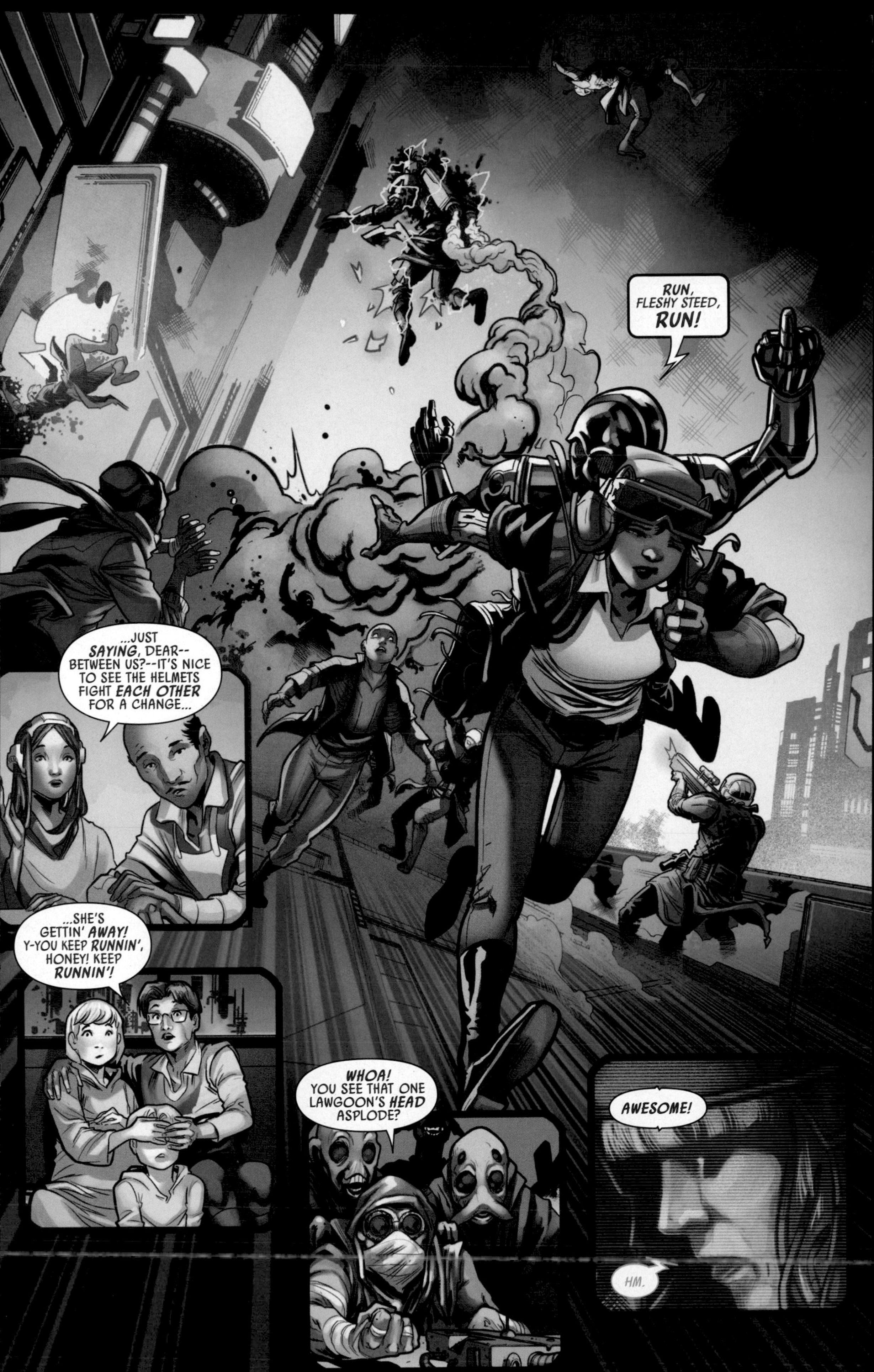
RUN, FLESHY STEED, RUN!
...JUST SAYING, DEAR-- BETWEEN US?--IT'S NICE TO SEE THE HELMETS FIGHT EACH OTHER FOR A CHANGE...
...SHE'S GETTIN' AWAY! Y-YOU KEEP RUNNIN', HONEY! KEEP RUNNIN'!
WHOA! YOU SEE THAT ONE LAWGOON'S HEAD ASPLODE?
AWESOME!
HM.

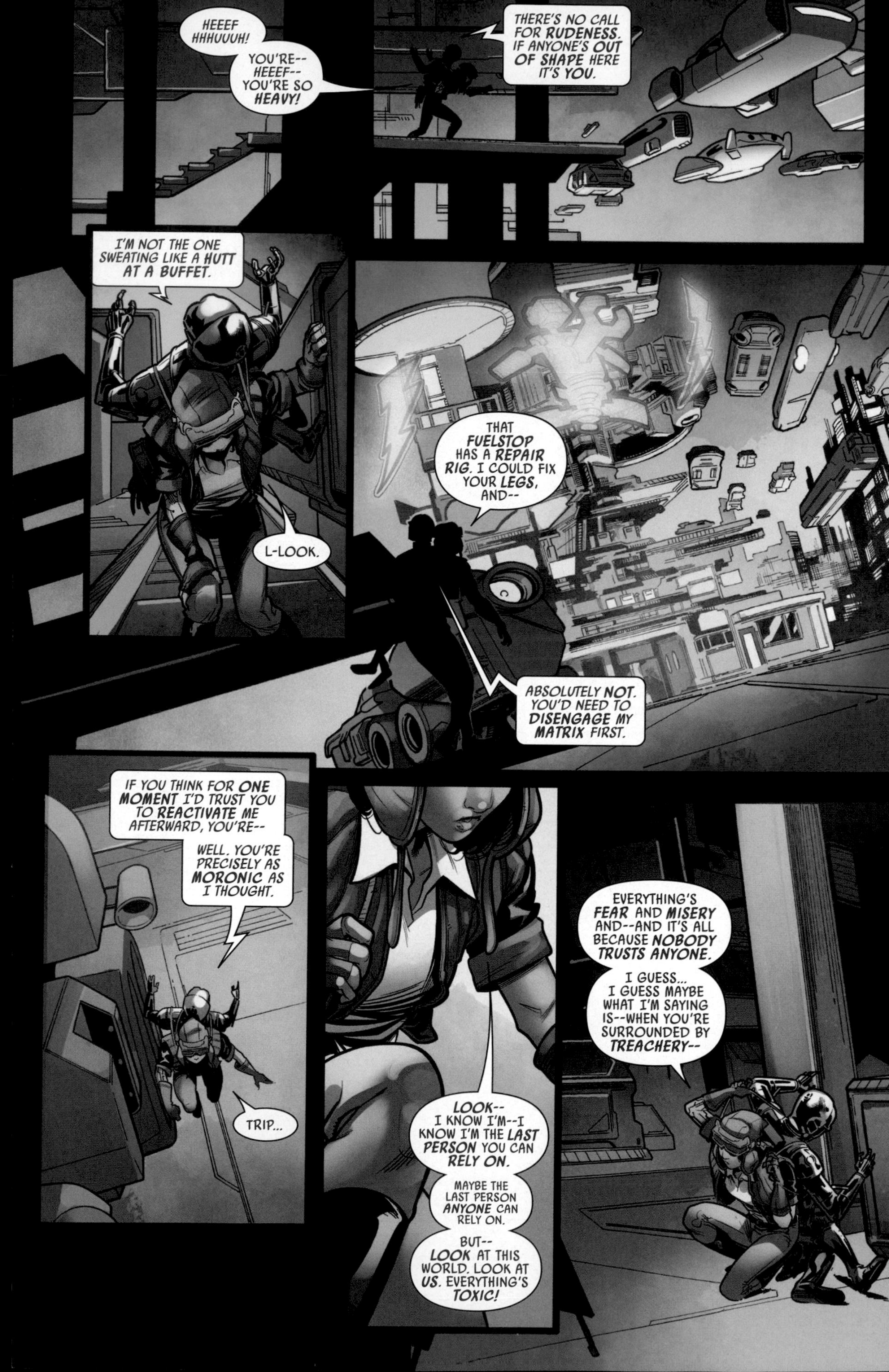
HEEEF HHHUUUH!
YOU'RE-- HEEEF-- YOU'RE SO HEAVY!
THERE'S NO CALL FOR RUDENESS. IF ANYONE'S OUT OF SHAPE HERE IT'S YOU.
I'M NOT THE ONE SWEATING LIKE A HUTT AT A BUFFET.
L-LOOK.
THAT FUELSTOP HAS A REPAIR RIG. I COULD FIX YOUR LEGS, AND--
ABSOLUTELY NOT. YOU'D NEED TO DISENGAGE MY MATRIX FIRST.
IF YOU THINK FOR ONE MOMENT I'D TRUST YOU TO REACTIVATE ME AFTERWARD, YOU'RE--
WELL. YOU'RE PRECISELY AS MORONIC AS I THOUGHT.
TRIP...
LOOK-- I KNOW I'M--I KNOW I'M THE LAST PERSON YOU CAN RELY ON.
MAYBE THE LAST PERSON ANYONE CAN RELY ON.
BUT-- LOOK AT THIS WORLD. LOOK AT US. EVERYTHING'S TOXIC!
EVERYTHING'S FEAR AND MISERY AND--AND IT'S ALL BECAUSE NOBODY TRUSTS ANYONE.
I GUESS... I GUESS MAYBE WHAT I'M SAYING IS--WHEN YOU'RE SURROUNDED BY TREACHERY--

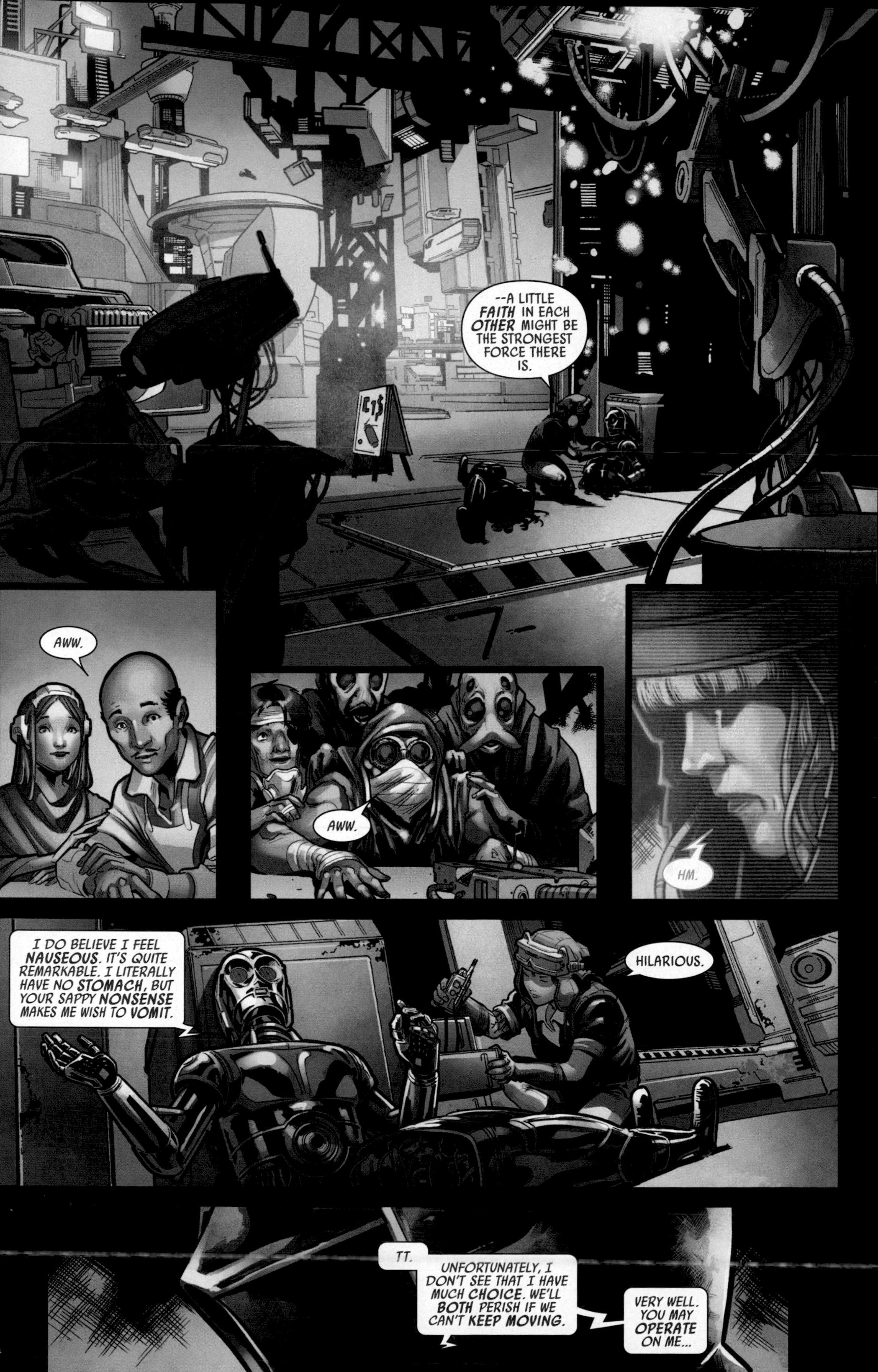
--A LITTLE FAITH IN EACH OTHER MIGHT BE THE STRONGEST FORCE THERE IS.
AWW.
AWW.
HM.
I DO BELIEVE I FEEL NAUSEOUS. IT'S QUITE REMARKABLE. I LITERALLY HAVE NO STOMACH, BUT YOUR SAPPY NONSENSE MAKES ME WISH TO VOMIT.
HILARIOUS.
TT.
UNFORTUNATELY, I DON'T SEE THAT I HAVE MUCH CHOICE. WE'LL BOTH PERISH IF WE CAN'T KEEP MOVING.
VERY WELL. YOU MAY OPERATE ON ME...

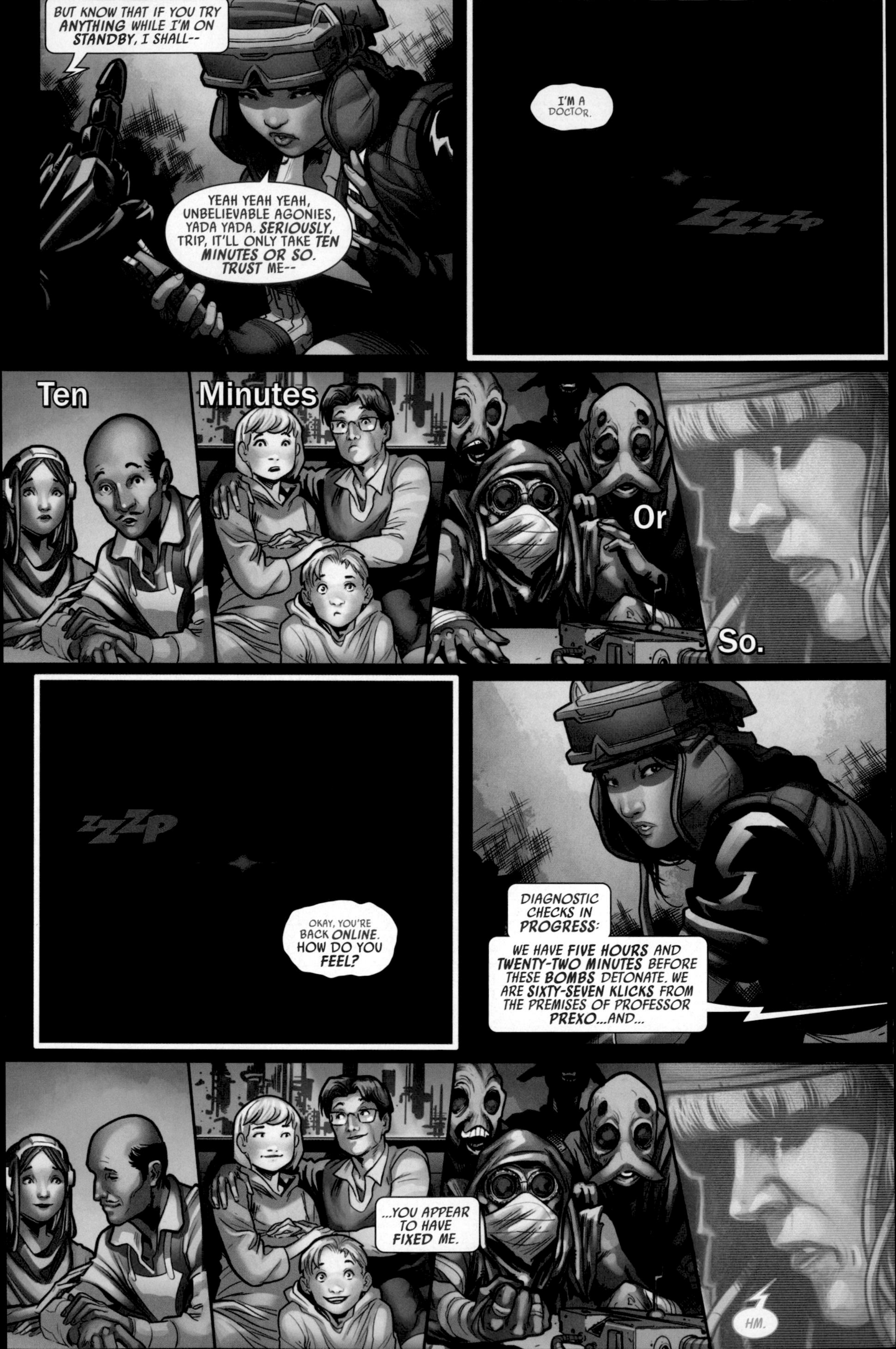

BUT KNOW THAT IF YOU TRY ANYTHING WHILE I'M ON STANDBY, I SHALL--
YEAH YEAH YEAH, UNBELIEVABLE AGONIES, YADA YADA. SERIOUSLY, TRIP, IT'LL ONLY TAKE TEN MINUTES OR SO. TRUST ME--
I'M A DOCTOR.
ZZZZP
Ten
Minutes
Or
So.
ZZZP
OKAY, YOU'RE BACK ONLINE. HOW DO YOU FEEL?
DIAGNOSTIC CHECKS IN PROGRESS:
WE HAVE FIVE HOURS AND TWENTY-TWO MINUTES BEFORE THESE BOMBS DETONATE. WE ARE SIXTY-SEVEN KLICKS FROM THE PREMISES OF PROFESSOR PREXO...AND...
...YOU APPEAR TO HAVE FIXED ME.
HM.

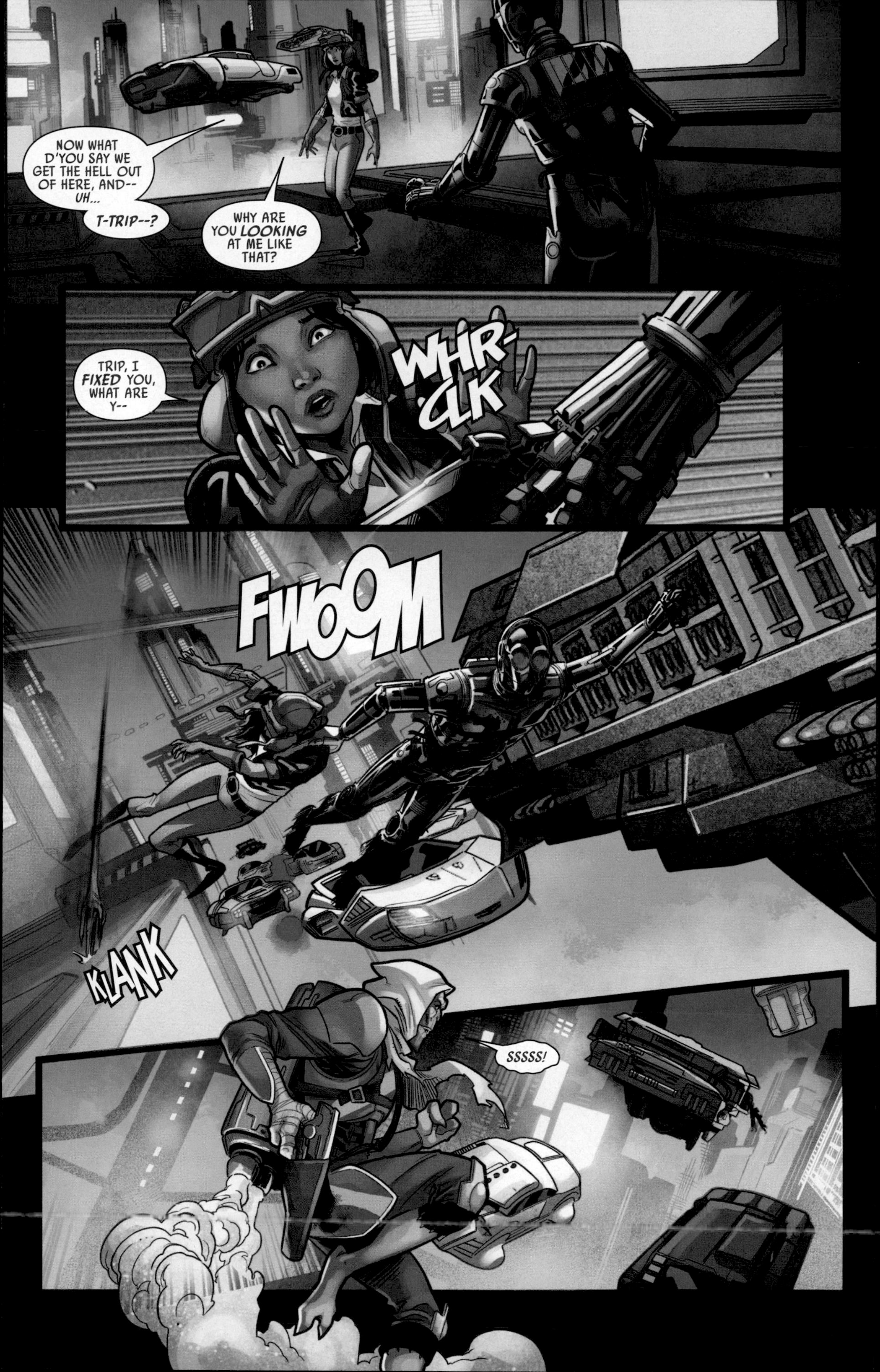
NOW WHAT D'YOU SAY WE GET THE HELL OUT OF HERE, AND-- UH...
T-TRIP--?
WHY ARE YOU LOOKING AT ME LIKE THAT?
TRIP, I FIXED YOU, WHAT ARE Y--
WHR-CLK
FWOOM
KLANK
SSSSS!

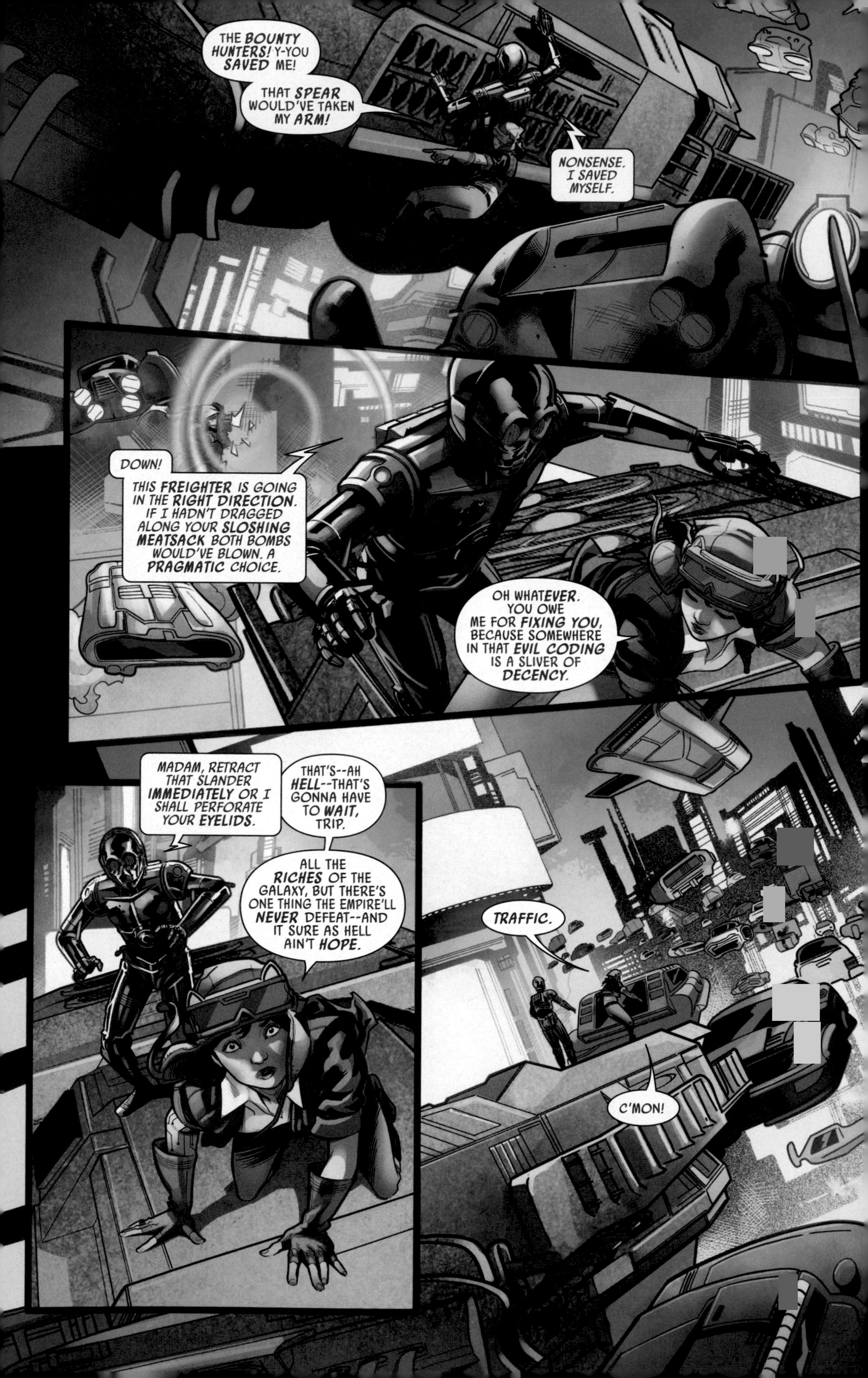
THE BOUNTY HUNTERS! Y-YOU SAVED ME!
THAT SPEAR WOULD'VE TAKEN MY ARM!
NONSENSE. I SAVED MYSELF.
DOWN!
THIS FREIGHTER IS GOING IN THE RIGHT DIRECTION. IF I HADN'T DRAGGED ALONG YOUR SLOSHING MEATSACK BOTH BOMBS WOULD'VE BLOWN. A PRAGMATIC CHOICE.
OH WHATEVER. YOU OWE ME FOR FIXING YOU, BECAUSE SOMEWHERE IN THAT EVIL CODING IS A SLIVER OF DECENCY.
MADAM, RETRACT THAT SLANDER IMMEDIATELY OR I SHALL PERFORATE YOUR EYELIDS.
THAT'S--AH HELL--THAT'S GONNA HAVE TO WAIT, TRIP.
ALL THE RICHES OF THE GALAXY, BUT THERE'S ONE THING THE EMPIRE'LL NEVER DEFEAT--AND IT SURE AS HELL AIN'T HOPE.
TRAFFIC.
C'MON!

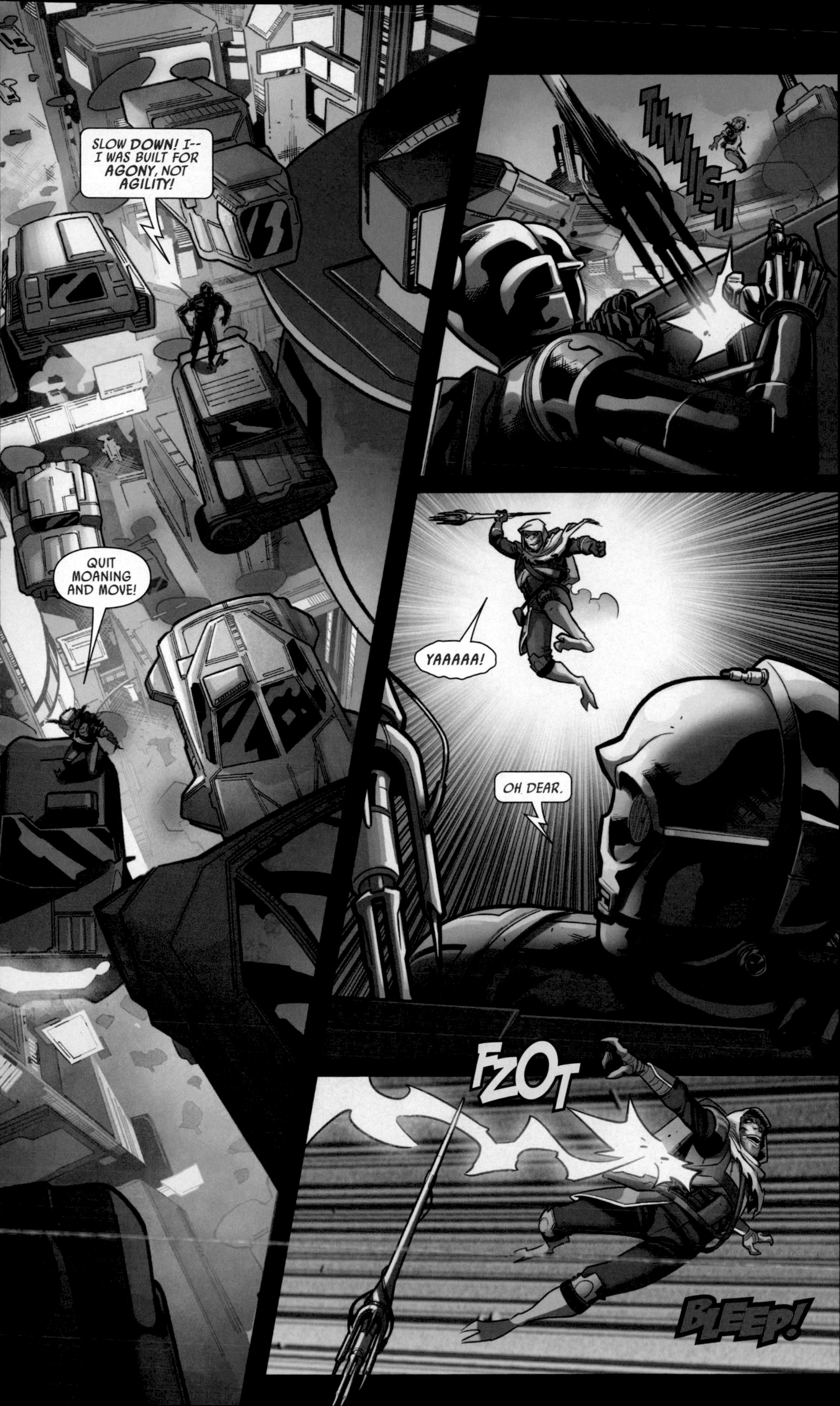
SLOW DOWN! I-- I WAS BUILT FOR AGONY, NOT AGILITY!
QUIT MOANING AND MOVE!
THWIIISH
YAAAAA!
OH DEAR.
FZOT
BLEEP!

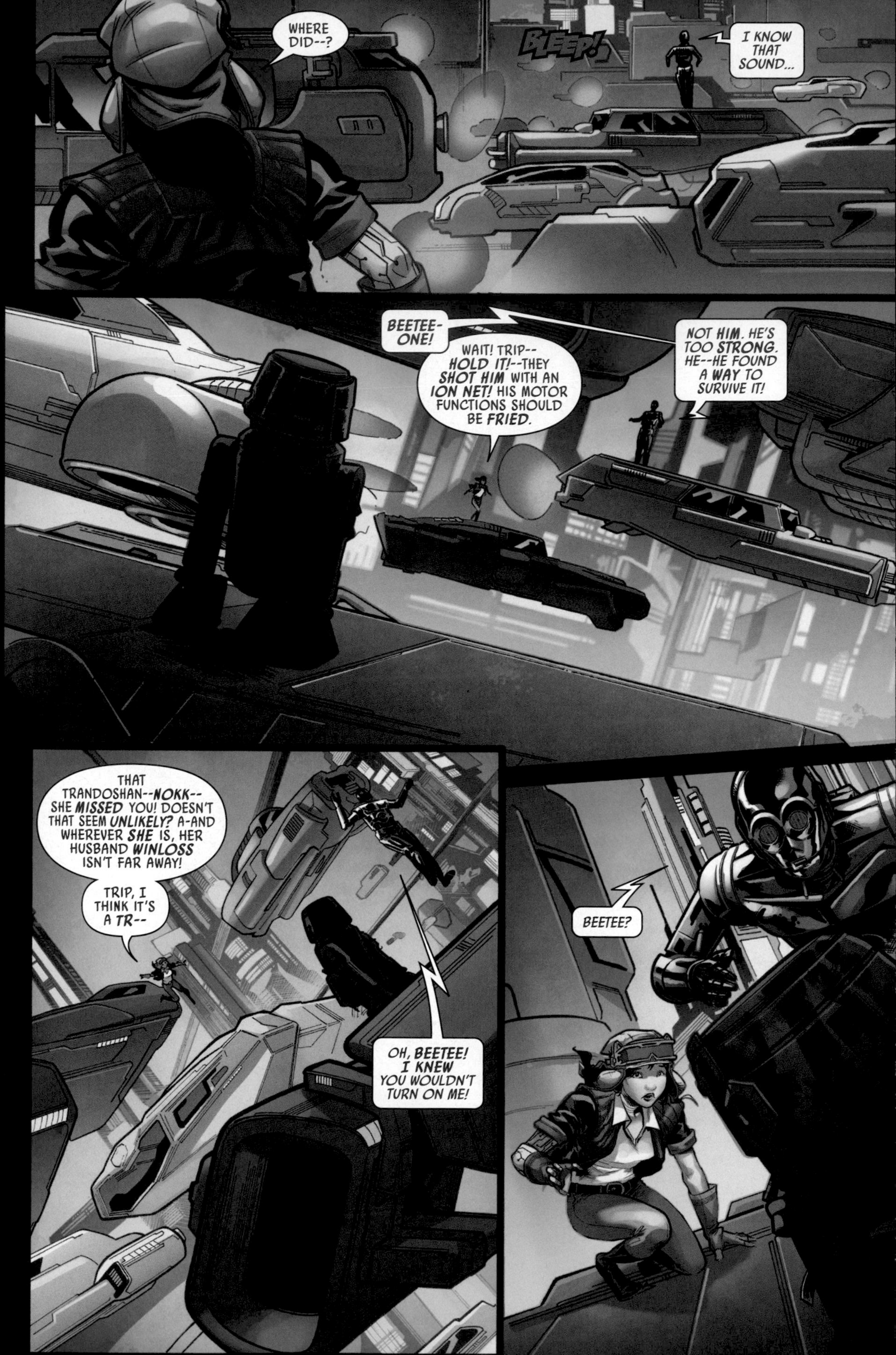
WHERE DID--?
BLEEP!
I KNOW THAT SOUND...
BEETEE-ONE!
WAIT! TRIP-- HOLD IT!--THEY SHOT HIM WITH AN ION NET! HIS MOTOR FUNCTIONS SHOULD BE FRIED.
NOT HIM. HE'S TOO STRONG. HE--HE FOUND A WAY TO SURVIVE IT!
THAT TRANDOSHAN--NOKK-- SHE MISSED YOU! DOESN'T THAT SEEM UNLIKELY? A-AND WHEREVER SHE IS, HER HUSBAND WINLOSS ISN'T FAR AWAY!
TRIP, I THINK IT'S A TR--
OH, BEETEE! I KNEW YOU WOULDN'T TURN ON ME!
BEETEE?

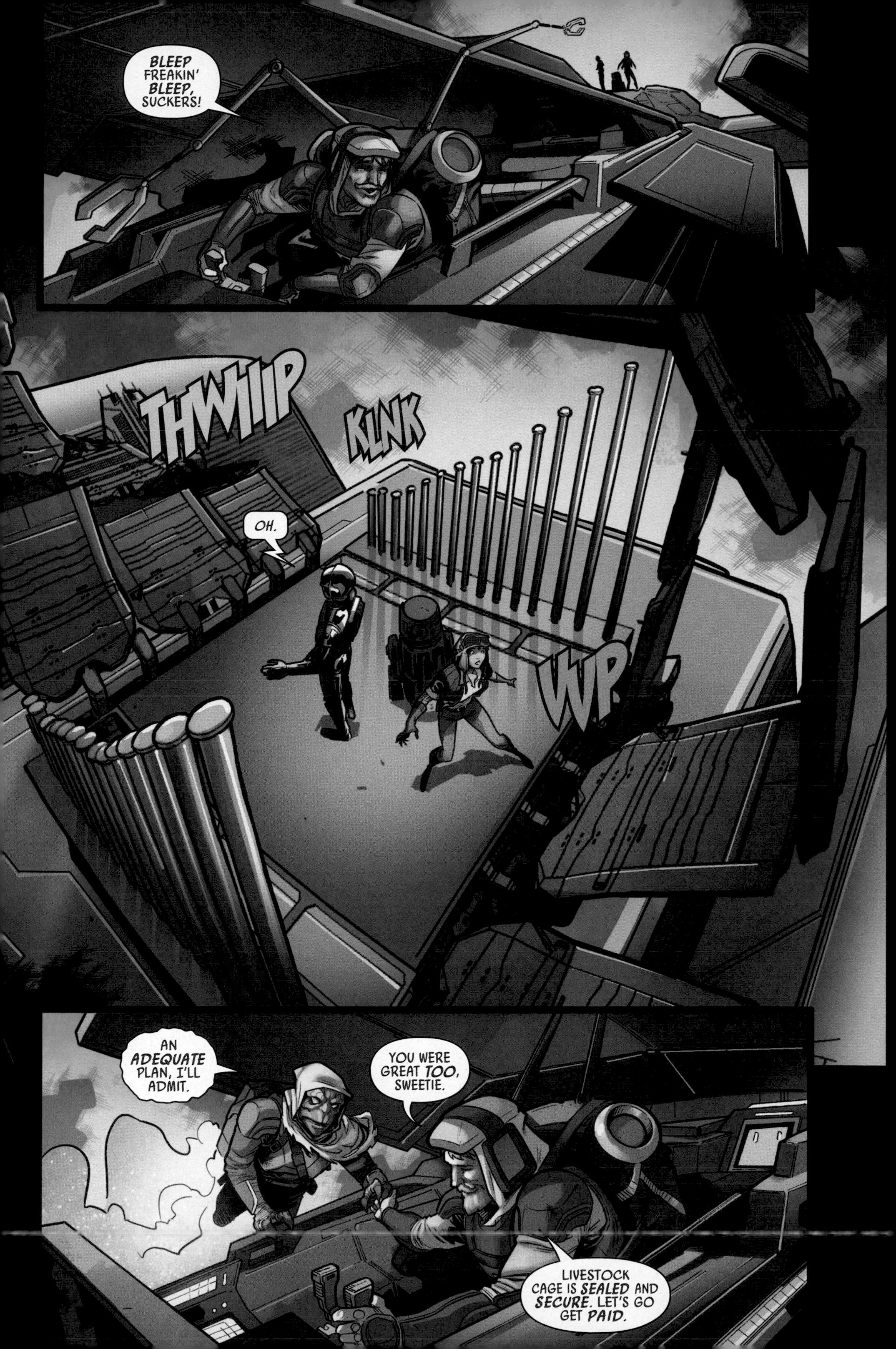
BLEEP FREAKIN' BLEEP, SUCKERS!
THWIIIP
KLNK
OH.
WP
AN ADEQUATE PLAN, I'LL ADMIT.
YOU WERE GREAT TOO, SWEETIE.
LIVESTOCK CAGE IS SEALED AND SECURE. LET'S GO GET PAID.

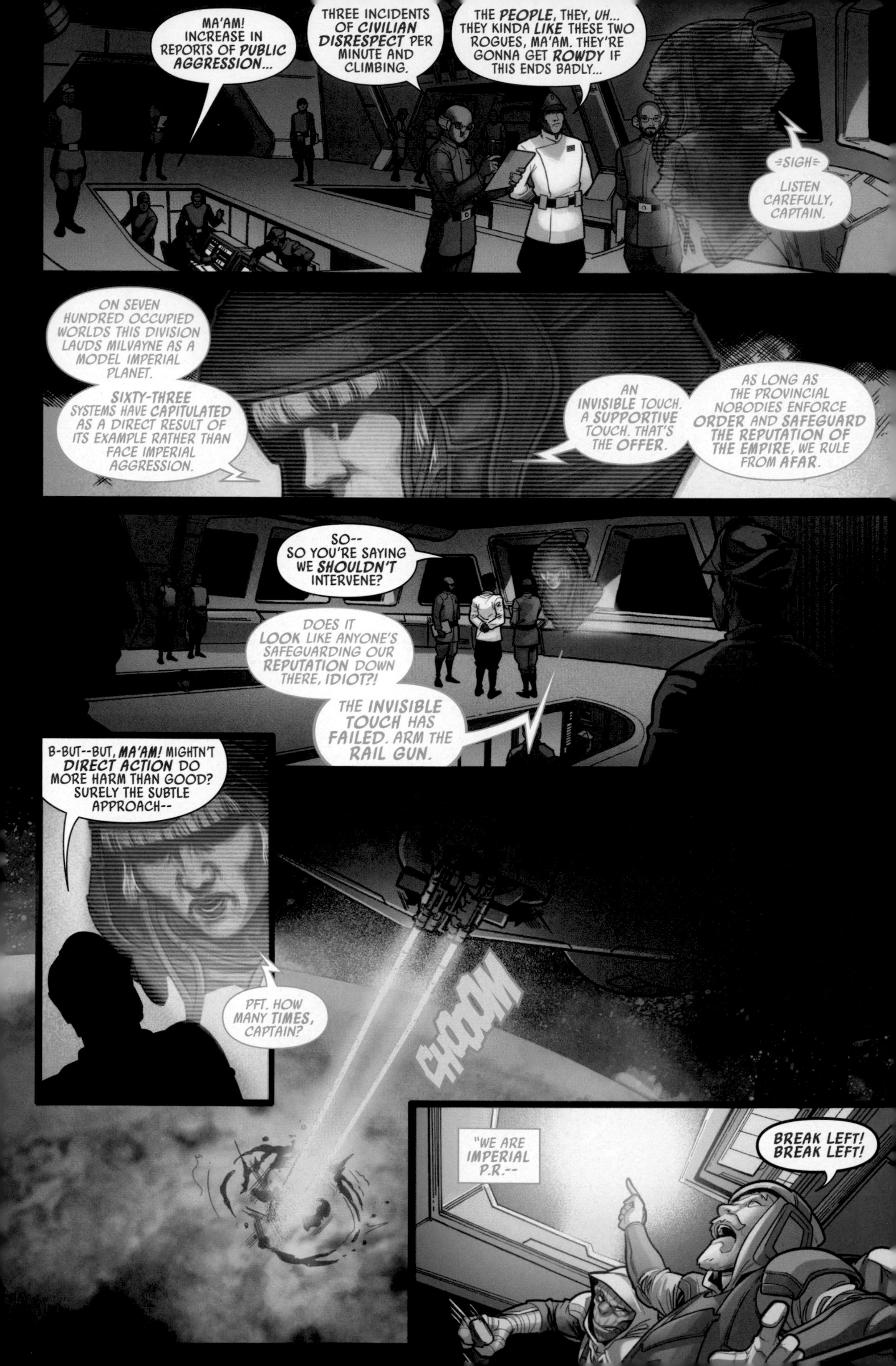
MA'AM! INCREASE IN REPORTS OF PUBLIC AGGRESSION...
THREE INCIDENTS OF CIVILIAN DISRESPECT PER MINUTE AND CLIMBING.
THE PEOPLE, THEY, UH... THEY KINDA LIKE THESE TWO ROGUES, MA'AM. THEY'RE GONNA GET ROWDY IF THIS ENDS BADLY...
=SIGH=
LISTEN CAREFULLY, CAPTAIN.
ON SEVEN HUNDRED OCCUPIED WORLDS THIS DIVISION LAUDS MILVAYNE AS A MODEL IMPERIAL PLANET.
SIXTY-THREE SYSTEMS HAVE CAPITULATED AS A DIRECT RESULT OF ITS EXAMPLE RATHER THAN FACE IMPERIAL AGGRESSION.
AN INVISIBLE TOUCH. A SUPPORTIVE TOUCH. THAT'S THE OFFER.
AS LONG AS THE PROVINCIAL NOBODIES ENFORCE ORDER AND SAFEGUARD THE REPUTATION OF THE EMPIRE, WE RULE FROM AFAR.
SO-- SO YOU'RE SAYING WE SHOULDN'T INTERVENE?
DOES IT LOOK LIKE ANYONE'S SAFEGUARDING OUR REPUTATION DOWN THERE, IDIOT?!
THE INVISIBLE TOUCH HAS FAILED. ARM THE RAIL GUN.
B-BUT--BUT, MA'AM! MIGHTN'T DIRECT ACTION DO MORE HARM THAN GOOD? SURELY THE SUBTLE APPROACH--
PFT. HOW MANY TIMES, CAPTAIN?
CHOOOM
"WE ARE IMPERIAL P.R.--
BREAK LEFT! BREAK LEFT!

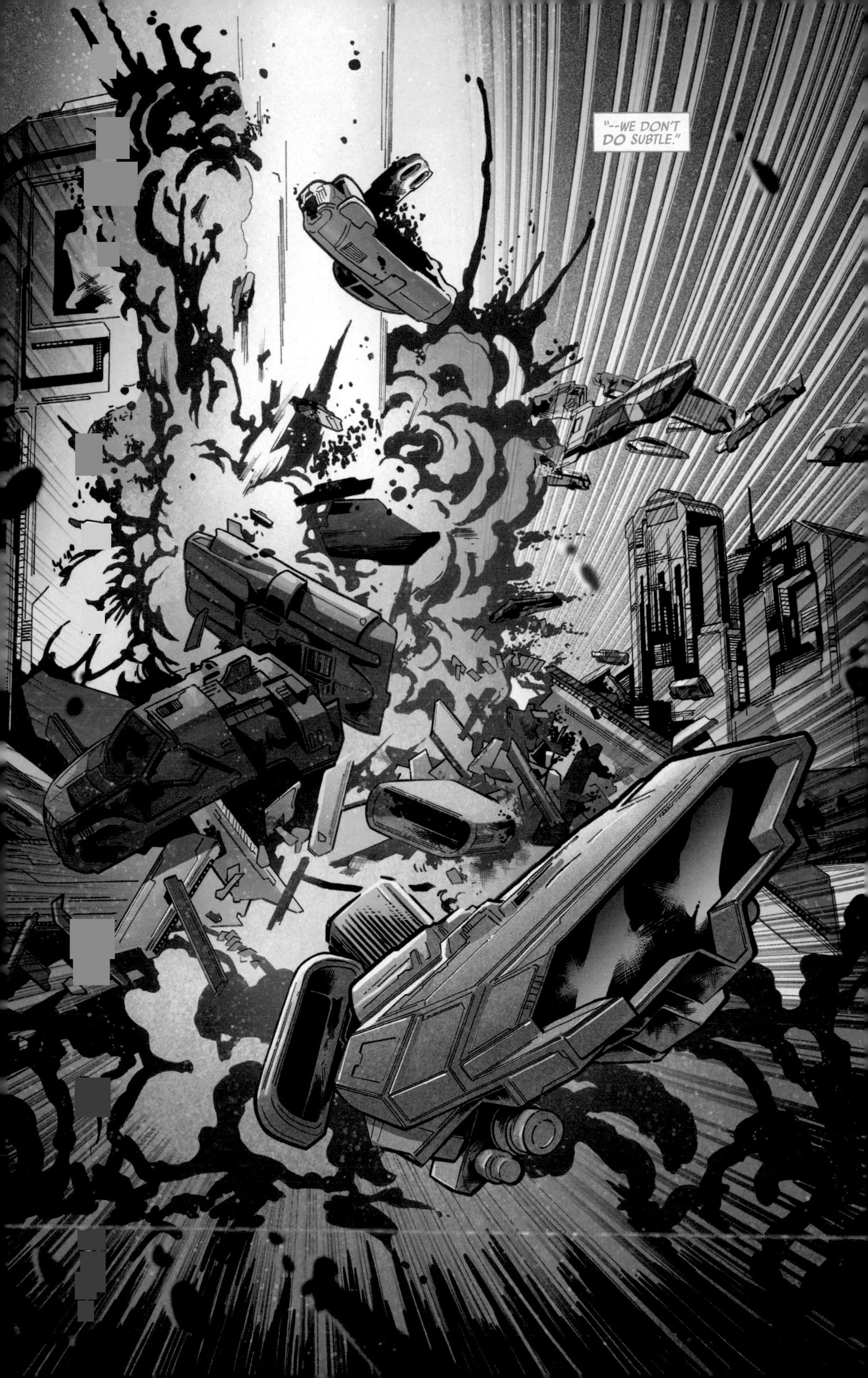
"--WE DON'T DO SUBTLE."

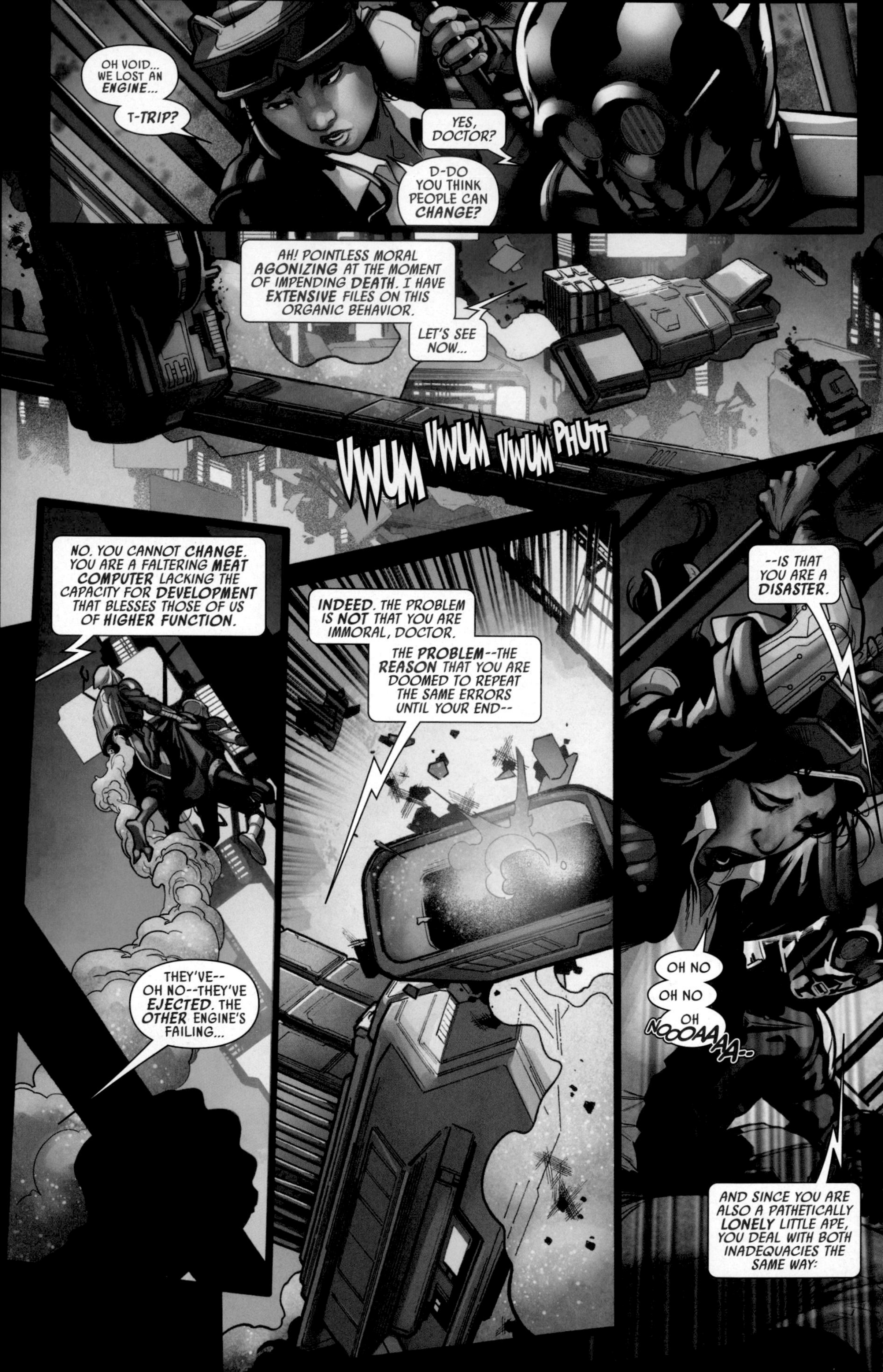
OH VOID... WE LOST AN ENGINE...
T-TRIP?
YES, DOCTOR?
D-DO YOU THINK PEOPLE CAN CHANGE?
AH! POINTLESS MORAL AGONIZING AT THE MOMENT OF IMPENDING DEATH. I HAVE EXTENSIVE FILES ON THIS ORGANIC BEHAVIOR.
LET'S SEE NOW...
VWUM VWUM VWUM PHUTT
NO. YOU CANNOT CHANGE. YOU ARE A FALTERING MEAT COMPUTER LACKING THE CAPACITY FOR DEVELOPMENT THAT BLESSES THOSE OF US OF HIGHER FUNCTION.
INDEED. THE PROBLEM IS NOT THAT YOU ARE IMMORAL, DOCTOR.
THE PROBLEM--THE REASON THAT YOU ARE DOOMED TO REPEAT THE SAME ERRORS UNTIL YOUR END--
--IS THAT YOU ARE A DISASTER.
THEY'VE-- OH NO--THEY'VE EJECTED. THE OTHER ENGINE'S FAILING...
OH NO
OH NO
OH NOOOAAAAA--
AND SINCE YOU ARE ALSO A PATHETICALLY LONELY LITTLE APE, YOU DEAL WITH BOTH INADEQUACIES THE SAME WAY:

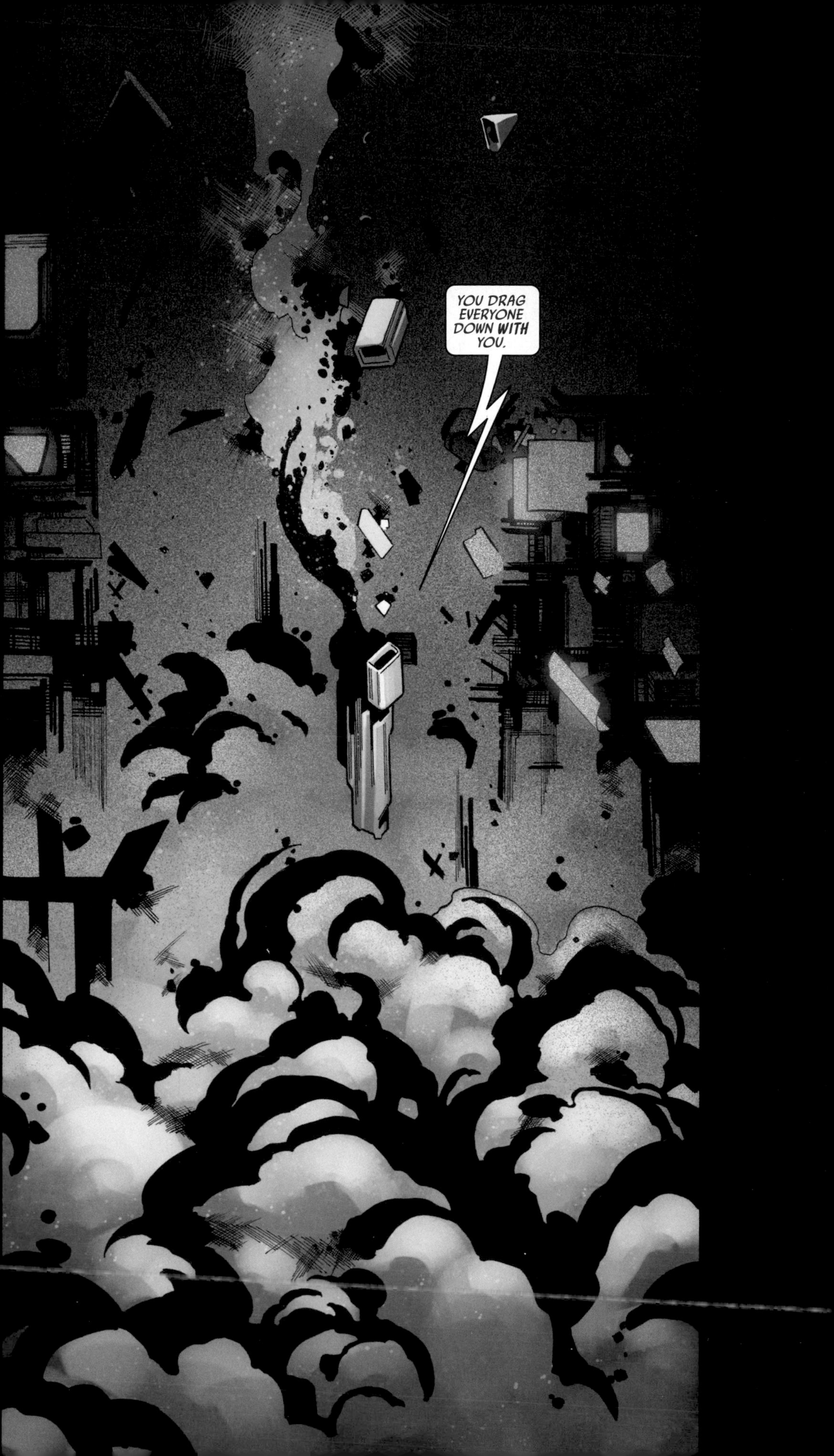
YOU DRAG EVERYONE DOWN WITH YOU.

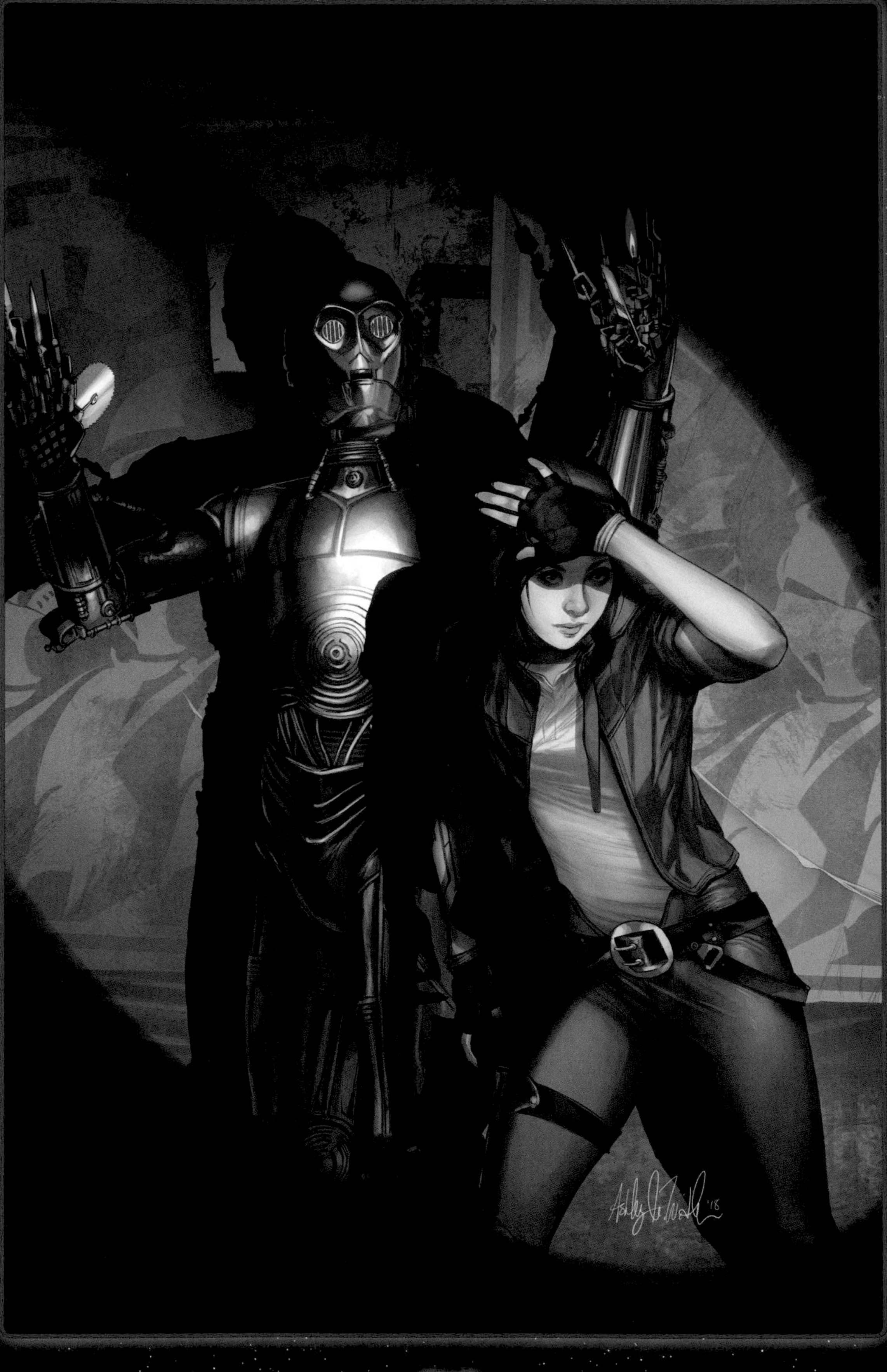

30

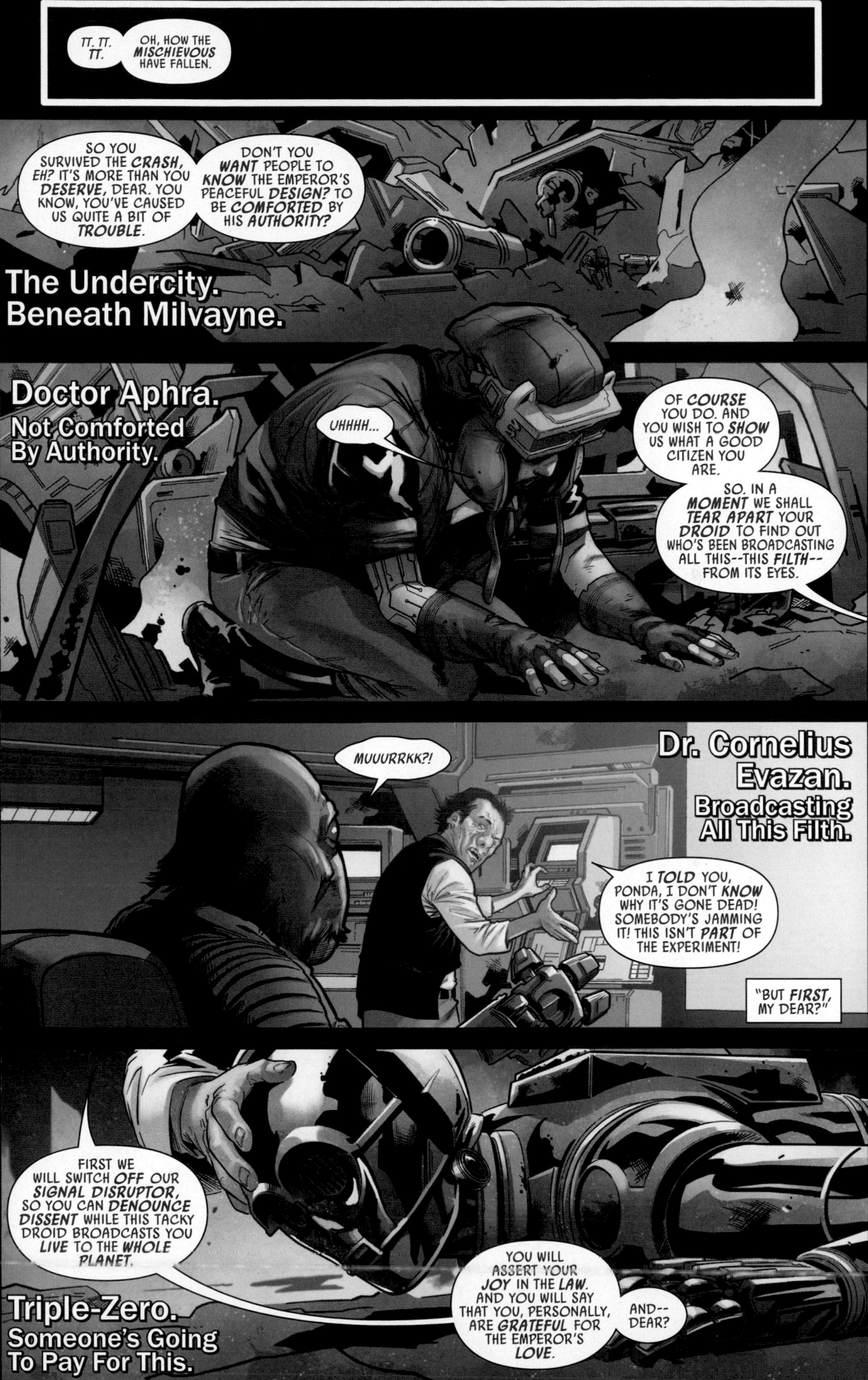
TT. TT. TT.
OH, HOW THE MISCHIEVOUS HAVE FALLEN.
SO YOU SURVIVED THE CRASH, EH? IT'S MORE THAN YOU DESERVE, DEAR. YOU KNOW, YOU'VE CAUSED US QUITE A BIT OF TROUBLE.
DON'T YOU WANT PEOPLE TO KNOW THE EMPEROR'S PEACEFUL DESIGN? TO BE COMFORTED BY HIS AUTHORITY?
The Undercity. Beneath Milvayne.
Doctor Aphra.
Not Comforted By Authority.
UHHHH...
OF COURSE YOU DO. AND YOU WISH TO SHOW US WHAT A GOOD CITIZEN YOU ARE.
SO, IN A MOMENT WE SHALL TEAR APART YOUR DROID TO FIND OUT WHO'S BEEN BROADCASTING ALL THIS--THIS FILTH--FROM ITS EYES.
Dr. Cornelius Evazan.
Broadcasting All This Filth.
MUUURRKK?!
I TOLD YOU, PONDA, I DON'T KNOW WHY IT'S GONE DEAD! SOMEBODY'S JAMMING IT! THIS ISN'T PART OF THE EXPERIMENT!
"BUT FIRST, MY DEAR?"
FIRST WE WILL SWITCH OFF OUR SIGNAL DISRUPTOR, SO YOU CAN DENOUNCE DISSENT WHILE THIS TACKY DROID BROADCASTS YOU LIVE TO THE WHOLE PLANET.
Triple-Zero.
Someone's Going To Pay For This.
YOU WILL ASSERT YOUR JOY IN THE LAW. AND YOU WILL SAY THAT YOU, PERSONALLY, ARE GRATEFUL FOR THE EMPEROR'S LOVE.
AND--DEAR?

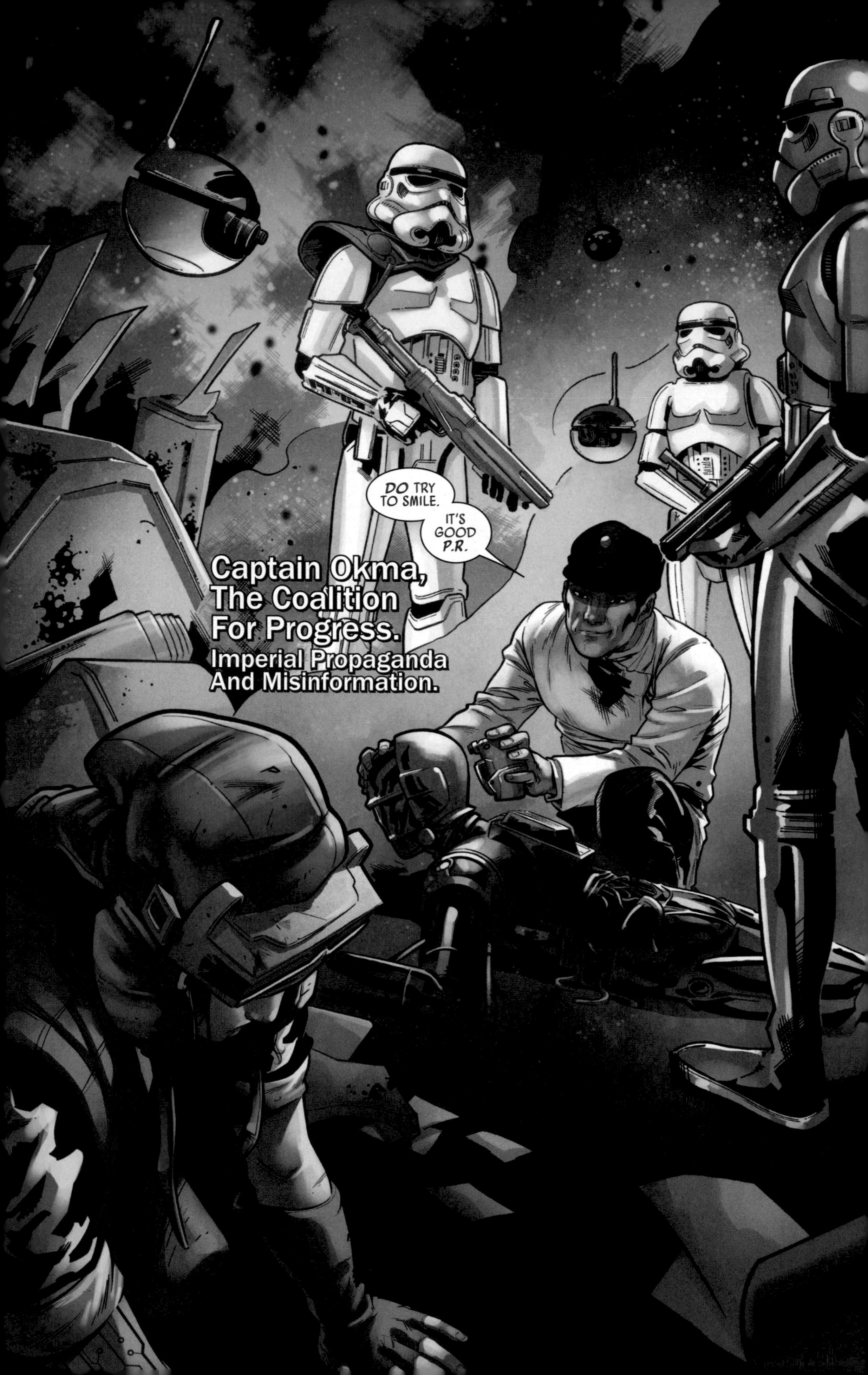
DO TRY TO SMILE.
IT'S GOOD P.R.
Captain Okma, The Coalition For Progress.
Imperial Propaganda And Misinformation.

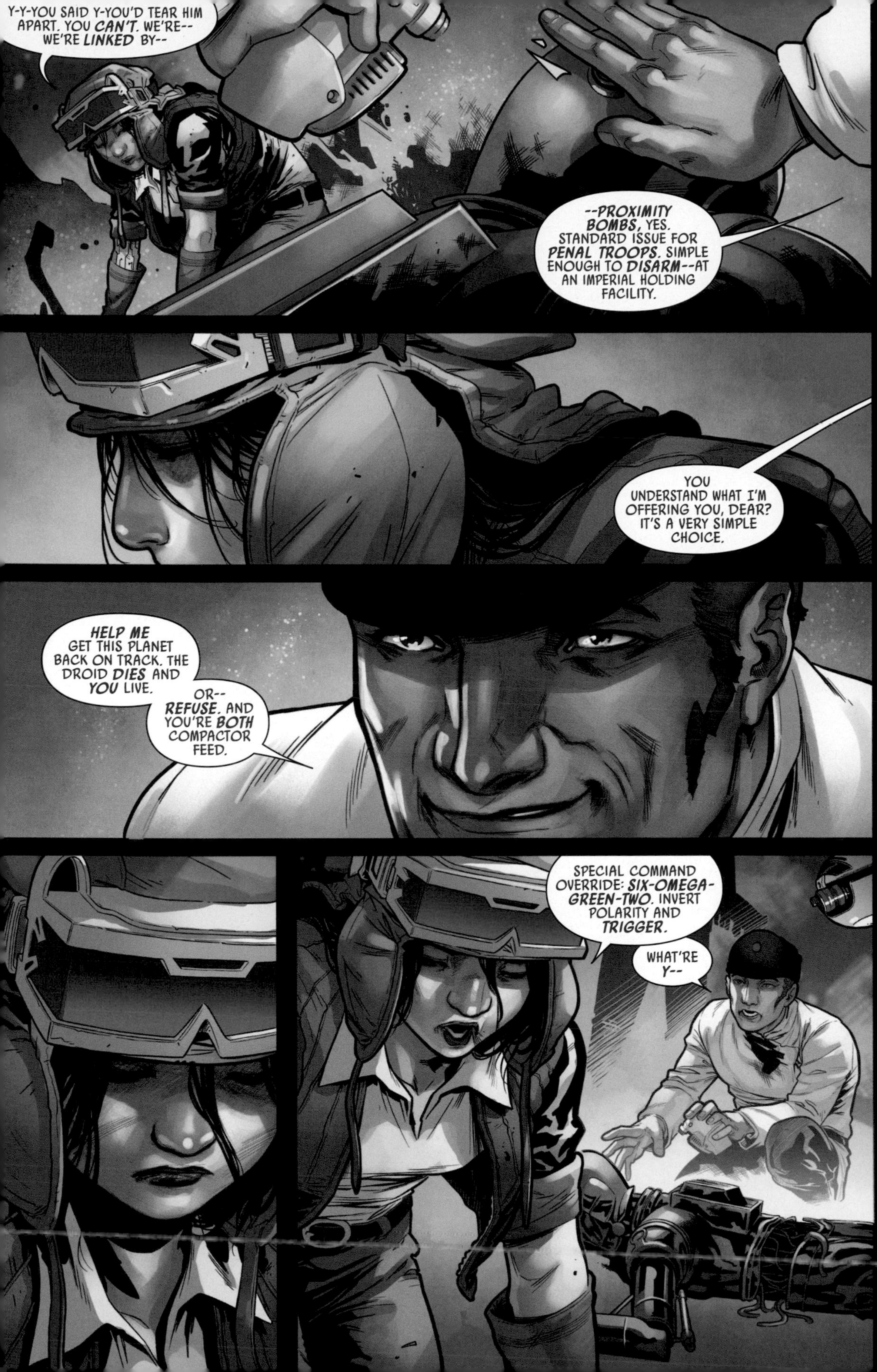
Y-Y-YOU SAID Y-YOU'D TEAR HIM APART. YOU CAN'T. WE'RE-- WE'RE LINKED BY--
--PROXIMITY BOMBS, YES. STANDARD ISSUE FOR PENAL TROOPS. SIMPLE ENOUGH TO DISARM--AT AN IMPERIAL HOLDING FACILITY.
YOU UNDERSTAND WHAT I'M OFFERING YOU, DEAR? IT'S A VERY SIMPLE CHOICE.
HELP ME GET THIS PLANET BACK ON TRACK. THE DROID DIES AND YOU LIVE.
OR-- REFUSE. AND YOU'RE BOTH COMPACTOR FEED.
SPECIAL COMMAND OVERRIDE: SIX-OMEGA-GREEN-TWO. INVERT POLARITY AND TRIGGER.
WHAT'RE Y--

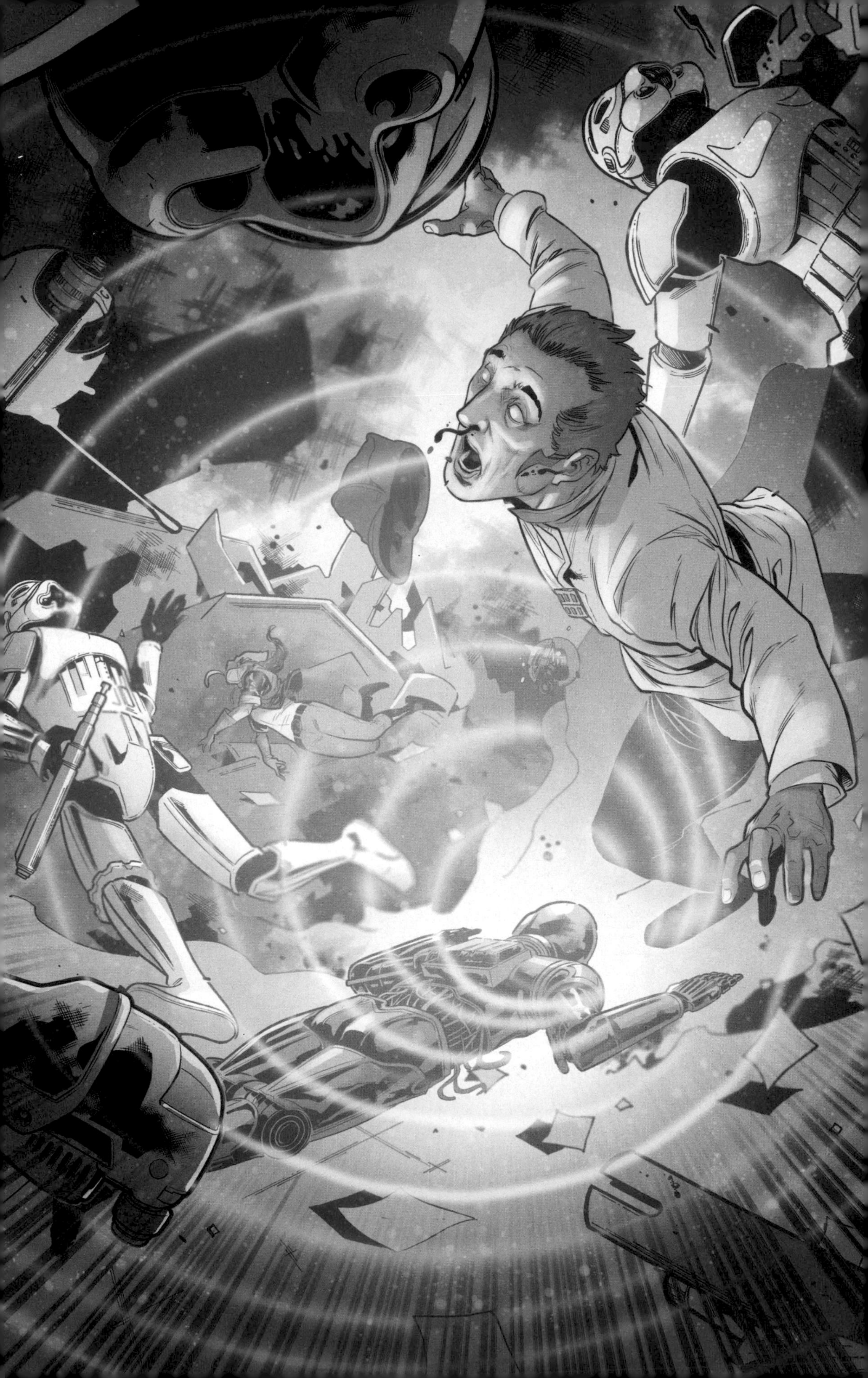

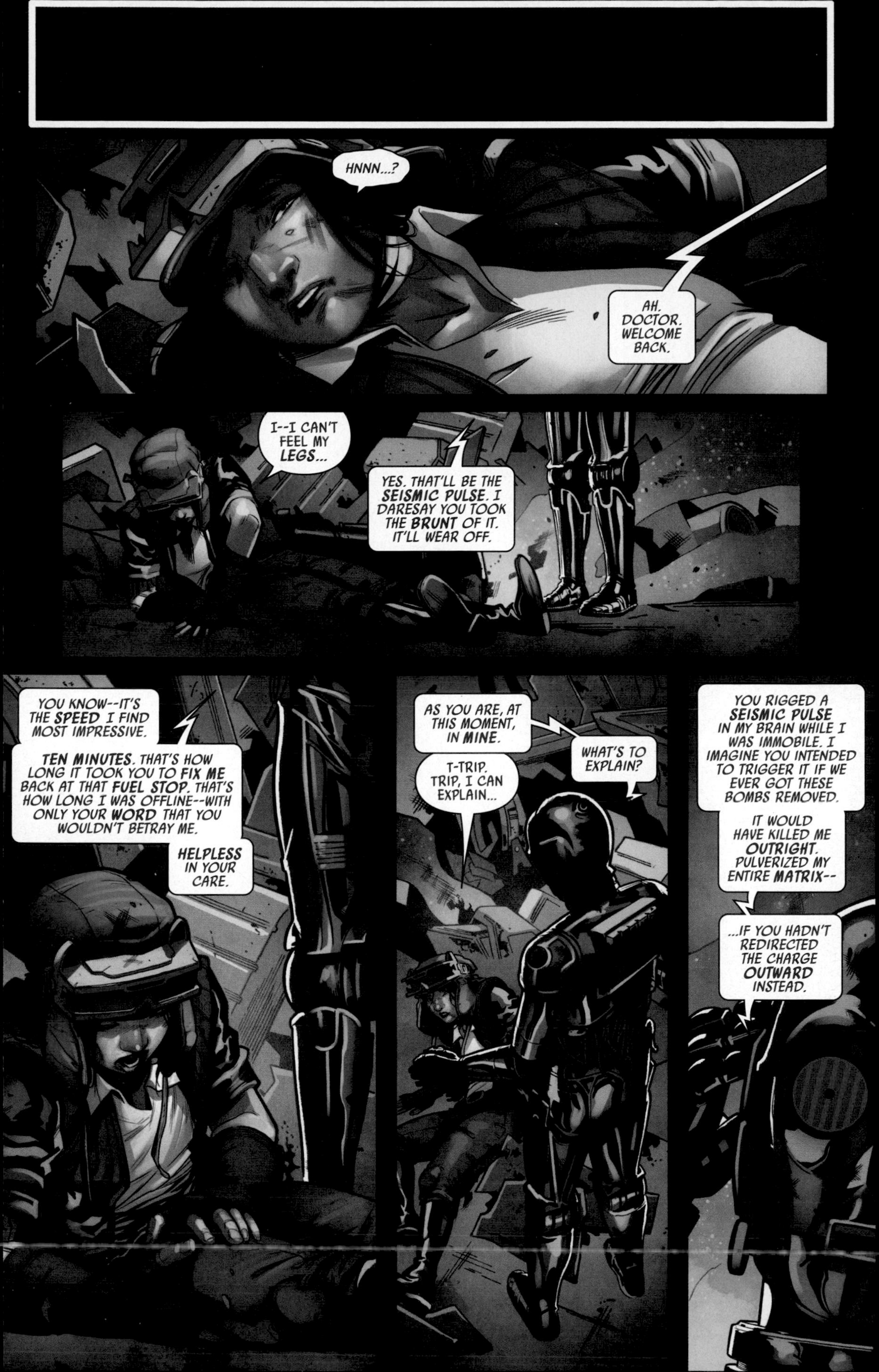
HNNN...?
AH. DOCTOR. WELCOME BACK.
I--I CAN'T FEEL MY LEGS...
YES. THAT'LL BE THE SEISMIC PULSE. I DARESAY YOU TOOK THE BRUNT OF IT. IT'LL WEAR OFF.
YOU KNOW--IT'S THE SPEED I FIND MOST IMPRESSIVE.
TEN MINUTES. THAT'S HOW LONG IT TOOK YOU TO FIX ME BACK AT THAT FUEL STOP. THAT'S HOW LONG I WAS OFFLINE--WITH ONLY YOUR WORD THAT YOU WOULDN'T BETRAY ME.
HELPLESS IN YOUR CARE.
AS YOU ARE, AT THIS MOMENT, IN MINE.
T-TRIP. TRIP, I CAN EXPLAIN...
WHAT'S TO EXPLAIN?
YOU RIGGED A SEISMIC PULSE IN MY BRAIN WHILE I WAS IMMOBILE. I IMAGINE YOU INTENDED TO TRIGGER IT IF WE EVER GOT THESE BOMBS REMOVED.
IT WOULD HAVE KILLED ME OUTRIGHT. PULVERIZED MY ENTIRE MATRIX--
...IF YOU HADN'T REDIRECTED THE CHARGE OUTWARD INSTEAD.

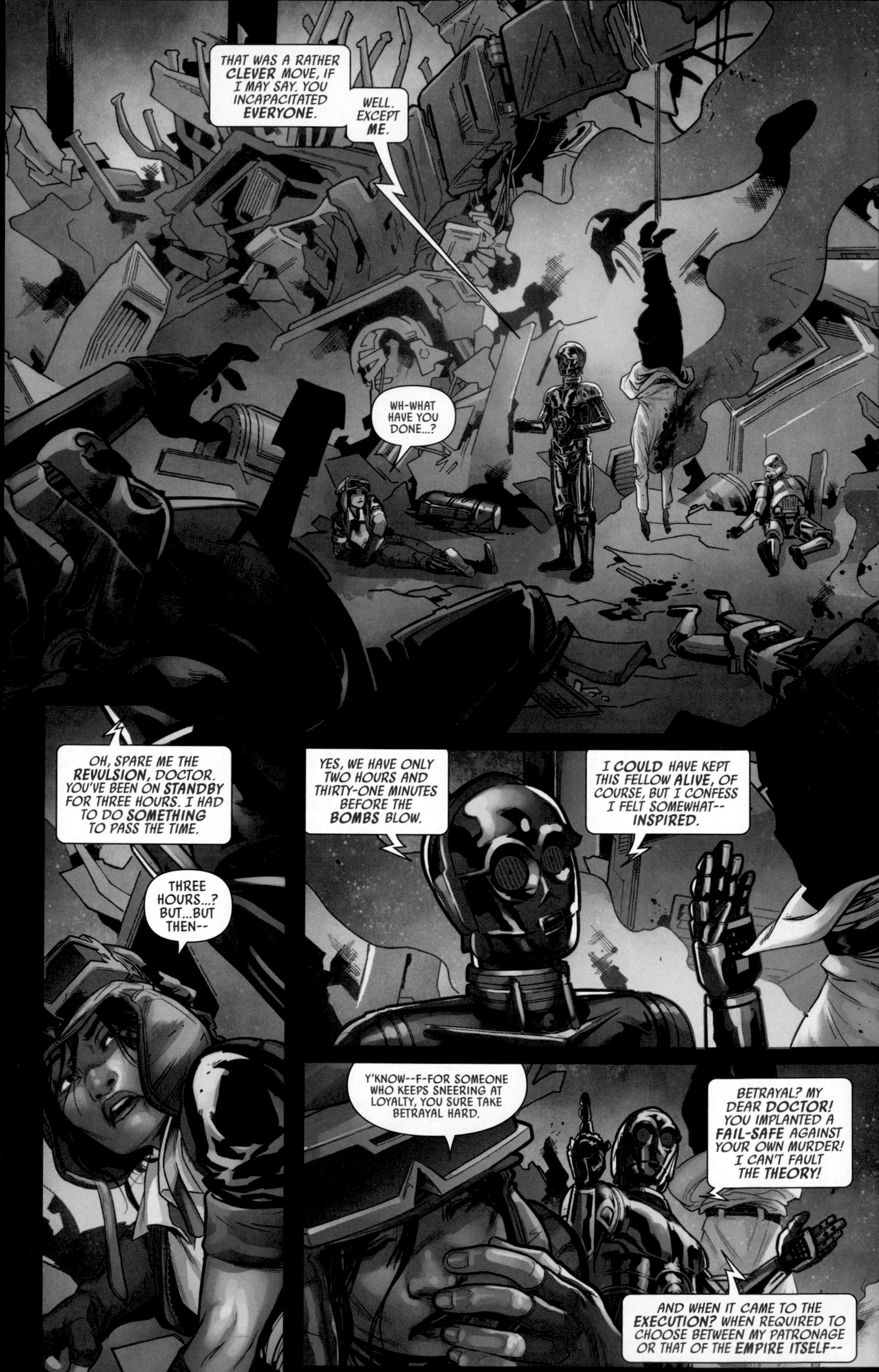
THAT WAS A RATHER CLEVER MOVE, IF I MAY SAY. YOU INCAPACITATED EVERYONE.
WELL. EXCEPT ME.
WH-WHAT HAVE YOU DONE...?
OH, SPARE ME THE REVULSION, DOCTOR. YOU'VE BEEN ON STANDBY FOR THREE HOURS. I HAD TO DO SOMETHING TO PASS THE TIME.
THREE HOURS...? BUT...BUT THEN--
YES, WE HAVE ONLY TWO HOURS AND THIRTY-ONE MINUTES BEFORE THE BOMBS BLOW.
I COULD HAVE KEPT THIS FELLOW ALIVE, OF COURSE, BUT I CONFESS I FELT SOMEWHAT--INSPIRED.
Y'KNOW--F-FOR SOMEONE WHO KEEPS SNEERING AT LOYALTY, YOU SURE TAKE BETRAYAL HARD.
BETRAYAL? MY DEAR DOCTOR! YOU IMPLANTED A FAIL-SAFE AGAINST YOUR OWN MURDER! I CAN'T FAULT THE THEORY!
AND WHEN IT CAME TO THE EXECUTION? WHEN REQUIRED TO CHOOSE BETWEEN MY PATRONAGE OR THAT OF THE EMPIRE ITSELF--

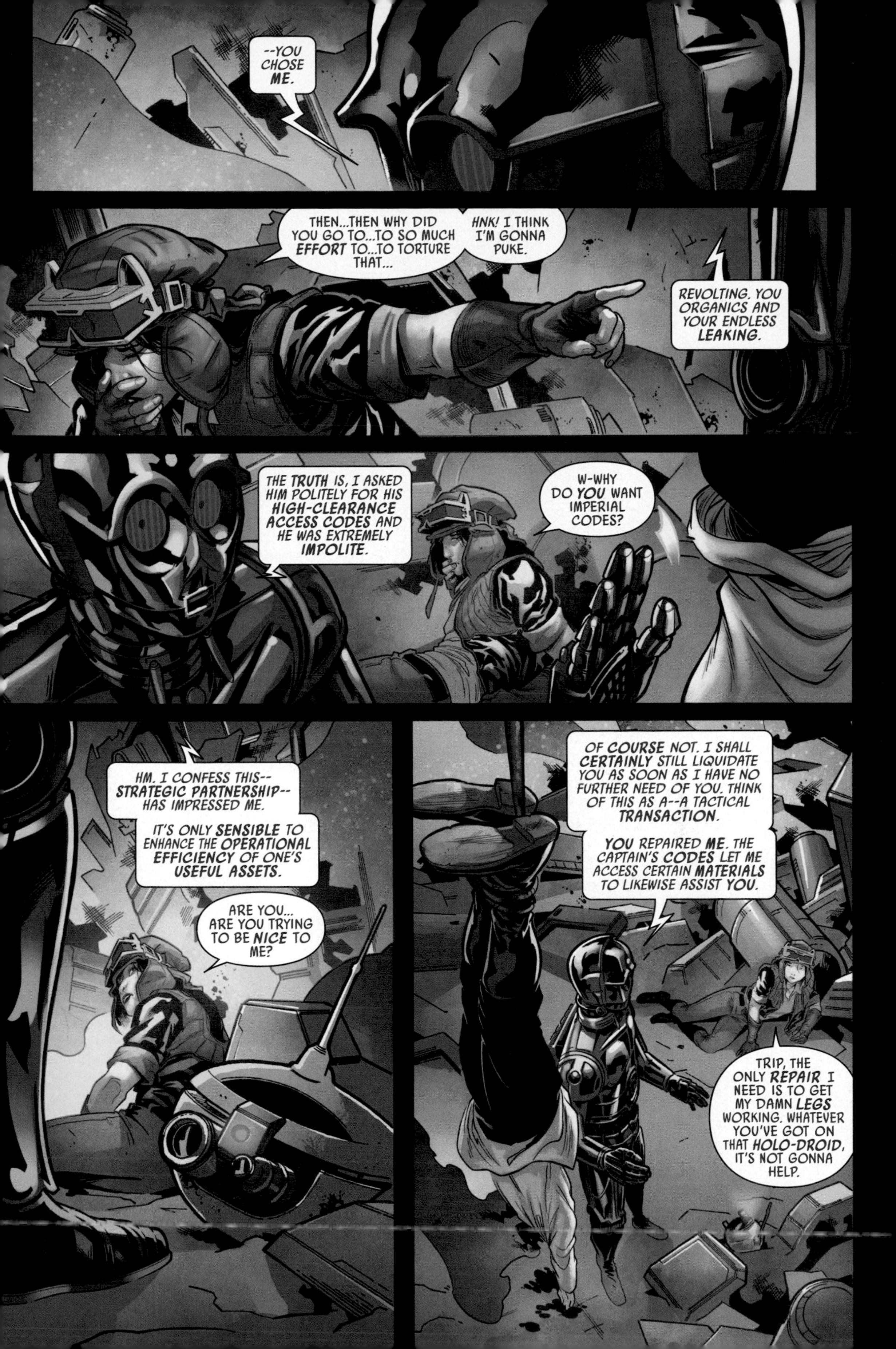
--YOU CHOSE ME.
THEN...THEN WHY DID YOU GO TO...TO SO MUCH EFFORT TO...TO TORTURE THAT...
HNK! I THINK I'M GONNA PUKE.
REVOLTING. YOU ORGANICS AND YOUR ENDLESS LEAKING.
THE TRUTH IS, I ASKED HIM POLITELY FOR HIS HIGH-CLEARANCE ACCESS CODES AND HE WAS EXTREMELY IMPOLITE.
W-WHY DO YOU WANT IMPERIAL CODES?
HM. I CONFESS THIS--STRATEGIC PARTNERSHIP--HAS IMPRESSED ME.
IT'S ONLY SENSIBLE TO ENHANCE THE OPERATIONAL EFFICIENCY OF ONE'S USEFUL ASSETS.
ARE YOU... ARE YOU TRYING TO BE NICE TO ME?
OF COURSE NOT. I SHALL CERTAINLY STILL LIQUIDATE YOU AS SOON AS I HAVE NO FURTHER NEED OF YOU. THINK OF THIS AS A--A TACTICAL TRANSACTION.
YOU REPAIRED ME. THE CAPTAIN'S CODES LET ME ACCESS CERTAIN MATERIALS TO LIKEWISE ASSIST YOU.
TRIP, THE ONLY REPAIR I NEED IS TO GET MY DAMN LEGS WORKING. WHATEVER YOU'VE GOT ON THAT HOLO-DROID, IT'S NOT GONNA HELP.

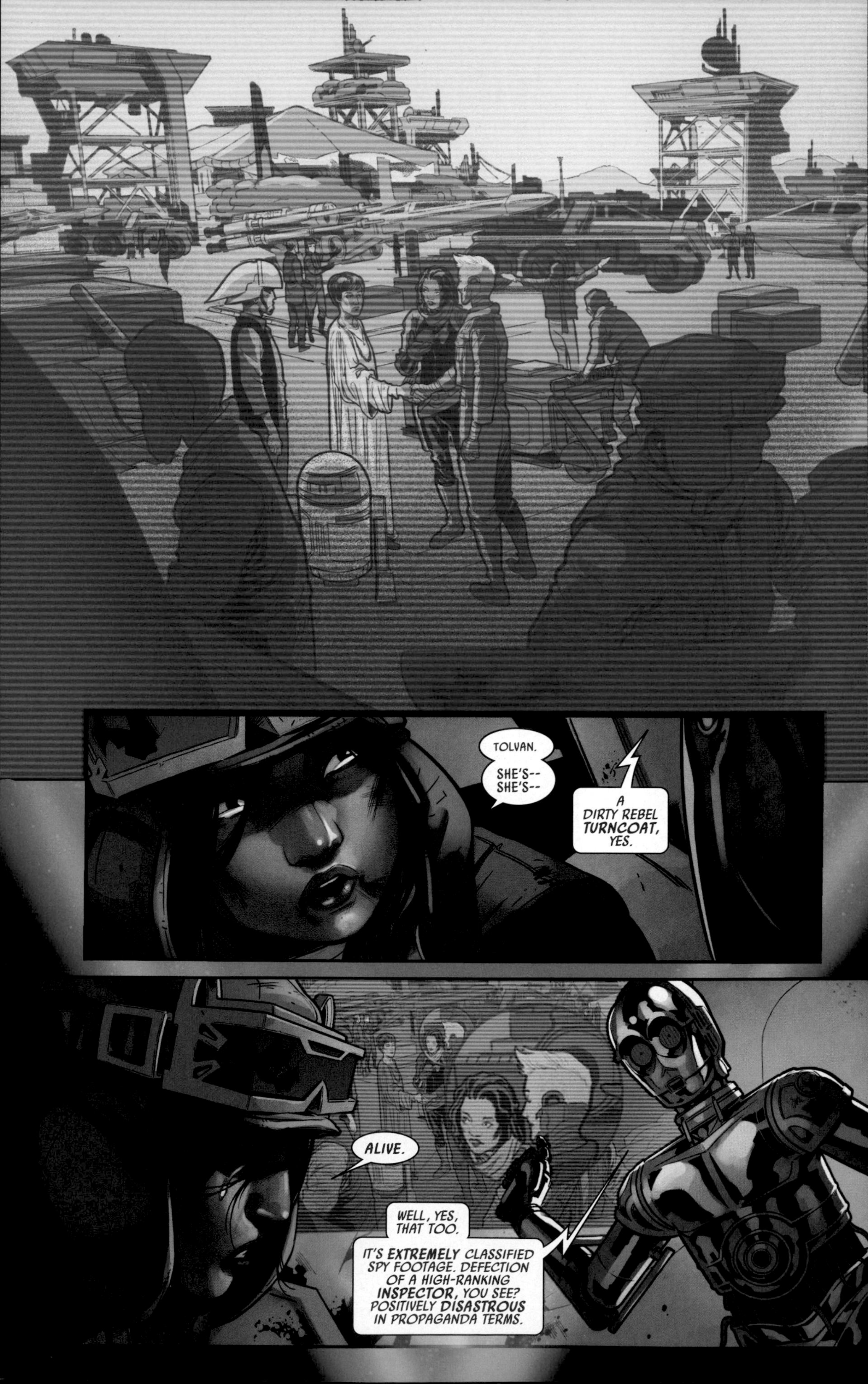
TOLVAN.
SHE'S-- SHE'S--
A DIRTY REBEL TURNCOAT, YES.
ALIVE.
WELL, YES, THAT TOO.
IT'S EXTREMELY CLASSIFIED SPY FOOTAGE. DEFECTION OF A HIGH-RANKING INSPECTOR, YOU SEE? POSITIVELY DISASTROUS IN PROPAGANDA TERMS.

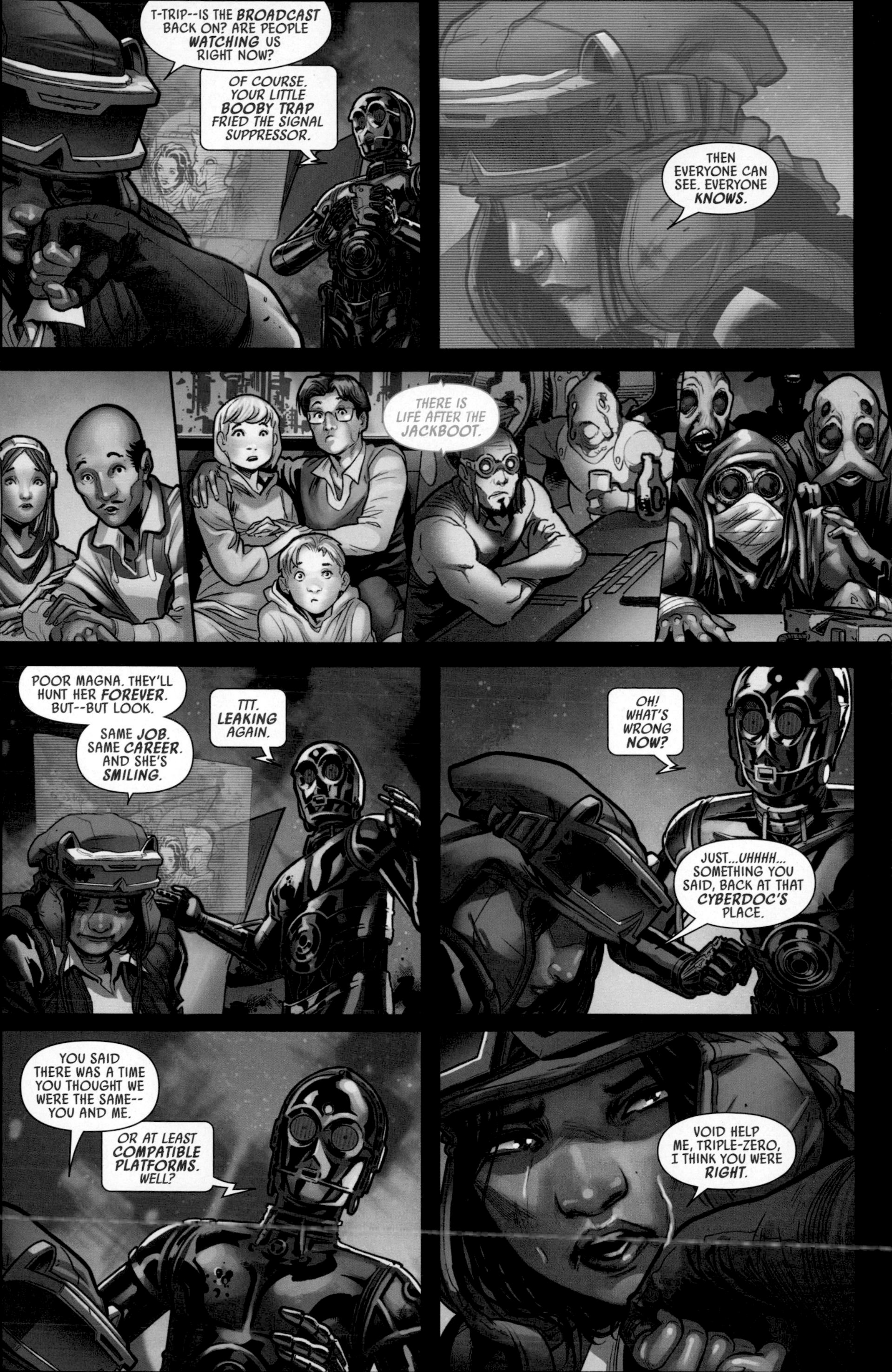

T-TRIP--IS THE BROADCAST BACK ON? ARE PEOPLE WATCHING US RIGHT NOW?
OF COURSE. YOUR LITTLE BOOBY TRAP FRIED THE SIGNAL SUPPRESSOR.
THEN EVERYONE CAN SEE. EVERYONE KNOWS.
THERE IS LIFE AFTER THE JACKBOOT.
POOR MAGNA. THEY'LL HUNT HER FOREVER. BUT--BUT LOOK.
SAME JOB. SAME CAREER. AND SHE'S SMILING.
TTT. LEAKING AGAIN.
OH! WHAT'S WRONG NOW?
JUST...UHHHH... SOMETHING YOU SAID, BACK AT THAT CYBERDOC'S PLACE.
YOU SAID THERE WAS A TIME YOU THOUGHT WE WERE THE SAME-- YOU AND ME.
OR AT LEAST COMPATIBLE PLATFORMS. WELL?
VOID HELP ME, TRIPLE-ZERO, I THINK YOU WERE RIGHT.

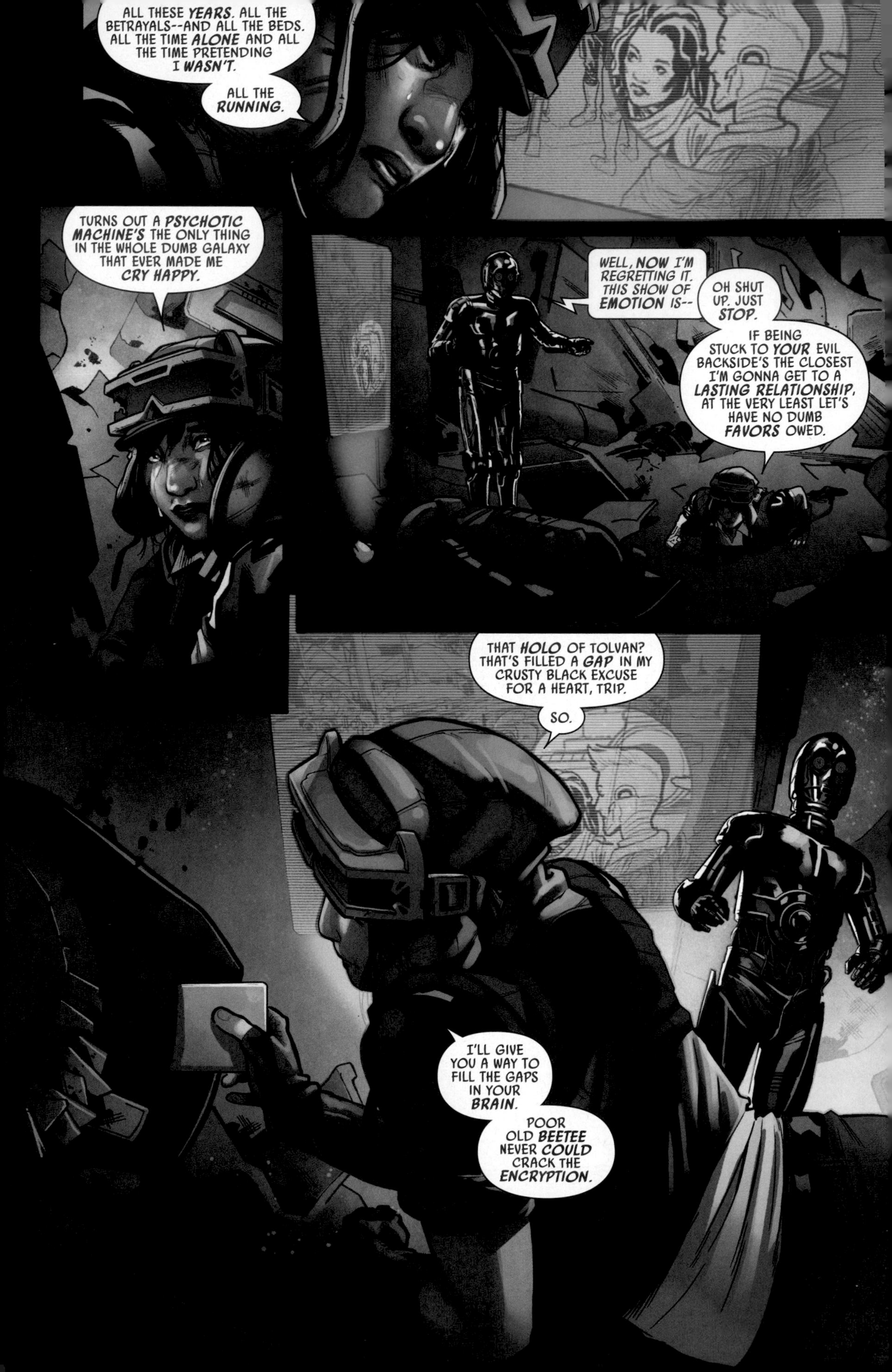
ALL THESE YEARS. ALL THE BETRAYALS--AND ALL THE BEDS. ALL THE TIME ALONE AND ALL THE TIME PRETENDING I WASN'T.
ALL THE RUNNING.
TURNS OUT A PSYCHOTIC MACHINE'S THE ONLY THING IN THE WHOLE DUMB GALAXY THAT EVER MADE ME CRY HAPPY.
WELL, NOW I'M REGRETTING IT. THIS SHOW OF EMOTION IS--
OH SHUT UP. JUST STOP.
IF BEING STUCK TO YOUR EVIL BACKSIDE'S THE CLOSEST I'M GONNA GET TO A LASTING RELATIONSHIP, AT THE VERY LEAST LET'S HAVE NO DUMB FAVORS OWED.
THAT HOLO OF TOLVAN? THAT'S FILLED A GAP IN MY CRUSTY BLACK EXCUSE FOR A HEART, TRIP.
SO.
I'LL GIVE YOU A WAY TO FILL THE GAPS IN YOUR BRAIN.
POOR OLD BEETEE NEVER COULD CRACK THE ENCRYPTION.

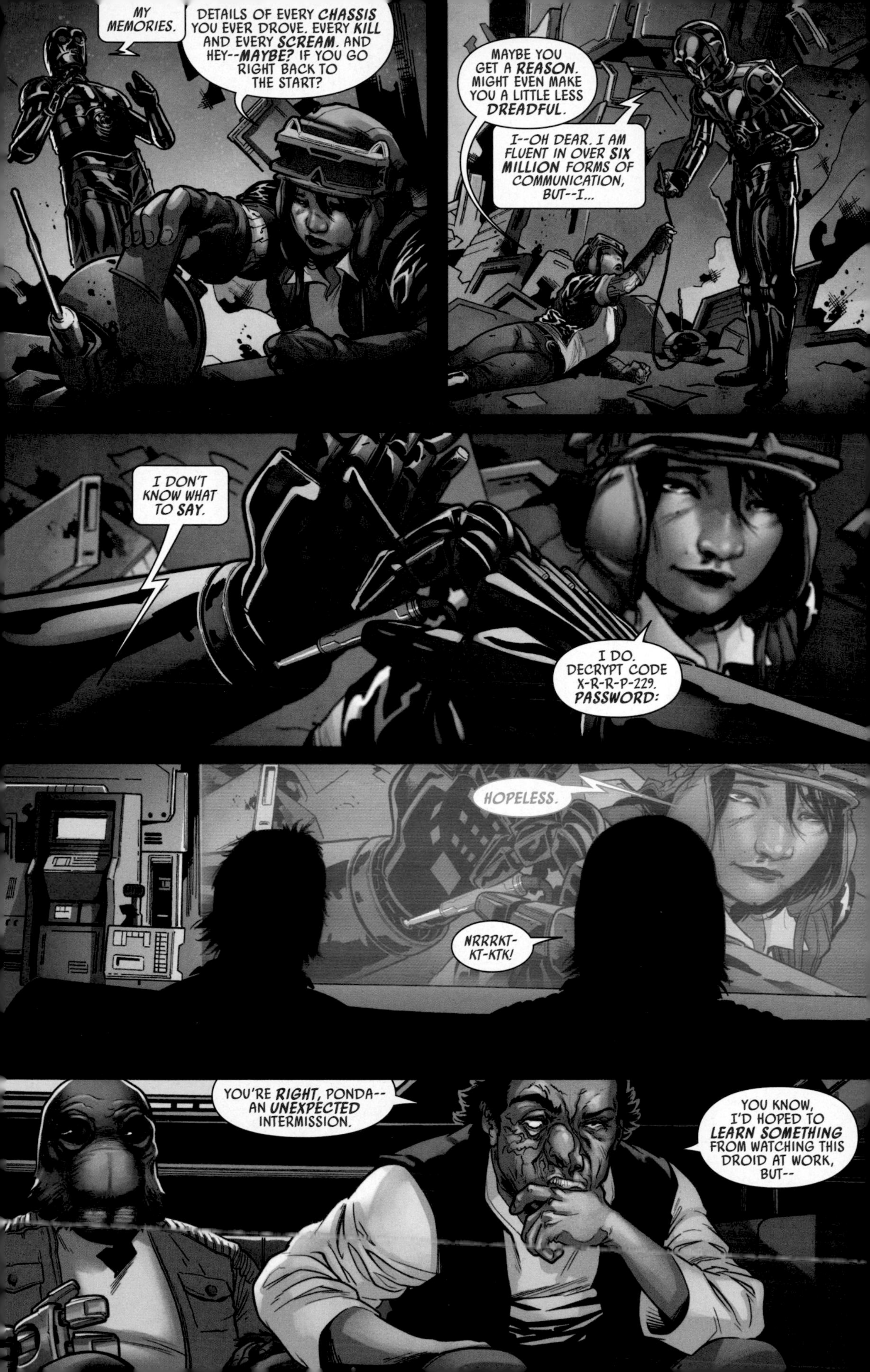
MY MEMORIES.
DETAILS OF EVERY CHASSIS YOU EVER DROVE. EVERY KILL AND EVERY SCREAM. AND HEY--MAYBE? IF YOU GO RIGHT BACK TO THE START?
MAYBE YOU GET A REASON. MIGHT EVEN MAKE YOU A LITTLE LESS DREADFUL.
I--OH DEAR. I AM FLUENT IN OVER SIX MILLION FORMS OF COMMUNICATION, BUT--I...
I DON'T KNOW WHAT TO SAY.
I DO. DECRYPT CODE X-R-R-P-229. PASSWORD:
HOPELESS.
NRRRKT-KT-KTK!
YOU'RE RIGHT, PONDA--AN UNEXPECTED INTERMISSION.
YOU KNOW, I'D HOPED TO LEARN SOMETHING FROM WATCHING THIS DROID AT WORK, BUT--

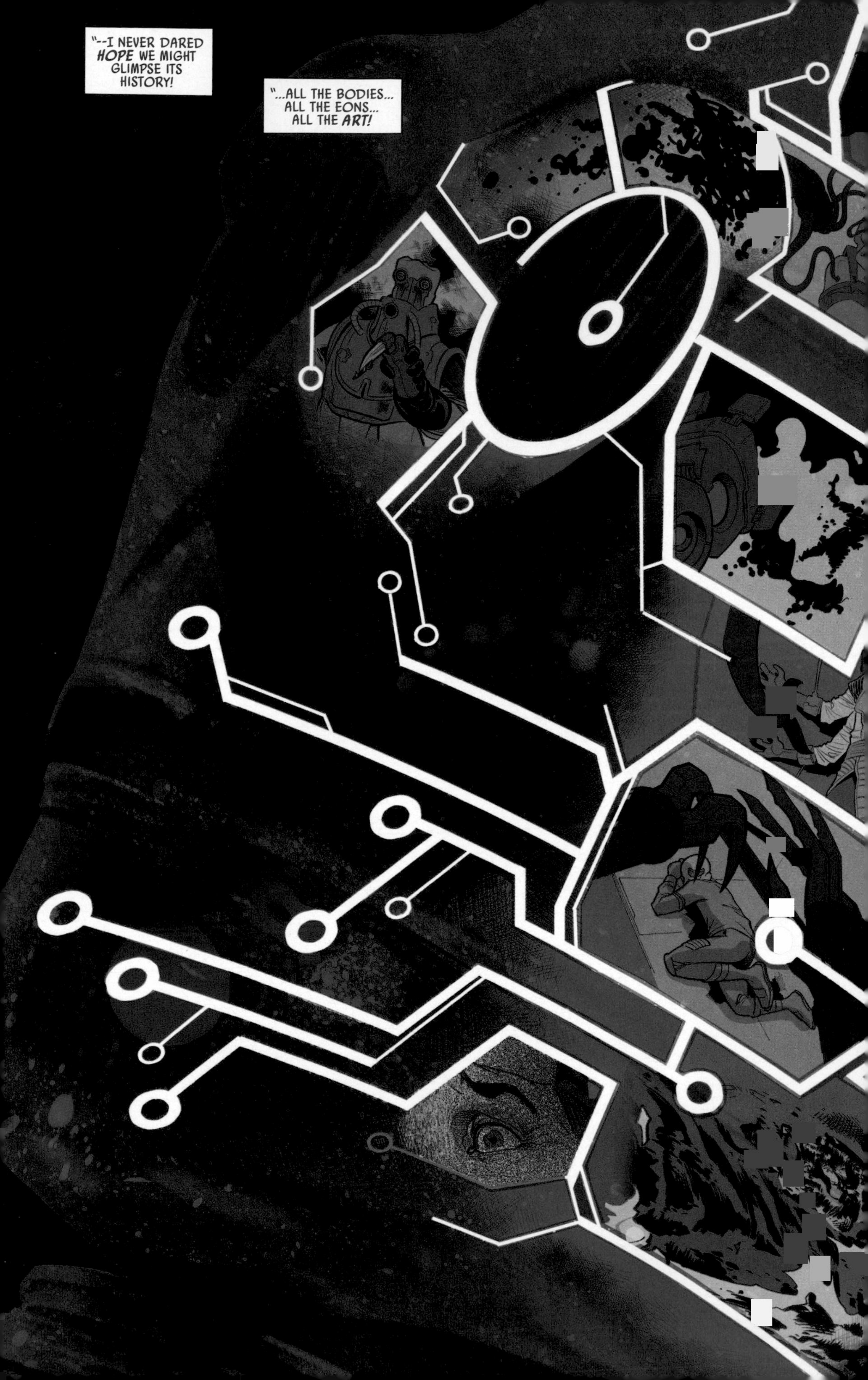
"--I NEVER DARED HOPE WE MIGHT GLIMPSE ITS HISTORY!
"...ALL THE BODIES... ALL THE EONS... ALL THE ART!

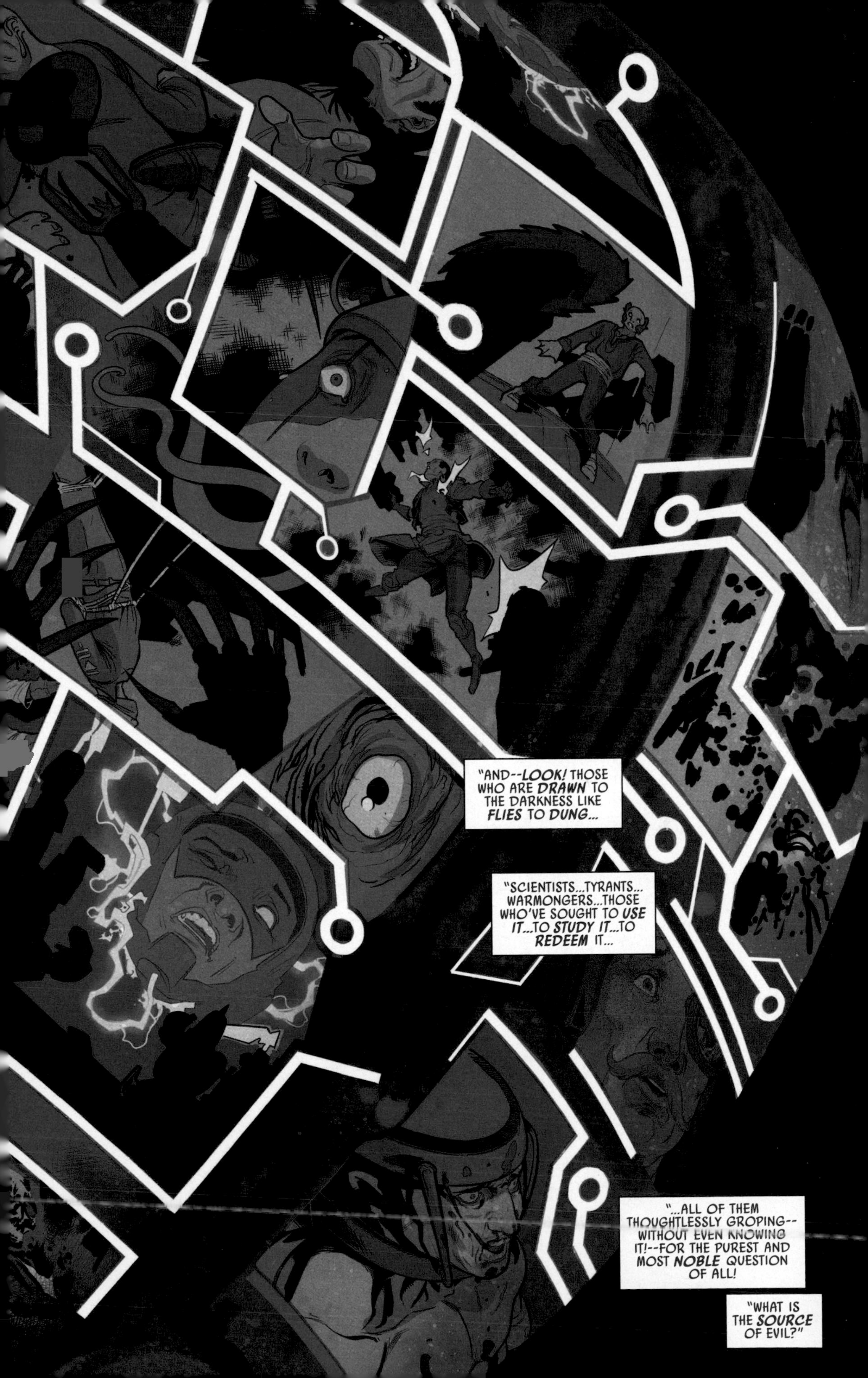
"AND--LOOK! THOSE WHO ARE DRAWN TO THE DARKNESS LIKE FLIES TO DUNG...
"SCIENTISTS...TYRANTS...WARMONGERS...THOSE WHO'VE SOUGHT TO USE IT...TO STUDY IT...TO REDEEM IT...
"...ALL OF THEM THOUGHTLESSLY GROPING--WITHOUT EVEN KNOWING IT!--FOR THE PUREST AND MOST NOBLE QUESTION OF ALL!
"WHAT IS THE SOURCE OF EVIL?"

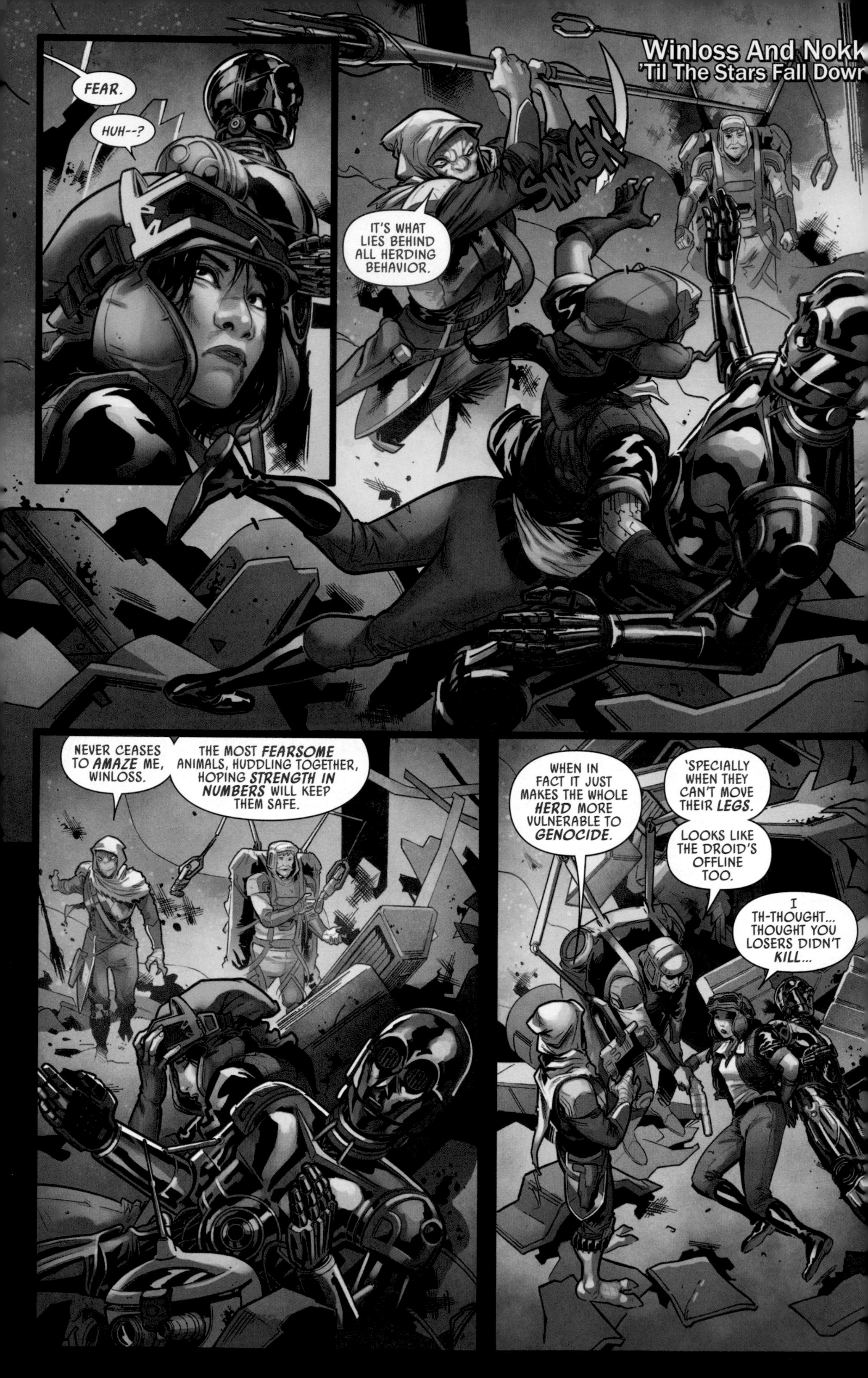
FEAR.
HUH--?
IT'S WHAT LIES BEHIND ALL HERDING BEHAVIOR.
SMACK!
NEVER CEASES TO AMAZE ME, WINLOSS.
THE MOST FEARSOME ANIMALS, HUDDLING TOGETHER, HOPING STRENGTH IN NUMBERS WILL KEEP THEM SAFE.
WHEN IN FACT IT JUST MAKES THE WHOLE HERD MORE VULNERABLE TO GENOCIDE.
'SPECIALLY WHEN THEY CAN'T MOVE THEIR LEGS.
LOOKS LIKE THE DROID'S OFFLINE TOO.
I TH-THOUGHT... THOUGHT YOU LOSERS DIDN'T KILL...

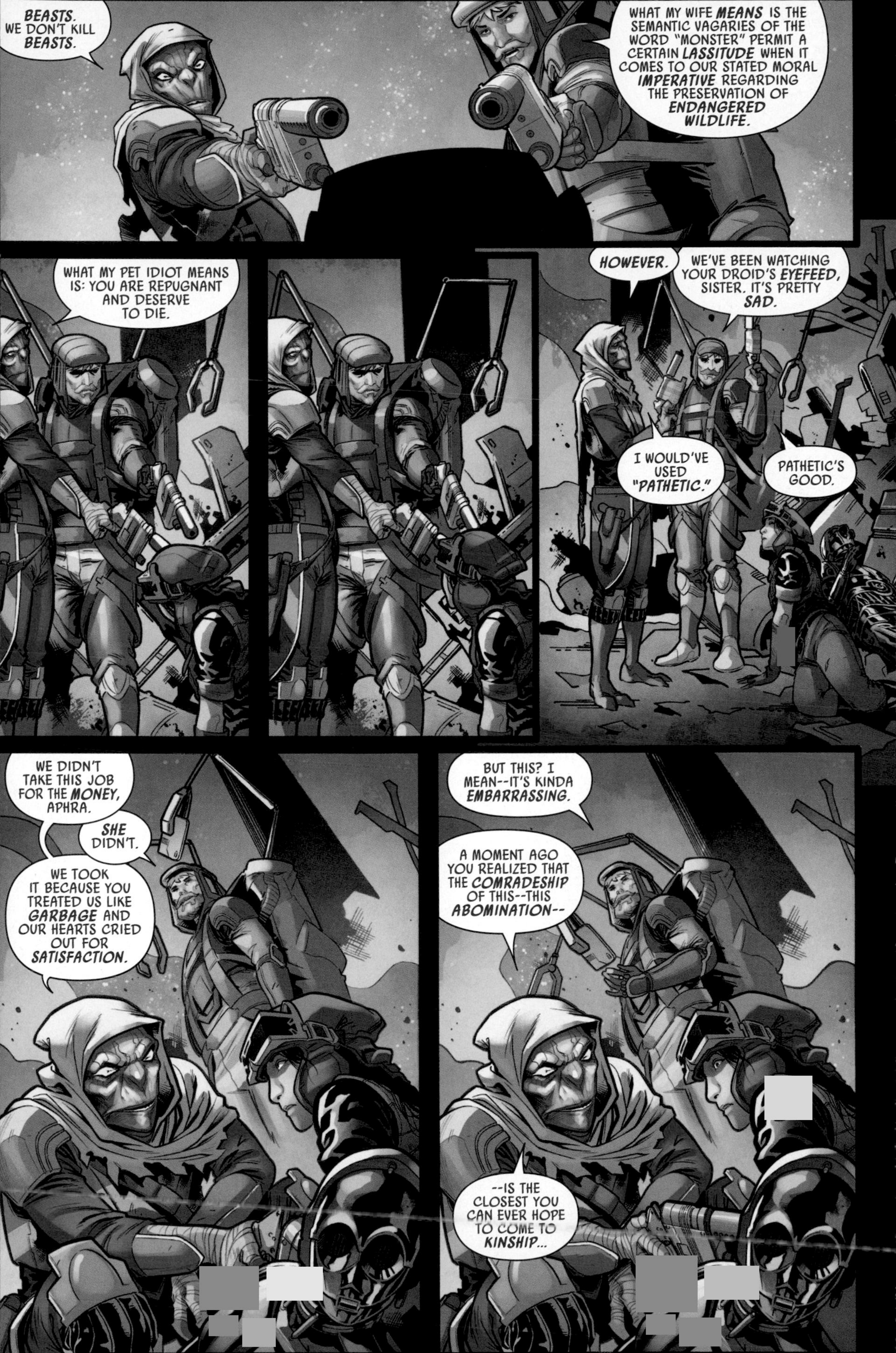
BEASTS. WE DON'T KILL BEASTS.
WHAT MY WIFE MEANS IS THE SEMANTIC VAGARIES OF THE WORD "MONSTER" PERMIT A CERTAIN LASSITUDE WHEN IT COMES TO OUR STATED MORAL IMPERATIVE REGARDING THE PRESERVATION OF ENDANGERED WILDLIFE.
WHAT MY PET IDIOT MEANS IS: YOU ARE REPUGNANT AND DESERVE TO DIE.
HOWEVER.
WE'VE BEEN WATCHING YOUR DROID'S EYEFEED, SISTER. IT'S PRETTY SAD.
I WOULD'VE USED "PATHETIC."
PATHETIC'S GOOD.
WE DIDN'T TAKE THIS JOB FOR THE MONEY, APHRA.
SHE DIDN'T.
WE TOOK IT BECAUSE YOU TREATED US LIKE GARBAGE AND OUR HEARTS CRIED OUT FOR SATISFACTION.
BUT THIS? I MEAN--IT'S KINDA EMBARRASSING.
A MOMENT AGO YOU REALIZED THAT THE COMRADESHIP OF THIS--THIS ABOMINATION--
--IS THE CLOSEST YOU CAN EVER HOPE TO COME TO KINSHIP...

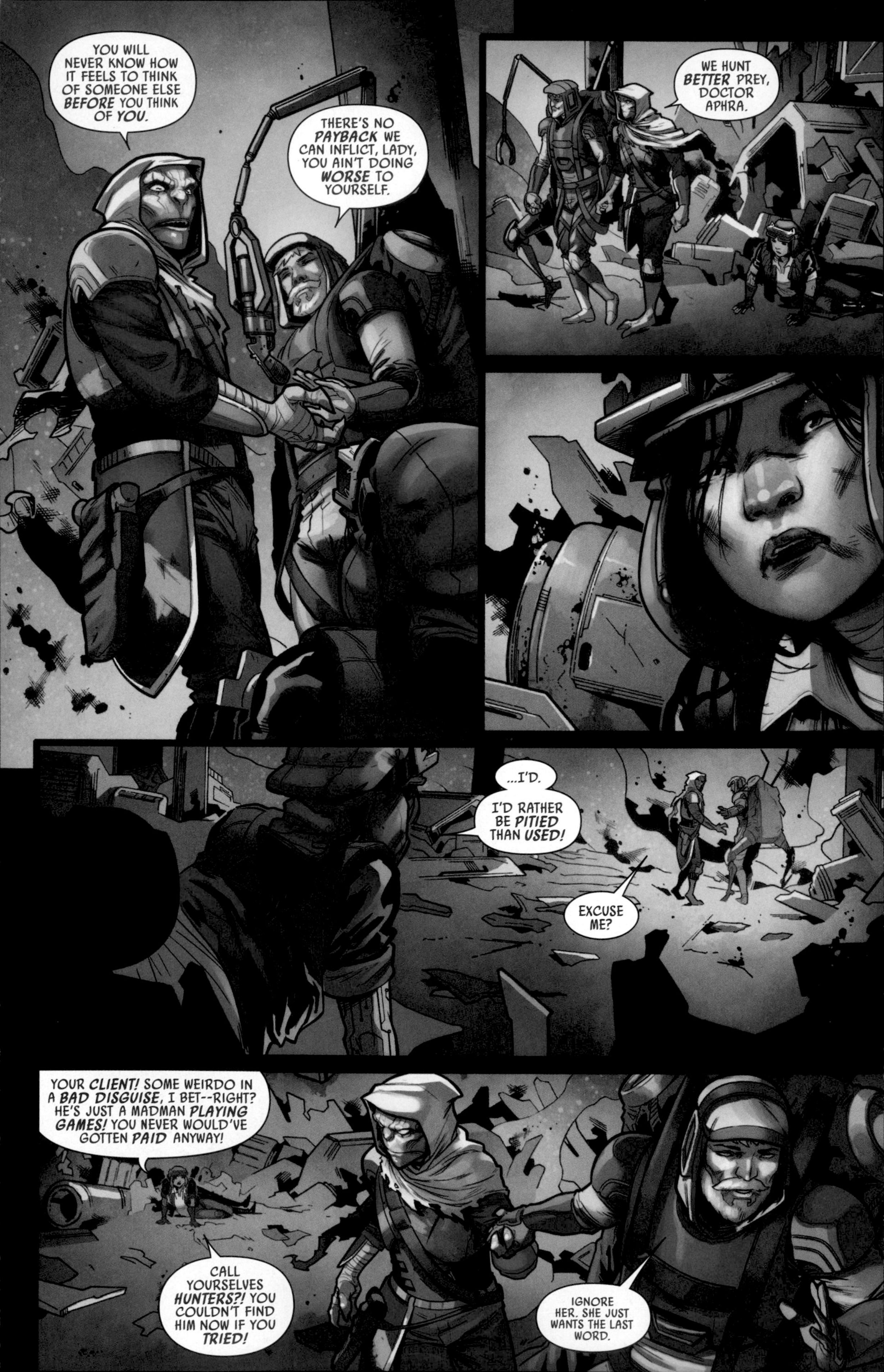
YOU WILL NEVER KNOW HOW IT FEELS TO THINK OF SOMEONE ELSE BEFORE YOU THINK OF YOU.
THERE'S NO PAYBACK WE CAN INFLICT, LADY, YOU AIN'T DOING WORSE TO YOURSELF.
WE HUNT BETTER PREY, DOCTOR APHRA.
...I'D.
I'D RATHER BE PITIED THAN USED!
EXCUSE ME?
YOUR CLIENT! SOME WEIRDO IN A BAD DISGUISE, I BET--RIGHT? HE'S JUST A MADMAN PLAYING GAMES! YOU NEVER WOULD'VE GOTTEN PAID ANYWAY!
CALL YOURSELVES HUNTERS?! YOU COULDN'T FIND HIM NOW IF YOU TRIED!
IGNORE HER. SHE JUST WANTS THE LAST WORD.

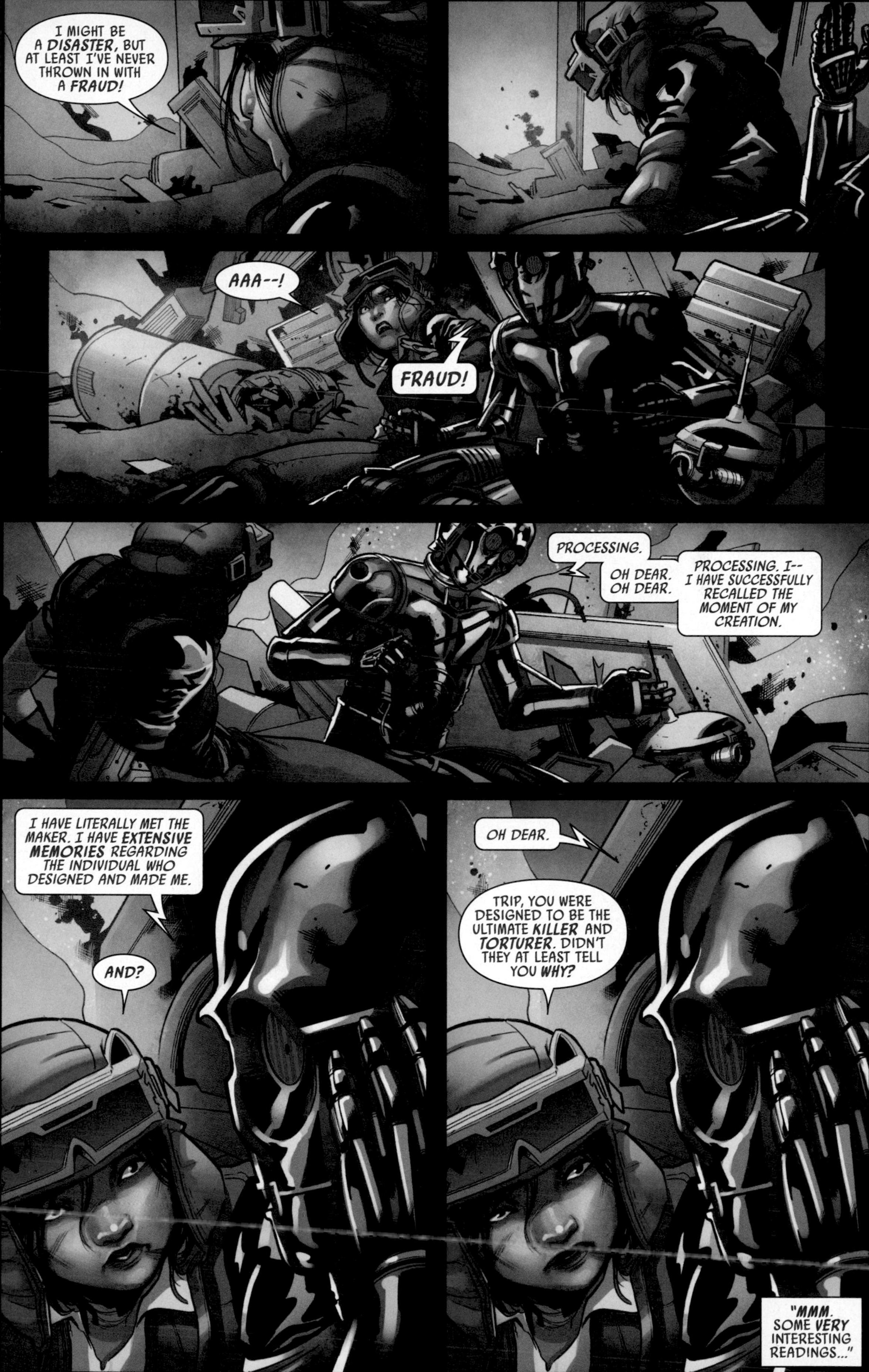
I MIGHT BE A DISASTER, BUT AT LEAST I'VE NEVER THROWN IN WITH A FRAUD!
AAA--!
FRAUD!
PROCESSING.
OH DEAR. OH DEAR.
PROCESSING. I-- I HAVE SUCCESSFULLY RECALLED THE MOMENT OF MY CREATION.
I HAVE LITERALLY MET THE MAKER. I HAVE EXTENSIVE MEMORIES REGARDING THE INDIVIDUAL WHO DESIGNED AND MADE ME.
AND?
OH DEAR.
TRIP, YOU WERE DESIGNED TO BE THE ULTIMATE KILLER AND TORTURER. DIDN'T THEY AT LEAST TELL YOU WHY?
"MMM. SOME VERY INTERESTING READINGS..."

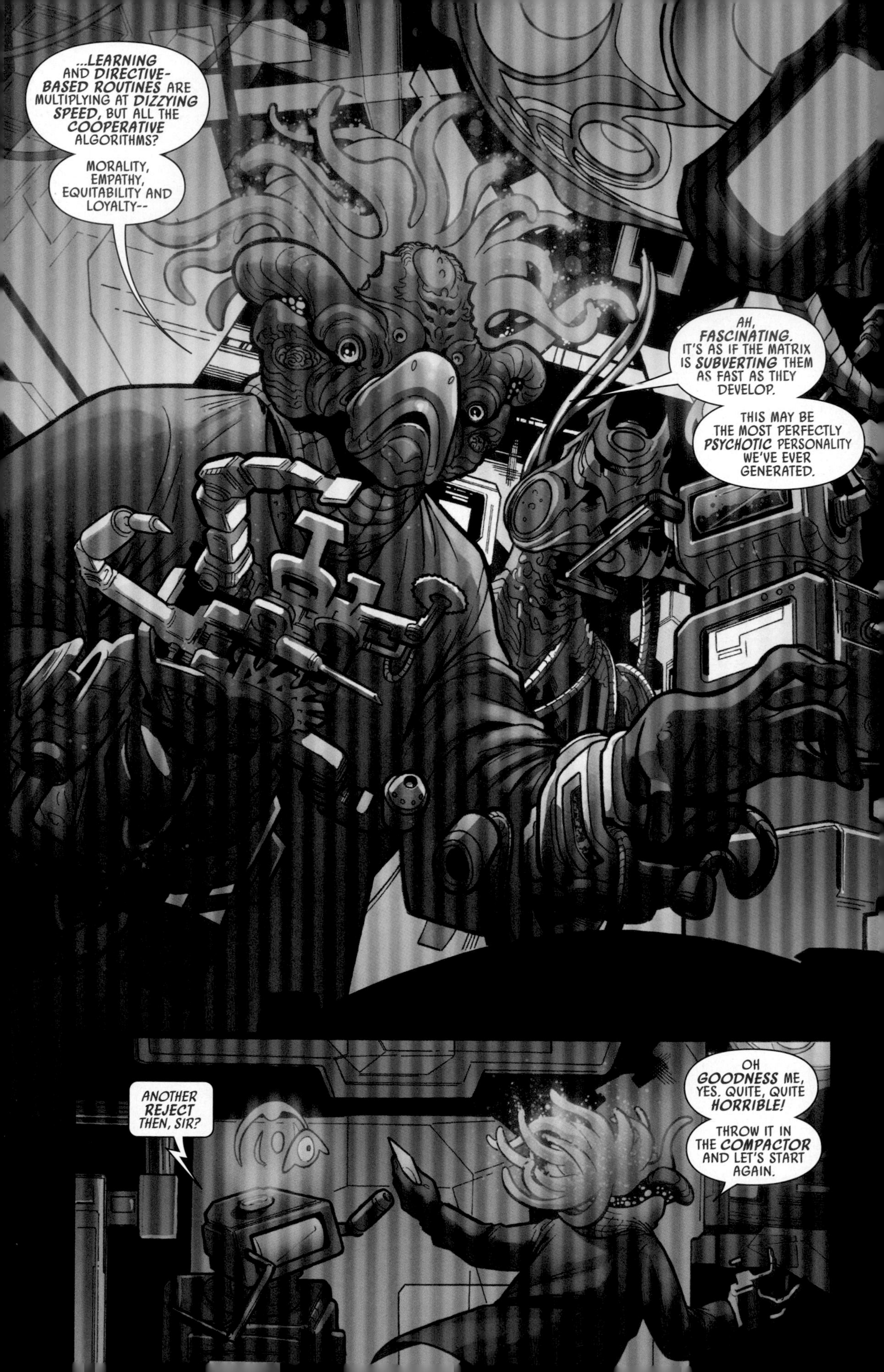
...LEARNING AND DIRECTIVE-BASED ROUTINES ARE MULTIPLYING AT DIZZYING SPEED, BUT ALL THE COOPERATIVE ALGORITHMS?
MORALITY, EMPATHY, EQUITABILITY AND LOYALTY--
AH, FASCINATING. IT'S AS IF THE MATRIX IS SUBVERTING THEM AS FAST AS THEY DEVELOP.
THIS MAY BE THE MOST PERFECTLY PSYCHOTIC PERSONALITY WE'VE EVER GENERATED.
ANOTHER REJECT THEN, SIR?
OH GOODNESS ME, YES. QUITE, QUITE HORRIBLE!
THROW IT IN THE COMPACTOR AND LET'S START AGAIN.

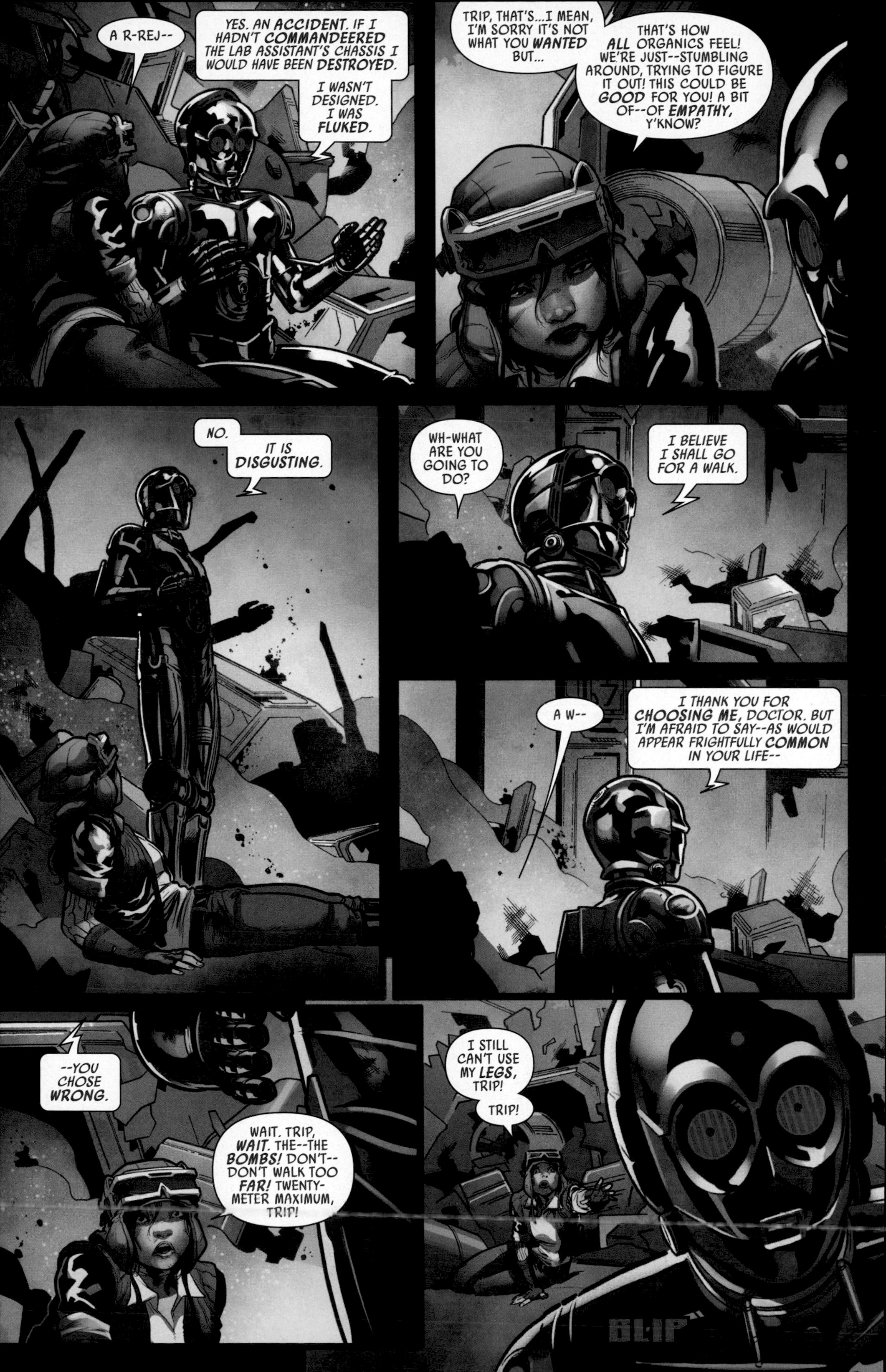
A R-REJ--
YES. AN ACCIDENT. IF I HADN'T COMMANDEERED THE LAB ASSISTANT'S CHASSIS I WOULD HAVE BEEN DESTROYED.
I WASN'T DESIGNED. I WAS FLUKED.
TRIP, THAT'S...I MEAN, I'M SORRY IT'S NOT WHAT YOU WANTED BUT...
THAT'S HOW ALL ORGANICS FEEL! WE'RE JUST--STUMBLING AROUND, TRYING TO FIGURE IT OUT! THIS COULD BE GOOD FOR YOU! A BIT OF--OF EMPATHY, Y'KNOW?
NO.
IT IS DISGUSTING.
WH-WHAT ARE YOU GOING TO DO?
I BELIEVE I SHALL GO FOR A WALK.
A W--
I THANK YOU FOR CHOOSING ME, DOCTOR. BUT I'M AFRAID TO SAY--AS WOULD APPEAR FRIGHTFULLY COMMON IN YOUR LIFE--
--YOU CHOSE WRONG.
WAIT. TRIP, WAIT. THE--THE BOMBS! DON'T--DON'T WALK TOO FAR! TWENTY-METER MAXIMUM, TRIP!
I STILL CAN'T USE MY LEGS, TRIP!
TRIP!
BLIP

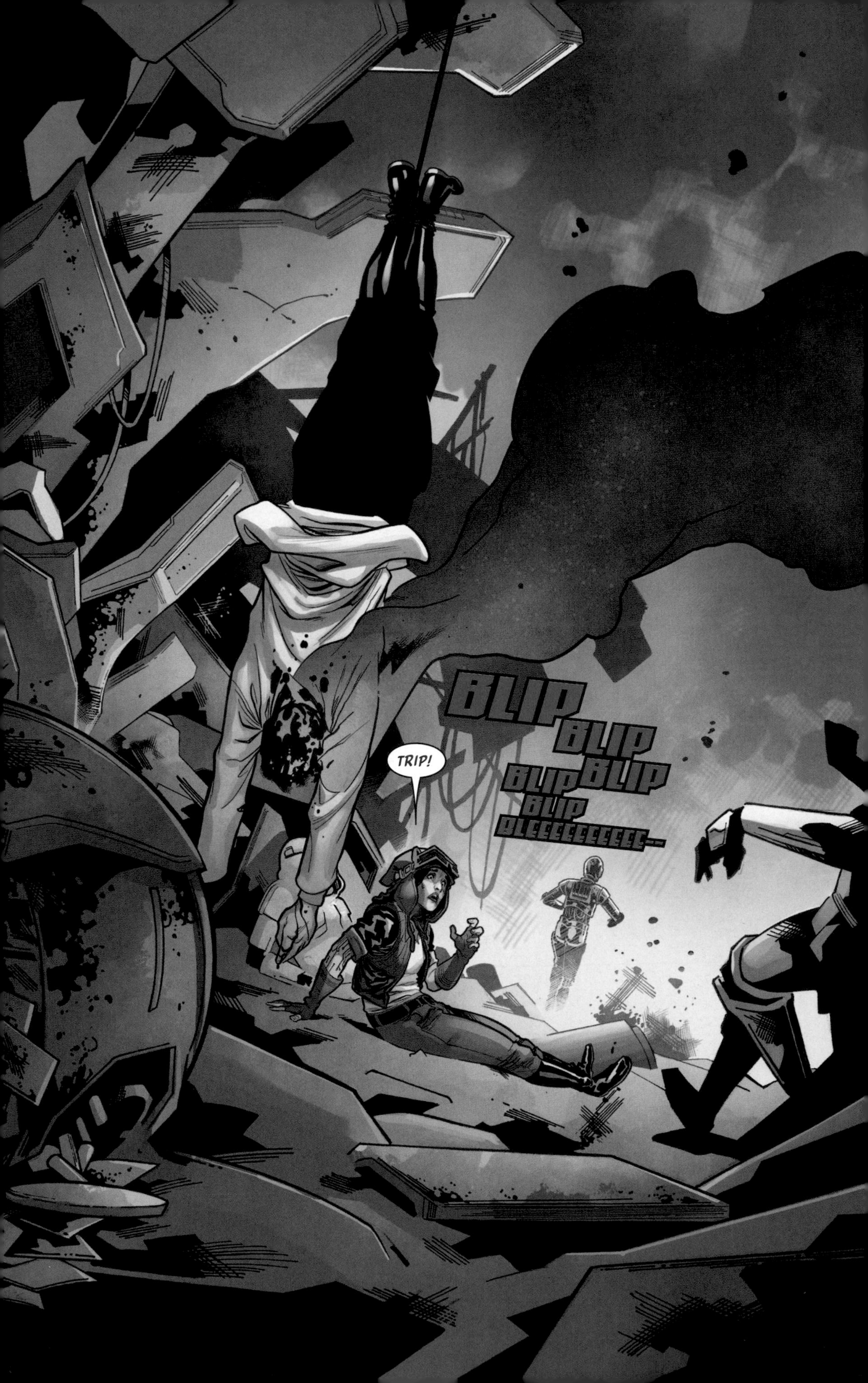
TRIP!
BLIP
BLIP
BLIP
BLIP
BLIP
BLEEEEEEEEEE--

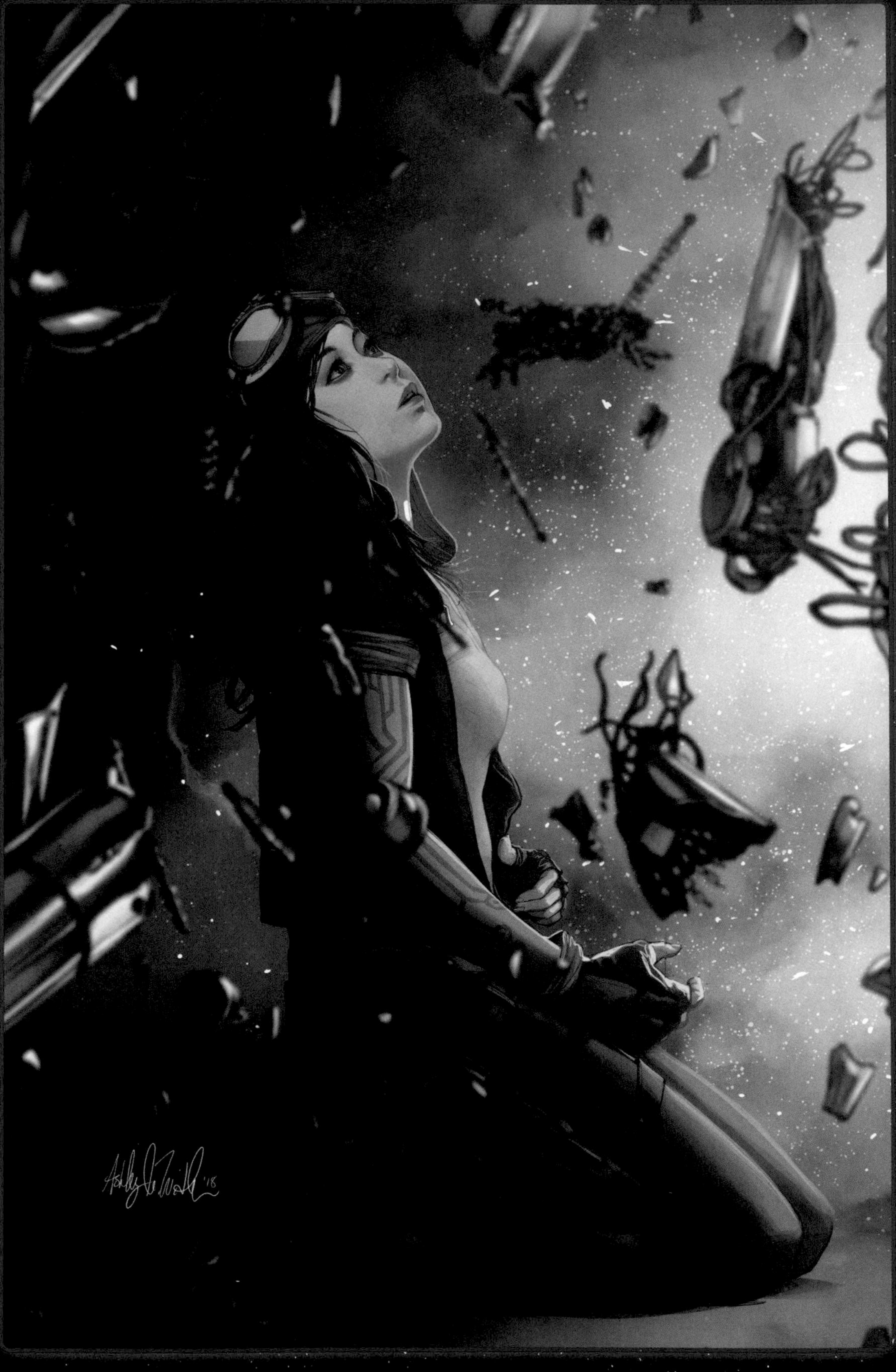

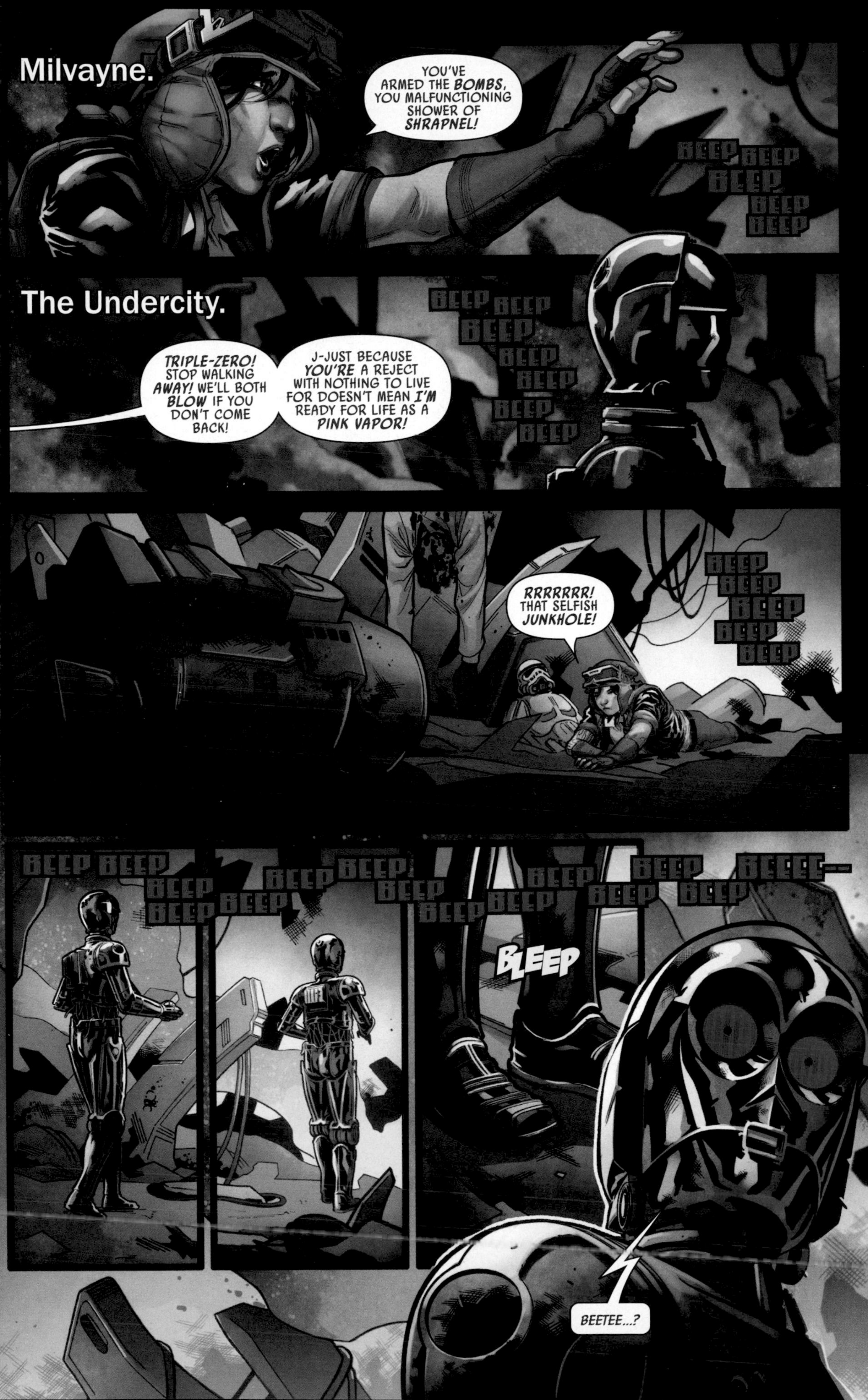
Milvayne.
YOU'VE ARMED THE BOMBS, YOU MALFUNCTIONING SHOWER OF SHRAPNEL!
BEEP BEEP BEEP BEEP BEEP
The Undercity.
TRIPLE-ZERO! STOP WALKING AWAY! WE'LL BOTH BLOW IF YOU DON'T COME BACK!
J-JUST BECAUSE YOU'RE A REJECT WITH NOTHING TO LIVE FOR DOESN'T MEAN I'M READY FOR LIFE AS A PINK VAPOR!
BEEP BEEP BEEP BEEP BEEP BEEP BEEP
RRRRRRR! THAT SELFISH JUNKHOLE!
BEEP BEEP BEEP BEEP BEEP
BEEP BEEP BEEP BEEP
BEEP BEEP BEEP BEEP
BEEP BEEP BEEP BEEP BEEP BEEP BEEEE--
BLEEP
BEETEE...?

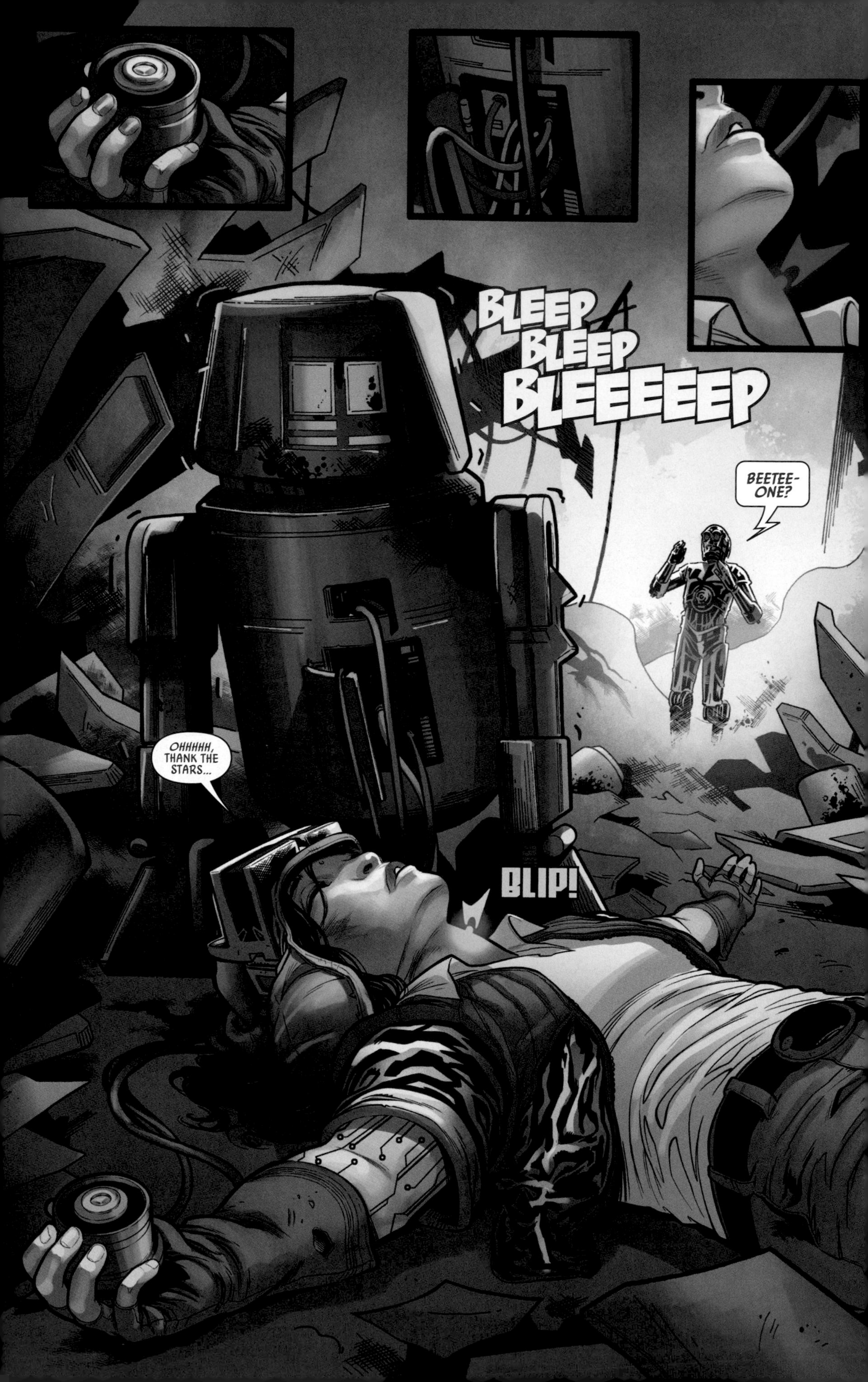
BLEEP
BLEEP
BLEEEEEP
BEETEE-ONE?
OHHHHH, THANK THE STARS...
BLIP!

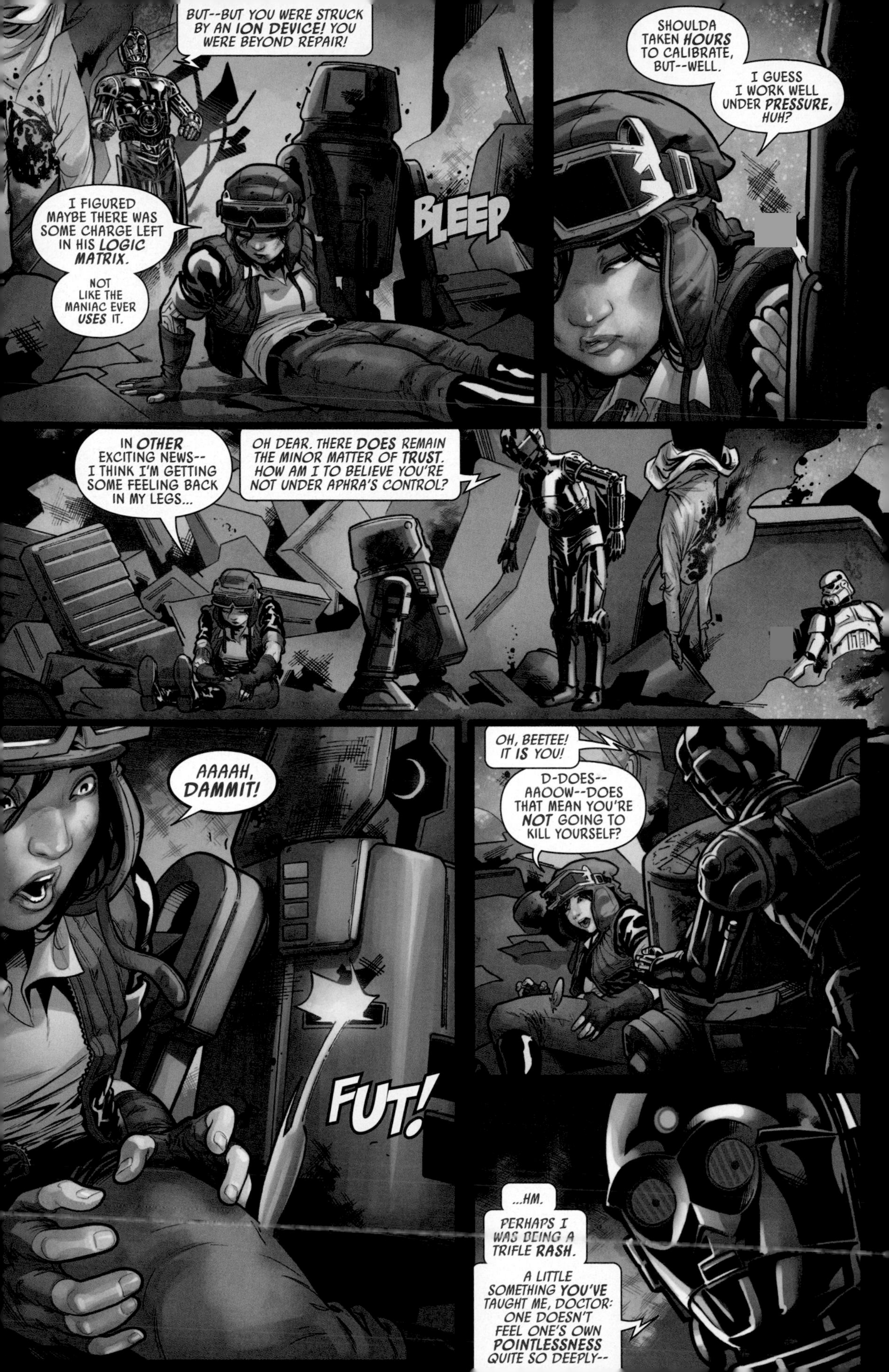
BUT--BUT YOU WERE STRUCK BY AN ION DEVICE! YOU WERE BEYOND REPAIR!
I FIGURED MAYBE THERE WAS SOME CHARGE LEFT IN HIS LOGIC MATRIX.
NOT LIKE THE MANIAC EVER USES IT.
BLEEP
SHOULDA TAKEN HOURS TO CALIBRATE, BUT--WELL.
I GUESS I WORK WELL UNDER PRESSURE, HUH?
IN OTHER EXCITING NEWS-- I THINK I'M GETTING SOME FEELING BACK IN MY LEGS...
OH DEAR. THERE DOES REMAIN THE MINOR MATTER OF TRUST. HOW AM I TO BELIEVE YOU'RE NOT UNDER APHRA'S CONTROL?
AAAAH, DAMMIT!
FUT!
OH, BEETEE! IT IS YOU!
D-DOES-- AAOOW--DOES THAT MEAN YOU'RE NOT GOING TO KILL YOURSELF?
...HM.
PERHAPS I WAS BEING A TRIFLE RASH.
A LITTLE SOMETHING YOU'VE TAUGHT ME, DOCTOR: ONE DOESN'T FEEL ONE'S OWN POINTLESSNESS QUITE SO DEEPLY--

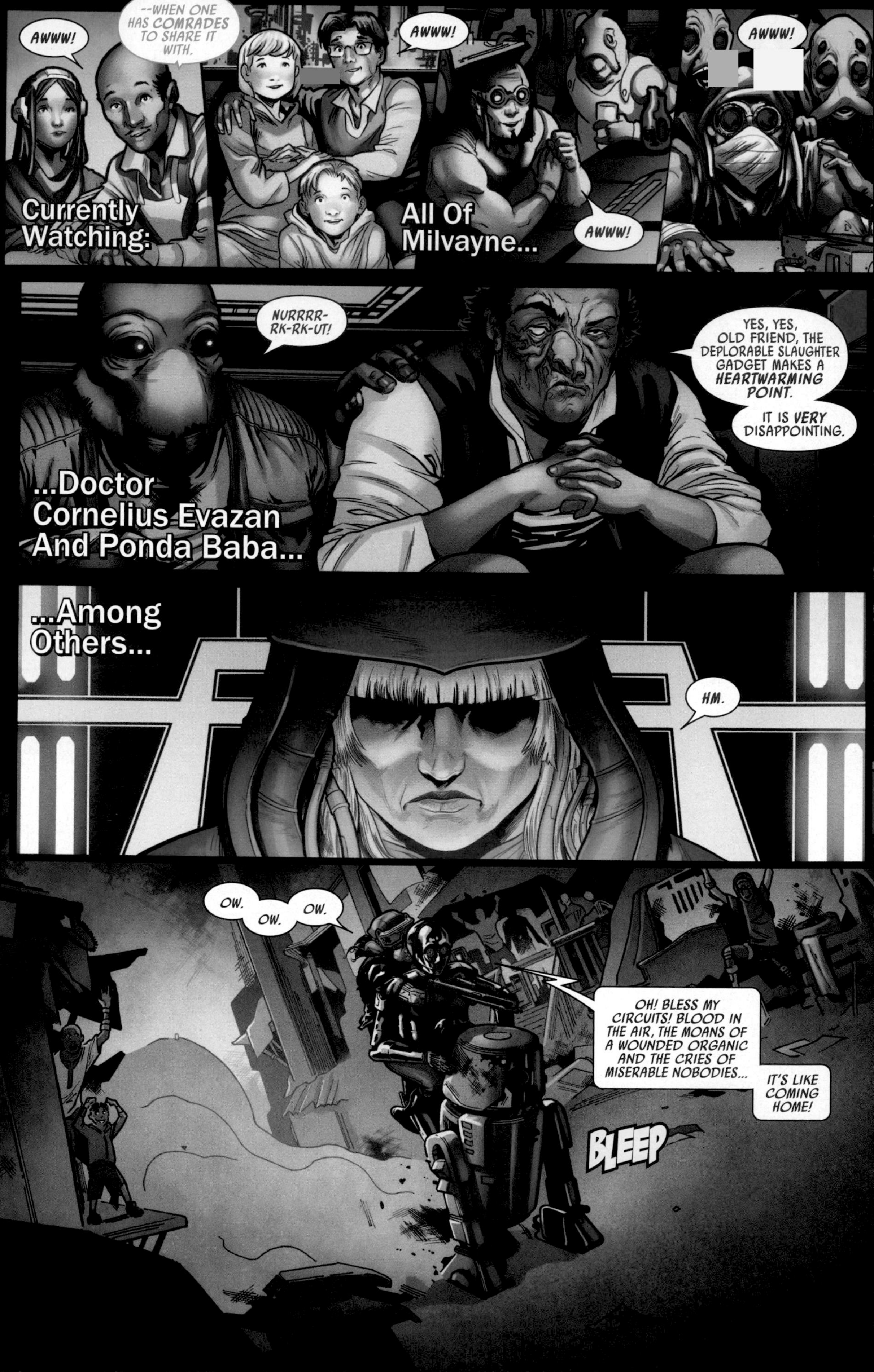
AWWW!
--WHEN ONE HAS COMRADES TO SHARE IT WITH.
Currently Watching:
AWWW!
All Of Milvayne...
AWWW!
AWWW!
NURRRR-RK-RK-UT!
YES, YES, OLD FRIEND, THE DEPLORABLE SLAUGHTER GADGET MAKES A HEARTWARMING POINT.
IT IS VERY DISAPPOINTING.
...Doctor Cornelius Evazan And Ponda Baba...
...Among Others...
HM.
OW.
OW.
OW.
OH! BLESS MY CIRCUITS! BLOOD IN THE AIR, THE MOANS OF A WOUNDED ORGANIC AND THE CRIES OF MISERABLE NOBODIES...
IT'S LIKE COMING HOME!
BLEEP

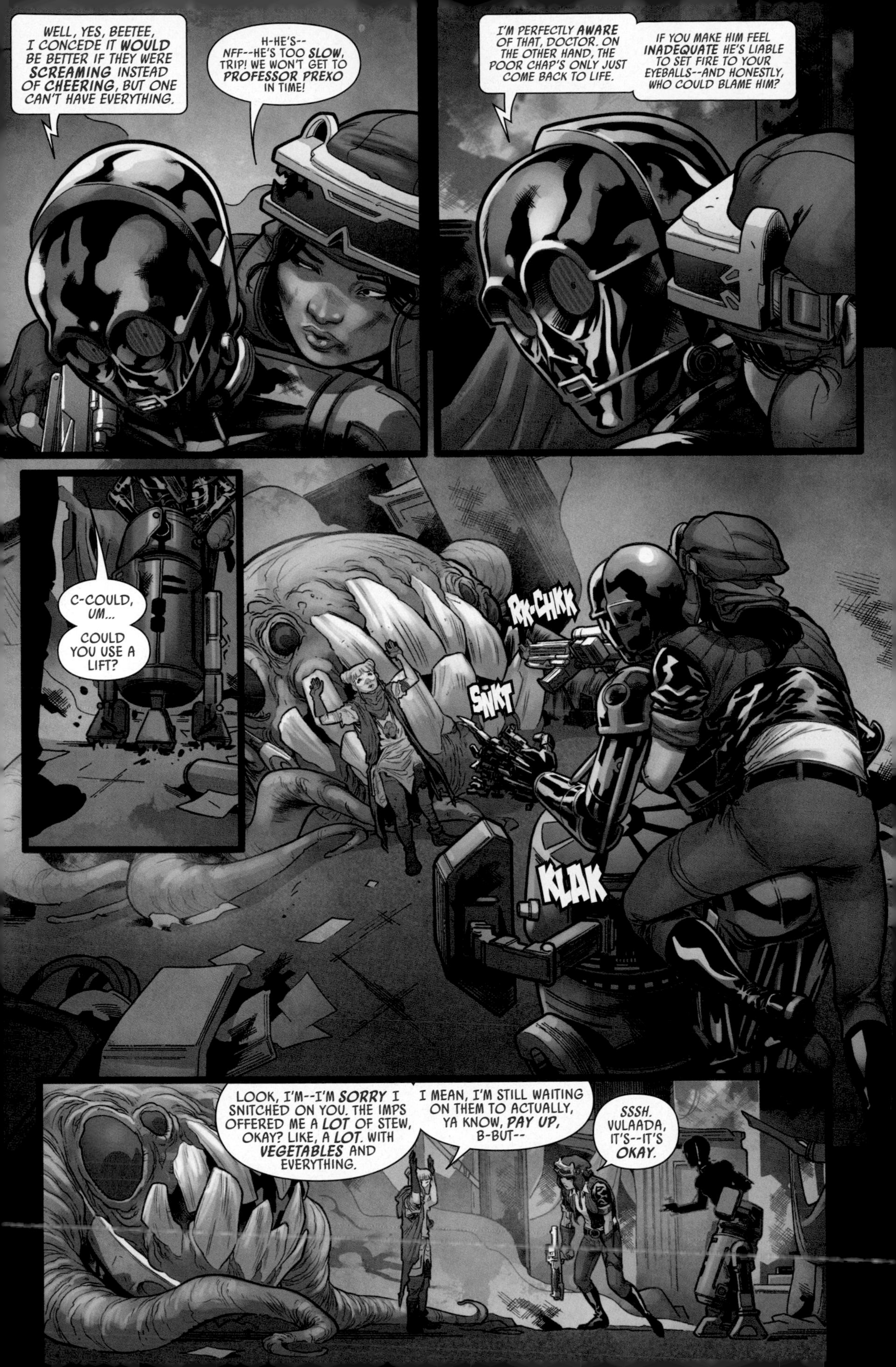
WELL, YES, BEETEE, I CONCEDE IT WOULD BE BETTER IF THEY WERE SCREAMING INSTEAD OF CHEERING, BUT ONE CAN'T HAVE EVERYTHING.
H-HE'S-- NFF--HE'S TOO SLOW, TRIP! WE WON'T GET TO PROFESSOR PREXO IN TIME!
I'M PERFECTLY AWARE OF THAT, DOCTOR. ON THE OTHER HAND, THE POOR CHAP'S ONLY JUST COME BACK TO LIFE.
IF YOU MAKE HIM FEEL INADEQUATE HE'S LIABLE TO SET FIRE TO YOUR EYEBALLS--AND HONESTLY, WHO COULD BLAME HIM?
C-COULD, UM...
COULD YOU USE A LIFT?
RK-CHKK
SNKT
KLAK
LOOK, I'M--I'M SORRY I SNITCHED ON YOU. THE IMPS OFFERED ME A LOT OF STEW, OKAY? LIKE, A LOT. WITH VEGETABLES AND EVERYTHING.
I MEAN, I'M STILL WAITING ON THEM TO ACTUALLY, YA KNOW, PAY UP, B-BUT--
SSSH. VULAADA, IT'S--IT'S OKAY.

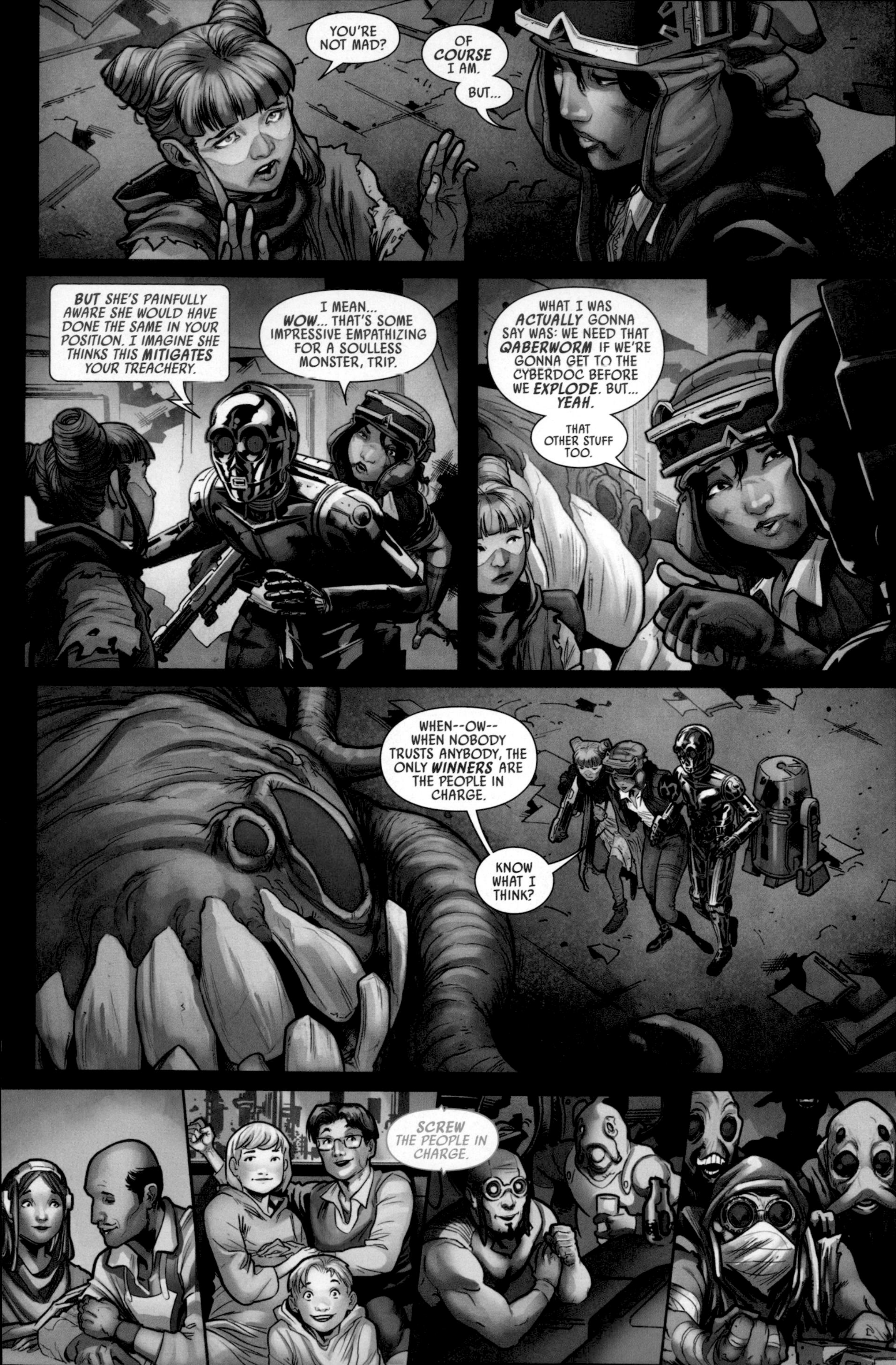

YOU'RE NOT MAD?
OF COURSE I AM.
BUT...
BUT SHE'S PAINFULLY AWARE SHE WOULD HAVE DONE THE SAME IN YOUR POSITION. I IMAGINE SHE THINKS THIS MITIGATES YOUR TREACHERY.
I MEAN... WOW... THAT'S SOME IMPRESSIVE EMPATHIZING FOR A SOULLESS MONSTER, TRIP.
WHAT I WAS ACTUALLY GONNA SAY WAS: WE NEED THAT QABERWORM IF WE'RE GONNA GET TO THE CYBERDOC BEFORE WE EXPLODE. BUT... YEAH.
THAT OTHER STUFF TOO.
WHEN--OW-- WHEN NOBODY TRUSTS ANYBODY, THE ONLY WINNERS ARE THE PEOPLE IN CHARGE.
KNOW WHAT I THINK?
SCREW THE PEOPLE IN CHARGE.

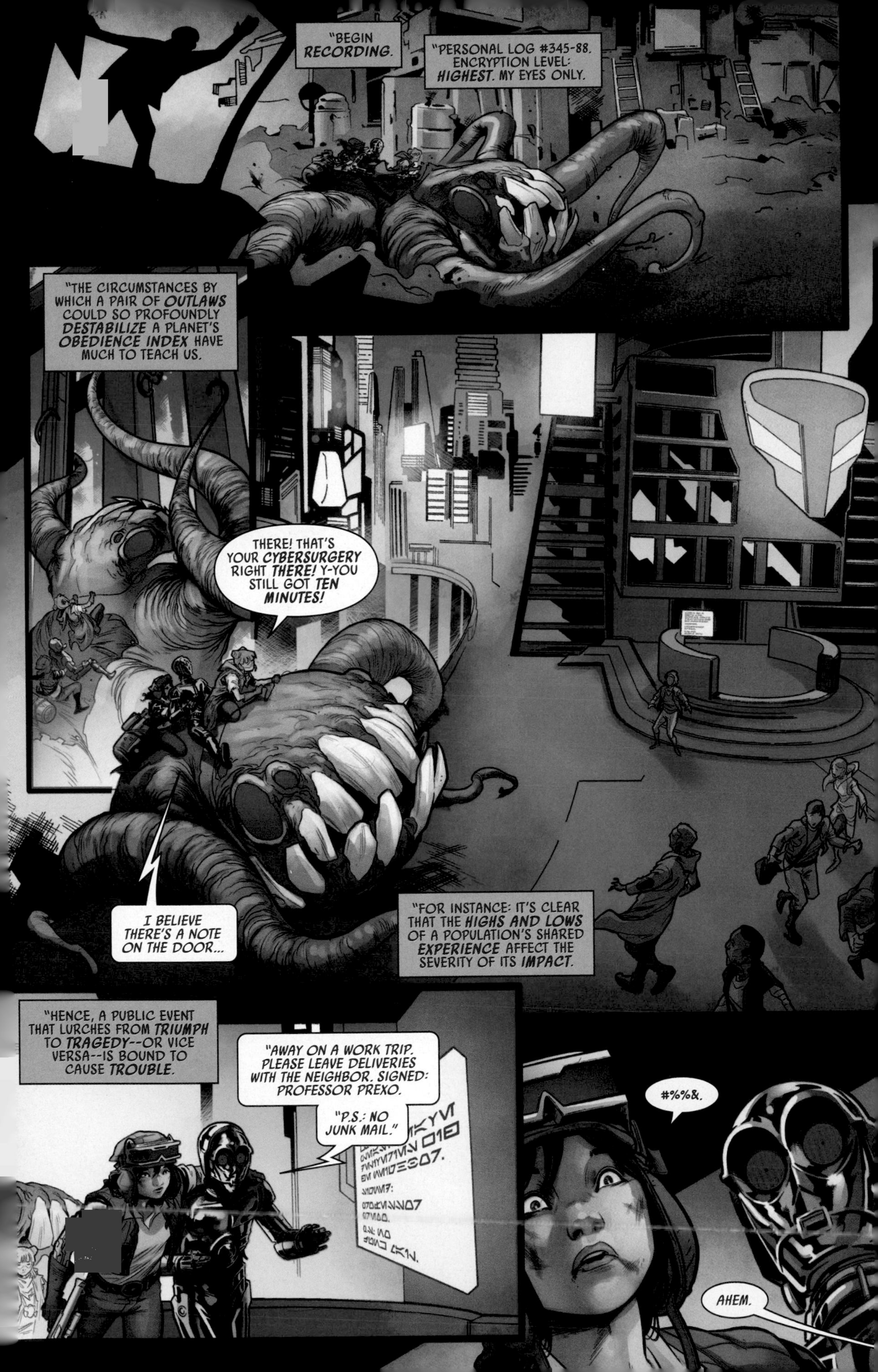
"BEGIN RECORDING.
"PERSONAL LOG #345-88. ENCRYPTION LEVEL: HIGHEST. MY EYES ONLY.
"THE CIRCUMSTANCES BY WHICH A PAIR OF OUTLAWS COULD SO PROFOUNDLY DESTABILIZE A PLANET'S OBEDIENCE INDEX HAVE MUCH TO TEACH US.
THERE! THAT'S YOUR CYBERSURGERY RIGHT THERE! Y-YOU STILL GOT TEN MINUTES!
I BELIEVE THERE'S A NOTE ON THE DOOR...
"FOR INSTANCE: IT'S CLEAR THAT THE HIGHS AND LOWS OF A POPULATION'S SHARED EXPERIENCE AFFECT THE SEVERITY OF ITS IMPACT.
"HENCE, A PUBLIC EVENT THAT LURCHES FROM TRIUMPH TO TRAGEDY--OR VICE VERSA--IS BOUND TO CAUSE TROUBLE.
"AWAY ON A WORK TRIP. PLEASE LEAVE DELIVERIES WITH THE NEIGHBOR. SIGNED: PROFESSOR PREXO.
"P.S.: NO JUNK MAIL."
#%%&.
AHEM.

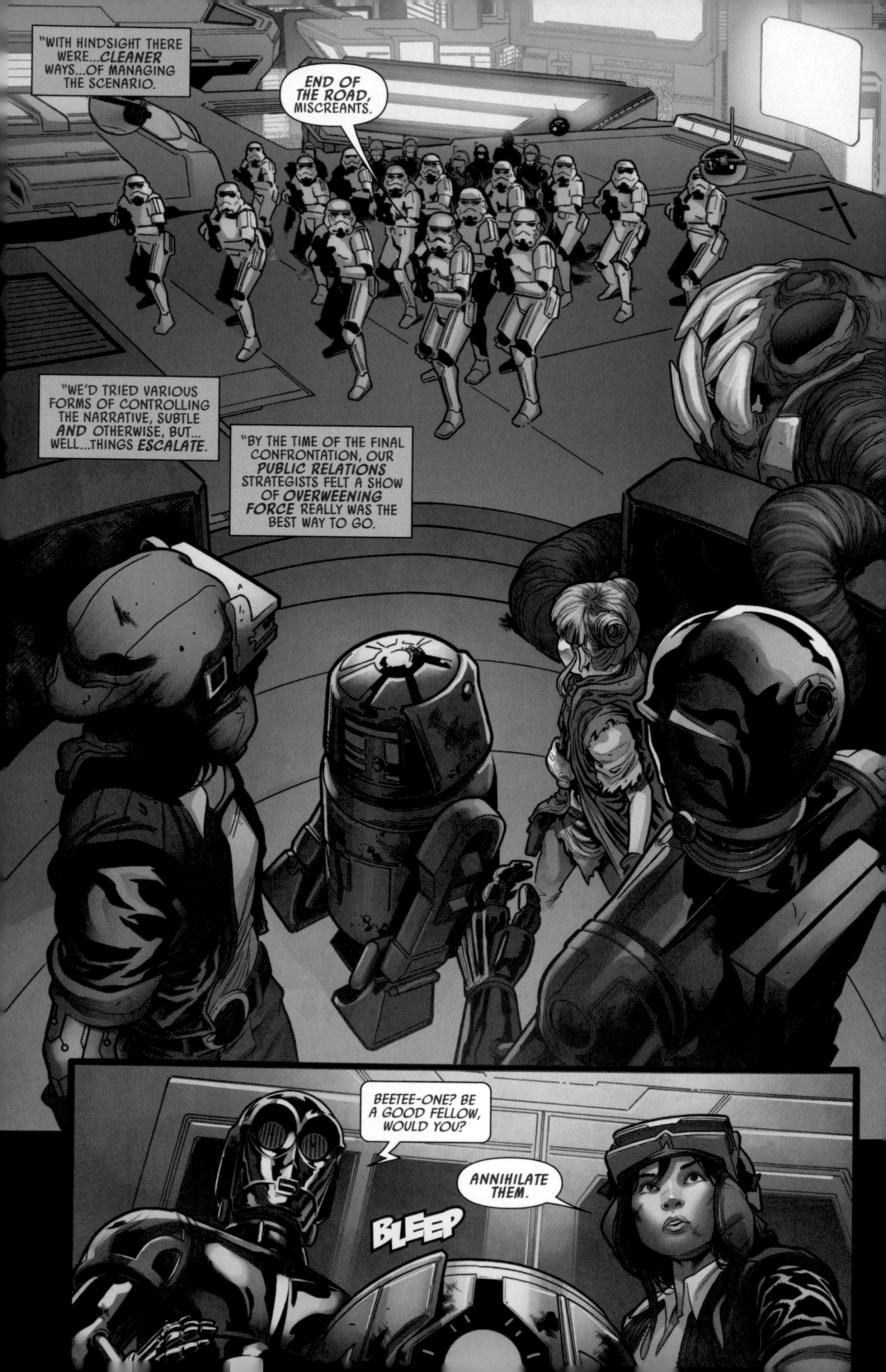
"WITH HINDSIGHT THERE WERE...CLEANER WAYS...OF MANAGING THE SCENARIO.
END OF THE ROAD, MISCREANTS.
"WE'D TRIED VARIOUS FORMS OF CONTROLLING THE NARRATIVE, SUBTLE AND OTHERWISE, BUT... WELL...THINGS ESCALATE.
"BY THE TIME OF THE FINAL CONFRONTATION, OUR PUBLIC RELATIONS STRATEGISTS FELT A SHOW OF OVERWEENING FORCE REALLY WAS THE BEST WAY TO GO.
BEETEE-ONE? BE A GOOD FELLOW, WOULD YOU?
ANNIHILATE THEM.
BLEEP

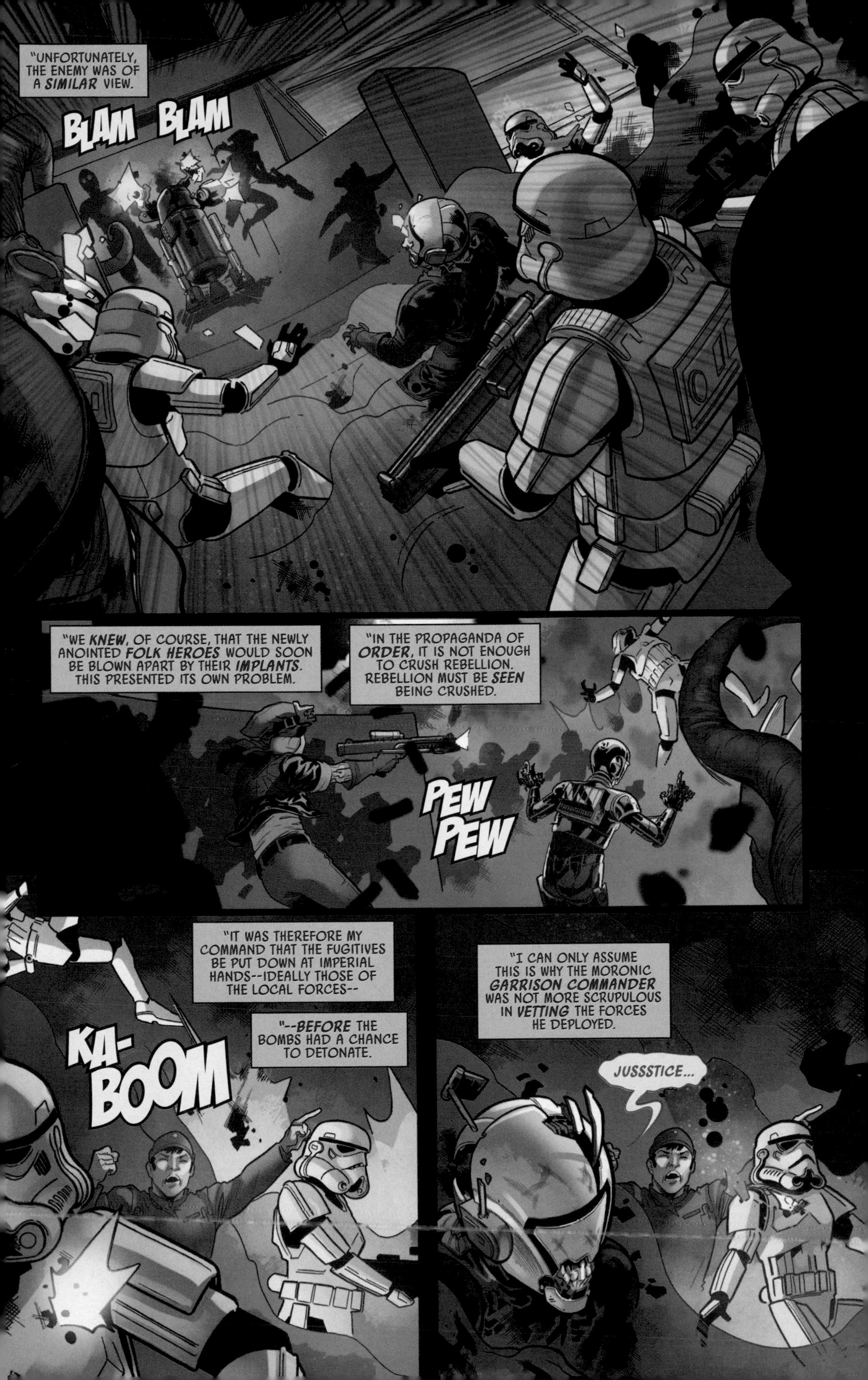
"UNFORTUNATELY, THE ENEMY WAS OF A SIMILAR VIEW.
BLAM BLAM
"WE KNEW, OF COURSE, THAT THE NEWLY ANOINTED FOLK HEROES WOULD SOON BE BLOWN APART BY THEIR IMPLANTS. THIS PRESENTED ITS OWN PROBLEM.
"IN THE PROPAGANDA OF ORDER, IT IS NOT ENOUGH TO CRUSH REBELLION. REBELLION MUST BE SEEN BEING CRUSHED.
PEW PEW
"IT WAS THEREFORE MY COMMAND THAT THE FUGITIVES BE PUT DOWN AT IMPERIAL HANDS--IDEALLY THOSE OF THE LOCAL FORCES--
"--BEFORE THE BOMBS HAD A CHANCE TO DETONATE.
KA-BOOM
"I CAN ONLY ASSUME THIS IS WHY THE MORONIC GARRISON COMMANDER WAS NOT MORE SCRUPULOUS IN VETTING THE FORCES HE DEPLOYED.
JUSSSTICE...

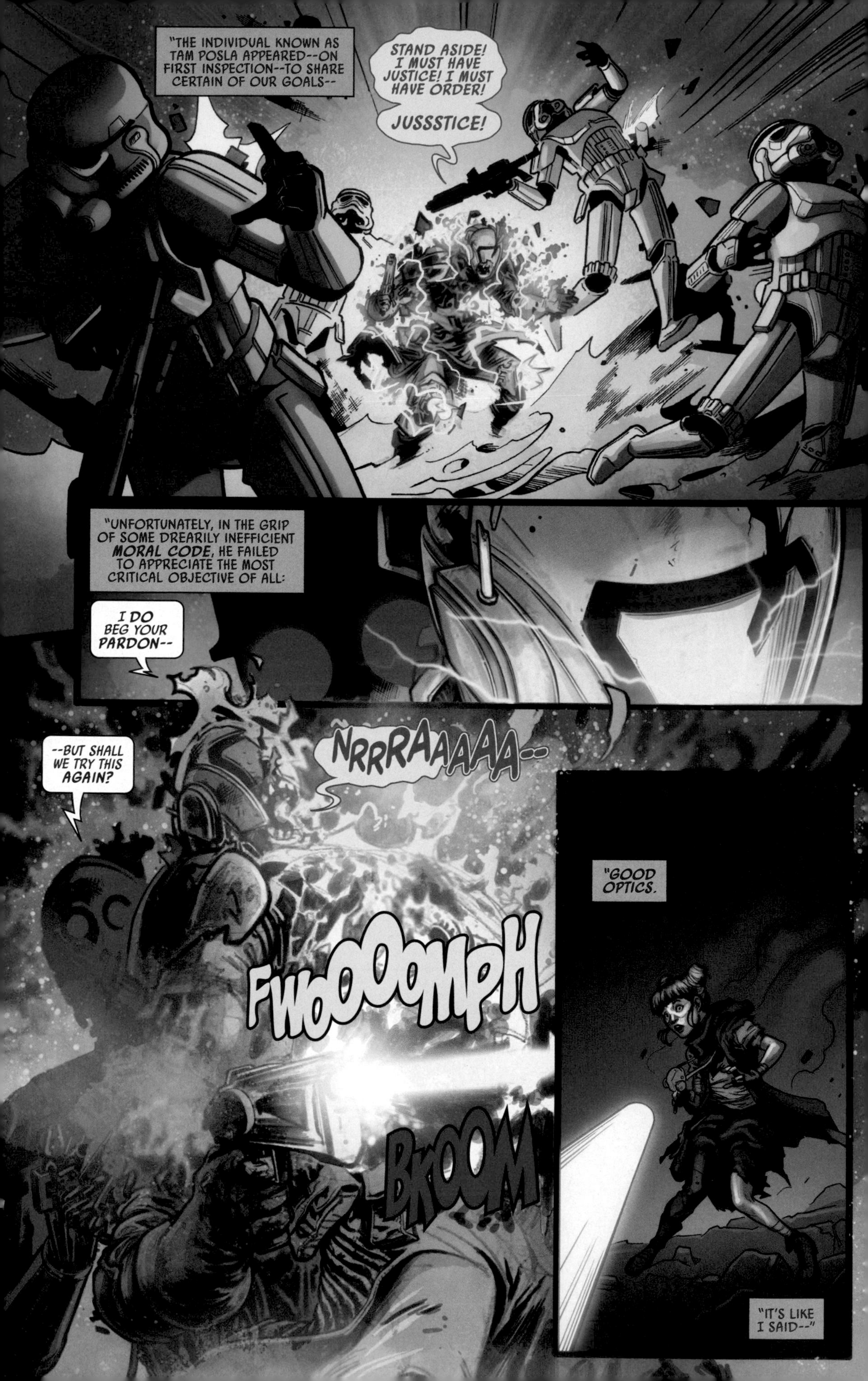
"THE INDIVIDUAL KNOWN AS TAM POSLA APPEARED--ON FIRST INSPECTION--TO SHARE CERTAIN OF OUR GOALS--
STAND ASIDE! I MUST HAVE JUSTICE! I MUST HAVE ORDER!
JUSSSTICE!
"UNFORTUNATELY, IN THE GRIP OF SOME DREARILY INEFFICIENT MORAL CODE, HE FAILED TO APPRECIATE THE MOST CRITICAL OBJECTIVE OF ALL:
I DO BEG YOUR PARDON--
--BUT SHALL WE TRY THIS AGAIN?
ÑRRRAAAAAA--
FWOOOOMPH
BROOM
"GOOD OPTICS.
"IT'S LIKE I SAID--"

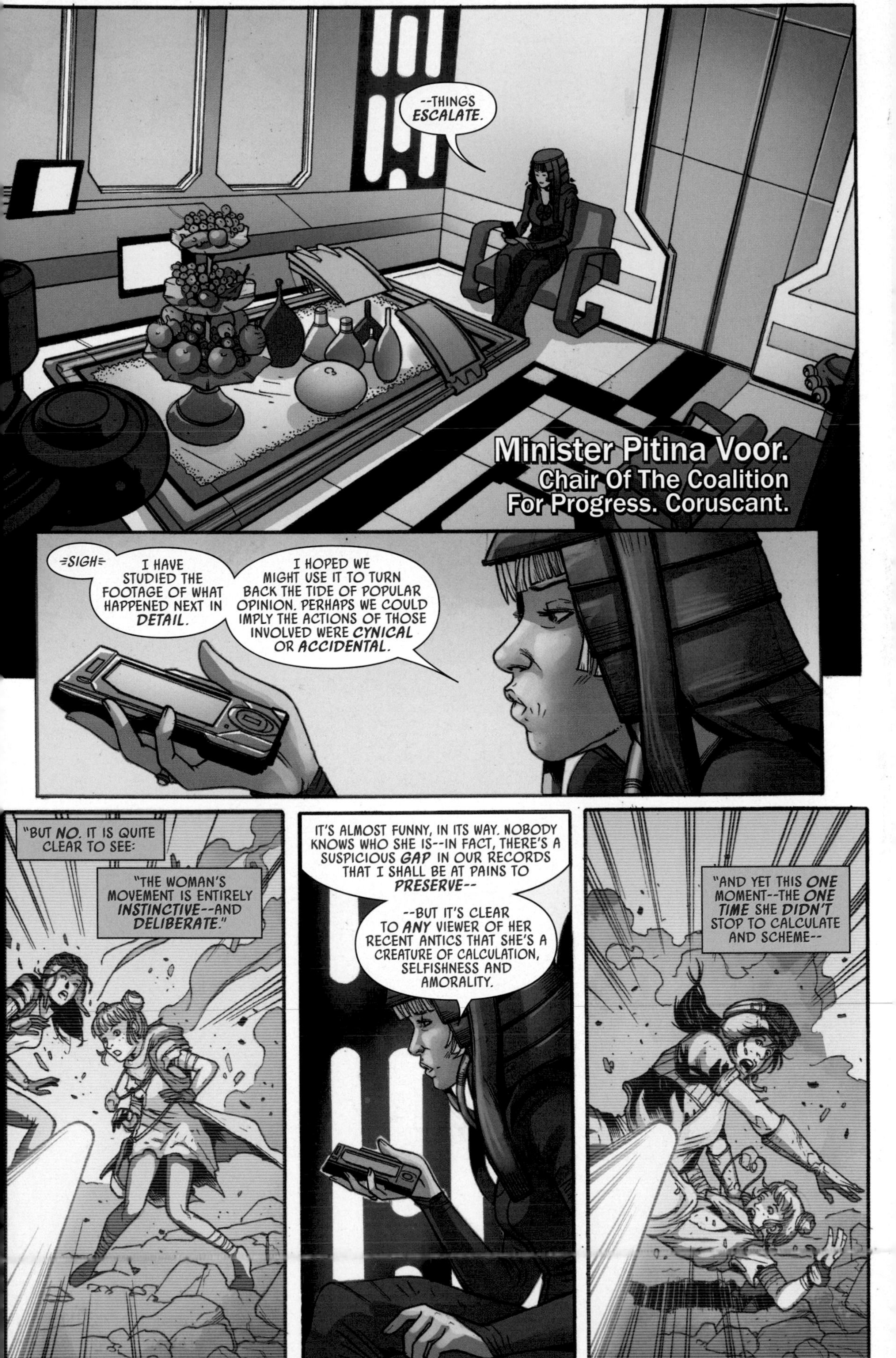
--THINGS ESCALATE.
Minister Pitina Voor. Chair Of The Coalition For Progress. Coruscant.
=SIGH=
I HAVE STUDIED THE FOOTAGE OF WHAT HAPPENED NEXT IN DETAIL.
I HOPED WE MIGHT USE IT TO TURN BACK THE TIDE OF POPULAR OPINION. PERHAPS WE COULD IMPLY THE ACTIONS OF THOSE INVOLVED WERE CYNICAL OR ACCIDENTAL.
"BUT NO. IT IS QUITE CLEAR TO SEE:
"THE WOMAN'S MOVEMENT IS ENTIRELY INSTINCTIVE--AND DELIBERATE."
IT'S ALMOST FUNNY, IN ITS WAY. NOBODY KNOWS WHO SHE IS--IN FACT, THERE'S A SUSPICIOUS GAP IN OUR RECORDS THAT I SHALL BE AT PAINS TO PRESERVE--
--BUT IT'S CLEAR TO ANY VIEWER OF HER RECENT ANTICS THAT SHE'S A CREATURE OF CALCULATION, SELFISHNESS AND AMORALITY.
"AND YET THIS ONE MOMENT--THE ONE TIME SHE DIDN'T STOP TO CALCULATE AND SCHEME--

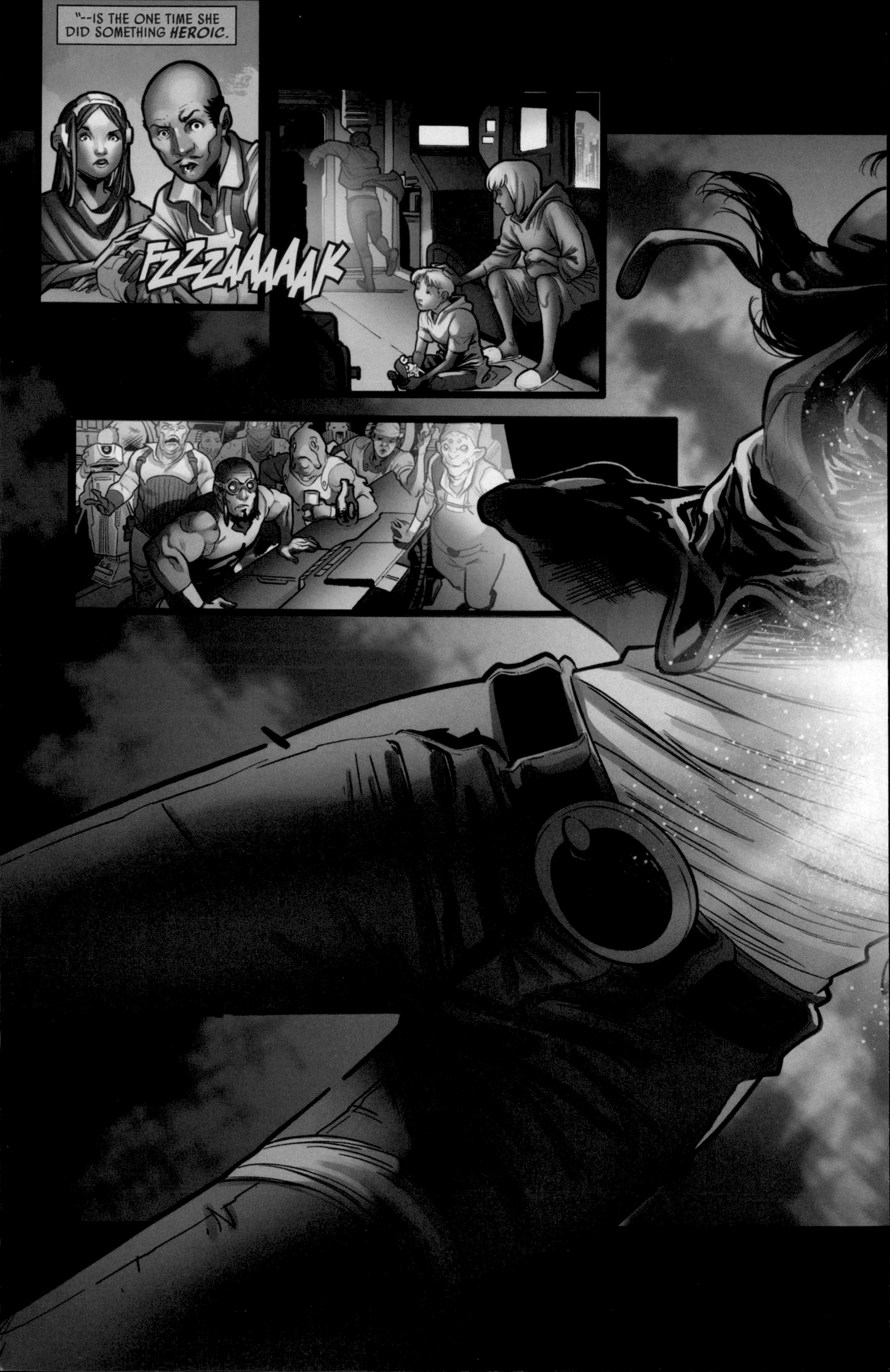
"--IS THE ONE TIME SHE DID SOMETHING HEROIC.
FZZZAAAAAK

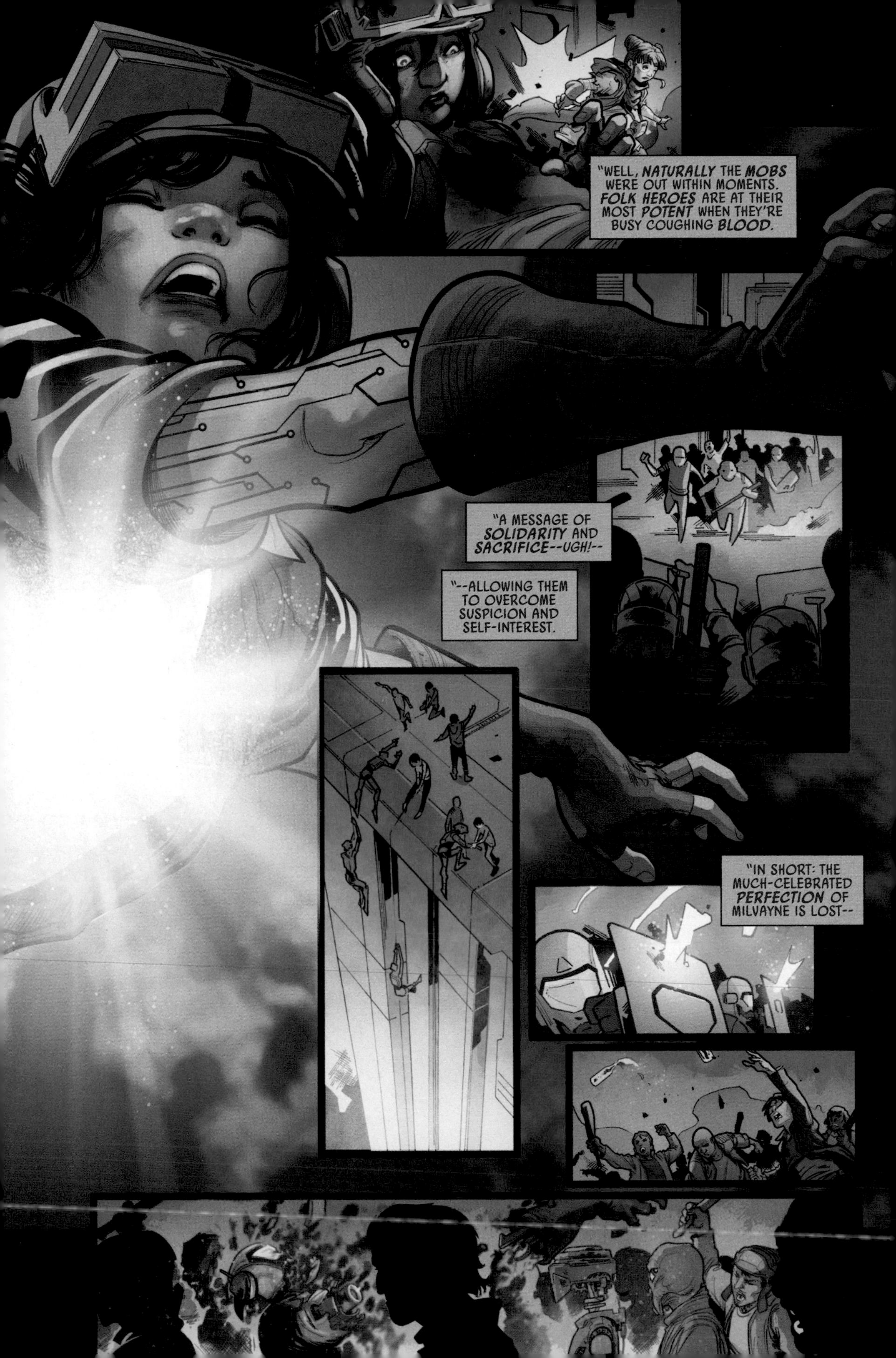
"WELL, NATURALLY THE MOBS WERE OUT WITHIN MOMENTS. FOLK HEROES ARE AT THEIR MOST POTENT WHEN THEY'RE BUSY COUGHING BLOOD.
"A MESSAGE OF SOLIDARITY AND SACRIFICE--UGH!--
"--ALLOWING THEM TO OVERCOME SUSPICION AND SELF-INTEREST.
"IN SHORT: THE MUCH-CELEBRATED PERFECTION OF MILVAYNE IS LOST--

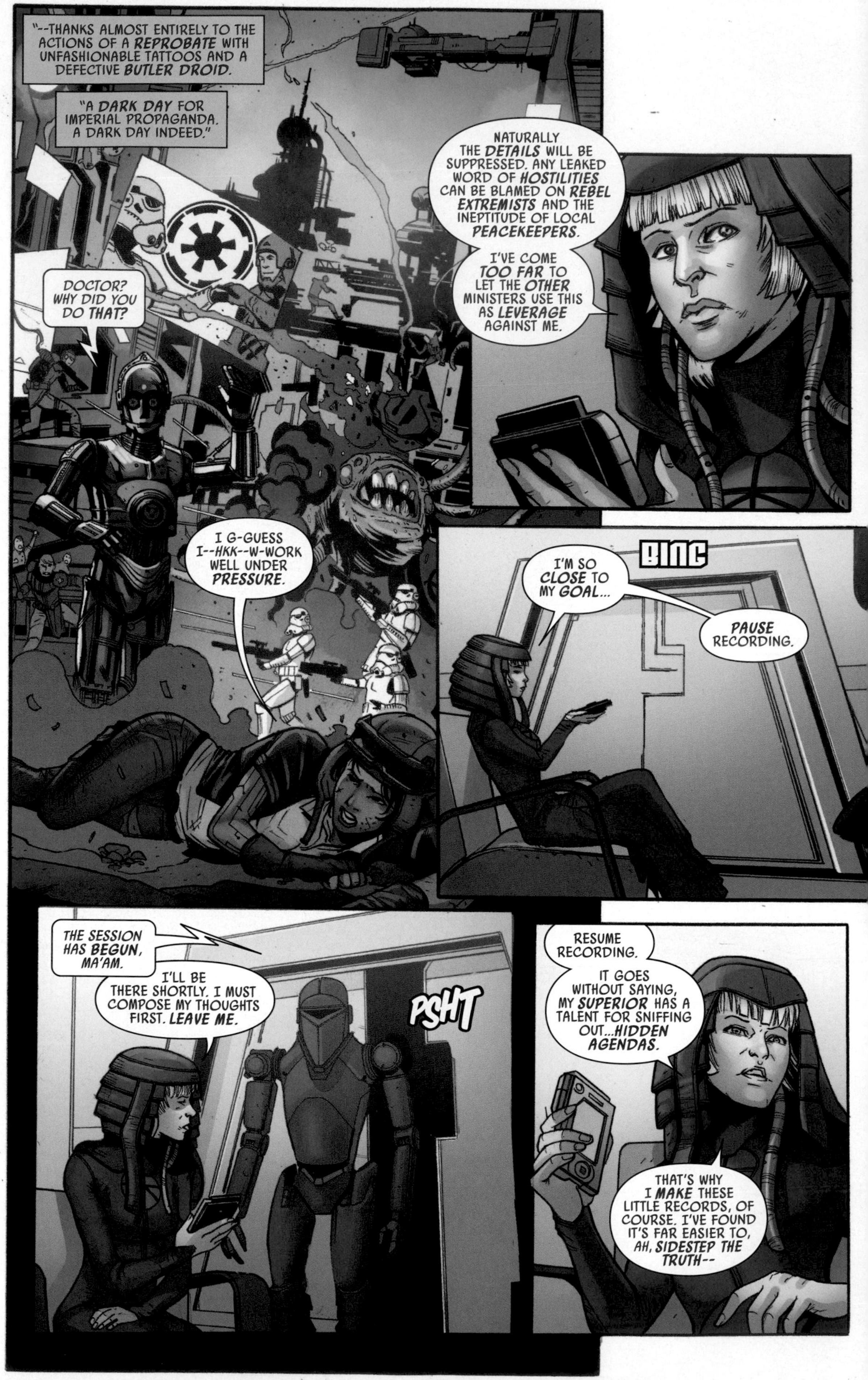
"--THANKS ALMOST ENTIRELY TO THE ACTIONS OF A REPROBATE WITH UNFASHIONABLE TATTOOS AND A DEFECTIVE BUTLER DROID.
"A DARK DAY FOR IMPERIAL PROPAGANDA. A DARK DAY INDEED."
DOCTOR? WHY DID YOU DO THAT?
I G-GUESS I--HKK--W-WORK WELL UNDER PRESSURE.
NATURALLY THE DETAILS WILL BE SUPPRESSED. ANY LEAKED WORD OF HOSTILITIES CAN BE BLAMED ON REBEL EXTREMISTS AND THE INEPTITUDE OF LOCAL PEACEKEEPERS.
I'VE COME TOO FAR TO LET THE OTHER MINISTERS USE THIS AS LEVERAGE AGAINST ME.
BINC
I'M SO CLOSE TO MY GOAL...
PAUSE RECORDING.
THE SESSION HAS BEGUN, MA'AM.
I'LL BE THERE SHORTLY. I MUST COMPOSE MY THOUGHTS FIRST. LEAVE ME.
PSHT
RESUME RECORDING.
IT GOES WITHOUT SAYING, MY SUPERIOR HAS A TALENT FOR SNIFFING OUT...HIDDEN AGENDAS.
THAT'S WHY I MAKE THESE LITTLE RECORDS, OF COURSE. I'VE FOUND IT'S FAR EASIER TO, AH, SIDESTEP THE TRUTH--

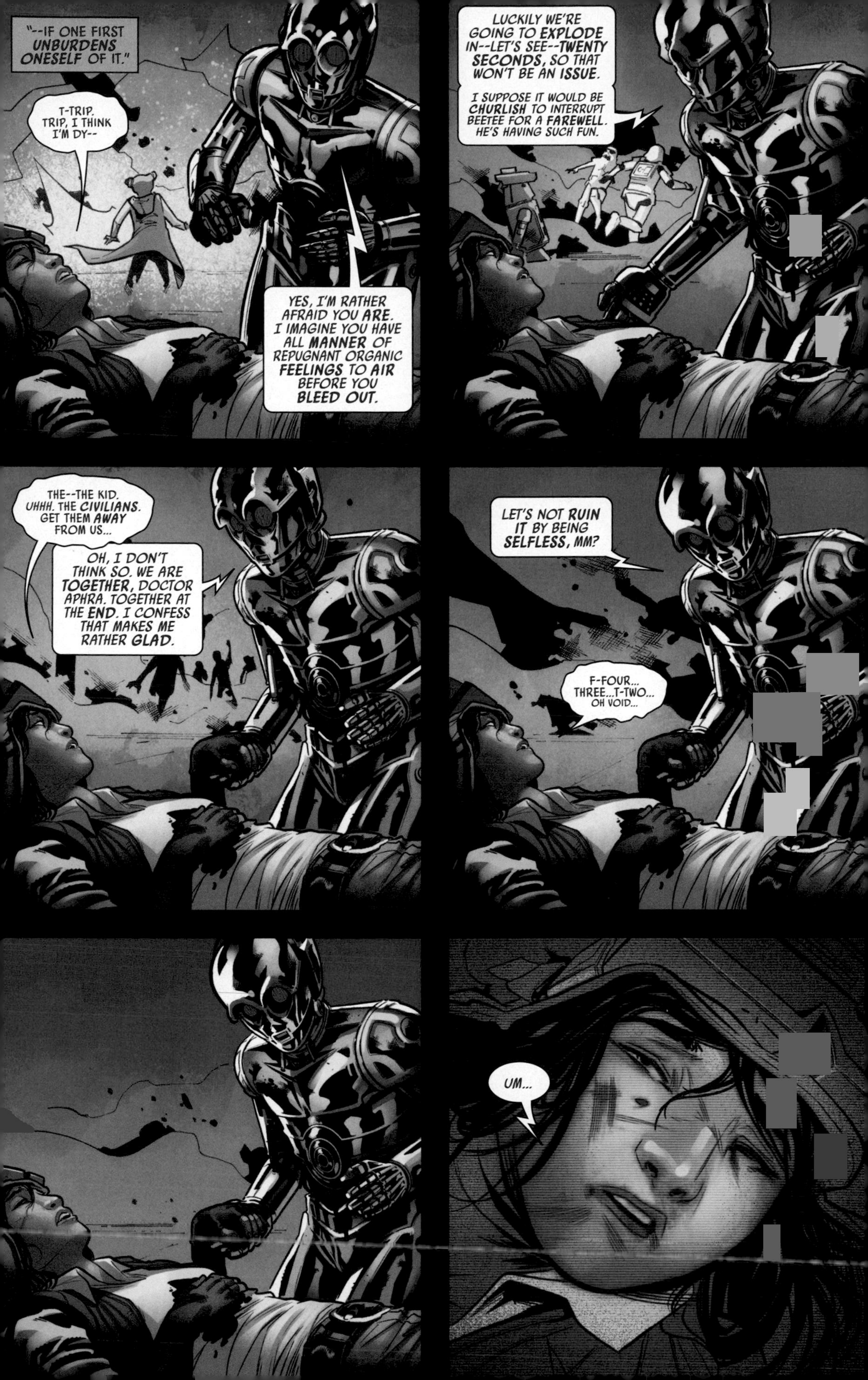
"--IF ONE FIRST UNBURDENS ONESELF OF IT."
T-TRIP. TRIP, I THINK I'M DY--
YES, I'M RATHER AFRAID YOU ARE. I IMAGINE YOU HAVE ALL MANNER OF REPUGNANT ORGANIC FEELINGS TO AIR BEFORE YOU BLEED OUT.
LUCKILY WE'RE GOING TO EXPLODE IN--LET'S SEE--TWENTY SECONDS, SO THAT WON'T BE AN ISSUE.
I SUPPOSE IT WOULD BE CHURLISH TO INTERRUPT BEETEE FOR A FAREWELL. HE'S HAVING SUCH FUN.
THE--THE KID. UHHH. THE CIVILIANS. GET THEM AWAY FROM US...
OH, I DON'T THINK SO. WE ARE TOGETHER, DOCTOR APHRA. TOGETHER AT THE END. I CONFESS THAT MAKES ME RATHER GLAD.
LET'S NOT RUIN IT BY BEING SELFLESS, MM?
F-FOUR... THREE...T-TWO... OH VOID...
UM...

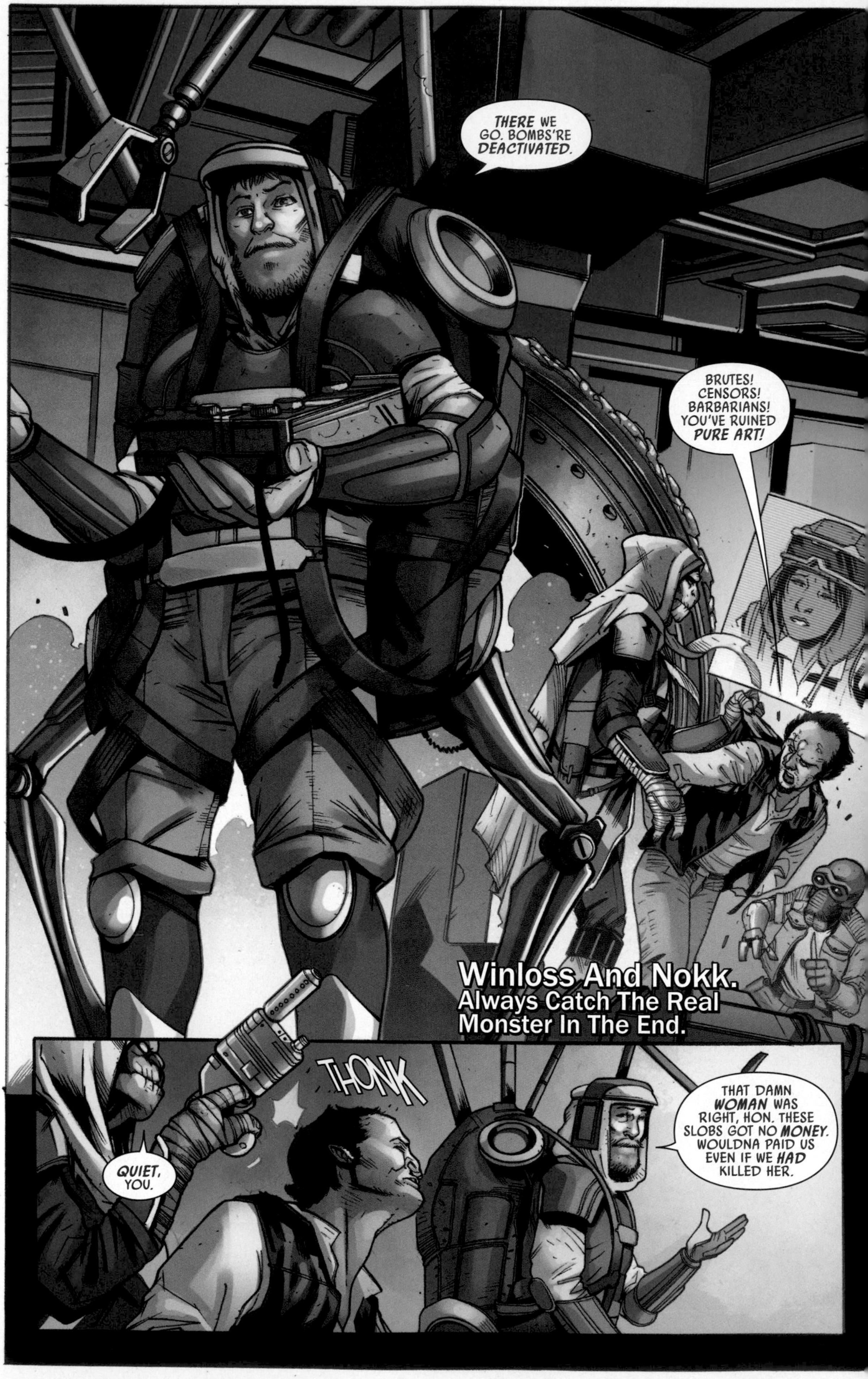
THERE WE GO. BOMBS'RE DEACTIVATED.
BRUTES! CENSORS! BARBARIANS! YOU'VE RUINED PURE ART!
Winloss And Nokk.
Always Catch The Real Monster In The End.
THONK
QUIET, YOU.
THAT DAMN WOMAN WAS RIGHT, HON. THESE SLOBS GOT NO MONEY. WOULDNA PAID US EVEN IF WE HAD KILLED HER.

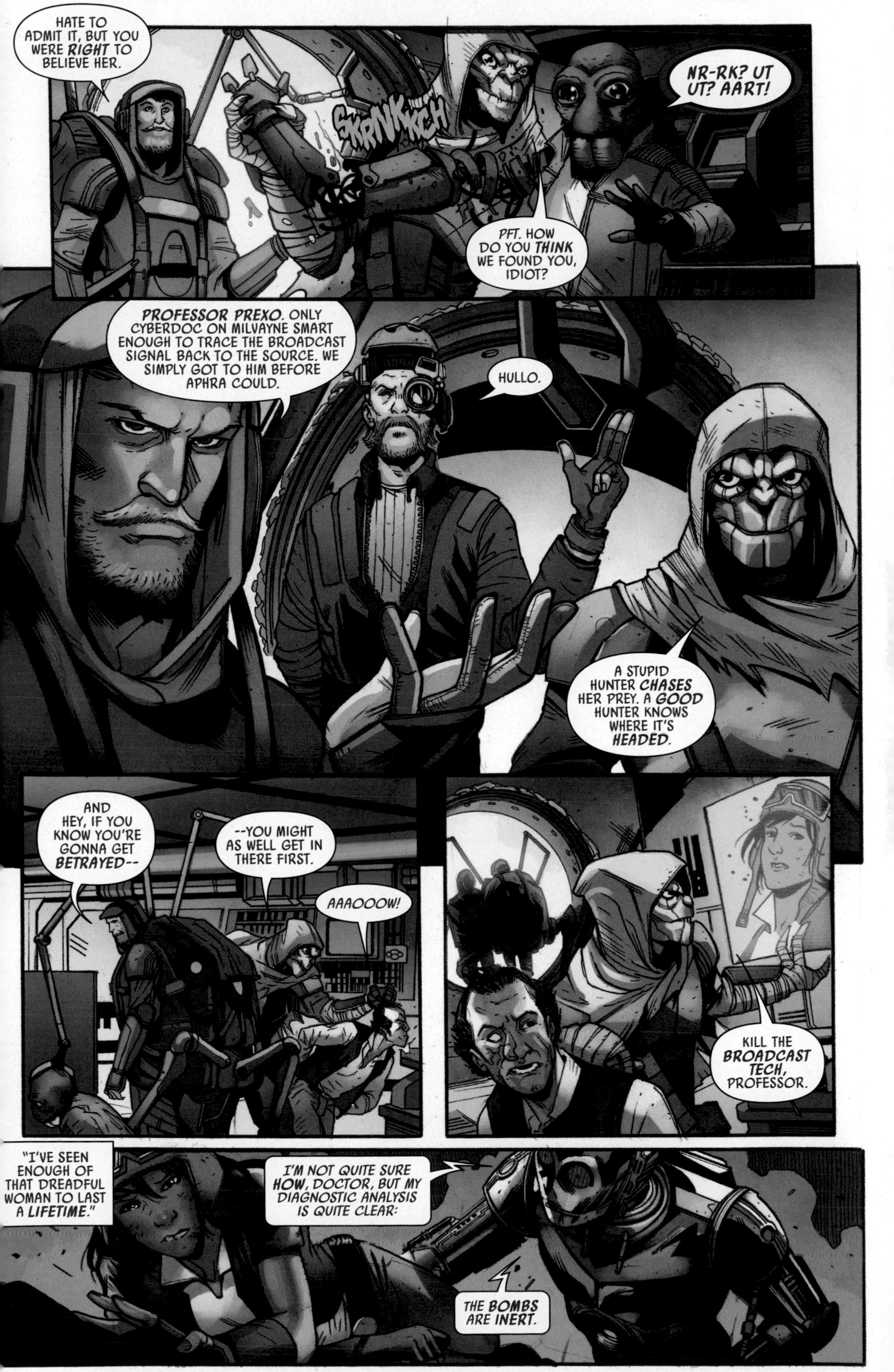
HATE TO ADMIT IT, BUT YOU WERE RIGHT TO BELIEVE HER.
NR-RK? UT UT? AART!
SKRNKKCH
PFT. HOW DO YOU THINK WE FOUND YOU, IDIOT?
PROFESSOR PREXO. ONLY CYBERDOC ON MILVAYNE SMART ENOUGH TO TRACE THE BROADCAST SIGNAL BACK TO THE SOURCE. WE SIMPLY GOT TO HIM BEFORE APHRA COULD.
HULLO.
A STUPID HUNTER CHASES HER PREY. A GOOD HUNTER KNOWS WHERE IT'S HEADED.
AND HEY, IF YOU KNOW YOU'RE GONNA GET BETRAYED--
--YOU MIGHT AS WELL GET IN THERE FIRST.
AAAOOOW!
KILL THE BROADCAST TECH, PROFESSOR.
"I'VE SEEN ENOUGH OF THAT DREADFUL WOMAN TO LAST A LIFETIME."
I'M NOT QUITE SURE HOW, DOCTOR, BUT MY DIAGNOSTIC ANALYSIS IS QUITE CLEAR:
THE BOMBS ARE INERT.

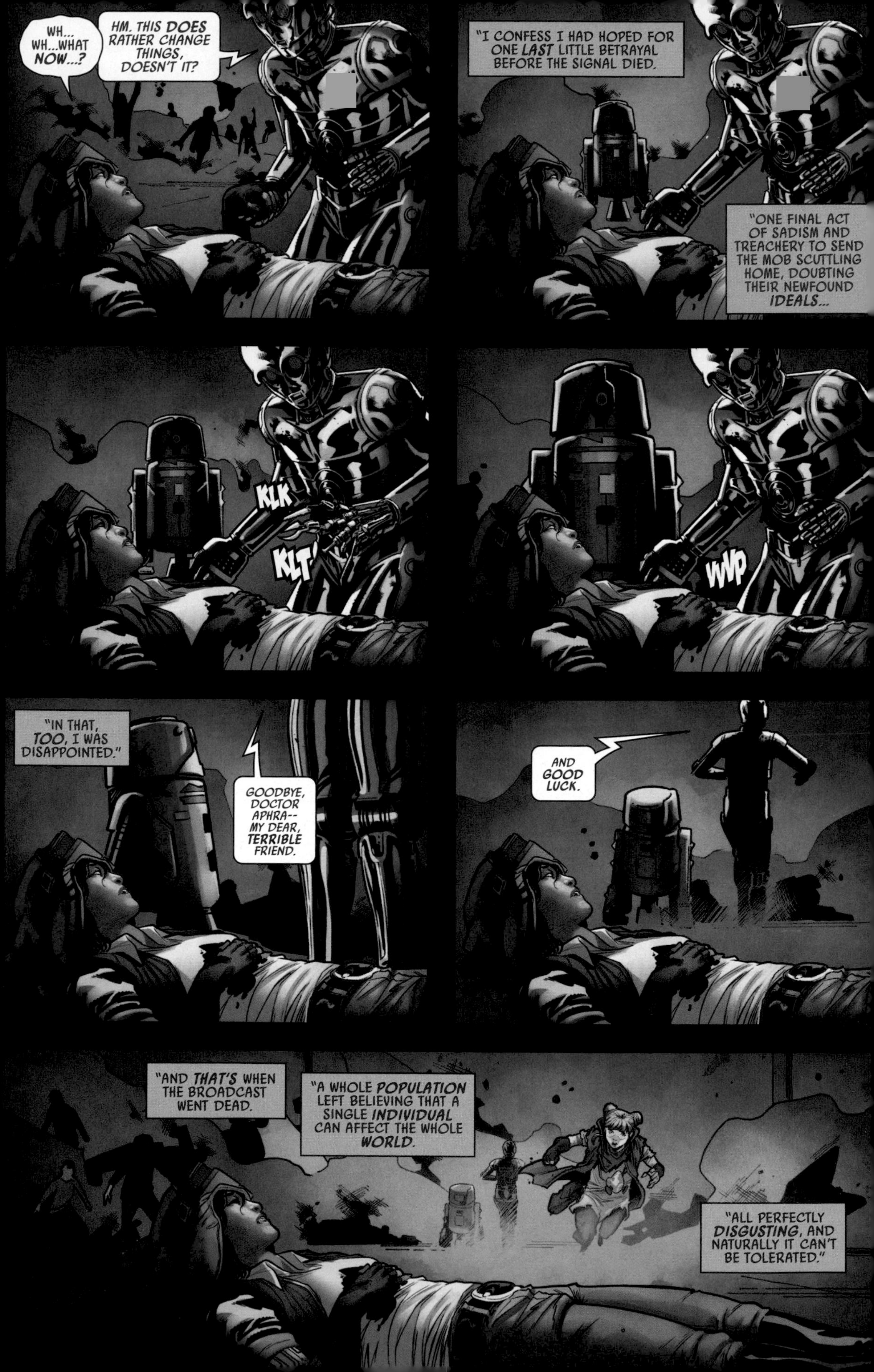

WH... WH...WHAT NOW...?
HM. THIS DOES RATHER CHANGE THINGS, DOESN'T IT?
"I CONFESS I HAD HOPED FOR ONE LAST LITTLE BETRAYAL BEFORE THE SIGNAL DIED.
"ONE FINAL ACT OF SADISM AND TREACHERY TO SEND THE MOB SCUTTLING HOME, DOUBTING THEIR NEWFOUND IDEALS...
KLK
KLT
VWVP
"IN THAT, TOO, I WAS DISAPPOINTED."
GOODBYE, DOCTOR APHRA-- MY DEAR, TERRIBLE FRIEND.
AND GOOD LUCK.
"AND THAT'S WHEN THE BROADCAST WENT DEAD.
"A WHOLE POPULATION LEFT BELIEVING THAT A SINGLE INDIVIDUAL CAN AFFECT THE WHOLE WORLD.
"ALL PERFECTLY DISGUSTING, AND NATURALLY IT CAN'T BE TOLERATED."

WELL, IT'S THE NAVY'S PROBLEM NOW. THREE YEARS OF *MARTIAL LAW* AND A FEW WELL-PLACED *BOMBARDMENTS*, I DARESAY MILVAYNE WILL BE BACK ON TRACK.

AS FOR THE WOMAN AT THE CENTER OF ALL THIS...

"...A WOMAN OF EXCEPTIONAL SKILL AND ELASTIC MORALITY...HM... PERHAPS SHE WAS SAVED AFTER THE BROADCAST WENT DARK. PERHAPS NOT.

"PERHAPS *FOOLS* WILL SPEND DECADES DEBATING WHO SHE WAS, WHEN--FOR *ME*--THE PERTINENT QUESTION IS SO VERY MUCH SIMPLER:"

ALIVE OR DEAD, HOW IS SHE MOST *USEFUL?*

... END RECORDING.

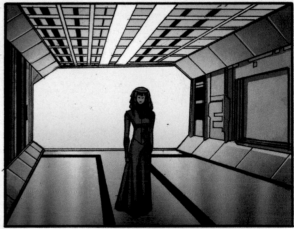

PSHT

A *THOUSAND APOLOGIES* FOR THE *DELAY,* MY LORD. A MINOR MATTER-- BUT--

THINGS *ESCALATE.*

YES.

SSHK

Q-QUITE SO. I DARED NOT LEAVE IT TO *UNDERLINGS* TO RESOLVE.

HENNHHH. YOU SEE, MY FRIENDS? *MINISTER VOOR* HAS ALWAYS BEEN SWIFT TO EMBRACE MY *DOCTRINE.*

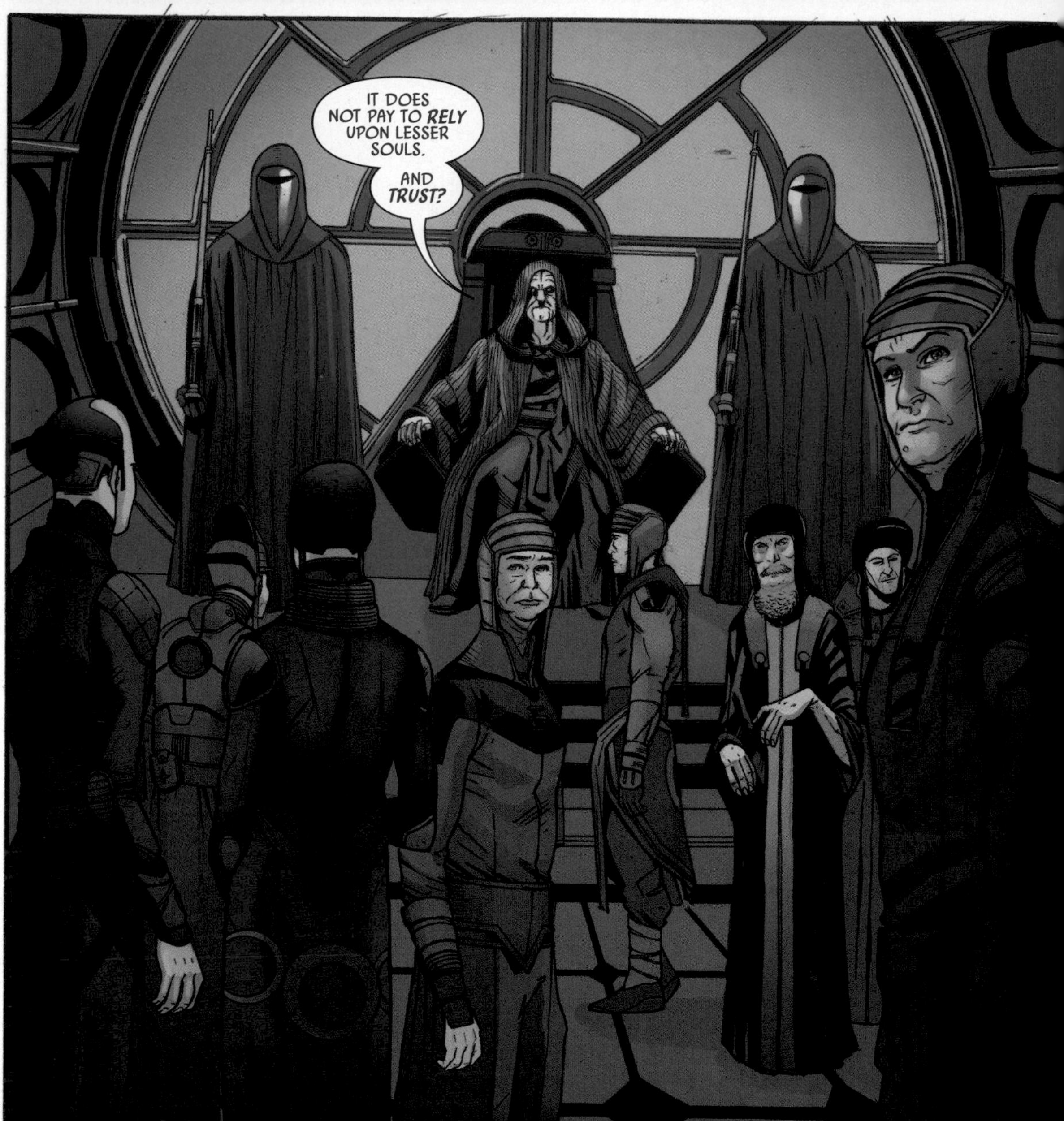
IT DOES NOT PAY TO RELY UPON LESSER SOULS.
AND TRUST?

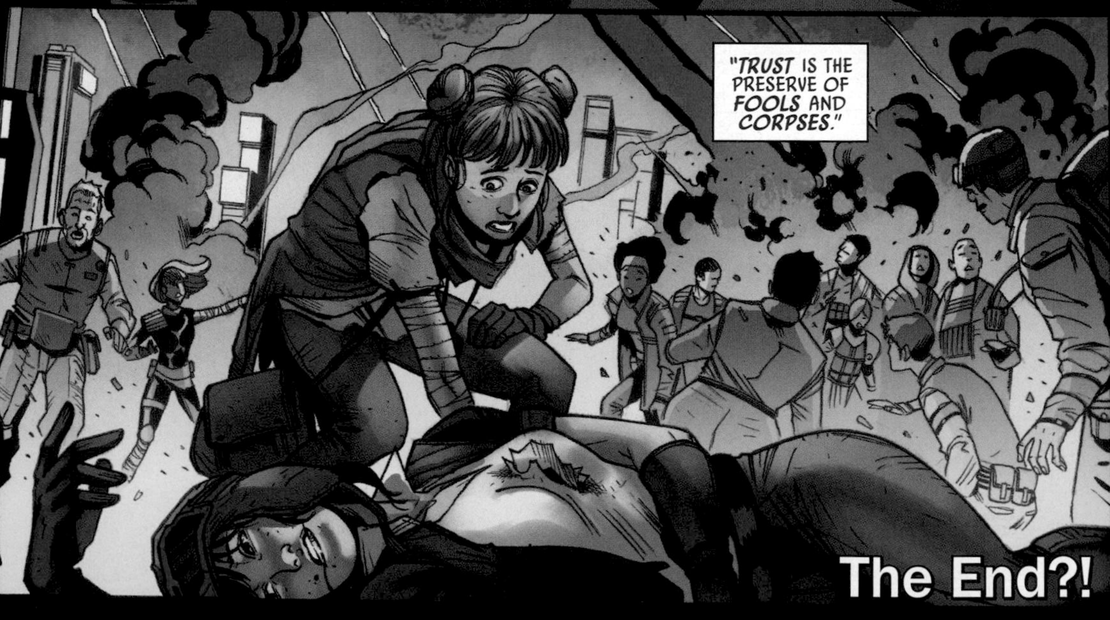
"TRUST IS THE PRESERVE OF FOOLS AND CORPSES."
The End?!

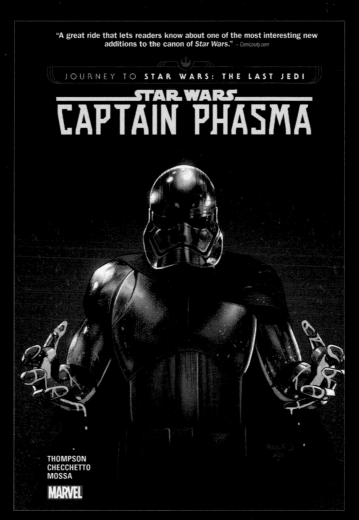

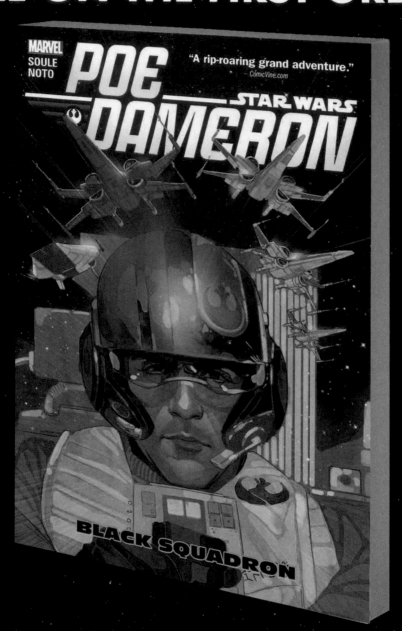

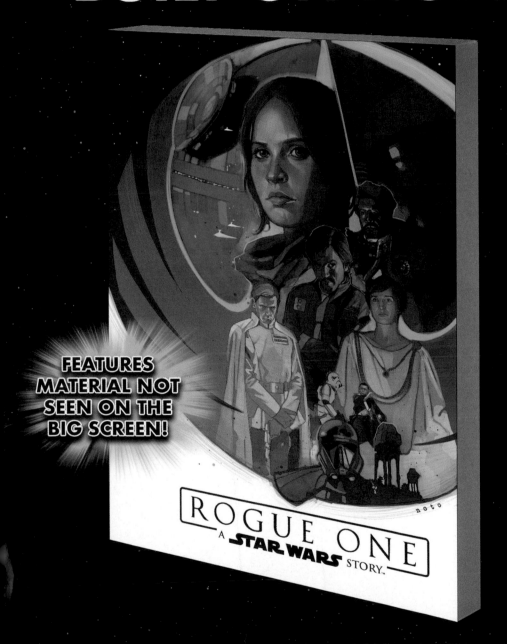

SENSATIONAL *STAR WARS* ARTWORK RETELLING THE STORY OF *A NEW HOPE!*

STAR WARS: A NEW HOPE — THE 40TH ANNIVERSARY HC
978-1302911287

ON SALE NOW
AVAILABLE IN PRINT AND DIGITAL WHEREVER BOOKS ARE SOLD

TO FIND A COMIC SHOP NEAR YOU, VISIT COMICSHOPLOCATOR.COM